Cultures of Compunction in the Medieval World

New Directions in Medieval Studies

Series Editors

Helen Young (Deakin University, Australia)
Andrew Elliott (University of Lincoln, UK)

This wide-ranging monograph series responds to emerging themes and interdisciplinary research methods in medieval scholarship, including the reception and reworking of the medieval in the post-medieval period. Particular concerns involve cataloguing the rich variety of experience of medieval people, re-evaluating medieval history from a global perspective, and exploring cultural transfer across different periods, places and groups. In doing so, New Directions in Medieval Studies seeks to contribute to the future directions and debates of medieval studies.

Published Titles

The Middle Ages in Popular Imagination, Paul Sturtevant
Medieval Literature on Display, Alexandra Sterling-Hellenbrand
Cultures of Compunction in the Medieval World, Graham Williams and Charlotte Steenbrugge (eds.)

Upcoming Titles

The Middle Ages in Modern Culture, Karl Alvestad and Paul Houghton (eds.)
Constructing Viking History, Thomas Smaberg
Laughter and Awkwardness in Late Medieval England, David Watt
The Cult of Thomas Becket, Paul Webster
Medieval Radicalism, Daniel Wollenberg

Cultures of Compunction in the Medieval World

Edited by

Graham Williams and Charlotte Steenbrugge

BLOOMSBURY ACADEMIC
LONDON • NEW YORK • OXFORD • NEW DELHI • SYDNEY

BLOOMSBURY ACADEMIC
Bloomsbury Publishing Plc
50 Bedford Square, London, WC1B 3DP, UK
1385 Broadway, New York, NY 10018, USA
29 Earlsfort Terrace, Dublin 2, Ireland

BLOOMSBURY, BLOOMSBURY ACADEMIC and the Diana logo
are trademarks of Bloomsbury Publishing Plc

First published in Great Britain 2021
This paperback edition published in 2022

Copyright © Graham Williams and Charlotte Steenbrugge, 2021

Graham Williams and Charlotte Steenbrugge have asserted their right under the Copyright, Designs and Patents Act, 1988, to be identified as Editors of this work.

For legal purposes the Acknowledgements on p. x constitute an extension of this copyright page.

Cover image: Jesus washing apostles' feet and Denial of St Peter © DeAgostini/Getty Images

All rights reserved. No part of this publication may be reproduced or transmitted in any form or by any means, electronic or mechanical, including photocopying, recording, or any information storage or retrieval system, without prior permission in writing from the publishers.

Bloomsbury Publishing Plc does not have any control over, or responsibility for, any third-party websites referred to or in this book. All internet addresses given in this book were correct at the time of going to press. The author and publisher regret any inconvenience caused if addresses have changed or sites have ceased to exist, but can accept no responsibility for any such changes.

Every effort has been made to trace copyright holders and to obtain their permissions for the use of copyright material. The publisher apologizes for any errors or omissions and would be grateful if notified of any corrections that should be incorporated in future reprints or editions of this book.

A catalogue record for this book is available from the British Library.

Library of Congress Cataloging-in-Publication Data
Names: Williams, Graham (Senior Lecturer), editor. | Steenbrugge, Charlotte, editor.
Title: Cultures of compunction in the Medieval World / edited by Graham Williams and Charlotte Steenbrugge.
Description: London ; New York : Bloomsbury Academic, 2020. | Series: New directions in medieval studies | Includes bibliographical references and index.
Identifiers: LCCN 2020025148 (print) | LCCN 2020025149 (ebook) | ISBN 9781788313445 (hb) | ISBN 9781350150379 (ePDF) | ISBN 9781350150393 (ebook)
Subjects: LCSH: Guilt–Religious aspects–Christianity–History–To 1500. | Emotions–History–To 1500. | Christianity and the arts–History–To 1500.
Classification: LCC BT722 .C85 2020 (print) | LCC BT722 (ebook) | DDC 274/.04–dc23
LC record available at https://lccn.loc.gov/2020025148
LC ebook record available at https://lccn.loc.gov/2020025149

ISBN:	HB:	978-1-7883-1344-5
	PB:	978-1-3502-1772-0
	ePDF:	978-1-3501-5037-9
	eBook:	978-1-3501-5039-3

Series: New Directions in Medieval Studies

Typeset by Integra Software Services Pvt. Ltd.

To find out more about our authors and books visit www.bloomsbury.com and sign up for our newsletters.

Contents

List of illustrations	vi
Notes on contributors	viii
Acknowledgements	x
Abbreviations	xi
Introduction *Graham Williams and Charlotte Steenbrugge*	1
1 Crying out with the compunction of the Prodigal Son: Byzantine hymns, liturgical emotions and icons of repentance *Andrew Mellas*	15
2 Repenting in their own words: Old English vocabulary for compunction, contrition and penitence *Daria Izdebska*	27
3 A concept without relevance? Compunction in Old Norse-Icelandic literature *Roland Scheel*	61
4 William of Auvergne and compunction: Describing the world through metaphors *Béatrice Delaurenti*	87
5 Seawater in flame: Compunction in the Lambeth and Trinity homilies *Ayoush Lazikani*	103
6 The expression of remorse in Old and Middle French literature *Corinne Denoyelle*	119
7 Peter's three tears *Véronique Plesch*	143
Notes	166
Bibliography	219
Index	253

Illustrations

Figures

1. Giovanni Canavesio, Denial of Peter, 1492, Notre-Dame des Fontaines, La Brigue (Photo: author) — 157
2. Giovanni Canavesio, Denial of Peter (detail), Notre-Dame des Fontaines, La Brigue (Photo: author) — 157
3. Giovanni Canavesio, Crowning with Thorns, 1492, Notre-Dame des Fontaines, La Brigue (Photo: author) — 158
4. Giovanni Canavesio, Mocking of Christ, 1492, Notre-Dame des Fontaines, La Brigue (Photo: author) — 158
5. Mocking of Christ, 1472, chapel of San Fiorenzo, Bastia Mondovì (Photo: author) — 159
6. Giovanni Canavesio, Christ before Caiaphas, after 1492, chapel of Notre-Dame des Douleurs des Pénitents Blancs, Peillon (Photo: author) — 159
7. Giovanni Canavesio, Remorse of Judas, 1492, Notre-Dame des Fontaines, La Brigue (Photo: author) — 160
8. Giovanni Canavesio, Pact of Judas, 1492, Notre-Dame des Fontaines, La Brigue (Photo: author) — 160
9. Giovanni Canavesio, Suicide of Judas, 1492, Notre-Dame des Fontaines, La Brigue (Photo: author) — 161
10. Giovanni Canavesio, Christ Washing the Feet of the Apostles, 1492, Notre-Dame des Fontaines, La Brigue (Photo: author) — 161
11. Giovanni Canavesio, Descent into Limbo, 1492, Notre-Dame des Fontaines, La Brigue (Photo: author) — 162
12. Giovanni Canavesio, Crucifixion, 1492, Notre-Dame des Fontaines, La Brigue (Photo: author) — 162
13. Giovanni Canavesio, Christ Washing the Feet of the Apostles (upper register) and Denial of Peter (lower register), 1492, Notre-Dame des Fontaines, La Brigue (Photo: author) — 163
14. Giovanni Canavesio, Last Judgment, 1492, west wall, Notre-Dame des Fontaines, La Brigue (Photo: author) — 164

15 Giovanni Canavesio, Last Judgment, detail: traitors and despairers, 1492, west wall, Notre-Dame des Fontaines, La Brigue (Photo: author) 165
16 Arches and springs below the sanctuary of Notre-Dame des Fontaines, La Brigue (Photo: author) 165

Tables

1 Overview of the lexical make-up of the word-families for compunction, contrition and penance 36
2 Distribution of word-families in the corpus in different text types by raw frequencies (RF) and normalized frequencies (NF) 40

Contributors

Beatrice Delaurenti is Associate Professor at the École des Hautes Etudes en Sciences Sociales (Paris). Her research interests focus on medieval intellectual controversies at the crossroads of religion, science and magic, dealing specifically with the question of action generated at a distance. She is currently working on doctrinal debates surrounding the evil eye, the active force of the gaze and the power of imagination in the fields of medieval medicine and natural philosophy. She has published *La Puissance des mots. Débats doctrinaux sur le pouvoir des incantations* (2007) and *La contagion des émotions. "Compassio", une énigme médiévale* (2016).

Corinne Denoyelle (PhD Paris III) is Professor (*maîtresse de conférence*) of Medieval French Literature and Old French Language at the University of Grenoble-Alpes (France). Her teaching and research interests are Old and Middle French prose and verse romances, especially Arthurian and Tristanian literature. Her research is situated at the crossroads between literature (narratology and stylistic) and linguistics (diachronic pragmatics), focusing on the structure and functions of dialogues in medieval romances and how the use of dialogues relates to the conception of the individual over the course of the Middle Ages.

Daria Izdebska is Lecturer in English Language at Liverpool Hope University where she teaches a wide range of courses related to historical linguistics, semantics and digital humanities. Her research interests and publications focus on the history of emotions, diachronic lexical semantics, corpus linguistics, and Old English language and literature. Her doctoral thesis, a semantic analysis of the vocabulary for ANGER in Old English, was completed at the University of Glasgow, where she also worked as Research Assistant in English Language and as Project Assistant on the AHRC-funded Mapping Metaphor with the Historical Thesaurus project.

Ayoush Lazikani is Lecturer in Old and Middle English at the University of Oxford. She specializes in devotional writing of the eleventh, twelfth and thirteenth centuries. Her research considers English, Latin and Anglo-Norman texts, and she has particular interests in literature written for religious recluses in the post-Conquest period. She has published widely in these areas, including in her first monograph *Cultivating the Heart: Feeling and Emotion in Twelfth- and Thirteenth-century Religious Texts* (2015). She is currently completing a comparative project across Christian and Islamic contemplative traditions, with a focus on emotion in Arabic and English texts.

Andrew Mellas is Senior Lecturer in Byzantine studies at St Andrew's Theological College, a member of the Sydney College of Divinity. Andrew has published various articles and chapters on Byzantine literature, hymnody and liturgy in peer-reviewed journals and edited volumes. He has recently published an edited and translated collection of hymns composed by Romanos the Melodist and a monograph entitled *Liturgy and the Emotions in Byzantium* (2020).

Véronique Plesch is Professor of Art History at Colby College (Waterville, Maine, USA). She is the author and editor of several books and has published over fifty articles in English, French, Italian and Spanish on subjects ranging from Passion iconography to art in the Duchy of Savoy, from Passion plays to early modern graffiti, and from artist books to contemporary art – many of them with a steady focus on word and image issues (she served three terms as President of the International Association of Word and Image Studies, from 2008 to 2017).

Roland Scheel is Junior Professor at Georg-August-Universität Göttingen at the Skandinavisches Seminar. His research focuses on Old Norse-Icelandic literature, its reception in modern times, transcultural relations between the North, Byzantium and Western Europe, and law and literature in the Scandinavian Middle Ages. His most recent books are a monograph on Scandinavia and Byzantium (*Skandinavien und Byzanz. Bedingungen und Konsequenzen mittelalterlicher Kulturbeziehungen*, 2015) and an edited volume *Narrating Law and Laws of Narration in Medieval Scandinavia* (2020).

Charlotte Steenbrugge is Lecturer in Medieval Literature at the University of Sheffield. She mainly works on medieval and sixteenth-century English, Dutch and French drama. She has a strong interest in the relationship between medieval theatre and devotion. Her most recent book is *Drama and Sermon in Late Medieval England: Performance, Authority, Devotion* (2017). She is currently working on an article on the absence of medieval English farces.

Graham Williams is Senior Lecturer in the History of English at the University of Sheffield. His most recent book is *Sincerity in Medieval English Language and Literature* (2018). His interests range across a hodgepodge of philological topics, mainly to do with the English Middle Ages and, in addition to emotions, currently including Anglo-Norman letters, English proverbs and the history of goblins.

Acknowledgements

The editors would like to thank the editorial and production team at Bloomsbury; everyone we have worked with has been nothing but supportive, attentive and patient. Feedback from the two anonymous reviewers of the manuscript proved indispensable, so much respect to them. And of course, especial thanks to the contributors for their work and collegiality through the process. It has been some time coming, but here we are.

Abbreviations

BNC	British National Corpus
B-T	Joseph Bosworth and T. Northcote Toller, *An Anglo-Saxon Dictionary Based on the Manuscript Collections of the Late Joseph Bosworth*
DMLBS	*Dictionary of Medieval Latin from British Sources*
chap.	chapters
CSCO	Corpus Scriptorum Christianorum Orientalium
DOE	*Dictionary of Old English*
DOEC	*Dictionary of Old English Web Corpus*
DOP	*Dumbarton Oaks Papers*
f	feminine
m	masculine
MED	*Middle English Dictionary*
MLN	*Modern Language Notes*
n	neuter
OED	*Oxford English Dictionary*
OCA	*Orientalia Christiana Periodica*
ODB	*Oxford Dictionary of Byzantium*
OE	Old English
p	person
PG	*Patrologia Graeca*
pl	plural
SC	*Sources Chrétiennes*
sg	singular
st.	stanza
TOE	*A Thesaurus of Old English*

Introduction

Graham Williams and Charlotte Steenbrugge

The initial inspiration for what would eventually culminate in this volume developed in a fairly typical academic fashion: its editors share a hallway and, by way of casual conversation, came to find that even though we work in fairly distinct areas of our department (i.e. medieval drama and historical linguistics) we share an interest in the history of emotions. Even more specifically, we had both recently conducted research related to medieval compunction and contrition; Charlotte had encountered manifestations of these emotions in her work on medieval drama and its relationship to sermons,[1] and Graham was finishing work on the relationship between medieval emotions of confession and the subsequent development of apologies in English.[2] If chance would have it that we were both independently thinking about medieval cultures of compunction and contrition, it stood to reason that there must be other medievalists from other areas of study, working with different languages and different media (e.g. the fine arts), who would welcome conversation in this vein. A panel was organized for the 2016 International Medieval Congress in Leeds, which served to confirm our suspicions, and we subsequently reached out to others to form a small but compelling network of scholars. And while these discussions did of course draw on a number of instrumental earlier studies,[3] it quickly became clear that there was a rationale for bringing together a multivariate collection of essays that addressed the culture of medieval contrition and compunction from distinct angles of investigation.

Previous studies of this emotion have approached compunction and contrition from the perspective of devotional practice, which has (for example) greatly enriched our understanding of developments in lay piety. Yet what remains less explored are the ways that Christian ideologies of guilt, shame and regret extended into medieval culture beyond the remit of devotional practice per se, and the culture of compunction that this book argues for had profound influence in the domains of medieval and post-medieval art, music, literature, language and thought. A number of previous studies have discussed compunction or related emotions to do with specific texts, individuals or areas of experience,[4] or specifically in the context of penance and confession,[5] yet there has been very little discussion of compunction across areas of experience. Nor has there been much attempt to look at the way in which compunction functioned and was formulated in different linguistic communities, especially vernacular ones. By bringing together expertise across disciplines and medieval languages, this collection of essays aims to demonstrate the ubiquity and impact of compunction for medieval life and suggests wider connections between devotional, secular and quotidian areas of experience.

The study of particular emotional cultures has proved to be one of the more productive strands of scholarship on the Middle Ages in the past several decades, and we now know that many of the emotions we presently take for granted and that form the bedrock of modern Western (and increasingly global) culture, e.g. romantic love and compassion,[6] were first culturally prioritized, idealized and in some cases conventionalized, in medieval contexts of linguistic, artistic and intellectual production and exchange. This volume illustrates some of the ways in which this was also true of compunction and contrition and provides a companion for those working on these cultures of emotion, medieval or otherwise. In this short introduction, we have chosen to focus on some of the key elements; in particular, we will use it as an opportunity to think about the wider culture of contrition and compunction (as guilt, etc.) and the words themselves, in the Middle Ages and the present day, mainly dealing with English.

The medievalism of guilt

Guilt, remorse and shame are fundamental emotions for Christian cultural institutions and their means of instituting emotional power structures, but these emotions have over the course of their long history been (re)interpreted, idealized and rejected in different ways at different times. Certainly, it should be abundantly clear that these emotions remain just as relevant today, and one need not live in a culture dominated by Christian faith to be surrounded by manifestations of what we might refer to as modern reflexes of compunction and contrition – even if some of those reflexes do have medieval, Christian origins in one way or another.

In Anglo-American culture, for example, expressions of guilt are a ubiquitous part of daily life, and in various ways this emotion is identifiable through aspects of present-day language, belief, art and entertainment. In a performative sense, guilt has been conventionalized in the context of English apologies, e.g. 'I am sorry', which originally derived from medieval cultures of compunction and confession – although today there is less frequently any communicative condition or expectation that a speaker actually feels sorry when they utter this phrase.[7] 'Bourgeois' or 'capitalist guilt' has been subject to editorial as well as historical comment and analysis.[8] But if guilt is something we deal with apropos our lifestyle, it is also something we indulge by way of drama; e.g. in October 2019 the BBC released a series entitled *Guilt*, in which the emotion leads to the unravelling of two men's lives after they commit a hit-and-run murder. Guilt is also funny, and characters riddled with this and other potentially neurotic emotions have been subjected to comedic treatment in film and on television, notably, for example, in the immensely successful television series *Seinfeld* – a show one might describe using another relevant modern phrase, i.e. *a guilty pleasure*.

Given the prominence of guilt in modern culture, it is not surprising that compunction and contrition are amenable to discussions of medievalism, as in cases where modern-day culture witnesses expressions of like emotions in ways somehow referential or analogous to medieval instantiations. For example, Angela Jane Weisl describes a medievalesque manifestation of 'confession, contrition and the rhetoric of tears' found in reality television shows, which feature 'excessive weeping' as a public performance: 'If many of the ritual functions of the Middle Ages are lost from modern life, in the seemingly contemporary phenomenon of reality television, tears continue to do a medieval kind of work.'[9] More specifically, this work involves contestants publically performing (to judges and audiences) their inner experiences of contrition and compunction apropos past actions or words spoken (to fellow contestants, for example), which in turn demonstrates, or proves, a redemptive sort of betterment in a way akin to the devotional function of displays of compunction in medieval art and literature, which features the contrite weeping of numerous saints, as well as figures like Margery Kempe (perhaps the English example par excellence when it comes to the blessing of tears of compunction). In both cases, public examples are meant to somehow affectively influence their audience (which also relates to another idealized emotion relevant to the Middle Ages, compassion). And while this example of medievalism is almost surely an unconscious one in its televised instantiations, this fact serves to demonstrate a long-standing ideology in the West that feeling bad about one's actions is integral to moral redemption and self-improvement. Whether this tradition of compunction is in any way attributable to medieval Christian influence relates to the question of how general the emotions involved are, i.e. are compunction and contrition universals of human experience? Another way of phrasing it: to what extent might one suggest that these emotions were 'invented' in the Middle Ages?

Universalities of expression?

The cross-cultural universality of emotion is relevant when treating the subject of emotions and their related cultures in a historically distant context; as L. P. Hartley once wrote, '[T]he past is a foreign country; they do things differently there.'[10] And whether or not we should consider the underlying emotions associated with compunction and contrition, i.e. guilt, shame and remorse, as universal for human experience is complicated by the fact that when we say 'emotion' we are almost always referring to something that happens in interaction, something produced (performed?) by one individual and interpreted by another in a particular cultural context. The question of universality is also of interest when discussing syncretic environments where one culture of emotion meets another (usually on unequal ground), as in the case of pagan vis-à-vis Christian contact. Chapters by Izdebska, on Old English, and Scheel, on Old Norse-Icelandic culture, treat questions of syncretism for Germanic peoples wherein Christian cultures of compunction interacted with, and in some cases clearly transformed, originally pagan words, practices and ideas. The fact that contact and syncretism are so ubiquitous to the Middle Ages can make it difficult to locate precisely where and when a particular aspect of emotional culture was introduced. Certainly the purpose of this introduction cannot be to settle questions of universality, but consideration of this issue serves to highlight at the outset that emotions are, more or less, conditioned by the 'cultures of emotion' in which they are interpreted.

Emotions do of course have felt psychological realities that distinguish one from another, which is to say that emotional cultures and the distinction of one emotion vs another are not purely ideational, as they relate to the bodily experiences of living subjects. Delaurenti's chapter in particular discusses the contrite body in pain from the medieval theological-physiological perspective of William of Auvergne, who took an especial interest in the physical experience of pricks and stings and how this related to emotional states. Mellas's chapter also focuses on the embodiment of emotion, namely as experienced by Byzantium writers and the congregations that performed hymns and the *kontakion* of Romanos the Melodist. Compunction, Mellas argues, was not merely an idea but instead a transformative, embodied experience that brought the faithful closer to divine emotion.

Embodiment also means that the subjective feeling of any one emotion is often reflected in the way that one looks and acts while experiencing it. Facial expressions in particular are important when it comes to performing and depicting compunction socially and artistically. The face can of course be controlled consciously, but it can also be more direct and immediately reflective of inward feeling, whereas in language feelings can be more easily disguised or dissembled. Agreed upon, cross-culturally identifiable facial expressions include happiness, disgust, anger, surprise, fear and sadness.[11] But to what extent is compunction an independent facial expression distinguishable from other forms of sadness? Considered in an interactional context, and especially when aided by linguistic means of disambiguation, an expression of sadness might be interpreted in relation to feelings of regret – see the cover of the present volume for a medieval representation of one such instance, i.e. a fresco depicting the apostle Peter as he breaks down in tears of repentance (i.e. experiences compunction) for having denied Jesus. Yet without the narrative context from the gospels, the expression of sadness on Peter's face here is not ipso facto indicative of compunction, and in fact it could be interpreted in multiple ways (tears of joy, tears of grief, etc.), which is also why the artist clarifies beyond doubt by painting the crowing cock foreseen by Jesus directly above Peter's head. Plesch's chapter elaborates more fully on the tears staining Peter's face and the depiction of penance more generally in the visual arts in medieval Italy and France. Scheel discusses facial expressions as communicated in Old Norse textual sources made up of language only, which further demonstrates the importance of the face when it cannot otherwise be seen (i.e. as it can in life and visual media). Thus compunction involves a facial expression of sadness, but it seems doubtful that one should be able to distinguish compunction based on facial expression alone, without the contextual clues needed to 'read' in more meaningful detail. The same might be said of the weeping and tears often attributed to compunction – i.e. tears are indicative of sadness, but one needs to know more in able to discern the concomitant emotions of contrition/compunction. In *The Book of Margery Kempe*, for example, Margery's frequent weeping is often glossed as deriving from one of these emotions, which serves as justification for what was otherwise interpreted (by many of her contemporaries in the narrative, for example) as antisocial or insincere behaviour: 'ower mercyful Lord vysytyd þis creatur wyth plentyuows teerys of contricyon day be day;[12] terys of compunccyon, deuocyon, & compassyon arn þe heyest & sekerest ȝyftys þat I ȝeue in erde'.[13] What's more, Lazikani's chapter explains that there were in fact a variety of types of tears even within the remit of medieval guilt; i.e. there were tears and there were *tears*!

The generalness and potential ambiguity of human facial expressions is where the specificity of linguistic categorization, i.e. words for socially recognized emotions, becomes important and telling of the ways in which particular emotions are prioritized in specific communities. In terms of emotion vocabularies, Hupka et al. (1999) found that out of sixty-four languages, ranging from minority languages with fewer than 1 million speakers (e.g. Mazahua) to global languages such as English, all had a word for an emotion concept approximating 'guilt'.[14] The only other universally acknowledged emotion in this sense was 'anger'. This led them to postulate that these two emotions were the first to be 'encoded', i.e. lexicalized in natural language development in a social-evolutionary way, and 'that the anger and guilt categories were encoded first suggests that the need to maintain social control may have been a priority in all societies. [...] Violation of standards tends to elicit the types of emotions in Shaver et al.'s (1987) anger and guilt categories'.[15] From this perspective, guilt and shame as psychological experiences are fundamental to the functioning of human society. And even though the past may be 'a foreign country', it seems relatively safe to submit Hupka et al.'s findings to the Middle Ages by way of uniformitarian principles; i.e. we can say that at the most basic level medieval people were not emotionally different from us in terms of what they were capable of feeling inwardly; certainly guilt (and anger for that matter) was instrumental to the power structures of medieval societies in the West. Yet the details of the cultural dimension are what makes the emotional building blocks socially and interactionally meaningful – and it is this dimension that did differ in the Middle Ages.

In conjunction with other socially imposed measures (e.g. the written law), basic human emotions provide crucial motivations for the maintenance of social rules – in fact, as discussed in a following section, many of the modern English uses of these terms are found in instances where someone who breaks a legal or moral law is described as having done so 'without compunction/contrition', wherein the lack of emotion explains and also compounds the offensiveness of the act. In the Middle Ages, the rules governing people's lives were of course predominantly directed by religious beliefs and church authorities, disseminated in the form of devotional instruction, in texts but also by way of figures such as priests and bishops. And, as is well known, medieval Christianity, perhaps more explicitly than most other institutions in Western history, exploited the relationship between guilt and the maintenance of power to extremely significant effect. They did this primarily through the doctrines of contrition and compunction.

Church doctrine served as a cultural catalyst for expressions and representations of guilt in the Middle Ages more generally, in terms of both the language used to describe and express emotions and also the ways in which ostensibly canonical contrition and compunction were integrated into medieval art, literature and thought. Not to say that more complex examples were divorced from religion (few, if any, things in the Middle Ages were), but the culture of compunction was a diverse and multifaceted one that went beyond the basic tenet that one must feel sorry for sin. Indeed, Denoyelle's chapter very clearly illustrates how the culture of 'remorse' (French *remords*) was to an extent independent of that of religious compunction, and just as religious texts utilized the force and transformative powers of contrition and compunction to great effect, the very intensity of remorse allowed romance writers to exploit this emotion to great literary effect.

Lexical labels for compunction and contrition cannot be taken on the surface as indicative of anything universal; they must be read closely for the semantic as well as discursive contexts that gave them meaning in their moment of production. What follows is a brief analysis of the words *compunction* and *contrition* as they are relevant to the history of English, which will include a consideration of how these words were used and where they were found in Middle English texts (the period when they were borrowed into English) and also some observations about their occurrence in Present-Day English. Clearly one cannot directly equate lexical representation, or lack thereof, with the presence or absence of an idea or concept of emotion in any one culture or time – and, as demonstrated by the plurality of medieval and modern guilt-words (e.g. medieval French *repentir* 'repentance' and *remords* 'remorse', discussed in Denoyelle's chapter), Latin and vernacular cognates for *contrition* and *compunction* do not cover the entire vocabulary used within medieval cultures of guilt, shame and regret (the latter modern English words also reflect this point). Yet words do perform a lot of work when it comes to the inculcation of concepts, ideals and ideologies. And given that the two main words in scholarship are *contrition* and *compunction*, we would like to spend a bit of time in this introduction outlining their Anglicization and subsequent, post-medieval history in English.

We have chosen to provide a brief overview of these words in medieval and modern Englishes in part because none of the chapters that follow do so in the way we have (thus the Introduction adds to the range of analysis; cf. Izdebska's chapter on British English), but also because looking at the terms and their use across these periods draws attention to the historical and contextual mutability that forms one of the underlying rationales for the present volume more generally.

Words in English

The word *compunction* is absent from *The Oxford Dictionary of the Christian Church* (ODCC), but *contrition* is there described as 'a form of interior repentance, defined by the Council of Trent [1545–1563] as "sorrow of heart and detestation of sin committed, with the purpose of not sinning in the future" (sess. xiv, cap. 4)'.[16] As Lazikani's chapter explores in more detail, contrition, more than just a feeling, was a transformative action, an inward 'grinding away'; the spiritual love for God that gave rise to contrite pain ground away sins in a devotee (vs *attrition*, which came to be distinguished as a form of fear of punishment and therefore less powerful than *contrition* in its redemptive potential). According to the ODCC, 'the classic utterance of the contrite heart in the Old Testament is the Miserere', i.e. the fourth penitential psalm, Psalm 50.19 (here from the Douay Rheims and Vulgate), where one finds the Latin reflex *contritum* used to describe David's inward state:

> [19] A sacrifice to God is an afflicted spirit: a contrite and humbled heart, O God, thou wilt not despise.
>
> (Sacrificium Deo spiritus contribulatus; cor contritum et humiliatum, Deus, non despicies.)

Originally in Latin *contritio* and *compunctio* were distinguished in meaning by the different types of literal, physical actions they referred to; namely the former was derived from 'Latin *contrītus* bruised, crushed, past participle of *conterĕre*, < con- together + *terĕre* to rub, triturate, bray, grind' (OED, *contrite*) and the latter 'Latin *compunctus*, past participle of *compungĕre* to prick severely, to sting, < com- intensive + *pungĕre* to prick' (OED, *compunct*). In this way they seem to have occupied related, although clearly distinct, areas of semantic meaning. Yet in medieval Latin, as in later vernacular appropriations of these words, both of these forms came to take on figurative senses in a way common to semantic change more generally, i.e. from concrete to abstract senses. In following with their unpleasantness in the original concrete meanings, both of these words took on subjective senses to do with an inner pain that was not merely intrinsic, but a gift from God and a devotional experience that could be fostered by way of prayer (see Mellas's chapter on Byzantium hymns). And it was these affectively orientated meanings that came to be appropriated so significantly in medieval Christian discourse, which is the context in which the Latin words were vernacularized in English.

There were other words in English that occupied the semantic space for 'guilt', 'shame' and 'regret' before the addition of *contrition* and *compunction* (see Izdebska as well as Lazikani in this volume for Old and Middle English), but none of the earlier forms would have been specific to the devotional context that came to be occupied by the latter. And while the literal (now obsolete) senses of physical puncturing and crushing were borrowed independently much later in the sixteenth and seventeenth centuries (possibly via a new wave of contact brought about as many texts were being translated into English from Latin), it was almost exclusively with their meanings to do with inward pain that they were used in Middle English. Unlike with more everyday words borrowed into Middle English, it is unlikely that either of these words had much currency in any register of spoken English before they appeared in writing in the fourteenth century. And while it is likely that reflexes for these terms in medieval French had contact influence on the borrowings in English, their presence is minimal in the corpus of Anglo-Norman texts: even accounting for spelling variation, there are only sixteen total hits for *contrition/contrite* and ten total for *compunction/compunct* in the Anglo-Norman textbase.[17] According to both the OED and the *Middle English Dictionary*, most of the earliest Anglicized contexts in which we find *compunction/compunct* and *contrition/contrite* are in biblical translations; e.g. the former appears in Richard Rolle's *Psalter*, 'Compunccioun for my synn is festid in my hert' (OED), and the latter in the Wycliffite Bible, from a translation of the previously mentioned Miserere, Psalm 50.19: 'Sacrifise to God, a spiritt holly trublid; a contrit herte and mekid, God, thou shalt not despise.'[18]

It would seem that although the words are well documented as having been Anglicized in late Middle English, both *contrition* and *compunction* were relatively rare in everyday medieval English (just as they are today), and their use was reserved mainly for references to penitential practice in written texts. For example, *compunction* appears nowhere in the works of Chaucer, and when Chaucer's Parson refers to the penitential 'weeping' that collocates with *compunction* in other texts (e.g. *The Book of Margery Kempe*) he uses more established Germanic words such as *shame* (from Old English) and *(be)wail*

(Old Norse) that were/are not exclusively devotional in their meaning. *Contrition* appears only once outside the *Parson's Tale* in the *Canterbury Tales*, namely in *The Tale of Melibee*, where we find a reference to the contrition of David from the Old Testament (as we have seen, the originator of devotional contrition par excellence) (1737).[19] Yet *contrition* occurs no less than twenty-nine times in the *Parson's Tale* – in fact, much of the Parson's contribution could be characterized as an exposition of the meaning of contrition for a lay audience, both in terms of the fiction of the narrative (i.e. the fellow pilgrims) and also as a lay devotional text for Chaucer's late medieval audience. According to the Parson, penitence is a tree, and 'The roote of this tree is Contricioun, that hideth hym in the herte of hym that is verray repentaunt' (113), and 'Contricioun is the verray sorwe that a man receyveth in his herte for his synnes' (129). Late medieval English sermons are likewise emphatic on the importance of contrition and compunction, although the latter term is less frequent, and again, altogether different terms might also be employed, e.g. the *forthinking* (from Old English) and *repentance* (from Anglo-Norman) from a mid-fifteenth-century sermon: 'Ʒe shall vndirstond that iij þinges makeþ a man acceptable to þe mercy of God. Þe first is for-þenkyng in herte, þat a man shuld repente hym for is synnes þat he haþ done aȝeyns God and is soule.'[20] Sermons not only outline the importance of contrition but also define its quality, associating it predominantly with the heart ('a sorowfull and a contrite herte')[21] and tears ('contriscion … thereof þu muste make a drynke, þat is to sey, thu muste wepe for þi synnes').[22] The analysis of contrition in the *Parson's Tale* is also telling, as one way of reading the tale is as a literary act of penance derived from Chaucer's own feelings of guilt towards his secular literature as a whole. This reading is of course debatable, but it seems significant in this respect that the pseudo-penitential Retractions directly follow the *Parson's Tale* in almost all of the manuscripts in which it is found.[23]

The Middle English *Prick of Conscience*, for which well over 100 copies survive from the Middle Ages, gestures directly towards a puncturing of the spiritual heart in its title and function but actually does not use the words *compunction* or *contrition* anywhere in its 9621 lines. In the sixth part, on 'þe paynes of helle', for example, the tears of the damned are described as burning as hot as molten lead, which may have been avoided had the sinful had *forthynkyng* ('regret; compunction/contrition') accompanied by the much sweeter tears of devotion in life (7126).[24] Nicholas Love's *Myrrour of the Blessed Lyf of Jesu Christ* (also a very 'popular' text), on the other hand, does use the Latinate forms of both words. Love's *Myrrour* was one of the most widely produced texts in the fifteenth century, and it is generally regarded as a milestone in lay devotion and also as a benchmark following Arundel's Constitutions, which were published in 1409.²⁵ In light of these facts, it should be reasonable to suggest that it was probably by way of Love's text that the word *compunction* was subjected to its first notable circulation in a clearly Anglicized context for a lay audience (whereas *contrition* is found elsewhere previously, most significantly throughout the *Parson's Tale*).

Regardless of their appearance in these more widely circulated texts, however, it is doubtful that either of these words ever had much currency in spoken registers of English. In Middle English, our data is of course entirely from written texts, but the fact that neither *contrition* nor *compunction* occurs with any frequency in the plentiful representations of spoken speech – e.g. rarely in medieval drama and only in the mouth of the Parson in *The Canterbury Tales* (vs the more dialogic tales that precede his tale) – makes it unlikely that many speakers would have used or even recognized these words as Anglicized. When one searches for these words more broadly using the *Corpus of Middle English Prose and Verse*, it becomes clear that by and large *contrition* was a much more frequent word in Middle English writing than *compunction*. Searching for <contrit*> and <contric*> to cover most spelling variants of *contrition/contrite* results in 797 hits; however, searching for <conp*> and <comp*> (again accounting for most spelling variants in Middle English) results in eighty-four examples of *compunction* or *compunct*, excluding examples of Latin sections of texts as well as Middle English bibles and psalters that are also found in the corpus.

Ambiguity naturally arose when the words were fully separated from their original, more literal senses, as they were in the process of vernacularization (save a brief period when they were used in their more distinct physical senses) and are in Present-Day English usage. In Present-Day English they mean much the same thing; albeit they are so rare that semantic competition between them presents relatively low stakes, which is possibly one reason why both words continue to exist. That is, because neither word is very common, there is less systemic linguistic pressure for one to be chosen over the other or for one to have connotations to do with register (e.g. as with the Present-Day English verbs *commence*, from French, and *begin*, from Old English). It seems likely that *contrition* and *compunction* will eventually fall out of use altogether, as there are other words in English that are more commonly used to describe the related set of emotions, e.g. *feeling bad, ashamed, guilty, sorry* etc. The OED online lists both within its Frequency Band 4 (from a range of 1–8, 1 being extremely rare and 8 being very common), which means they occur between 0.1 and 1.0 times per million words in typical modern English usage. [...] However, most

[Band 4] words remain recognizable to English-speakers, and are likely to be used unproblematically in fiction or journalism'.[26] So while *contrition* and *compunction* are relatively rare, the fact that they are seemingly recognizable to most English speakers probably indicates they have gained a considerable amount of currency since their introduction in the late Middle Ages – certainly they are no longer delimited solely to devotional contexts.

In Present-Day English the use of *compunction* seems to be highly phraseological. In the English *TV Corpus* of 325 million words (1950–2018; composed of US, Canadian, British, Australian and New Zealand Englishes),[27] *compunction* occurs only sixty-three times (making it very rare indeed), and it is used predominantly to reference 'having no … ' or being 'without compunction', frequently in the case of murder wherein one 'kills/murders without compunction'. There is one positive use of this emotion in this corpus, from a British television series called *Upstairs Downstairs* (a 1930s period drama): 'I felt a strong moral compunction to oppose the use of violence against my fellow man.' The two contemporary-set occurrences of the word that do not involve a negative phraseology are actually to do with not knowing what the word means, e.g. 'What's a compunction? […] Sounds dirty' (from *Two and a Half Men*, 2005).

Using the 14 billion word web corpus, *iWeb*,[28] reveals that *compunction* does occur in the English of present-day websites, specifically 2005 times, which equals 0.00014 occurrences every thousand words (i.e. still very infrequent). Again, most of these examples were used in relation to negative phraseologies with *no/without*. Reading all 2005 corpus occurrences in context would take too long, but in a randomized 100 example sample, 18 instances came from explicitly Christian websites, and four examples referred to medieval writers or saints. Of the few examples where it was used positively (i.e. to describe one who does exhibit the ideal of compunction), most were from a Christian devotional context and thus echo medieval usage in that they cite exemplary devotional practice. *Contrition* is only slightly more common, with 4,664 hits. Again, taking a 100 example sample, 14 came from explicitly Christian websites, and most of the other examples were used in a context where someone had committed a wrong and failed to express any regret.

In Middle English on the other hand, *compunction* and *contrition* are almost always used in a positive context, especially to exemplify ideals of Christian emotional culture, frequently in combination with the outward sign of tears. So of the eighty-four previously mentioned examples of *compunction/compunct* found in the *Corpus of Middle English Prose and Verse*, seventy-nine were with a positive reference, in the sense of describing someone (saint or otherwise) who feels or exhibits compunction in an ideal way or describing the ideal of compunction more abstractly. Only five of the examples were of individuals who lacked compunction when they should have felt it. All of the Middle English examples were clearly related to Christian practice, and twenty-four occurred in conjunction with reference to 'tears' or 'weeping' that served as external indicators of the prick of inward conscience. Given the much greater frequency of *contrition* in Middle English, it is not possible to read all instances in context, but a preliminary check suggests that the findings would be similar for this word, especially in terms of its use in relation to positive examples.

The dynamics of guilt, both as a grouping of historical words and as a culture of emotion, have been briefly explicated here, and this highly selective introduction also serves to highlight lines of inquiry that will be pursued in the chapters that follow. The acknowledgement of guilt as both word and concept, particularly in the multilingual, multicultural, multimodal remit of the European Middle Ages, begs questions to do with its various representations across languages (Latin and vernaculars) as well as media and traditions of devotion, but also of art, literature and scholarship. Christianity was to a large extent responsible for the idealization of guilt, shame and regret, but it did so within the specific remit of emotional reformation in the context of practising penance. Certainly, if one delimits their focus to the words deriving from Latin, i.e. *contrition* and *compunction*, most (although not all) references in the Middle Ages will refer to the practice of penance. Contributors in this volume of course do engage with this area of experience, in new and insightful ways, but authors also question the conceptual limits of the related emotions and the ways in which shame, guilt and remorse were represented, nuanced and in some cases complicated in other contexts. It is to those discussions that we now recommend our readers.

1

Crying out with the compunction of the Prodigal Son: Byzantine hymns, liturgical emotions and icons of repentance

Andrew Mellas

The ritual performance of hymns and Scripture devoted to the theme of the prodigal son as a paradigm of compunction and repentance during Great Lent[1] rendered this biblical figure an exemplar for Byzantine Christians. Hymnography composed for this liturgical event amplified the Lukan parable of the prodigal, portraying sin as exile from one's homeland and enslavement to depraved passion. However, it juxtaposed this estrangement with the feeling of compunction, a blessed passion that was intertwined with the experience of paradisal nostalgia and an outpouring of tears.[2] This chapter explores how this hymnody evoked and aroused the emotion of compunction by reimagining the performance of the hymns for this liturgical event in the *Triodion*, the liturgical hymnbook for Great Lent and Holy Week in Byzantium, and the *kontakion*[3] on the prodigal son composed by Romanos the Melodist in the sixth century. It argues that, for the Byzantine faithful, the emotion of compunction was not merely an ideational construct, but an embodied experience that was enacted through sacred song and liturgical mysticism.

Hymns were not simply a remembrance of biblical stories and events but the enactment of a sacred drama that staged the mystery of salvation. The liturgical world of Byzantium embodied 'the harmonious habitus that was ordered toward divine things' and it was there that heaven and earth converged in the hearts of the faithful.[4] Liturgy was the song of theology where the faithful experienced 'the concord of divine things, their selves and others' as one harmonious choir.[5] Through the mystagogy[6] of liturgy, human emotion could be transformed into divine emotion. Hymnody was the affective script that invited human feelings to become liturgical feelings. One precondition for this to occur was the nature of the ecclesial community the liturgy was portrayed as engendering. As John

Chrysostom remarked, this 'body of the faithful is one' and 'is divided by neither time nor place'.[7] The other precondition for this to occur was the Incarnation of the Logos, which 'taught [the flesh] to feel things beyond its nature' by uniting it to the divine in the person of Christ.[8] If Christ's emotions were not simply attributed to his human nature but ascribed to the one incarnate Logos who 'suffered in the flesh, and was crucified in the flesh, and experienced death in the flesh',[9] then, according to this tradition, what the Logos assumed, he also healed and transformed. It was in liturgical worship that such blessed emotions could be felt and the faithful could grasp this mystery.[10]

Compunction for the Byzantine faithful was an embodied phenomenon that can be reimagined by appreciating the 'literariness' of hymnography and reconsidering how it can serve as a historical source, 'not only as documentary witness reflecting or representing what already exists in a given culture but as "source" in the generative sense – as font, wellspring'.[11] Byzantine hymns were more than just literary texts; they served as performative scripts for the making of emotion in liturgy.[12] As scholars are increasingly revealing, emotions are not simply historicized phenomena, they can even change the course of history.[13] Compunction cannot simply be analysed through a text inhabiting the cultural and theological discourse of Byzantium; it must be understood as an intersubjective phenomenon that was embodied within an action and a practice. Compunction became meaningful within an 'affective field'[14] where the audience encountered the hymnographer's text and his or her protagonists in a liturgical experience.

The Sunday of the Prodigal Son in the *Triodion*

In the earliest extant manuscript of the *Triodion*, the tenth-century Sinai Graecus 734–735, the Lenten journey to Pascha[15] begins with hymns for the Sunday of the Prodigal Son, which was one of the preparatory Sundays in the liturgical calendar, before Great Lent formally began.[16] Indeed, according to the rubrics for the cathedral rite of Constantinople, the *Typikon of the Great Church*, this Sunday marked the beginning of the Lenten cycle and the gospel passage assigned for that day was Luke 15:11–32.[17] The first hymn for the Sunday of the Prodigal Son in Sinai Graecus 734–735 evokes how the prodigal son's journey home and restoration begin with compunction:

Ἀγκάλας πατρικὰς διανοῖξαί μοι σπεῦσον·
ἀσώτως τὸν ἐμὸν κατηνάλωσα βίον,

εἰς πλοῦτον ἀδαπάνητον ἀφορῶν τῶν οἰκτιρμῶν σου, σωτήρ·
νῦν πτωχεύουσαν μὴ ὑπερίδῃς καρδίαν·
σοὶ γάρ, Κύριε, ἐν κατανύξει κραυγάζω·
Ἥμαρτον, πάτερ, εἰς τὸν οὐρανὸν καὶ ἐνώπιόν σου.[18]

Make haste and open to me your fatherly embrace.
I have prodigally squandered my livelihood,
as I look to the inexhaustible wealth of your mercy, saviour,
do not now disregard my beggared heart,
for to you, Lord, in compunction I cry out:
'I have sinned, father, towards heaven and before you.'[19]

Perhaps the most striking characteristic of this poem is the first-person narrative that unveils the interiority of the prodigal son but also destabilizes Christian personhood, inviting the faithful to ponder the biblical narrative the hymn evoked and identify with the protagonist of the hymn. Through the singing of the hymn, this scriptural story could become the story of the faithful as they sang the song of the prodigal. The estrangement of the prodigal son became for the faithful their own alienation from divine grace and their own condition of disfellowship.

The journey is marked by the bonds of fatherhood and sonship. The Lukan parable and the hymn characterize the affection of the father for his son as always present. Even when the father allows his younger son to leave with his share of the inheritance and even when the son is isolated in a faraway land, feeding the swine, the actions and memory of the father reveal a relationship of freedom and love. The fatherly embrace embodies the bliss of a homeland that is never absent from the heart of the prodigal son and which becomes the catalyst for the moment of compunction that marks the beginning of the son's repentance. Indeed, in a profound image, the biblical story tells of how the prodigal son 'came to himself'[20] and arose to begin the journey home to his father.

Repentance emerges as a leitmotif of Scripture, especially in Luke–Acts,[21] and late antique Christian discourse.[22] However, repentance is a difficult concept to define.[23] The *Patristic Greek Lexicon* devotes several pages to defining repentance (μετάνοια).[24] Unlike modern audiences, which have inherited 'a somewhat distorted and incomplete view of repentance in late antiquity' as inextricably connected with ecclesiastical institutions of penitence, repentance's existential significance for Christianity went beyond penitential rites, embracing the totality of Christian life.[25] Byzantine hymns on the prodigal son dramatized the journey of repentance through narrative and song so that it could become the story and the voice of the faithful, illuminating the relationships between repentance, compunction and tears. Although the biblical tale of the prodigal son does not explicitly mention the tears of the prodigal, they emerge in the hymns that amplify the scriptural story:

> Ἴδε Χριστέ, τὴν θλῖψιν τῆς καρδίας, ἴδε μου τὴν ἐπιστροφήν, ἴδε τὰ δάκρυα Σῶτερ, καὶ μὴ παρίδης με, ἀλλ' ἐναγκάλισαι πάλιν δι' εὐσπλαγχνίαν, πληθύϊ σῳζομένων συναριθμῶν ὅπως ὑμνῶ εὐχαρίστως τὰ ἐλέη σου.[26]

> See, O Christ, the affliction of my heart; see my turning back; see my tears, O Saviour, and do not despise me. But embrace me once again through your compassion and number me with the multitude of the saved, that with thanksgiving I may sing the praise of your mercies.[27]

Appearing in the *Triodion* as part of the hymns for the Sunday of the Prodigal Son, this is the first strophe from the ninth ode of a *kanon*[28] on the prodigal, which may have been composed by Joseph the Stoudite in the late eighth century or early ninth century.[29] While the strophe continues the first-person narrative of the prodigal son, depicting his tears and repentance, it also voices the prayer of the faithful who are invited to feel like the prodigal son and sing his words.

Of course, in evoking a poignant image of tears and compunction, these hymns drew on a corpus of literature that had already cultivated these relationships in the Christian imagination. The Psalmist's exhortation, "'speak in your hearts and feel compunction on your beds" (λέγετε ἐν ταῖς καρδίαις ὑμῶν καὶ ἐπὶ ταῖς κοίταις ὑμῶν κατανύγητε)',[30] would have been familiar to an audience that ritually experienced the Psalms in its worship.[31] In the New Testament, repentance is linked with compunction (most notably in Acts 2:37–39)[32] and with tears (most vividly in Luke 7:36–50). A number of early Christian writers, including Origen, Gregory of Nyssa and John Chrysostom, develop these links.[33] The fourth-century theologian and poet Ephrem the Syrian[34] and the emergence of monasticism in Egypt and Syria also underscored the spiritual significance of tears.[35] Chrysostom had written about compunction as the '"mother of tears" (δακρύων ἐστὶ μήτηρ)'[36] and often linked tears and compunction in his homilies.[37] And the letters of the famous Old Men from sixth-century Gaza – Barsanuphios and John – reflect on 'weeping and compunction'.[38] Moreover, Isaac the Syrian's seventh-century writings often underscore the importance of weeping as an expression of repentance.[39]

The hymns of the *Triodion* reflected the liturgical atmosphere of Christian worship, which was a place of psalmody and compunction, even if that place of worship was the most magnificent church of Constantinople. A poem that was composed for – and possibly sung at – the inauguration of Hagia Sophia on 24 December 562 situates compunction within the liturgical context of this sacred space:

> Here, noetically, sacrifices in spirit and truth, not in odours of burnt offerings and streams of blood, are ceaselessly offered to God as a sweet-smelling fragrance. The tears of prayers with piety and the songs of psalmody for compunction are sung with instruments of spirit, putting to sleep the demonic impulses of the passions, creating prudent pleasure for salvation, which Christ gives to people, *the life and resurrection of all*.[40]

As in the hymns on the prodigal son in the *Triodion*, this poem portrays compunction as intertwined with prayer and psalmody. Far from eschewing feeling, the liturgical hymns and rites of Byzantium counteracted tainted passions with the remedial power of blessed emotions, such as compunction.

Romanos the Melodist's compunctious hymn on the prodigal son

A few centuries before the *Triodion* and its hymns for the Sunday of the Prodigal Son were composed and compiled, Romanos the Melodist composed a *kontakion* devoted to this biblical hero of repentance.[41] Romanos lived in Constantinople during the reign of Emperor Justinian (527–65) and his *kontakia* represents a unique fusion of classical rhetoric inherited from the Greek world of antiquity, the fourth-century Syriac poetry of Ephrem and the Christian discourse of the Cappadocian Fathers.[42] The *kontakion* was an integral part of the cathedral rite in Constantinople until the Fourth Crusade in 1204.[43] It formed part of the ritual of nocturnal worship known as the night vigil, which was celebrated towards the beginning of the major feasts in the liturgical calendar.[44] Although the manuscript tradition usually assigns each *kontakion* to a particular day in the liturgical calendar, this does not necessarily reflect when each hymn was sung in sixth-century Constantinople.[45] I recognize that our knowledge of liturgical practice and the lectionary in the sixth century is scant, owing to the fact that no liturgical books relating to Constantinopolitan worship survive from that century.

Nevertheless, as the faithful journeyed through Great Lent, Holy Week and other parts of the liturgical calendar, Romanos's hymns presented them with biblical exemplars of compunction, retelling scriptural stories and welcoming them to enter into these narratives. These hymns juxtaposed the parable of the prodigal son, the story of the harlot who washed Christ's feet with her tears[46] and other narratives of biblical heroes with counter-ideals such as the foolish virgins and Judas. However, Romanos's hymnography did not simply enrich biblical texts. His hymns sought to harness the iconic nature of the liturgy to incite a sacramental mimesis that could shape Christian identity.[47] The singing of these hymns by the faithful signified a liturgical imitation of these biblical exemplars, where the speech acts of Romanos's protagonists could become the song and confession of the congregation and where emotions could become intersubjective.[48] Singing the words of these biblical exemplars and entering the liturgical world of these scriptural stories, the faithful prayed for the tears and yearned to feel the compunction that were embodied in poetry, melody and sacred drama.

While it is unclear from the manuscript tradition whether Romanos's *On the Prodigal* was performed on the Second Sunday of Great Lent or on the first of the three preparatory Sundays preceding Lent, before the fourteenth century in Constantinople the Second Sunday of Lent had no particular theme.[49] Moreover, the *Typikon of the Great Church* does not assign Luke 15:11–32 as the gospel reading for that Sunday.[50] Instead, this biblical passage is prescribed for the first of the three preparatory Sundays preceding Lent – 'the Sunday before Carnival Sunday'.[51] Further evidence that this Sunday commemorated the parable of the prodigal son is found in two early manuscripts of the *Triodion*, which dedicate a number of hymns to the theme of the prodigal for this day.[52]

The two preludes in the hymn *On the Prodigal*, begin the hymn by asking the congregation to identify their 'senseless deeds' with those of the prodigal son who befouled 'the first robe of grace' – a baptismal image that is developed further in the fourth strophe – with 'the stains of passions'.[53] As the prodigal son 'came to himself'[54] and arose to return to his father's house, likewise the *kontakion* calls each of the faithful back to the 'mystical table'[55] – an image of the Eucharist:

> καὶ ὡς ἐκεῖνος προσπίπτω σοι καὶ ζητῶ τὴν ἄφεσιν, Κύριε·
> διὸ μὴ παρίδης με, ὁ τῶν αἰώνων δεσπότης καὶ κύριος.[56]
>
> and I fall down before you like him, O Lord, and seek forgiveness.
> Therefore, do not despise me,
> the Master and Lord of the ages.[57]

Romanos presents the prodigal son as a paradigm of humanity who travels to a faraway land and – not unlike Adam and his exile from Eden – acknowledges his fallenness, feels compunction and nostalgia, and begins the journey home.

Strangely though, the prodigal son only utters one line in the whole *kontakion* (in the third strophe). Romanos takes a strikingly different approach in his hymn *On the Harlot*, which explores the interiority of the harlot who, 'with compunction',[58] closely followed Christ's footsteps. The hymn embodies her conversion in the poetry and melody of the *kontakion*:

> Τὴν φρένα δὲ τῆς σοφῆς ἐρευνῆσαι ἤθελον
> καὶ γνῶναι πῶς ἔλαμψεν ἐν αὐτῇ ὁ Κύριος[59]
>
> I wish to search the heart of the wise woman
> and to know how the Lord shined in her.[60]

The *Triodion* also contained various compositions on this theme of the repentant harlot who became a wise woman, most notably the hymn *On the Sinful Woman* by the ninth-century hymnographer Kassia.[61]

Nevertheless, despite the absence of the voice of the rebellious son in the hymn *On the Prodigal* by Romanos, it is through the prism of the prodigal's repentance that the Melodist invites the faithful to see and hear every other monologue and dialogue in the hymn, as well as the Eucharistic and baptismal themes that emerge therein. Unlike his hymn *On the Harlot*, which delves into the protagonist's thoughts and feelings, Romanos here encourages the congregation to be more circumspect and ponder the entire drama of salvation at play. In the first and second strophes alone, the hymn employs the hortative voice or imperative mood on several occasions to invite the congregation to step into the liturgical world of the *kontakion*: 'let us contemplate'; 'hurry'; 'let us celebrate'; 'let us hasten'; 'let us banquet'; 'let us see'.[62]

The hymn likens the robe that the prodigal son is given upon his repentance to 'the first robe, which the baptismal font weaves for all'.[63] This 'first robe' symbolizes the ancient glory of Adam and Eve before they were given the 'garments of skin'[64] and represents the common gift of all Christians who have been 'baptised into Christ' and have 'put on Christ'.[65] Therefore in encouraging the faithful to imitate the prodigal son's repentance, Romanos unlocks the significance of his compunction for all Christians. And in dramatizing the father's compassion for his son with a monologue that does not appear in the Lukan narrative, the hymnographer demonstrates God's desire for all of his creation to be found worthy of forgiveness:[66]

> Ἴδον αὐτὸν καὶ παριδεῖν οὐ στέγω τὸν γυμνωθέντα·
> οὐ φέρω βλέπειν οὕτως τὴν εἰκόνα μου τὴν θείαν·
> ἐμὴ γὰρ αἰσχύνη τὸ ὄνειδος τοῦ παιδός μου·
> ἰδίαν δόξαν τὴν τοῦ τέκνου δόξαν ἡγήσομαι.[67]

> I saw him and I cannot allow myself to disregard his nakedness;
> I cannot bear to see my divine image in this way.
> For the disgrace of my child is my dishonour;
> I will consider the glory of my child my own glory.[68]

Here Romanos begins to allude to the salvific acts of Christ – the Crucifixion, descent into Hades and Resurrection – that will mark the climax of the Lenten journey. Although it is still the beginning of the Lenten season and these events have not yet come to pass, the ritual aesthetic and performance of Byzantine hymns create a rich dialectic between what has happened before and will occur again.

Romanos's exegesis of the fatted calf and the banquet that mark the festivities for the prodigal's return begins to collapse into the present liturgical moment events that took place long ago with what will be celebrated at the end of Great Lent and Holy Week. The human drama of the prodigal son's compunction and repentance unfolds amidst the divine drama of God's compassion, incarnation and sacrifice:

> Ἕλκετε, θύσατε τὸν ζωοδότην
> τὸν καὶ θυόμενον καὶ μὴ νεκρούμενον,
> τὸν ζωοποιοῦντα πάντας τοὺς ἐν ᾅδῃ,
> ἵνα φαγόντες ἐπευφρανθῶμεν[69]

> Drag in, sacrifice the giver of life,
> who is sacrificed and not put to death,
> who gives life to those in hell,
> so that, as we eat, we may rejoice in him[70]

The hymn's allusion to the Eucharist suggests that the celebration of the liturgy in Hagia Sophia and the other churches of Constantinople was imminent.[71] While the context of Romanos's hymns was the night vigil, this particular *kontakion* was chanted in anticipation of the Sunday liturgy, which renders its Eucharistic subtext all the more striking.

The repentance of the prodigal climaxes not simply in a reconciliation with his father, but in the Eucharistic celebration where all are given 'the Lover of mankind' as 'all-holy food'.[72] According to Romanos, this celebration is the nub of the parable, which gives meaning to and is the fulfilment of the prodigal son's compunction. Paradoxically, it is not a bishop or priest who presides but God himself who offers and is offered at this mystical banquet:

καὶ πάντες εὐφρανθέντες ἐμελῴδουν θεῖον ὕμνον·
ὁ πατὴρ μὲν πρῶτος κατήρξατο τῶν παρόντων,
«Γεύσασθε, λέγων, καὶ ἴδετε ὅτι Χριστός εἰμι».[73]

and as all were celebrating, they sang a divine hymn.
The Father, first of those present, began saying,
'Taste and see that I am good'.[74]

The speaker in the hymn invites the faithful to internalize the very communion that they were anticipating:

«Τὸ πάσχα τὸ ἡμέτερον
ἐτύθη νῦν Ἰησοῦς Χριστός,
ὁ τῶν αἰώνων δεσπότης καὶ κύριος.»[75]

'Our Passover has now been sacrificed, Jesus Christ,
Master and Lord of the ages.'[76]

On the Prodigal ends with a prayer to the 'Word of God' to accept 'through compassion' all those who like the prodigal son cry out with compunction: 'Give us tears, as you did the harlot [...] as you did the publican.'[77] Once again Romanos brings other scriptural characters into his story, offering these figures as paradigms of repentance. Moreover, in an unexpected twist to the familiar biblical narrative, Romanos adds a new ending to the Lukan account. The prodigal son's disgruntled elder brother, who in the gospel story refuses to enter the banquet and celebrate his younger brother's return, is persuaded by the love of the father to partake in the supper and sing with joy.[78]

Sacred music and compunction

An intrinsic aspect of Byzantine hymns and their compunctious effect was the sacred music that was wedded with the text. Reimagining the experience of chant and the overall sound of liturgical hymns in Byzantium may seem to be a fool's errand, however, through informed speculation and empirical research; 'it is still possible for us to draw meaningful conclusions about the soundscapes of Byzantine worship from those elements of its acoustic design that may be at least partially recovered'.[79] Scholars have recently begun exploring the soundscapes of Byzantine worship and investigating the significance of sacred music for the faithful.[80] However, one of the difficulties that is inevitably encountered is the absence of an extant treatise devoted entirely to a theory of sacred music in Byzantium. While the sixth book of Augustine's *On Music* suggests that this sacred art is a quest for truth that embodies the beauty of God, the influence of the Bishop of Hippo's writings in Byzantium is uncertain.[81] Nevertheless, Augustine's view of music as being able to stir the emotions of the soul through 'a mysterious inner kinship' between the various modes of chant and feeling reflected Byzantine views on the affective power of sacred song.[82] Byzantium followed Aristotle in believing that melodies affected the listener's soul, as well as being representations of the ordered harmonies underpinning the universe of Plato's *Timaeus*.[83]

Byzantine patristic texts often pondered the effect of music on the emotions. Gregory the Theologian's *On His Own Verses* reflects on how the delight and pleasure of music and poetry could have a role to play in cultivating spirituality, extending beyond the sensual and cultivating the hearts of the faithful:

> Ὥσπερ τι τερπνὸν τοῦτο δοῦναι φάρμακον,
> Πειθοῦς ἀγωγὸν εἰς τὰ χρησιμώτερα,
> Τέχνῃ γλυκάζων τὸ πικρὸν τῶν ἐντολῶν.
> Φιλεῖ δ' ἀνίεσθαί τε καὶ νευρᾶς τόνος·
> Εἴ πως θέλεις καὶ τοῦτο· εἰ μή τι πλέον,
> Ἀντ' ᾀσμάτων σοι ταῦτα καὶ λυρισμάτων.[84]

> My verse could be given as a delightful potion,
> Leading them towards more beneficial things by persuasion,
> Sweetening by art the bitter taste of laws.
> Verse helps us to relax the tightened strings,
> If we but will, even if it be no more
> Than lyric odes and tunes on the lyre.[85]

According to Athanasius of Alexandria, psalmody could become like a mirror to the emotions of the soul and a source of therapy and correction suited for these emotions.[86] The Psalms presented the faithful with emotions for internalization through a text and melody that became their own words and their own song through meditation and participation in devotional practices. In hearing the song, they were 'moved by compunction'[87] and received the words of others in the Psalm as being about their very selves:

> And it seems to me that these words become like a mirror to the person singing them, so that he might perceive himself and the emotions of his soul, and thus affected, he might recite them. For in fact he who hears the one reading receives the song that is recited as being about him, and either, when he is moved to

compunction by his conscience, he will repent, or hearing of the hope that resides in God, and of the succour available to believers – how this kind of grace exists for him – he rejoices greatly and begins to give thanks to God.[88]

Similarly, hymnody did not hesitate to draw upon scriptural stories, asking the faithful to enter into the sacred drama unfolding before them and feel the emotions of biblical characters such as the prodigal son.

Concluding remarks

Hymns on the theme of the prodigal son by Romanos and in the *Triodion* evoked the mystery of compunction and repentance in Byzantium. They aroused liturgical emotions by presenting the prodigal as an icon of repentance and inviting the faithful to feel the emotions of biblical characters through the affective mysticism of hymnody. Scriptural exemplars of repentance, such as the prodigal and the harlot, were often characterized by their 'tears of compunction'[89] and their desire to experience the merciful embrace of Christ. Although William Blake will tell us that 'a tear is an intellectual thing', insofar as we cry because we think, the spiritual valency of tears for Eastern Christianity is profound.[90] Tears were eschatological rebirth into the life of the age to come and yet a return to the paradisal bliss of old:

> I do not have a sorrowful heart to search for you, I do not have repentance, I do not have compunction nor tears which return children to their homeland.[91]

The prodigal's compunction showed how liturgical emotions were not simply a natural phenomenon but a gift or a way:

> As I ponder the quality of compunction, I am amazed. How does grief and so-called sadness, joy and gladness, mingle inside us like honeycomb? What can we learn from this? That this compunction has been properly ordained a gift of God. Then there is no disagreeable pleasure in the soul, since God secretly brings consolation to those who are contrite in heart.[92]

Compunction could trace a pathway to the divine, deconstructing the dichotomy of interiority vs exteriority and mediating the liminal space between God and the faithful.

Compunction in the *Triodion* and in Romanos's hymn *On the Prodigal* emerges as an act of vulnerability and a desire for restoration. Hymnody performed scriptural narrative and invited the Byzantine faithful to become protagonists in the sacred story of salvation. The hymns sung during the Lenten cycle became a collective space of liturgical action that sought to draw in the faithful and invite them to experience the sacred drama that unfolded in Constantinople and beyond. The congregation could follow in the footsteps of, and identify with, the prodigal as he journeyed towards repentance. And, insofar as human emotion could become liturgical emotion, they could cry with the compunction of the prodigal son and experience the tears that circumscribed 'the path that leads towards the new age'.[93]

2

Repenting in their own words: Old English vocabulary for compunction, contrition and penitence

Daria Izdebska

Introduction

A look in the British National Corpus, which was 'designed to represent a wide cross-section of British English from the later part of the 20th century' in both its written and spoken forms,[1] shows that in terms of frequency of occurrence the words *compunction* and *compunctions* come at 0.68, while *contrition* and *contrite* come at around 1.18 instances per million words (henceforth, wpm).[2] As is to be expected due to a relatively low importance of these concepts in modern life, this is not a very high number. However, to put it into contrast with related emotions that are perhaps more familiar, a search for *repent** comes at 2.15, *remors**[3] at 4.16 and *regret**[4] at 31.98 wpm. To give a broader comparison still, the adjectives *angry* and *happy* yield 40.66 and 115.1 wpm, respectively, even without accounting for such variations as *anger* or *happiness*. There may be a lesson here on the differences between basic and complex emotions, or about the affective preoccupations of the speakers of British English, but suffice it to say that, overall, Present-Day English (PDE) does not place a heavy emphasis on directly discussing the experiences of remorse or regret, let alone contrition or compunction in overt terms.

Though an interesting question in its own right, it is not in the remit of this chapter to discuss the ways in which these terms function in Present-Day English, but rather to investigate a period when the affective experiences denoted by them were first being introduced into the language, with the arrival of the Christian religion and its associated ideas. Even so, the modern corpus query brings our attention to the difficulties in disentangling concepts from the terms used to denote them and the deceptiveness of cognate vocabulary. The adjective *contrite*, as it appears in the BNC, though sometimes entrenched in Christian contexts (e.g. 'for all the sins which you confess with a **contrite** heart'),[5] has lost much of its previous force and is more frequently found in situations where *remorseful* or *sorry* would have been equally appropriate (as indeed, in this example from a work of fiction depicting an altercation between a mother and a daughter: 'She was not **contrite** or sorry or any of the things she should have been').[6] To modern perceptions the etymology of this word, from Latin *conterĕre* 'to rub together, grind',[7] is entirely opaque, and its literal senses 'bruised, crushed, worn, broken', attested rarely up until the seventeenth and eighteenth centuries, are now obsolete.[8] The embodied connotations which evoke an emotion strong enough to be compared to violent physical pain are no longer available to speakers of Present-Day English.

Even though we may not discuss *regret* very often, we instinctively recognize what it is. The previous sentence quoted from the BNC is a good example for another reason. It represents a scenario, a conceptual frame of behaviour, which seems so familiar to us that we do not pause to think about its significance. If one does something wrong, it is culturally accepted to reflect on it, acknowledge one's responsibility and make amends by verbally apologising and, often, making further reparations. If the script is not followed when someone is clearly to blame, the perpetrator's behaviour may be deemed inappropriate, rude, and perhaps even invite accusations of a lack of a moral compass. The inability to feel remorse, in extreme cases, may even be considered a mark of a sociopathic personality disorder.[9]

Words such as *compunction*, *contrition*, *repentance* and *penitence* entered the English language in the Middle English period from Latin via Anglo-Norman or Old French.[10] The concepts behind these words, however, were introduced much earlier, with the arrival of Christianity in Anglo-Saxon England. They were either directly defined through patristic and monastic texts or described as part of the course of Christian praxis. These were not merely abstract ideas, but as a component part of the doctrine of penitence and the practice of confession, they constituted a complex affective experience which needed to be taught and explained to the believers by the clergy. It was an experience that could be constructed from already existing emotions (regret, sadness, fear, love, hope) and involved cognitive decision-making regarding future behaviour. Rather than borrowing words directly from Latin, as will be seen in the course of this chapter, Old English chose to render these emotions either through a set of loan translations or by semantic extensions to already existing vocabulary. The way in which these linguistic and lexical adaptations occurred will throw light on the act of adopting and adapting the emotions of compunction into the Old English conceptual structures. To what extent this transposition of emotions was successful at the level of lay practitioners is impossible to tell, as there is no surviving evidence to illustrate everyday experiences. The literature of the period was written down (if not necessarily composed) in monastic contexts, which makes any attempts at reconstructing pre-Christian mindsets even more difficult. However, the first step to understanding emotional experiences of distant cultures is to look at the vocabulary they use, and this approach will be adopted for the purpose of this chapter.

The main aim of this chapter is, therefore, to examine the Old English vocabulary for *regret* and *compunction* via a corpus-based lexical-semantic analysis and determine patterns of usage, frequency and distribution of occurrence. I shall also look at the range of senses of selected word-families in order to establish the level of integration of these new ideas into the Old English language and thought.

Analysing complex emotions cross-culturally: Did Anglo-Saxons feel regret?

The evolving understanding of emotions from a psychological and neurobiological point of view has moved away from the simplistic in favour of seeing emotions as 'composite, multi-component constructs'[11] that 'emerge from the dynamic interactions between large-scale brain networks'.[12] To this complexity, we also have to add the difficulties faced by the analysis of emotions diachronically and cross-culturally, particularly in linguistic and anthropological contexts, which have been discussed at length elsewhere.[13]

For the purpose of this discussion, it is worth distinguishing between different levels on which any emotion could be analysed: (1) the emotion as an internal experience that arises from the physiological responses in the body, often difficult to encapsulate in words; (2) the emotion as a mental concept: how it is represented in the mind, but also the cognitive structures associated with that emotion which involve appraisal of the situation, expectations, memories, judgment and planning; (3) emotion as tied to behaviour that involves e.g. body language and facial expressions (some innate, some acquired as part of cultural norms and scripts); (4) *emotion* as a word that denotes this mental concept, i.e. the linguistic sign with the emotion as a referent; and (5) the linguistic and pragmatic expression of this emotion, i.e. what phrases and words are used to express it in a communicative speech act. While there is a lot of overlap between these levels, the main challenge lies in the fact that they do not correspond to one another fully. It puts us in a precarious epistemological position – without access to live participants to observe and ask questions of, can we really reconstruct emotions on all these five levels? The copious research on the history of emotions would suggest that textual evidence can be a good enough approximation of at least some of them, but, as a healthy degree of caution is advised, we should keep in mind the distinctions on these levels. As a primarily linguistic investigation, this discussion will be most interested in levels 2 and 4 outlined above, with brief mentions of levels 3 and 5.

Regret can be seen as the obvious basis from which the Christian emotions of compunction/contrition developed. While usually not counted among the basic emotions,[14] and often subsumed under sadness or shame as a tertiary emotion,[15] it is still considered universal by some. Breugelmans et al. acknowledge the difficulties in translating emotions from one language to another, and yet they find in their comparison of distinct cultures (the United States, Israel, Taiwan and the Netherlands) that regret is associated with similar thoughts and feelings in all four. The items found as indicative were: 'I felt *regret*. I felt *angry* with myself. I thought that I was *responsible* for the situation. I thought that I had made a *mistake*. I wanted to *correct* my mistake.'[16] In other psychological studies, regret is defined as 'an emotion associated with a decision that turns out badly, […] elicited by a comparison (counterfactual [1–3]) between the outcome of a choice (reality) and the better outcome of foregone rejected alternatives (what might have been) … thus inducing a disposition to behavioral change'.[17]

In very simplistic terms, we could then define the concept of regret (borrowing some aspects of the language of semantic primes from Wierzbicka and Goddard's Natural Semantic Metalanguage (NSM), but without constructing the whole explication), as: 'I did something bad or did not do something I or people wanted me to do. Now I feel bad. I want to think: I didn't do this. I know it's not true. I want to do something to make it good.' Regret is, thus, often combined with the evaluation of past actions, the acceptance of one's role in them and the wish to make amends either through speech acts or through deeds, and therefore is tied with apologies and the notions of sincerity and forgiveness.[18]

The theme of correction and amendment is very strong in both of the above discussions of remorse or regret. However, to use a contemporary, cross-linguistic example and to move away from a more Anglo-centric view of this emotion, it is not always this straightforward in all languages. In Polish, for instance, the closest equivalent to the Present-Day English word *regret* is *żal*. This word can be variously translated as 'grief', 'sadness', 'sorrow', 'regret' and even 'longing'. However, it is also a 'culturally specific feeling', which 'does not correspond to any of these words individually'[19] and has been discussed in relation to its untranslatability and the uniqueness of its experience as a distinct category of emotion.[20]

To expand on these observations, the word *żal* often encodes sadness or grief at something that has happened, but the component of correction of one's own actions seems cognitively separate to native speakers. One can maintain the state of *żal* without ever learning from it. The emotion is more directed towards the past – the reliving of the unpleasant memories or feeling pity for oneself at having done something bad. It is less directed towards the future. Though regret can be considered universal, it does not mean it is universally important or understood in the same way in different cultures, nor that it always maps fully on to the schema described above. Thus, we need to start our investigation by asking, how did Anglo-Saxons feel regret in pre-Christian times? In order to understand how compunction and contrition were superimposed upon the Old English notions of *regret*, we need to first determine its shape.

Williams's study on sincerity has brought attention to the lack of pragmatic apologies in Old English, and his discussion of the reconstructed mores of early Germanic society clearly shows that cultural norms can greatly influence the inner affective landscape and its external linguistic expression.[21] Similarly, Kohnen finds in his corpus-based pragmatic analysis that, though there are some extracts in the extant data that could be considered apologies, all of them belong 'to genres of religious instruction and prayer'.[22] He concludes that the very act of apologising was likely not common in the secular sphere of life in a Germanic warrior society and was likely strongly influenced by the Christian acts of penitence, which can be seen as 'precursors of apologies'.[23]

If the Anglo-Saxons did not place the same emphasis on apologies and forgiveness, the feelings of remorse or regret would not necessarily hold the same cultural value, nor would they be as heavily lexicalized as other concepts. That is not to say the emotion would be absent or non-existent, but rather that it was not prioritized.

Fulkerson's book-length study on the concept of remorse in pre-Christian Classical Antiquity throws light on some of the types of differences we could expect to see:

> Regret and remorse have rather different roles to play in ancient and modern cultures. It is not [...] that there was no place for remorse or regret in pagan Greece or Rome, but rather that these emotions occurred and were evaluated according to different rules. In general, the modern Western viewpoint esteems the feelings of regret and particularly remorse as a part of a beneficial rethinking and learning process – even as the need for them shows an initial aberration in behaviour. Their appearance shows that one has made progress, has become a better person, and moved past the original incidents. The ancients have a different intuition, believing that one should refrain from doing in the first place things that one will later need to regret.[24]

She further states that the increasing influence of monotheistic religions eventually morphs the feelings of remorse into the Christian virtue of repentance, but that the process lasted at least several centuries, with old paradigms remaining relevant for a considerable period.[25] This could provide a broad parallel to the developments within Anglo-Saxon culture – which was similarly polytheistic and centred around the ideas of heroism and fate – and developed into a monotheistic culture which held remorse and forgiveness in high regard. Certainly, when it comes to other emotions, such as compassion or even pity, they have been influenced by Christian doctrine in Anglo-Saxon times as well. Stanley concludes his overview of vocabulary for various forms of compassion in legal and homiletic writings and charitable provisions, stating that though the Anglo-Saxons had a 'social conscience', it was inextricably linked with the ideas of eternal reward and punishment, unlike our own.[26]

The integration between pre-Christian notions and Christian doctrine worked on the level of concepts and behaviours, but also on the level of vocabulary. As Pascual notes, 'many native Old English words gradually changed their meanings after the advent of Christianity, losing older connotations and assuming new ones in order to adapt to novel concepts and ideas'.[27]

According to the *Historical Thesaurus of English*, Old English could express the idea of regret with a variety of lexical means, such as the following verbs: *gnornian, sorgian (after), hrēowan, besargian, heofan, sican after, bemǣnan*.[28] For none of these, however, 'to regret' was a core meaning.[29] Rather, the core meanings focus on various degrees of sadness that are related either to external manifestation of sadness (such as 'moan', 'lament', 'sigh') or to the physical experience of emotional pain (such as 'wound', 'feel pain'). In fact, a large portion of vocabulary relating to negative emotions has a strong somatic motivation, as initially discussed by Nicholson.[30] 'Regret' as a meaning of these words is, therefore, much more context-dependent than inherent – it can be understood as a specific type of the more general experience of grief and sadness.

Penance and compunction in Anglo-Saxon England

The doctrine of compunction has been investigated in much detail in the Early Medieval period, particularly in Sandra McEntire's work on the subject,[31] and can be considered 'central to the spirituality of medieval monasticism in the West'.[32] Initially, before Gregory the Great and the sixth-century monastic rules, the doctrine was concerned simply with mourning for one's sins, but Gregory developed the notion of *compunctio cordis* 'the compunction of the heart'. In his writings – such as the *Dialogi* translated into Old English by Werferth – Gregory discusses two types of compunction, one that arises from the feelings of fear for eternal punishment, the other that is motivated by the love of God and the desire for his closeness. He further differentiates between two types of tears as those of repentance and sorrow, which are inferior, and those of desire, love and joy, which are superior.[33] Compunction is thus not only a complex affective experience, but also a God-inspired and God-given grace that is given to those most pure of heart and evidenced through the free-flowing tears, which can act as a 'conduit between the human and the divine'.[34]

Anglo-Saxons would have been aware of the doctrine of compunction either through the works of early Church fathers in Latin (Isidore, Gregory, Jerome) or through the various *regularis concordia* (e.g. the *Rule of Chrodegang*). The texts most relevant to compunction, such as the Gregory's *Dialogi* and the *Pastoral Care* or the Benedictine rule, were also translated into Old English,[35] and Alcuin himself wrote on compunction in his *Liber de Virtutibus et Vitiis*.

As tears are considered the 'most readily identifiable feature' of compunction,[36] it is often through the depictions of weeping that this affective experience is analysed in Old English poetry, such as McCormack's work on *Christ*, Palmer's analysis of *The Wanderer* or Cooper's discussion of Cynewulfian poems.[37]

Though for the purposes of this chapter compunction, contrition and penitence are treated together, according to McEntire compunction and penance were clearly delineated in the early Church writings,[38] where penance is understood as specifically the act of amending wrongs and following confession. The literature on penance and penitence is extensive, both in terms of the Old English texts and scholarly work discussing it,[39] and the descriptions and prescription of practice as well as theological explanations are found in a significant proportion of prose works in Old English from this period. The confessor's job was to prescribe appropriate acts of penance (fasting, almsgiving), but also to assess the penitent's sincerity and level of compunction, views reflected both in Alcuin's writings (compunction was a necessary precondition for God's forgiveness) and in practice, such as in *Egbert's Penitential*.[40] This brings us to the conclusion that, at least in theory, a measure of affective response was required from the sinners, one that had to be taught and learned. The materials for penitential practice were complex, but in theory they had to 'reach far downward from royal and episcopal levels to the world of a poorly trained clergy and uninstructed laymen'.[41]

Methodology and data

The first step to obtain lexical data for the analysis of the lexical field of compunction was to consult the electronic versions of both the *Historical Thesaurus of English* (HTE) and *A Thesaurus of Old English* (TOE)[42] to cross-reference and determine the range of lexemes associated with the emotions falling under the compunction umbrella.[43] The two thesauri have different conceptual hierarchical structures, with differing levels of depth of vertical classification.[44] This is a result of the adopted editorial processes – the TOE editors 'allowed the taxonomy to emerge from the data' to reflect as far as possible the Anglo-Saxon world views.[45] As the HTE needs to deal with the entirety of the history of English diachronically, where conceptual structures would have changed significantly over time, it is more guided by modern classifications than the TOE, which only has to cover the Old English period.

In this sense, it is the TOE classification that is more relevant, while HTE data only serves as a control, to make sure the appropriate vocabulary is captured. In TOE the relevant compunction-words can be found predominantly in the category 08.01.03.02.01 (n.) 'Bad feeling, sadness:: Discontent:: Compunction, remorse, contrition', but also to some extent in 16.02.04.07.02.01 (n.) 'Religion:: Faith:: Worship, honour, praise:: Confession:: Penitence,' and 12.08.02.02.01 (n.) 'Social interaction:: Principle, character:: Integrity, absence of moral flaw:: Reform, correction'. These categories reflect well the position of this emotion in the Anglo-Saxon world view as an affective experience that is tied to Christian religion and moral conduct and often has a corrective effect on behaviour.

Following the methodology adopted in previous studies of a similar nature,[46] the selected vocabulary found in the thesauri was then arranged into word-families,[47] i.e. all the derived forms that share the same root. These word-families were analysed in relation to their etymologies and senses, based on a selection of lexicographic resources to give an indication of potential semantic motivations behind them, including any metaphors or metonymies, and to make it easier to establish whether these etymologies are transparent or opaque when words are used in context.

The underlying methodological and theoretical assumptions of this study rest on the application of corpus-linguistic methods to the *Dictionary of Old English Web Corpus* (DOEC),[48] particularly the distribution and frequency of occurrence of word forms in different text types (verse, prose and glosses) within the framework of cognitive historical semantics that takes a two-pronged, onomasio- and semasiological approach. The quantitative data was then complemented by a close manual philological analysis of verse and prose samples within their co-text and context to establish most common senses and patterns of usage. The analysis also takes into consideration collocations, connotations and possible synonyms. This study looks only at the direct discussion of the emotions through the words or terms which reference them, rather than indirect behavioural displays of emotions (such as tears or weeping).

Texts from the period in question exist on a continuum – from original texts composed in Old English, through texts composed in Old English but inspired by Latin originals to close translations of Latin source texts (e.g. Gregory's *Dialogues* or the *Pastoral Care*), to interlinear glosses of Latin texts. However, the linguistic data found in the glosses can be considered a class of their own, separate enough to warrant a different approach. Rather than analyse the patterns of usage, correspondences between Latin and Old English are traced throughout the corpus in both directions – with the search performed on both Latin terms (and which Old English words are used to translate them) and on Old English terms (and which Latin words render them). This is aimed at determining the stability of the lexical equivalence and whether the equivalence is exclusive (one word always corresponding to another) or free (one word has more than one potential translation). This method will throw light on how polysemous the Old English terms were.

Another methodological concern when attempting to map out diachronic changes within the Old English period itself is the lack of certainty regarding the date of composition of many of the texts from which we draw our linguistic data – some can be placed in time with greater certainty than others (particularly when associated with identified figures, e.g. prose works from the court of King Alfred the Great or the later compositions by Ælfric or Wulfstan). However, as the majority of the material is anonymous and, particularly in case of verse, often found in manuscripts with a later date of production than the believed date of composition, there are ongoing debates.

An overview of the semantic field of COMPUNCTION/ REPENTANCE

The words chosen for analysis are those which from the evidence of dictionaries and thesauruses have 'compunction', 'contrition' or 'repentance' as one of their senses and appear with this meaning frequently enough to warrant an analysis.[49] Based on these criteria, six word-families were selected (see Table 1), though each one of them required an analysis tailored to its individual characteristics. In some cases, the senses of compunction were not found in all of the words derived from the same root; in some cases, the entire word-family and all its derivatives could have that sense.[50]

Table 1 Overview of the lexical make-up of the word-families for compunction, contrition and penance

Word-family	Word category	Lexemes	Senses from *Dictionary of Old English* (DOE) or Bosworth-Toller (B-T)[51]
HRĒOW	Verbs	behrēowsian (ge)hrēowan hrēowian hrēowsian	'regret, lament, repent', 'to feel pity' (1)'distress, grieve, cause sorrow', (2) 'cause pity, compassion,' (3) 'cause regret, remorse', (4) 'to repent' 'to sorrow, grieve, lament', 'to repent' (1) 'to grieve, lament, bewail', (2) 'to regret, repent', (3) 'to make an open demonstration of repentance, do penance'
	Nouns	behrēowsung behrēowsungtīd gehrēow (ge)hrēownes hrēow hrēowsung	'repentance' 'time of penitence' 'sorrow, remorse, lamentation' 'penitence, repentance, sorrow, contrition' (1) 'sorrow, grief, sadness', (2) 'regret, remorse, repentance, penitence, penance' 'sorrow, penitence, repentance'
	Adjectives	hrēow hrēowcearig hrēowig hrēowigmōd hrēowlīc	'sorrowful, repentant' 'troubled, anxious, sorrowful' 'sad, sorrowful' 'sad at heart' 'grievous, miserable, pitiful, sad'
	Adverb	hrēowlīce	'miserably, cruelly, grievously'

Word-family	Word category	Lexemes	Senses from *Dictionary of Old English* (DOE) or Bosworth-Toller (B-T)[51]
BRYRD	Verbs	ābryrdan inbryrdan onbryrdan	'spur, prod, stimulate', 'make contrite', 'incite with fear' (1) 'spur, stimulate, incite, inspire', (2) 'inspire to compunction, remorse, contrition, compassion' 'instigate, stimulate', 'excite to compunction'
	Nouns	bryrding bryrdnes gebryrdnes inbryrdnes onbryrdness onbryrding	'compunction, instigation' 'a pricking, goading, stimulation' glossing *compunctio*: 'compunction, stimulus' 'inspiration, animation, compunction, feeling' 'instigation, stimulus, inspiration, compunction' 'an exciting, a stimulus'
DǢDBŌT	Verbs	dǣdbētan	'to repent, do penance, to regret'
	Nouns	dǣdbeta dǣdbētere dǣdbōt dǣdbōtlīhting dǣdbōtnes	'a penitent' 'a penitent' 'repentance, penitence, penance' 'mitigation of penance' 'penitence'
ÞRǢST	Verbs	forþrǣstan þrǣstan	glossing *conterere*: 'crush, shatter', 'contrite', 'stifle' 'twist, writhe, roll about'
	Nouns	forþrǣstednes þrǣsting (ge)þrǣstnes	'bruise, wound, breach', 'affliction, distress, grief' 'torment, affliction' 'affliction, contrition'
FOR/ TŌBRȲT*	Verbs	forbrȳtan tōbrȳtan	'break utterly', 'destroy' 'to break in pieces, crush, bruise', 'to make contrite'
	Nouns	forbrȳtednes forbrȳtnes tōbrȳtedness	'bruise, wound', 'affliction, distress, grief', 'contrition' 'affliction, distress, grief' 'a bruise, breach', 'trouble, sorrow'
FORGNID	Verbs	forgnīdan	'to crush, break to pieces' pp. *forgniden* 'crushed, contrite'
	Nouns	forgnidennes	glossing *contritio*: 'crushing, bruise, affliction'

Etymologies and semantic change

HRĒOW is of central interest to this chapter as a word-family with a range of senses predominantly relating to emotions. As the lexicographic evidence in Table 1 illustrates, *HRĒOW* covers different types of the 'basic' emotion of sadness, and these different senses will be discussed in more detail below. However, particularly for the later, prose evidence, *HRĒOW* develops the Christian sense of 'repentance, penitence'. The words from this family have received some attention in terms of morphological and derivational patterns and their significance for dialect identification in Old English.[52] The family is also the most productive when it comes to derivational variants.

Its cognates can be found in Old Saxon, Old High German and Old Norse, and the Old Saxon range of lexemes is likewise derivationally rich.[53] The Proto-Germanic strong verb is either reconstructed as **xrewwanan*[54] or, more recently, as **hrewan* < **kréu(H)-e-*,[55] with the sense of 'to be sad, to make sad, to grieve'. The earliest recorded senses for the Old High German cognate noun *(h)riuwa*, from the eighth century, are given as 'Leid, Trauer, Schmerz, Unglück, Klage'[56] (roughly equivalent to Present-Day English *grief, sorrow, pain, misfortune, lamentation*). Pfeifer et al. suggest that in the course of the Middle Ages the senses developed from a spiritual or emotional pain into regret and then repentance and contrition.[57] This seems a pattern common to the West Germanic branch, with Old Saxon and Old English likely undergoing similar processes.

Old Norse has the verb *hryggva* 'to distress, grieve', the adjective *hryggr* 'afflicted, grieved, sad', and the noun *hryggð* 'affliction, grief, sorrow', plus a range of compounds formed with the noun as base, which add the senses of 'mourning' and 'lamentation', such as *hrygðar-búnaðr* 'a mourning dress'.[58] The association of these lexemes with the superordinate category of SADNESS is further evidenced, as when translating Christian concepts from Latin, *hryggð* is used for *tristitia*,[59] i.e. 'sadness', rather than *poenitentia, compunctio* or *contritio*.[60]

The potential cognates in other Indo-European families could include Lithuanian *krùšti* 'to pound', Greek *krū́ein* (κρούειν) 'to strike, smite' or Old Slavic *sъkrušiti* 'break, rip, smash'.[61] Perhaps initially in Proto-Germanic the root may have had a similar sense, but most sources treat the further origin of the word as uncertain.[62] No evidence in the Old English sources suggests that *HRĒOW* ever denoted any literal physical sense of 'crushing, grinding,' though violent physical motivations for strong, painful emotions are not unheard of.[63] Nevertheless, it is notable that in earlier word history this physical meaning could have been present, considering that the semantic motivation of Latin *contritio* as physical breaking apart was definitely transparent to the speakers of Old English.

DǢDBŌT, which includes the noun *dǣdbōt* 'repentance, penitence, penance' and the verb *dǣdbētan* 'to repent, do penance', will be discussed in more detail below but will not be analysed within the corpus itself. As the main focus of this chapter is the emotional experience of compunction and penitence, rather than the resulting acts (which these words refer to), a decision was made to look at *DǢDBŌT* only when it throws light on the affective aspects of these concepts.[64] The words are coinages within the Old English period and their etymology is transparent and easily analysable in terms of the modifier *dǣd* 'deed, act' and the heads: *bōt* 'atonement, fine, compensation' and *bētan* 'to make good, amend, correct, atone for', but also 'to compensate, to pay a fine'. They have no direct parallels in other Germanic languages.

BRYRD comprises both verbs and de-verbal nouns formed with the suffix *-nes*. The base for this family is the verb *bryrdan* 'to prick, goad, prod, spur', from Germanic **bruzdjanan* 'to prick', from **bruzdaz* 'sharp point'. The Old English verbs formed with the prefixes *on-* or *in-* could have been formed by analogy with the Latin *con-punctio*.[65] The lexicographic evidence shows that from the literal sense of 'pricking', two metaphoric senses developed, one dealing with inspiration, the other specifically with compunction, but inspiration seems more prototypical (the verb *onbryrdan* often means 'to instigate, stimulate, incite').

In case of *ÞRǢST*, *BRYT* and *FORGNID*, the term 'word-family' is not entirely adequate. Word-family suggests that all members of this family derived from the same root will share meaning(s) at least in some of their occurrences (like in the case of *HRĒOW*). However, in the case of these three sets of expressions it is only a few lexemes that directly refer to the notions of compunction/contrition. These expressions (to borrow Diaz Vera's term), which are used in glosses for Latin *contritio*, are mostly de-verbal nouns. They take as base an existing Old English verb that denotes a form of physical breaking or injury of some sort: *þrǣstan* 'to twist, writhe, torture', *brytan* 'crush, grind, break', and *gnidan* 'crush, grind'. The prefix *for-* has an intensifying function of an action being done 'very, extremely or utterly', often used 'with sense of destructive, painful or prejudicial effect',[66] and *to-* denotes separation or division. Sometimes, past participles of the verbs are also used with the sense 'contrite'. It is only the prefixed forms that denote contrition. These words are semantic loans or loan translations of the Latin noun *contritio*, and the verb *contero* 'to grind, bruise, pound, wear out',[67] which range from senses denoting physical breaking to the specific Christian emotion of contrition.[68]

Table 2 Distribution of word-families in the corpus in different text types by raw frequencies (RF) and normalized frequencies (NF).

Word-Family	RF	Size of the subcorpus	NF
HRĒOW			
Verse (A)[69]	34	177,480	19.15708812
Prose (B)	435	2,128,781	20.43422973
Gloss (C + D)	86	726,204	11.84240241
Total	**555**	**3,032,465**	**18.30194248**
DǢDBŌT			
Verse (A)	1	177,480	0.563443768
Prose (B)	421	2,128,781	19.77657636
Gloss (C + D)	69	726,204	9.501462399
Total	**491**	**3,032,465**	**16.19144821**
BRYRD			
Verse (A)	14	177,480	7.888212756
Prose (B)	155	2,128,781	7.281162318
Gloss (C + D)	82	726,204	11.291593
Total	**251**	**3,032,465**	**8.277094707**
FOR/TOBRYT*			
Verse (A)	0	177,480	0
Prose (B)	24	2,128,781	1.127405778
Gloss (C + D)	104	726,204	14.32104478
Total	**128**	**3,032,465**	**4.220988536**
ÞRÆST*			
Verse (A)	1	177,480	0.563443768
Prose (B)	24	2,128,781	1.127405778
Gloss (C + D)	82	726,204	11.291593
Total	**107**	**3,032,465**	**3.528482604**
*of which forþræst**			
Prose	*1*	2,128,781	0.046975241
Gloss (C + D)	*53*	726,204	7.298224741
FORGNID*			
Verse (A)	0	177,480	0
Prose (B)	0	2,128,781	0
Gloss (C + D)	73	726,204	10.05227181
		3,032,465	**2.407282524**

Distribution in the corpus

Table 2 illustrates the distribution of the word-families in the corpus by both raw and normalized frequencies (per thousand words) to make comparisons of the distribution between the subcorpora more meaningful. The searches were constructed to account for the variation in spelling of different words to enhance recall, so words from the *HRĒOW* family could be searched as *hreo**, *hreu** or even *hrev**, etc.

In absolute terms, out of the six word-families, *HRĒOW* words are the most commonly occurring in the DOEC (555 occ., NF = 18.3), followed by *DǢDBŌT* (491 occ., NF = 16.19). The difference in the overall occurrences of the two in the corpus is not significant at first glance, but the two word-families show a markedly different distribution in the text-type subcorpora. The normalized frequencies for *HRĒOW* in verse and prose are broadly similar, showing a comparable rate of occurrence in proportion to the size of the subcorpus. The word-family is slightly less frequent in glosses, but not by very much. *DǢDBŌT*, on the other hand, occurs predominantly in prose, half as frequently in glosses, and virtually not at all in verse. *DǢDBŌT* likely had a more specialized meaning of penance and recompense which would have been discussed in the kinds of texts that form the majority of the prose corpus: homilies, penitentials, handbooks and so on. If an additional analysis were to be performed on the religious senses of the verb *bētan* (see below), the number of occurrences in prose could have been even greater. *HRĒOW* is much more evenly distributed, due to its broader range of affective senses.

BRYRD is the third largest family (with 251 occ., NF = 8.27), but it is only about half the size of the previous two. It occurs with similar frequency in verse and prose but is slightly more common in glosses. The remaining loan translations are far less frequent, being confined almost entirely to glosses.

A point of note with regard to the frequency of occurrence in the glosses is that raw numbers and even the normalized frequencies can be misleading as they assume regular distribution and uniqueness of occurrence. Unlike in a representative corpus, they do not take into account the existence of several versions of the same (or similar) text. Latin texts were glossed more than once by different glossators from different traditions, and particularly in the case of the Old English Psalter glosses (which constitute a large part of this subcorpus), a Latin word in the same passage from a single psalm could occur in the corpus up to fifteen times being glossed with the same Old English word.[70] While the linguistic and historical differences between these glosses mean that they cannot be treated as the same text for philological purposes, a computational analysis of their occurrence is problematic and therefore will not be fully attempted.

DǢDBŌT and compensation

DǢDBŌT occurs in the TOE both in the category of emotional experience (08.01 'Bad feeling, sadness') and in the category for religious practice (16.02.04.07 'Worship, honour, praise'), which suggests that it was used to denote the feeling of repentance as well as an act of penance and making amends. Literally, the verb *dǣdbētan* means simply 'to make good or to remedy a deed' (DOE), and the range of senses in the DOE clearly shows that the core meaning and focus of this word-family are shifted towards the acts of penance, rather than the affective experience.[71]

As previously mentioned, the semantic motivation of the noun *dǣdbōt* and the verb *dǣdbētan* is transparent. Alongside compound words we see phrasal units as well, clearly marked as such by case morphology (e.g. *dǣdum bētan*). What is more, *bōt* and *bētan* on their own can also take on the specialized meaning of 'repentance, atonement for sin' and 'repent, atone' (DOE), without the need for the pre-modifier. Both the noun and verb also exhibit a wider range of senses that can throw light on our understanding of the adaptation of the idea of repentance or penance in Old English. The base sense is related to the ideas of repairing, mending, healing and generally making good. These general senses can be used also in more technical settings – such as the Christian act of penance – but also, crucially, in legally restricted contexts of a complex system of monetary compensations for injuries and infractions,[72] common in early Germanic laws.[73] *Wergild* – the price for manslaughter of differing value depending on the social standing of the victim and the perpetrator – was set so that vengeance and feuding could be avoided.[74]

One of the earliest Anglo-Saxon laws, the Æthelberht's code, provides a good representation of the usage of the verb to refer to payment, a practice found in later laws as well. Though it survives in a twelfth-century copy in the *Textus Roffensis*, it is thought to have been issued around the year 600,[75] so barely a few years after the arrival of the mission of St Augustine and king Æthelberht's conversion to Christianity.[76]

[11] Gif in cyninges tune man mannan of slea, L scill **gebete.**
'If a person should kill someone in the king's dwelling, let him pay 50 shillings.'

[42] Gif eage of weorð, L scillingum **gebete**.
'If an eye is gouged out, let him pay 50 shillings.'[77]

The relationship between penitentials and secular law codes is a complex and dynamic one, with influences likely going both ways, particularly for the late Anglo-Saxon period.[78] As Hough notes, by the time of the laws of Cnut, the Old English *bōt* develops the dual meaning of 'spiritual atonement' and 'of rendering a debt to society', both senses juxtaposed and complementing one another, particularly in the prose of Wulfstan.[79] However, there is little evidence that the penitentials influenced the earlier Anglo-Saxon laws.

It is interesting that in modern judicial contexts, for instance in present-day American jurisprudence, remorse for one's actions (or lack thereof) is often one of the factors which influences the judges' decisions when it comes to sentencing.[80] One of the features of the Anglo-Saxon laws, which Hough argues was likely an earlier aspect not influenced by Christian culture,[81] is that the severity of the punishment could be based on the assessment of the intentionality of the crime, rather than remorse. Alfred, ch. 36 outlines a situation of an accidental killing or maiming of a person by a spear positioned on the shoulder of the bearer. The intent seems to be judged by external circumstances of the deed (how high was the spear positioned at the time), but the *wergild* is to be paid regardless. Whether a fine would also be added on top of that may depend on whether any accusations of intent are levied against the perpetrator and how he clears himself in proportion to the deed.[82] Hough, discussing this passage in relation to the possible influences of penitentials, notes the parallels with earlier fifth-century Burgundian and Frisian laws. The Germanic act of clearing oneself under oath is very different from the admission of remorse. Williams observes, in the context of oaths and their importance to early heroic Germanic culture, that 'it was not so much a matter of whether or not a speaker meant what they said, but whether or not they would maintain resolve when the oath was tested' – the individual interior perspective is therefore far less important than the social ties that are affected by external actions.[83] The verb *getrēowian* used in this law has the meaning of 'making something true' or 'making one's self out to be true' (B-T) and could be considered a performative speech act by which the act of stating something to be true, akin to an oath, makes it true, because the moral integrity of the one who swears it is on the line, especially if it is done before the lord or king.

In the context of early tribal society guided by a heroic code and strictly determined fines, any potential feelings of remorse or regret at having caused an injury or death to another – even if potentially present – may simply not have been relevant to the social mores and expectations; they do not feature within the established script. Whether the incident happened by accident or not, a *wergild* is due to the kin of the victim, and the intentions of the slayer are judged not within the frame of apologies, but within the culture of oaths.

It is likely that initially the idea of penance was understood in the context of performing an act of compensation akin to the monetary fines determined in legal codes. In fact, in some law codes it often is not clear whether *gebētan* refers to 'financial' or to 'spiritual reparation', and in others it can refer to both at the same time.[84] There are also instances where the Anglo-Saxon legal codes influenced the penitentials in the practice of commutations, i.e. monetary compensations, instead of spiritual acts of penance, leading to such 'exchange rates' as can be found in the *Pseudo-Egbert Penitential* where 'an dæges fasten man mæg mid anum penige alysan, oþþe mid twam hund sealmum' (one day's fast can be redeemed with a penny, or with two hundred psalms).[85]

Semantic loans and loan translations

This larger group comprises four word-families or expressions, i.e. FOR/TŌBRŸT*, ÞRÆST, FORGNID and BRYRD, with the latter being the most frequent. In terms of distribution and meaning the first three can be discussed together, as they show very similar patterns. BRYRD behaves a little differently, not the least because it occurs in verse, unlike the other three, and therefore will be discussed separately.

FOR/TŌBRŸT, ÞRÆST, FORGNID

With the exception of one occurrence of ÞRÆST in verse, all of the occurrences for this group of expressions can be found in either prose or, more typically, in glosses. While on the surface, there seems to be a significant difference between the number of occurrences in glosses in comparison to prose (see Table 2), the previous caveat regarding duplication of occurrences, particularly in relation to Psalter Glosses, has to be reiterated. Typically, the prose texts represented are homilies, lives of saints, the Heptateuch, the Gospels and various historical texts (Gregory's *Dialogues* and Bede's *Historia Ecclesiastica*).

In prose, *FOR/TŌBRȲT* and *ÞRÆST* are always found as verbs (or past participles) with the meaning 'broken, crushed, afflicted'. *TŌBRȲT* is entirely physical, with the objects of the verb being usually statues, false idols, body parts (e.g. heads) and, more metonymically, armies. In prose, *ÞRÆST* is mostly literal (e.g. a broken arm, a young monk crushed by a wall), but there are also figurative uses as in 'mentally broken', broken 'with hunger' or afflicted with heaven's fire, and it co-occurs with such Old English verbs as *(ge)brecan* 'to break, bruise, crush' or *geþrēan* 'to afflict'.

In glosses, all these expressions are mostly found in Psalter Glosses and render Latin *contero* or *contritio*, both in the emotional and the physical sense, but the physical sense predominates, with the object of the verb being: teeth, bread, arm, bow, ships and bones. The emotional senses are confined to the nouns and adjectives, but these only account for about 15 per cent of all occurrences. Whenever other Latin words are being glossed, they still focus on physical destruction, such as *comminuo*, *confringo* 'to break into (small) pieces', *allido* 'crush, bruise' or *elido* 'shatter, crush', and are accompanied by alternative Old English translations, such as *tōbrecan* 'to break entirely'.[86]

The single occurrence of *ÞRÆST* in the *Paris Psalter*, in the phrase 'heorta **geðræste**' in Psalm 146 (147), translates Latin *contritos corde* 'brokenhearted', mirroring its prose and gloss usage.

More generally, Latin *contritio* or *contritus* are occasionally glossed with Old English words that directly evoke the emotions of sadness or mental affliction, rather than the sense of breaking, such as *unrotness/unrottan* 'sadness/sad', *getirged* 'afflicted' or *gesaroged* 'afflicted, troubled' (though the later could also mean 'damaged').

BRYRD

This family is evenly distributed between verse (14 occ., NF = 7.8) and prose (155 occ., NF = 7.8), and more frequently occurring in glosses (82 occ., NF = 11.3), though again there is a certain amount of duplication in the Psalter Glosses.

Verse

The verse occurrences of *BRYRD* are all found in religious poetry, particularly in poems on the lives of saints (*Andreas, Elene, Guthlac, Juliana, Judith*). These occurrences are found in the context of saints being inspired by God with faith, courage, strength and joy, such as Judith when she experiences lack of resolution before killing Holofernes, bishop Cyriacus when he is inspired to look for nails of the Holy Cross, or Guthlac when he requires courage to fight devils:

> Heo þæt deofol teah,
> breostum **inbryrded**, bendum fæstne,
> halig hæþenne   *Jul*, ll. 534–6.[87]
> (She, <u>inspired</u> in her breast,
> dragged the devil, fastened in bonds,
> the saint [dragged] the heathen.)

> Him of heofonum wearð
> **onbryrded** breostsefa bliðe gæste.   *GuthA,B*, ll. 335–6.
> (His inner heart became <u>incited</u>
> with a joyful spirit from heavens)

A common, alliterative formula that conceptualizes the 'incitement' or 'inspiration' as a pricking of the breast can be found in more than half of the poetic occurrences, i.e. *breostum in/onbryrded* (5 occ.) or *in/onbryrded breostsefa* (4 occ.). However, the inspiration does not always have to be positive or divine. In *Juliana*, the devil describes leading men astray, by how he '**onbryrdan** beorman' (incite[s them] with my barm/leaven/foam), to hinder them in the spiritual war. In *Andreas*, the hungry cannibals, rather gruesomely, are incited by the thoughts of eating a young body ('ymb þæs geongan feorh breostum **onbryrded**').

Prose

Some of the earliest prose occurrences for *BRYRD* show evidence for the meaning of inspiration (often by divine grace) in political contexts that legitimize privileges, wealth and power. In a charter from 883, which grants privileges to Berkeley Abbey, ealdorman Æðelred was made wealthy with a large portion of Mercia, '**inbryrdendre** Godes gefe' (by the inspiration of God's grace/by God's inspiring grace). In version F of the *Anglo-Saxon Chronicle* for the year 694, king Wihtred is 'inspired/urged on by the heavenly king and inflamed with the anger of righteousness' ('fram ðan heouenlice cinge **onbryrd** & mid <andan> ðare rihtwisnesse anæld'), to make sure that lands once given to the church will not be taken away.

The Old English prose translations of Latin texts, likely produced at the court of King Alfred, such as Orosius's *Historiae Adversus Paganos*, Bede's *Historia Ecclesiastica*, Gregory's *Dialogues* or his *Pastoral Care*, are on the whole a fairly close rendition of the Latin originals, but occasionally phrases are added or passages restructured, both for clarification and stylistic effect.[88] In these translations, *BRYRD* most often refers to inspiration in general, but sometimes more specifically to the grace of compunction, translating variously Latin *compunctio, instigates, instinctu* and *inspirante*, among others. Gregory's works, in particular, refer to compunction extensively, and most of the occurrences of *BRYRD* from the translations of *Dialogues* or *Pastoral Care* regularly translate *compunctio* (e.g. *syndon tu cyn þære* **inbryrdnesse** 'there are two kinds of compunction'). However, even in the *Dialogues* we can find an exception where *BRYRD* is used to mean inspiration, rather than compunction, suggesting both senses were available to the translator:

> hi mid haliges gastes gife in heora heortan ingehigdum **onbryrde** & gelærde wæron.
>
> (They, by the grace of the Holy Spirit, were inspired and taught in the understanding (inner-thoughts) of their hearts.)

Here, the passage relates to some people (like John the Apostle or Moses) not requiring teachers, but rather being taught and instructed inwardly by divine inspiration. The Latin passage (*per magisterium Spiritus intrinsecus docentur*) is not translated directly word for word, but more freely by adding the physical locus of inspiration (heart, where the mind is located in Old English psychologies), but also by juxtaposing *gelærde* 'taught' with *onbryrde* 'inspired' in a doublet[89] that is introduced to render *docere*, but which emphasizes the divine inspiration of the teaching and the educational effect of God's grace.

Still, the translation of Bede's *Historia Ecclessiastica* uses *onbryrded* more frequently in the contexts of divine (or demonic) inspiration than is found in Old English translations of Gregory, for instance, when Gregory is inspired to send St Augustine to convert the English.

> Se wæs mid godcundre **inbryrdnesse** monad   Bede 1 [0205 (13.54.27)]
> (He was prompted by divine inspiration)
>
> **inbryrdendum** þæm feonde ealra goda   Bede 3 [0504 (16.226.29)]
> (incited/goaded by the enemy of all that is good)

In various rules and confessionals, such as the Rule of Chrodegang (*ChrodR*), Theodulf's *Capitula* (*ThCap*), or the Benedictine Rule (*BenR*), which was first translated by St Aethelwold at the turn of the ninth and tenth centuries as part of the English Benedictine Reform, the sense of compunction predominates:

> & hine gebidde na mid hludre stefne ac mid teara wope and mid his heortan **abryrdnysse** BenRWells [0010 (52.80.9)]
> (And pray to him not in a loud voice, but with the weeping of tears and with the compunction of his heart)

Similarly, in later homiletic writings (mostly Ælfric's), compunction is found more frequently than inspiration:

> gif hi heora synna mid **onbryrdre heortan** gode anum andettað
> ÆCHom I, 8 [0039 (243.68)]
> (if they confess their sins with a heart moved to compunction to God alone)

> þæt is twyfealdlic **onbryrdnes**. eges & lufe   ÆCHom I, 9 [0040 (251.86)]
> (there are two types of compunction, of fear and of love)

Glosses

In glosses BRYRD very consistently renders Latin *conpunctio* and related expressions, deviating from this pattern only seven times out of eighty-two. Where it does deviate, it translates either words related to penitence or recompense (*penitudinis, rependito*), contrition (*contritum*) or those related to inspiration (*instinctu, instigauit*), though, in comparison to prose, the latter is a rare meaning.

The semantic loans and loan translations from Latin, FOR/TŌBRŸT, ÞRÆST, FORGNID and BRYRD, which were used to directly translate *compunctio* or *contritio*, follow the Latin etymology and the literal senses closely. In fact, the literal senses of various violent physical experiences ('crushing, breaking') occur much more frequently than those of contrition or compunction, rendering a range of Latin vocabulary of a similar scope. With the exception of BRYRD, however, the majority are still marginal in the surviving corpus, predominantly found in glosses, not very well integrated into prose compositions and virtually absent from verse. BRYRD *is* the exception as it occurs moderately frequently with the meanings of 'inspiration', 'compunction' and occasionally the literal sense of 'pricking', but the sense of inspiration is found almost as commonly as 'compunction'. Perhaps, then, whenever BRYRD is used to refer to compunction, the aspect that is particularly emphasized through the connotations of this word-family is the divine grace and inspiration needed to achieve true compunction.

HRĒOW

A manual analysis of over 500 of occurrences of *HRĒOW* in the DOEC was not deemed feasible for this study. Instead, all thirty-four occurrences in poetry were analysed. Then, a random sample of a 100 occurrences was generated from the prose subcorpus, and the occurrences were analysed in their co-text and context.[90]

Verse

Judging solely by the thematic content of the poems, with the exception of two occurrences in *Beowulf*, HRĒOW is confined almost exclusively to overtly religious poetry. However, the represented poems seem to range in dates from quite early works to much later ones (bearing in mind, of course, the notorious difficulty of dating Old English poetic texts).[91] The earliest occurrence comes from *Genesis A*, of the Cædmonian group, from which at least some of the texts can be dated to the first half of the eighth century. Arguably, these could be joined by the two occurrences in *Beowulf* (however due to the debate on *Beowulf*'s date of composition, it would be hard to base the argument for sense development on just those two occurrences). The Cynewulfian group is strongly represented by occurrences from *Guthlac B* and *Juliana*.[92] From around the middle of the ninth century, we have the occurrences from the *Meters of Boethius* and the English translation (or 'transliteration') of the Old Saxon *Genesis*, and finally the later poems are represented by the *Metrical Paris Psalter*. Arguably, the earliest occurrences come from *Genesis A* (1 occ.) and *Beowulf* (2 occ.). The largest number of occurrences per text in verse can be found in *Genesis B* (i.e. 7 occ.) and two of those can be directly paralleled by the surviving Old Saxon text: OE *hreowige* (*GenB*, l.799) for OS *hriuuig* and OE *hyge hreowan* for OS *hugi hriuuuig*, which suggests the remaining five could have been found in the Saxon version as well.

For the majority of the verse occurrences HRĒOW covers a range of senses that could be best rendered by PDE *regret, sorrow, grief, pity* or a combination thereof, and the passages in which the word-family is used often portray complex affective states with co-occurrences of other words for sadness and grief in the surrounding text (particularly in the case of Cynewulfian poems and *Genesis B*). Often, the emotion is a result of something going wrong, either because of the actions or situation of the one who experiences HRĒOW or, to the contrary, because someone else is in a difficult situation and the one affected by HRĒOW is unhappy about it. The differences lie in the cognitive acknowledgement of one's own personal involvement or responsibility in the situation, but the affective state itself seems broadly comparable.

The sense of sorrow and emotional pain appears in the context of noticing someone else's suffering or feeling an acute loss. To this effect, the transitive constructions with the verb *(ge)hrēowan* and a personal pronoun in the accusative can be used, but other *HRĒOW* words appear as well. In the passages below one of the apostles comes to save St Guthlac from the demons who oppress him, noticing his suffering. In the second, Christ expresses grief and sadness at the original sin and consequent dooming of all mankind. And in the third Guthlac's young servant mourns Guthlac's departure from this world:

> Is þæt min broþor, mec his bysgu **gehreaw**.   *GuthA,B* [0211(714)]
> (He is my brother, his affliction pains/grieves me.)

> Ða mec ongon **hreowan** þæt min hondgeweorc
> on feonda geweald feran sceolde,   *ChristA,B,C* [0383 (1414)]
> (Then it began to grieve me that my handiwork
> must pass into the power of fiends.)

>   He þæs færspelles
> fore his mondryhtne modsorge wæg,
> hefige æt heortan. Hreþer innan swearc,
> hyge **hreowcearig**, þæs þe his hlaford geseah
> ellorfusne   *GuthA,B* [0314 (1052)]
> (Because of this sudden news he carried sorrow in his mind for his master, heavy at the heart. The breast darkened within, the sorrowful mind, because he saw his lord so eager to go elsewhere.)

As I have discussed elsewhere,[93] the *Guthlac* passage is rich in vocabulary for SADNESS/GRIEF, with words denoting weeping, mourning and painful emotions, and in this sense, the reading of 'regret' is perhaps justified, insofar as it eschews any personal responsibility.

However, the same verbal construction that in *Christ* or *Guthlac* denotes sadness or pain, in *Genesis A*, has a much stronger component of regret, with the additional overtones of anger, when God sees that his people begin choosing wives among the kin of Cain:

>   **Hreaw** hine swiðe
> þæt he folcmægþa fruman aweahte,
> æðelinga ord, þa he Adam sceop,
> cwæð þæt he wolde for wera synnum
> eall aæðan þæt on eorðan wæs,
> forleosan lica gehwilc
> (It grieved him / he regretted it greatly, that he awoke the origin of the kinspeople, the origin of the nobles, when he created Adam, said that he wished, because of the sins of men, to lay waste to all that was on earth, to destroy each body)

In this instance, God's reaction to the transgressions committed by men is to regret ever having created them in the first place, to be angry at their behaviour and to wish to correct his mistake by eliminating it entirely. This passage follows the universal schema of REGRET discussed previously the most closely out of all the other analysed occurrences of *HRĒOW*.

The experience of *HRĒOW* can also be a result of the difficulties heaped on the one affected by this emotion, whether through one's own bad choices or external circumstances:

> Þæt wif gnornode,
> hof **hreowigmod**, hæfde hyldo godes,
> lare forlæten,   *GenB* [0265 (770)]
> (The woman wailed, lamented sad at heart,
> that she let go of the grace and teaching of God.)

> Ongan þa **hreowcearig**
> siðfæt seofian, sar cwanian,
> wyrd wanian   *Jul* [0146 (536)]
> (Then the sorrowful one began to complain
> about his expedition, bewail his injury, mourn his fate.)

> Hi ða **hreowigmode** wurpon hyra wæpen of dune,
> gewitan him werigferhðe on fleam sceacan.   *Jud* [0073 (289)]
> (Then they, desolate at heart, threw their weapons down,
> they knew, weary-hearted to take flight.)

> Þæt wæs <Hroðgare> **hreowa** tornost
> þara þe leodfruman lange begeate.   *Beo* [0590 (2129)]
> (That was to Hrothgar the most grievous of sorrows
> That plagued the lord of the people in a long time)

Both Eve and the Devil in *Juliana* clearly regret their bad choices, whether it is the eating of the forbidden fruit or going against a saint who proves too powerful a match, and while in the first case there may be some suggestion of penitence in Eve's lament, the devil can hardly be seen as repentant. In both cases, however, their affective states are depicted through verbal expressions of distress: *gnornode* 'wailed', *hof* 'lamented', *seofian* 'to lament, complain', *wanian* 'lament', and the devil is specifically commenting on his *sar* 'pain, hurt, sorrow', which could be seen as both physical – due to the violent thrashing he receives from Juliana – and emotional, at the engendered feelings of helplessness, fear and regret for his bad choices. He goes on to plead with Juliana to cease with the torment and thus makes for a truly pitiful figure (but not in the sense of engendering compassion).

In the passage from *Judith*, the warrior who ventures into the tent and discovers the beheaded body of Holofernes, his leader, falls to the ground and starts tearing at his hair in a visible external demonstration of mental distress and pain. The soldiers outside the tent react, instead, with a complete loss of heart. As they stand outside *unrot* 'sad, dejected', the news makes them abandon their weapons (and thus, any hope of winning the battle). The apposition of *werigferhð* 'weary-hearted, disconsolate, depressed' lends its connotations to *hreowigmod*, which here expresses a numbing sorrow and loss not only of a lord, but also of direction. Seen through the lens of a heroic society that praises courage and loyalty to one's lord above all else, abandoning weapons and fleeing is condemnable, but when that lord is no longer there, the strength that keeps the army together disappears and the sense of direction is taken away. A parallel can be drawn here with the passage from *Guthlac B*, discussed above, where the master-servant hierarchical relationship is likewise left without the lord or master, leaving the retainer in mental distress.

Beowulf also uses HRĒOW to refer to the loss of one party to a hierarchical relationship, but in an inverted sense. In l. 2129, where *hrēow* occurs for the first time, it refers to Beowulf's description of the grief that Hrothgar experiences following the death of his most beloved advisor, at the hands of Grendel's mother. The grief is particularly strong as Æschere can be neither buried nor cremated. It is not clear whether Hrothgar would feel in any way personally responsible, but the focus is on the mental anguish at a loss of human life, rather than culpability. Even so, Hrothgar's immediate reaction is to ask Beowulf to track down Grendel's mother and compensate for the loss of life with retaliation.

In the second passage where *hrēow* appears, Beowulf himself experiences this emotion. It is caused by the death of his own people and the melting of his throne, the metonymic symbol of his role as a ruler, in the dragon's fiery attack:

> Þæt ðam godan
> wæs **hreow** on hreðre, hygesorga mæst,
> wende se wisa þæt he wealdende
> ofer ealde riht, ecean dryhtne,
> bitre gebulge breost innan weoll
> þeostrum geþoncum swa him geþywe ne wæs.   Beo [0643 (2327)]
>
> (then the good one felt grief/regret in the heart, the greatest of sorrows; he knew then, the wise one, that he had bitterly angered the Lord, the Eternal Ruler over the old law. His breast welled within him with dark thoughts, as was not his custom.)

This passage is problematic, but also interesting, for two reasons. A particularly Christian context is added to the scene, placing the blame squarely on Beowulf's shoulders for his pagan faith and thus suggesting a penitential reading for *hrēow*. On the other hand, *hrēow* is linked to sorrow and grief through the apposition with *hygesorga* and the metaphoric *þeostrum geþoncum* 'dark thoughts', which also suggest sadness.[94] What is more, the phrase *swa him geþywe ne wæs* on the one hand implies that it was not usual for Beowulf to be given to grief, but also that it is not appropriate for a warrior, a hero to deliberate and give in to sorrowful thoughts. In fact, rather than mourning for too long, Beowulf readies himself for vengeance ('wræce leornode').

Whether both or any of the two occurrences of *hrēow* in *Beowulf* should be read with religious and penitential connotations, I am not certain. But what emerges from these passages is that while the grief of HRĒOW can be a natural reaction to the loss of human life, the heroic code suggests that rather than deliberate on the emotion itself, one should perform restitution by deeds.[95] This fits more generally into the accepted analyses of grief in heroic poetry, which lacks in depictions of tears (though there are ritualized lamentations, mostly performed by women) and where emotions should be locked within the chest and contained.[96]

Some instances of HRĒOW are more ambiguous and could be read as either a general sense of sorrow or regret.

> Ne bisorgað he synne to fremman,
> wonhydig mon, ne he wihte hafað
> **hreowe** on mode þæt him halig gæst
> losige þurh leahtras on þas lænan tid.   ChristA,B,C [0429(1555)]
> (Nor is he sorry/anxious to commit a sin,[97] the foolish man, nor does he have any regret/sorrow in his heart that the Holy Spirit will be lost to him through his vices in this transitory time.)

In the above passage, the implicature of the negations is that the sinner should feel regret and sorrow, yet not so much *for* the sins he committed, but rather *that* the path to God is closed to him. While there may be some penitential overtones here in the implicit warning about the possibility of damnation, the construction *þæt* ... forces the reading of regret/sorrow, which is strengthened by the co-occurrence with *besorgian*.

In rare instances in poetry, where the Christian meaning of 'repentance' is clearly intended, the passages in question draw directly on the doctrine of penance and typical phrasing found in prose works, as in:

> An is ærest þæt he ofte do wop and **hreowe** for his misdæda.   *Instr*, A44, [0005(13)]
> (One is first that he often weeps and <u>repents</u> for his sins.)
>
> Gif mon mid ealra <innancundre> heortan <gehygde> **gehreowað** his synna   *Instr*, A44, [00046(166)]
> (If one with all of his innermost heart's thoughts <u>regrets/repents</u> his sins)
>
> hu mære is seo soðe **hreow** synna and gylta?   *JDay II*, A17, [0012(53)]
> (How much greater is the true <u>repentance</u> of sins and wrongs?)

Co-occurrences of words that stress weeping and committed sins occur frequently in prose, and the adjective *soðe* 'true' is also a common modifier (c.13 occ. in the prose sample, e.g. in the *Vercelli Homilies* and the Old English version of Bede's *Historia Ecclesiastica*).

Rice has made the argument that the adjective *hrēowcearig* (which can be found in *The Dream of the Rood* and *Juliana*, among others), even in contexts that do not overtly call for the reading of 'repentance', would still have a religious, and more specifically, penitential, sense.[98] However, while *HRĒOW* is used in religious texts, it did not appear suddenly in the Christian Old English period but developed from an earlier sense of 'grief, distress'. While it is possible that religious texts would have used *HRĒOW* to indicate some sort of *penitential* connotation, it is equally possible that because *HRĒOW* had stronger connotations with regret than e.g. *GNORN* or *SORG*, it lent itself more readily to be adapted to the Christian idea of penitence and thus was used in religious texts. Whether the poets had intended one sense to indicate another, or indeed whether *all* occurrences of *HRĒOW* should be read with a penitential overtone, is up for debate.

Though (my) native speaker intuitions are not reliable to the extent that quantitative evidence is, as mentioned before, the Polish noun *żal*, the verb *żałować*, and the related family of expressions seem to correspond to *HRĒOW* much better than any of the Present-Day English vocabulary. *Żal* family depending on the context and form (e.g. additional prefixation) denotes sorrow, grief, grudge, pity, longing, compassion, mourning, regret, as well as, in a religious sense, contrition or penitence. The existence of a specialized meaning of regret for one's sins (*żal za grzechy* 'contrition, penitence', literally 'regret for sins') does not have any bearing on the other senses and is seen as quite distinct from e.g. *żal ścisnął jej gardło* 'a sense of loss and sorrow gripped her throat' or *żal mi cię* 'I really pity/feel for you'.[99] The 'sense of loss' or 'pity' simply does not have any penitential connotations.

Unfortunately, without access to native speaker intuitions, it is hard to determine how separate or overlapping the senses of polysemous words would have been in the mental lexicon of the speakers of Old English. However, the evidence from poetry suggests that HRĒOW covers a variety of different situations of mental anguish and distress that often can (but does not necessarily have to) lead to regret.

Prose

The *HRĒOW* family occurs in prose a little over 400 times, predominantly in texts that are focused on expounding the doctrine of penance. This includes various confessionals and handbooks for the use of confessors in their practice (34 occ., NF = 118), the Old English translation of Gregory's *Pastoral Care* (67 occ., NF = 94), and assorted homiletic writings (both anonymous and those authored by Ælfric, at around 166 occ., NF = 31). These taken together amount to around two-thirds of total occurrences, which dictates the types of contexts in which the words will be found.

In the analysed sample, the majority, seventy-five occurrences, are without a doubt related to repentance and penance within religious contexts and denote explicitly 'penitence' or 'penance'.[100] Extrapolating to the entire population, around 75 per cent of occurrences in the corpus can be expected to occur with such senses (± 8 per cent). These figures are in stark contrast to poetry, where the majority of occurrences were ambiguous or broadly suggestive of grief, pity or regret, but not explicitly related to penitence, despite the poetic texts in which *HRĒOW* occurs with religious themes as well.

In texts which are translations of Latin originals, *paenitentia* is the most common equivalent, but there are also instances of *fletum/flere*, and *plango*, all with the notions of 'pity, lament, mourning, and weeping', which suggests that *HRĒOW* could have had some conceptual links with compunction, due to the association with tears. It may conversely suggest that in some cases the more general concept of sadness was present in those translations as well. This link to tears can also be found in penitential writings, where *HRĒOW* covers the notion of *penitence* understood primarily as the sorrow for one's sins, which is one of the first sources for compunction, and the origin of 'inferior' tears.

Typically, however, we find *HRĒOW* most often in exhortations to appropriate Christian behaviour. These often talk about true ('sōð') penitence, linking it with earnest confession, humility, and making amends as the necessary conditions for achieving God's forgiveness and admission into heaven. In these types of depictions there are frequent co-occurrences with the verbs *bētan* 'to make amends', *dædbōt* 'penance', and *andettan* 'to confess', as well as variations on humility (*eadmodlice* 'humbly', *eadmodness* 'humility'):

> þæt eadmodlice mid micelre **hreowsunga** and mid godum dædan betan HomS 13 (Ass 11)
> (that [we] make amends for it humbly with good deeds and great repentance)

> Þæt bið seo soþe **hreow** þæt mon þa geworhtan synna andette & georne bete HomS 8 (BlHom2)
> (It is the true repentance that one confesses and eagerly makes amends for the committed sins)

> Hit is neod [...] þæt þurh soðe eadmodnysse and andytnysse betan þæt **hreowsiende** ChrodR1
> (It is necessary [...] that we make amends for it [i.e. sins], repenting, with true humility and confession.)

> se þe nele his synna on ðissere worulde andettan mid soðre **behreowsunge** ÆLS (Ash Wed)
> (He who will not confess his sins in this world with true repentance)

Often, the reflection on one's sins and committed crimes is associated with weeping and tears, and the interiority of the experience (as taking place in the heart/mind, either *mōd* or *hēort*) is stressed, which aligns it with the doctrine of compunction:

> **Hreowsiað** ærest on eowrum mode [...] & geclænsiað mid eowrum tearum CP [2214 (54.425.36)]
> (Repent first in your mind/heart [...] and cleanse yourself with your tears.)

> Gehwyrfað to me & gecyrrað mid eowrum heorte & mid fæstenum & mid wope, & mid **hreowsunga** eowra synna   HomM 8 (Murfin) [0041 (168)]
> (Turn to me with your heart and with fasting and with weeping and with the repentance of your sins)

In a common pattern, the trifecta of regret/repentance, recompense and confession appears as necessary conditions for God's forgiveness:

> eallum þam forgifnesse selest, <eallum> þam þe nu þurh soðe **hreowe** & þurh dædbote & þurh andetnesse   HomS 2 (ScraggVerc 16) [0044 (121)]
> (To all you give forgiveness, to all those who now through true repentance, and through recompense and through confession)

The instances where *HRĒOW* in prose does not refer to repentance overtly are few. Fewer than 20 per cent of instances in the sample are ambiguous or could be expressed with 'regret' as well as 'repentance', and in even fewer (barely 5 per cent) repentance can be ruled out as a possibility, which is in stark contrast to the verse subcorpus. Those rare instances echo the meanings more typically found in poetry, that is related to sadness or sorrow, as in the following passages:

> ða eode se Wisdom near [...] minum **hreowsiendum** geþohte   Bo [0023 (3.8.24)]
> (then Philosophy came close to my sorrowing thoughts)
>
> ða ongan se Wisdom **hreowsian** for þæs Modes tydernesse   Bo [0027 (3.9.9)]
> (then Philosophy began to lament/take pity on the Mind's weakness.)
>
> na þæt an mænan mihton and heora eorfeða **behreowsian**   LS 34 (SevenSleepers) [001700 (77)]
> (now they could bemoan and lament their hardships)

Particularly in the broader context of these passages, as in the first example from the translation of Boethius's *Consolation of Philosophy*, both context and the co-occurrence of other SADNESS words (such as *geomriende*, *murnende* and *sorgum*), help with the disambiguation.

It is also worth noting that in penitential writings, *HRĒOW* covers the notion of *penitence*, understood primarily as the sorrow for one's sins, which is one of the first sources for compunction, and the origin of the 'inferior' tears.

Glosses

In the glosses *HRĒOW* is consistently used to translate the Latin noun *poenitentia* or the verb *penitere* almost 80 per cent of the time (75 occ. out of 86). Some of the occurrences come from various Psalter glosses, so the same Latin passages are translated or represented more than once. Unlike in other word-families, however, Psalter glosses are not the main source of occurrences (only 14), though there are some additional occurrences from Canticles. Rather, it is the glosses from the Lindisfarne and Rushworth Gospels (22 occ.) and Defensor's *Liber Scintillarum* (17 occ.) that make up the bulk of the gloss occurrences. The Lindisfarne glosses can be dated to 950 and represent Northumbrian/Anglian dialect.

There are eleven instances of deviation from the otherwise fairly stable equivalence of *HRĒOW* with *poenitentia*. These often have the sense of 'grieving, lamenting, mourning' in Latin. These are *hreoweþ* for *miserior*[101] and *hrywð* for *miserebitur*,[102] *hreowlice* for *lugubriter*[103] and *hreow* for *lugubre*, *hreowsedan* for *doluerunt*,[104] and *behreowsygende* for *plangens* (although in this final instance, the context is directly related to mourning or lamenting one's sins – *plangens peccata*).

In two instances, other Old English words for sadness are provided as an alternative to the gloss, i.e. *sarig* and *bemænan*, but in the latter case both *behreowsiaþ/reowsiað* and *bemænan* refer to compunction by glossing Latin *compungimini*,[105] suggesting at least some degree of interchangeability, however localized. Where *hreowlice* is rendered by *calamitosum*, Old English *earmlice* is given as well, which suggests a sense of 'lamentable, miserable'. Stanley, discussing the range of *hrēowan*, cites a passage from the Peterborough Chronicle where *earmlice* and *reowlic* are also in apposition and suggests 'piteous' as an appropriate translation.[106]

From these examples we can see that in the glosses HRĒOW is associated primarily with repentance; however, it still refers to a range of emotions, not necessarily in a penitential context. In Matthew 15:34 *miserior* refers to Jesus feeling sorry for the people who came to listen to him and have no food to eat (and this is followed by the miracle multiplication of bread), and similarly in PsCaI, it translates a passage where 'the Lord judges his people and he has pity/feels sorry for his servants'.[107] Though relatively infrequent, these gloss occurrences echo the usage found in poetry, where HRĒOW is felt when someone else is in a difficult situation.

Conclusions

Did the Anglo-Saxons experience regret in pre-Christian times? Regret and remorse are often considered universal emotions, regardless of the available lexical means to express them. However, there are no monosemous words to denote *regret* in Old English and, unlike sadness, *regret* is not heavily lexicalized. Taken together, the evidence suggests that early Anglo-Saxons may have framed and evaluated *regret* according to a different model, most likely informed by the structures and mores of an early Germanic heroic society that placed more emphasis on physical or monetary means of recompense, physical retaliation within the structures imposed by the feud and a fatalistic determinism, rather than an affective acknowledgment of wrong-doing.

In pre-Christian times and perhaps in early Old English as well that portion of the emotional spectrum which in modern Western thought (or perhaps simply the experience of Present-Day English native speakers) would be clearly defined as regret, i.e. the sense of 'being sad at something one has done or failed to do,' but also 'something that has happened to others', was likely subsumed under the superordinate category of SADNESS, which was represented by a host of other expressions that could also be applied to situations of 'regret' (such as *sorgian* or *gnornian*). Paralleling similar developments in Old High German, the *HRĒOW* word-family in Old English initially had a broader semantic range of 'emotional suffering, grief' that could be felt in a variety of situations (including those we could label as 'regret') and, due to processes of semantic narrowing under the influence of the Christian ideas of penitence, compunction and contrition, took on the specialized meaning of 'regret, penitence' not only in religious, but also in secular contexts. The introduction of a set of new affective practices and the sociocultural changes that created a need for overt displays of emotions for committed wrongs, rather than just performing (monetary) compensation, made the linguistic expressions of feeling and expressing regret more necessary and allowed for the changes that made the phrase *rue the day* possible.

3

A concept without relevance? Compunction in Old Norse-Icelandic literature

Roland Scheel

Ancient heroes and saga protagonists do not regret their deeds. At least that is the impression gained from the surfaces of 'classical' vernacular Scandinavian texts, especially from the famous Icelandic Family Sagas (*Íslendingasögur*). These were composed in the thirteenth and fourteenth centuries and deal with conflicts between historical figures of the Icelandic upper class during the period of Iceland's settlement and into the first decades following the conversion to Christianity (late ninth–early eleventh century). Consequently, the texts portray their characters in the pursuit of honour, avenging perceived wrongs or compensating for a loss of face in other ways, looking for favourable alliances, securing a good reputation and, ultimately, peace. In doing so, the protagonists occasionally run out of options and must do what the code of honour demands from them, when they for instance kill a perpetrator in revenge instead of accepting compensation.[1] This especially applies to the more well-known 'canonical' sagas. Such a tragic structure, which in some cases approximates Old Norse heroic legend,[2] calls for a stoic attitude in the hero and precludes compunction or at least any display thereof. Furthermore, the sagas centre on action and the narration is externally focalized, which contributes to the impression that the characters are devoid of emotions. While research in recent years has demonstrated that emotions do play a major part in saga literature,[3] regret and remorse are not among the predominant feelings expressed in the sagas.

This absence is not only a consequence of the contents. Saga characters suffer from the pain felt at the death of family members or from shame resulting from the loss of honour. They feel anger towards persons who have killed their relatives or diminished their social standing. They envy others, they laugh at funny occasions and sometimes in the face of disaster, they blush with rage or embarrassment, and they swell with grief. Compunction as a rather complex concept, however, is not unambiguously linked to one of the facial expressions viewed as innate and universal: happiness, anger, sadness, fear, disgust/contempt, interest, surprise.[4] As the inner thoughts of the characters are never described, emotions often have to be inferred through bodily signs and gestures,[5] which greatly reduces complexity or at least precision. How, for instance, does one exhibit a bad conscience? Moreover, the saga narrator never qualifies the action, so even if a described deed was commonly viewed as a sin by the author and the public, a precondition for compunction and penance in the Christian sense of the word, the modern reader remains unaware. Thus, as moral attitudes must also be inferred and the overall focus of the Family Sagas on the descriptive surface centres on honour in local history rather than on edification, compunction appears to be a concept without relevance to the 'saga world', the social space constructed in the approximately forty *Íslendingasögur*. The study of emotions as well as anthropological approaches to Old Norse literature in general has so far mainly focused on these Family Sagas, and compunction has been declared alien or at least secondary to the allegedly heroic, honour-centred value system of the 'saga world' – although all these texts were written by Christians and for the most part by clerics in Christian communities.[6]

Iðran (compunction) and *iðrask* (to regret): The early evidence

A closer look at the lexicon reveals that this somewhat impressionist outline is misleading, first and foremost because the Family Sagas are neither identical with Old Norse-Icelandic literature, nor do they represent the vast array of genres and ways of literary expression. As a matter of fact, words related to compunction (*iðran* f. and the verb *iðrask*) appear rather frequently, with the exception of the Family Sagas. The same applies to the world field connected to the concept: confession (*skript/skriptumál* and *skripta*), forgiveness/absolution (*fyrirgefning* and *fyrirgefa*), conscience (*hugr/hugskot/hugvit/samvizka*).[7] Compunction is not absent from Scandinavian literature and law in the vernacular, but sharp distinctions between genres have kept the 'religious' and the 'secular' sphere apart in research.

The reason why aspects of culture, including norms and emotions, were first and sometimes only investigated on the basis of the Family Sagas is doubtlessly related to their uniqueness within a global framework. The frequent reference to oral tradition, the anonymity of the authors, the stateless society they describe and the consequent absence of the edifying tone in the narrator's voice give a strong impression of genuineness. This renders the Family Sagas especially attractive as representatives of the 'real' attitudes in the society that produced and listened to them.[8] The rationale behind this is a rather simple equation based upon the idea of an 'indigenous' culture, whose essence may be recognized by subtracting what is known to be universal in European Latinate culture and therefore is viewed as cultural 'import'. Consequently, the Family Sagas have received more attention than other genres.

Yet while their secular, worldly focus is beyond doubt, the assumption of their genuine and 'pure' representation of sociopolitical norms is a misconception:[9] Genuineness may also be constructed. This is further emphasized through the sagas' dating. As a genre, the Family Sagas are surrounded by numerous translations of theological texts from Latin, in the form of homilies, translations of saints' lives (*Heilagra manna sögur*), texts on ancient history, the lives of local saints and bishops (*Biskupasögur*) and the Kings' Sagas. Virtually at the same time as the first *Íslendingasögur*, c. 1220, prose translations of Anglo-Norman and French romance (*Riddarasögur*) were also being written. And while they do transform the emotional richness of their models into a terser saga style, the inner emotional life of their figures is much more vivid than in the Family Sagas[10] – which in turn influences later Icelandic romance as well as the *Fornaldarsögur* about fictitious ancient heroes from the North. In other words, the Family Sagas are a later product than those genres that quite naturally integrate the discourse on conscience, compunction and conversion into both fiction as well as universal and local history. These latter texts also significantly outnumber the *Íslendingasögur* when it comes to manuscript transmission. The Family Sagas' rather unemotional narrative style, moreover, becomes even more uniform over time within the genre as well as within the manuscript transmission.[11] This serves to underline that the resulting impression of stoic saga protagonists, who act in the pursuit of honour and are prone to suffering but display neither doubt nor regret, is the result of a consciously chosen literary strategy. In this regard, it is also worth pointing out how small the number of authors and scribes of Family Sagas actually was in pre-Reformation Iceland.

All of this shows that one cannot ascertain the 'emotional communities' of Iceland or Norway from the twelfth to the fourteenth century through one genre alone.[12] Therefore, the saga 'classics' will be addressed in the second part of this chapter once the earlier written discourse on compunction is established. In order to assess the importance of compunction in Old Norse literature more generally a semasiological look at the occurrences of *iðran/iðrask* documented in dictionaries proves rewarding as a first step. It is unfortunate that no comprehensive corpus of Old Norse texts is available in machine-readable versions, let alone in lemmatized versions, with the exception of the most famous 'classics'.[13] Therefore, one has to rely on the *Ordbog over det norrøne prosasprog* which lists a large number of occurrences.[14] What the results reveal is impressive proof that Icelandic and Norwegian clerics knew, understood and to an extent popularized the concept of *compunctio* in Old Norse as early as the twelfth century.

The translation of Alcuin's *De virtutibus et vitiis*, preserved in a manuscript from the early thirteenth century, translates *compunctio cordis* as *tármelti hjartans* (melting of the heart into tears) and *poenitentia* as *iðran*.[15] In other texts, especially the Old Norse Homily Book (*Gamal Norsk Homiliebok*) and the *Icelandic* or *Stockholm Homily Book* from around 1200, *iðran* occurs extremely frequently, also in the combination *gera iðran* (*poenitentiam agere*).[16] The semantics remain close to the classical, biblical meaning of μετάνοια and represent the contrite change of mind and the inner conversion[17] rather than the aspect of *satisfactio* included in *poentitentia*, although they potentially integrate both meanings. This is nicely demonstrated by the Old Norse *Elucidarius*, a translation of Honorius Augustodunensis's catechism from before 1200, which stands out due to its precise and often idiomatic language:[18]

> *Discipulus* Hve morgom hattom firi gevaz synðer
> *Magister* Sv hin fyrsta synða lavsn er skirn. Onnvr er pinsl. Þriðia er at *ganga i iðran*. Fiorða er bęna halld ok tara fall. Fimta er ǫlmoso gørð. Setta er at firir geva ovinvm. Sivnda er ost ok heilagr goðr vili.
> *Discipulus* In how many ways are sins forgiven?
> *Magister* The first forgiving of sins is baptism. The second is martyrdom. The third is to go into repentance/compunction. The fourth is holding prayers and shedding tears. The fifth is giving alms. The sixth is to forgive one's enemies. The seventh is love and saintly good will.[19]

And further:

> *Discipulus* Hverer hial-pasc ídome.
> *Magister* Þeir er gerþo miskun-nar verk ílogsamlegom hiuscap oc þeir es svnþer sinar botto meþ *iþrunn* oc olmoso gøþe.
> *Discipulus* Who shall be saved in the judgement?
> *Magister* Those who did works of charity in lawful marriage and those who compensated their sins with compunction/repentance and alms.[20]

Other texts that use the noun *iðran* are the early translations of classical and recent saints' lives and lives of the Apostles (*Heilagra manna sögur*), but also translations of different parts of the Old Testament written during the Middle Ages (*Stjórn*).[21]

Two interesting and momentous aspects are already visible in these (mostly) early translations, which predate the 'classical' texts and are supposed to have influenced the development of written expression in the vernacular and the narrative style of the sagas.[22] First, the noun *iðran* denotes the compunction of the 'inner man'. The visible consequences of *iðran* are expressed in legal, secular terminology: sin required *bœtr*, 'compensation', to God and is therefore similar to other crimes in that payment was due, as will be demonstrated later. This is hardly surprising given the close connection between tariff penance established in the Early Middle Ages and legal thought in societies with compensational law.[23] Second, the abstract noun is mainly found in direct translations from Latin. This implies that the introduction, stabilization and dissemination of a concept are not necessarily signified by the emergence of an abstract noun, which has been observed in texts written in a tradition based on Latin.[24] *Begriffsgeschichte*, the analysis of concepts, cannot be based on the semantics of single nouns when it comes to narrative texts in the vernacular. This applies especially to those which are not based on a Latin original.

In fact, when they are not strictly translating the noun *compunctio* or *poenitantia*, writers seem to prefer the verb *iðrask*, which is more frequent than the noun, especially in texts pertaining to Scandinavian matters. One good example is the *Veraldar saga*, a short world chronicle in Old Norse from the second half of the twelfth century. Its author used different sources, among them the works of Isidore, Bede and Sigebert of Gembloux.[25] In the chapter on the *prima aetas*, the author opens the story of the universal flood:

> gvð mælti við Noa. þik virði ek mann goþan oc retlatan i minv avgliti En ek *iðrvmz* er ek hefi manin skapaðan kvað gvð þvi at alðydan er havll til illzkv oc synþa.
>
> God said to Noah: 'I consider you good and righteous before me. But I regret that I have created man', said God, 'as mankind is always inclined towards evil and sins.'[26]

The passage is in accordance with the text of the Vulgate:

> Videns autem Deus quod multa malitia hominum esset in terra, et cuncta cogitatio cordis intenta esset ad malum omni tempore, *poenituit* eum quod hominum fecisset in terra. Et tactus dolore cordis intrinsecus.
>
> (Genesis 6,5f.)

This reflects God's compunction at the nature of His creation, His change of mind and thus the salvation plan.[27]

As was already hinted at, the verb appears not only in edifying texts like homilies, Gregory the Great's *Dialogues* and hagiography, but also in other, sometimes secular, contexts. Examples of this include the Christian law sections of the early law books and the Old Norse Kings' Mirror (*Konungs skuggsjá*). It also occurs in the 'classical' sagas, although rather infrequently and at first glance seemingly at random – a point to which I will return.[28]

The etymology of *iðrask* is unclear, especially as there are no parallels in other Germanic languages, but it is likely that there exists a connection to *iðrar*, 'intestines' (f. pl.), mirroring the idea that an uneasiness of conscience and the resulting feeling is connected to parts of the human body.[29] This would also account for the medio-passive form; the transitive verb *iðra* (to make regret) is virtually non-existent. Clearly in the case of compunction, the local idiom offered a viable word. On the other hand, while *conscientia* was occasionally translated with *hugr* (thought), *hugskot* (spirit, soul) or *hugvit* (understanding), stressing the intellectual side of recognizing a wrong, the loan translation *samvizka* was established in the thirteenth century.[30] Since these words for *conscientia* allude to the field of thought and knowledge, it seems reasonable to assume that *iðrask* came to be associated with the emotional side of compunction in a complementary way.

The 'oral' sphere: Eddic and skaldic poems

Is it possible to trace potentially older meanings of the verb *iðrask*? As the Family Sagas are definitively younger than the old translations, an examination of eddic and skaldic poetry with their roots in the Late Iron Age seems attractive. While doubtlessly open to manipulation during oral tradition, skaldic poetry was already considered especially stable by medieval historiographers such as Snorri Sturluson, obviously due to its strict form.[31] One further advantage with regard to the verse corpus is that the occurrences of words are listed in dictionaries and in an electronic database.[32]

In the Poetic Edda, *iðrask* occurs in only two heroic poems, *Sigurðarkviða in skamma* and *Atlamál in grœnlenzko*. The scarcity is not surprising, as the action of the heroic lays is tragic and requires a stoic attitude, as mentioned earlier. More revealing, however, is the fact that these two poems are reworkings of older ones treating the Nibelungen legend, which are also (partly) preserved in the *Codex regius* of the Poetic Edda from the second part of the thirteenth century. While the poems were not fixed on parchment prior to the twelfth or thirteenth century, scholars generally distinguish two chronological layers in the preceding oral tradition, represented by the older *Ereignislied* and the younger elegies.[33] While the former focuses on grand heroic settings and action, the latter are longer, and they focus on grief. The most extreme form of the latter are retrospective poems dominated by a monologue of the female character. As a result of the story, suffering is mandatory in heroic legend, but the discussion of feelings and the inner disposition of the figures are much more prominent in these later poems.[34] The elegies focus on Brynhildr, who is in love with Sigurðr Fáfnisbani but is tricked into marrying King Gunnarr with the help of Sigurðr disguised as Gunnarr, and on Guðrún, who is married to Sigurðr instead. Due to this betrayal and the resulting *mésalliance*, Brynhildr forces her husband to have Sigurðr killed. This in turn brings about Brynhild's suicide, elicits Guðrún's grief and subsequent marriage to King Atli, Brynhild's brother, who orders the death of Guðrún's brothers Gunnarr and Hǫgni. Consequently, Guðrún later kills the sons she has with Atli.

Our first example, *Sigurðarkviða in skamma* (The short lay of Sigurðr), a relatively young reworking of an older *Ereignislied*,[35] starts with the situation which arose after Guðrún revealed to Brynhildr that she was tricked into marrying Guðrún's brother Gunnarr with the help of Sigurðr, whom Brynhildr loves. It is not clear from the poem whether Brynhildr and Sigurðr had met before or even vowed to marry each other, which is the way *Vǫlsunga saga* tells the story.[36] The saga was composed around 1250 and is based upon the poems which are partially lost. It is clear from the surviving poems, however, that Brynhildr feels betrayed. The contextualization of *iðrask* is peculiar:

5. Hon sér at lífi   lǫst né vissi
oc at aldrlagi   ecci grand,
vamm þat er væri   eða vera hygði.
Gengo þess á milli   grimmar urðir.

6. Ein sat hon úti   aptan dags,
nam hon svá bert   um at mælaz:
'Hafa scal ec Sigurð   – eða þó svelti! –,
mǫg frumungan,   mér á armi.

7. Orð mæltac nú,   *iðromc* eptir þess,
qván er hans Guðrún,   enn ec Gunnars;
liótar nornir   scópo oss langa þrá.'[37]

5. She was not aware of any guilty pleasure in her life,
and in her fortunes there was no hurt,
nor any flaw that she could imagine.
The terrible fates intervened in this.

6. Alone she sat outside, one day in the evening,
quite openly she began to speak to herself:
'I shall have Sigurðr – or he must die! –
that very young man, in my arms.

7. 'Words I spoke now, I regret them afterwards,
Guðrún is his wife, and I am Gunnar's;
the ugly norns created a long torment for us.'

The story is the same as in the older *Brot af Sigurðarkviðo* (Fragment of the Poem about Sigurðr) but it elaborates on Brynhild's feelings and the inner conflict between her conscience and the role she must play. This is stressed by her characterization against the stroke of fate. Her compunction in the face of her decision that she will either have Sigurðr as her love or have him killed contrasts with the plans of the Norns, who bring this unbearable situation upon her. In stanza 10, she incites herself ('hvetiaz at vígi') and goads Gunnarr to order the death of the hero.[38] The psychological insight into Brynhild's feelings, a trademark of the younger poems, is quite in line with the Christian concept of compunction. Brynhildr utters a monstrous intention; she recognizes immediately that already her wish is wrong and thus enters an emotional state expressed through the word *iðrask* and its relation to *þrá* (torment).[39] The application here allows for an expansion of the tragic aspect, culminating in her suicide, without altering the course of action. In *Helreið Brynhildar*, a shorter poem where Brynhildr justifies her deeds before a giantess on her way to Hel after suicide, she stresses that she has been deceived and shall now be united with Sigurðr in death. The aggressive self-defence despite the giantess' accusation that she 'washed her hands in blood'[40] fits nicely with the agony befitting her ill fate.[41]

The second occurrence of *iðrar* in *Atlamál*, however, demonstrates that the connection to compunction is arbitrary. Here, Guðrún's new husband, King Atli, has her brothers killed, and Guðrún reacts to his confession by threatening him that 'á muno þér iðrar' ('regret shall overcome you') – which she ensures later on by killing the sons she has with Atli. The moment when Atli's *iðrar* are due is marked explicitly, though not by Atli himself,[42] which implies that Atli's decision was the catalyst for the abysmal events that transpire. It is marked by the prophecy of *iðrar*, although the feeling is not spelled out when disaster inevitably strikes. This constellation of one figure commenting on a critical decision or deed leading to perdition in the future tense ('you/we will come to regret this') and silence with regard to the figures' inner thoughts in the moment the prophecy is fulfilled is a trademark of the Family Sagas.[43]

There are more aspects which connect the poems to the prose corpus. *Atlamál* is an extended reworking of the older *Atlakviða*, and although the late dating on the basis of moral attitude and emotionality has been contested, *Atlamál* must be counted among the youngest ones, just like *Sigurðarkviða in skamma*.[44] They focus on the suffering of the characters involved and in the case of *Atlamál* on the poisoned marriage and the disintegration of the family rather than on Gunnar's heroic death. Moods and sentiments are stressed both in character voice and narrative voice, and these voices are also recognizable in the prose of the *Vǫlsunga saga*, which was written on the basis of these poems. The saga does not adopt the long elegiac monologues, but it employs the prediction of future 'regret' in another context, when Sigurðr warns his wife Guðrún not to quarrel with Brynhildr.[45] While *Sigurðarkviða* stresses the emotional aspect of regret related to conscience, *Atlamál* and *Vǫlsunga saga* allude to a secular meaning in the sense of a decision which is recognized as wrong and thus regretted afterwards. Both stress the predictability of the outcome and thus the implications of individual decisions, even though the figures must adhere to a tragic pattern.

This similarity to the saga discourse fits nicely with the overall style, lexicon, even phrases, and the metre of *Atlamál*, which are particularly close to prose.[46] All this implies that our examples are late adaptations of the material, most probably from the twelfth or thirteenth century. The language used to describe 'regret' is in fact reminiscent of the early translations of Latin texts. It seems that Christian discourse actually was a decisive inspiration for dealing with the *homo interior* in younger witnesses of heroic legend, while this discourse on conscience is absent in the oldest surviving layer of eddic poetry. It is revealing, then, that the style of the Family Sagas prefers the unemotional focus on action and heroic posture found in the older versions of the poems.[47]

When it comes to reliable dating, however, skaldic poems seem more promising as a source, as the classical praise poems are transmitted as quotations of single stanzas in saga prose with the name of the skald. The praise poems, commonly memorized by the elites, are mostly regarded as authentic, and nearly all the occurrences of *iðrask/iðran* (*iðrask* 13 times, *iðran* 15 times)[48] address the Christian concept of compunction. This is evident as early as the middle of the eleventh century in Sigvatr Þórðarson's *Erfidrápa Óláfs helga*.[49] While most of

Sigvat's poetry focuses on warlike exploits, the main subject of skaldic praise, his *Erfidrápa*, a memorial poem in classical *dróttkvætt* metre on St Óláfr Haraldsson, who had died in the battle of Stiklestad in 1030, is clearly hagiographic in nature. It is obvious from the stanzas, which recount his accession to power and then focus on the final battle, his miracles and his veneration, that the concept, which includes compunction of those who killed the saint, was understood by the mostly illiterate retinue. The oldest surviving chronicle on Norwegian history, *Historia de antiquitate regum Norwagiensium*, written between 1183 and 1188, states that the Norwegians were 'moved by compunction of the crime' ('poenitentia ducti pro scelere').[50] *Ágrip af Nóregs konunga sögum*, in this part a translation of the *Historia*, similarly states: 'því at men fundu misræði sín ok iðruðusk ok vildu þá þat bœta' ('because the people saw their misdeeds and regretted them and then wanted to compensate for this').[51] It is interesting to see that the Icelandic *Morkinskinna*, a more elaborate collection of Kings' Sagas finished between 1217 and 1222, the first comprehensive history of Norway after Óláfr and a direct forerunner of Snorri Sturluson's *Heimskringla*, chooses a different wording:

> Í þenna tíma lét Guð mjǫk birtask helgi ins heilagra Óláfs konungs, ok sáu þá margir satt mál um sína hagi ok fundu nú *misræði* sitt ok *glœp* þann er þeir hǫfðu gǫrt ok þóttusk nú þann veg helzt mega sýna at *bœta* þat nú á syni hans er þeir hǫfðu á sjálfum honum *misgǫrt*.[52]
>
> At this time, God let the sanctity of King Óláfr come to the fore, and many saw the truth of his status and realised now their ill-advised deed and the wickedness they had committed, and they thought now to demonstrate this in the way that they compensated his son for what they had committed against himself.

This obvious use of the (juridical) language of compensation[53] was already visible in *Ágrip*. It is accompanied by a focus on the display of the attitude rather than on the inner man, while the *Legendary Óláfs saga helga* (c. 1220) and subsequent hagiographic versions stick to the term *iðrask*. We shall return to this effect. The skaldic stanza, in any case, proves that the surviving secular elite included the concept into cultural memory quite early. Sigvatr says this shortly after 1030:

> 11. Fór i fylking þeira
> framm *iðrask* nú miðri
> – snarir fundusk þar – Þrœnda
> þess verks búendr merki.

In prose syntax:

> Merki Þrœnda fór framm í miðri fylking þeira; snarir fundusk þar; búendr *iðrask* nú þess verks.
>
> The standard of the people from Trøndelag advanced in the middle of their [the enemies'] ranks; the farmers now regret this deed.[54]

This rare insight into emotional states is an exception from the rule that secular court poetry does not address feelings but praises heroic deeds.[55] We know that Óláfr was venerated in England as early as the mid-eleventh century,[56] but Sigvat's praise poem is the oldest witness in Old Norse. This particularly early occurrence is the only one from secular discourse related to conscience and conversion which has its origins in an 'oral' past.

Sin, praise, edification: Skaldic poetry and law

If one takes an onomasiological perspective and looks at the actions related to the concept of penance and takes the confession of and compensation for sins into account, the principle becomes apparent in more places.[57] Thus we get to know from Þórarinn loftunga (Praise-tongue), a contemporary of Sigvat's and an adherent of Óláf's former enemy and successor Sveinn jarl Hákonarson, that Óláfr died 'synðalauss' ('without sin') and saved his soul before death.[58] This poem contains hagiographic statements too, and the hope for the resurrection of their king's soul is uttered by skalds as early as the turn of the millennium.[59] The aspect of penance also comes to the fore in praise of crusaders and pilgrims, such as King Erik Ejegod of Denmark (1095–1103), who died in Cyprus on his way to Jerusalem, where he, according to his skald Markús Skeggjason, wanted 'to cure his inner wounds' ('læknask sǫr in iðri').[60] More explicit is a poem on the pilgrimage of Sigurðr slembidjákn (d. 1139), an illegitimate son of King Magnús berfœttr and later king of Norway, who went to Rome and Jerusalem between 1128 and 1135. In the words of his skald, he 'expiated his sins' ('synðum hrauð') and 'washed away [his] sins' ('þvægi af sér synðir') in the river Jordan.[61]

Crusades are motivated by conscience as well as the pursuit of honour; both occur in Markús's stanza, and the examples may serve to demonstrate that the concept of sin, compunction and penitence had successfully amalgamated with the secular encomiastic discourse by the twelfth century. This in turn allowed for the integration of the heroic into the representation of crusades. In the case of King Sigurðr Jórsalafari of Norway (1103–30), the two skalds treating his crusade (1108–11) do not mention or allude to sin and penance in the quoted stanzas but rather evoke his similarity to the mighty kings of old when they describe the preparations,[62] a literary and political strategy also found in a Latin chronicle of the Third Crusade written in Denmark. It is made a matter of conscience to emulate the heroic heathen forefathers who fought solely for their fame when the possession of the Holy Land is at stake.[63] In the case of King Sigurðr, the religious aspect is found in the surrounding prose of *Morkinskinna*, where his motivation is said to have been 'at kaupa sér Guðs miskunn ok góðan orðstírr' ('to acquire God's pardon and a good reputation').[64] Man's relationship to God comes first, fame second. This is altered later in Snorri's *Heimskringla*,[65] and again this mirrors a secularization of language over time and follows further developments of genre, something we already saw above in the fate of Norwegian compunction in relation to Óláf's sanctity.

Nearly all the other occurrences of compunction are found in early Christian religious poetry.[66] The best example is *Harmsól* ('Sun of Sorrow'), a long skaldic poem written by Gamli kanóki, an Augustinian canon from Þykkvibœr in the second half of the twelfth century. It is a life and praise of Christ in the form of a full-fledged *drápa* and a haunting sermon in verse at the same time, which urges the listeners to repent their sins. In the context of the Crucifixion, the amalgamation of skaldic praise and edification is nicely illustrated in st. 25:

> Hollostu gefr hæsta
> hring-Þrótt með sér dróttinn
> saðr, þeims *sinna iðrask*
> *synða*, lausn ok ynði.
> Ern skóp hauðr ok hlýrni
> heims valdr sem kyn beima;
> orrs ok ǫllu dýrri
> élsetrs konungr betri.

In prose:

> Saðr dróttinn gefr hring-Þrótt, þeims *iðrask synða sinna*, hæsta hollostu, lausn ok ynði með sér. Ern valdr heims skóp hauðr ok hlýrni sem kyn beima; ǫrr konungr élsetrs es ǫllu betri ok dýrri.
>
> The true Lord gives the ring-Þróttr [= man] who repents of his sins the highest faith, absolution and delight with him. The powerful ruler of the world created earth and heaven as well as the kinsfolk of men; the generous king of the storm-seat [= king of the sky/Heaven = God] is better and more precious than everything.[67]

Þróttr is one of Óðin's names, and 'ring-Óðinn' stands for 'man' in this context. The kenning 'ring-Þróttr' also alludes to the repenting thief who is also crucified and called a 'gatherer of rings' ('tínir baugar') in st. 23.⁶⁸ The poem presents a perfect harmony of traditional language and Christian concepts some decades before the 'classical' sagas. Sinning men are seafarers and warriors under stormy skies and Christ is the triumphant all-ruler in accord with the heroic discourse, but the overall focus is on conscience, compunction and penance. *Iðran* and *iðrask* each occur twice, and it is no wonder that even this sermon stresses the aspect of compensation. One such example is when Gamli states that no man will be saved 'unless he makes reparation for deeds done out of habit' ('nema bœti verk gǫr af venju').⁶⁹

The degree to which penance had become part of vernacular discourse can also be inferred from the Christian law sections in the provincial laws and from the Icelandic *Grágás* laws,⁷⁰ which inculcate the duty to do penance especially after major crimes. Even more revealing are the *Gulaþingslǫg*, the provincial law for Western Norway, a 'private' collection by experts, which is viewed as the oldest surviving provincial law. The oldest manuscript is from *c*. 1250, and as the text contains many archaic features, its origin dates back as far as the early twelfth, if not the late eleventh, century.⁷¹ In the section pertaining to 'criminal law', *fullréttisorð* are treated, i.e. calling a man the passive part in homosexual intercourse or a woman a whore, which entitle the addressee to take revenge. Here, the law states: 'Iðrazt megu men orða sinna oc aptr taca ef vilia'⁷² ('Men have the chance to regret their words and to take them back if they wish'). It is remarkable that the action of formally taking back a mortal insult is not enough, but that the 'inner' aspect of remorse is addressed in the law; this becomes especially remarkable given that these law texts are normally preoccupied with formal procedure. Evidently, and perhaps unexpectedly, the attitude of the repenting sinner is required from a lawman's point of view.

The aspect of conscience (*samvizka*) in legal procedure is also repeatedly found in the Norwegian *Landslov* and in *Jónsbók*, new 'official' law codes for the whole of Norway and for Iceland introduced in 1274/76 and 1281, respectively. Conscience primarily concerns judgements and oath formulae and thus adds a moral aspect to matters of procedure.⁷³ This introduction of conscience in judgements concerning both friends and enemies effectively turns the exploitation of legal procedure against one's adversaries, a recurrent problem in saga disputes, into a sin. What we see in skaldic verse, the surrounding saga prose and the laws is a close relationship and a free exchange between discourse on self-reflection required in penance and discourse on action and, in this case, compensation preferred in secular texts. Consequently, no specifically 'old' semantics of *iðran/iðrask* come to the fore. The rather infrequent secular use with the meaning of 'regret' also addresses the inner disposition of the figure and is close to the idea of compensation and thus tariff penance. As a result, no different 'original' concept is discernible, a fact which also underlines the immersion of Christian doctrine in contemporary thought. If one looks at the dates of the poems and texts, it is clear that the aspect of compunction developed in the early translations is also present in the oldest surviving texts with indigenous contents. However, it does seem that in certain genres, notably the well-known Family Sagas, the lexicon of compunction and regret is consciously avoided, which coincides with their typical focus on action. This lexical absence can actually serve as a useful guideline in approaching saga literature.

Acting out compunction? Kings' Sagas

Compunction is addressed directly in historiographical texts in the widest sense. The concept is manifest to a greater degree the closer the respective texts are to Latin discourse and to the genre conventions of hagiography. One good example is the aforementioned *Ágrip af Nóregs konunga sǫgum*, a reworking of Latin chronicles. Here, King Hákon inn góði (the Good, 934–61) is excused for his acceptance of pagan practices. He had been raised in England and was a Christian but took part in a pagan sacrifice and was buried in pagan fashion – which strictly speaking turned him, a 'good' king who had guaranteed peace and prosperity, into an apostate, which is also stressed by the twelfth-century *Historia Norwegie*. *Ágrip*, however, states that when Hákon realized that he would die, 'he regretted much his offences against God' ('iðraðisk hann mjǫk mótgerða við guð').[74] As a result, he refused to be brought to England to be buried there in Christian soil, due to his belief that having lived among heathens, he was unworthy of anything but a heathen burial; instead, he chose to rely solely on God's mercy. This trick helps transform the fact that Hákon did not receive the sacrament of penance before his death into the virtue of humility and subsequently turns a pagan burial into a last push to be counted among the just.

We encounter a somewhat similar inverted display of conscience in the case of the infamous cruelty of King Óláfr Tryggvason (995–1000). In an attempt to have this Óláfr canonized, a Latin *vita* was written in the Icelandic monastery of Þingeyrar by the monk Oddr Snorrason shortly before 1200, of which only vernacular redactions survive.[75] As the story goes, one day Óláfr punishes an Icelander who had killed one of his retainers. The Icelander was outlawed at home for his deed, and the king takes further revenge on him by having him bitten to death by his dogs in front of the court, although his retinue advised against it. Óláfr was severely rebuked for this by his bishop and performed an act of public penance: 'he fell to his knees and confessed before God his wickedness (*glœpr*) and what he had committed (*misgert*) in this cruel deed, and the king did great penance (*mikla iðran*) for this'.[76] The words indicating sin are familiar from the example concerning St Óláfr and his son Magnús in *Morkinskinna* treated above.

Compunction is alluded to when acts of compensation for obvious sins are mentioned, as in *Orkneyinga saga*, a history of the jarls covering the period between the ninth century and the time around 1200 when the text was written. The centre of the text is the legend of St Magnús Erlendsson (1108–17), a jarl and martyr. His death came at the hands of Jarl Hákon Pálsson (1103–23), who had shared the realm with Magnús before he laid a trap for his cousin. Nothing is said about his compunction, and he tries to prevent the burial of Magnús's remains in a church. After the first miracles, however, he is overcome with tears and gives his permission for the burial before going on pilgrimage to Rome and Jerusalem. After his return, he makes better laws and becomes a popular ruler.[77] It is beyond doubt that Hákon and his change for the better were driven by compunction, but since there are no skaldic stanzas stating this, his emotional motives are either concealed behind or rather expressed through his deeds and through his tears. Tears are, of course, traditionally linked with compunction, as various contributions in this volume show, and this link was also made in Old Norse and Icelandic literature, as shown by the translation of *compunctio* as *tármelti* (melting into tears) in Alcuin's treatise.

If one turns towards the performative side of penance, one finds it virtually everywhere. The writing of *Sverris saga*, one of the oldest Kings' Sagas and the first extensive non-hagiographic biography of a single Norwegian king, started under the king's supervision, when the author, the abbot Karl Jónsson of the Icelandic monastery at Þingeyrar, was staying in Norway between 1185 and 1188/89. It is a peculiar text, as its aim is to justify the kingship of Sverrir, who was the son of a king born out of wedlock and who was responsible for the death of King Magnús Erlingsson. Magnús was not a king's son and had actually no legitimate claim to kinghsip, but he was the son of a king's daughter and powerful magnate, who succeeded in having him elected after decades of feuds between different pretenders in 1161. Magnús became the first crowned and anointed king of Norway.[78] Sverrir is staged in his saga as a second David sent to punish the arrogant who violated the old law, a theme developed especially in his dreams and his long speeches. As Sverrir had been educated to become a priest and the text was written by a monk, his long speeches showcase scholastic argumentation and theological knowledge (as well as secular rhetoric and humour).[79] Compunction is never mentioned, but Sverri's actions, which for the most part consist of military operations recorded in laconic saga style, are informed by a clear code of norms and values.

The fictional Sverri's speech after the decisive battle at Kalvskinnet in 1179, at which Magnús's father Jarl Erlingr fell, addresses the fact that the archbishop of Niðaróss (Trondheim) had misleadingly declared the war a crusade against the 'usurper'. It ends with an insistent plea to pray for the souls of the enemies who fell in this unjust conflict without the Eucharist or confession ('þjónustulausir ok skriftalausir') and with a 'hostile mind' ('grimmr hugr').[80] Sverrir underscores that praying for the souls of his enemies who were not adequately prepared for death will be rewarded, and he himself states that he will forgive ('fyrirgefa') them for all their crimes committed against him ('allt þat er þeir hafa misgort við mik'). It does not matter for the present study that this is political propaganda in a struggle for power. However, it does point to the fact that the author and King Sverri's party were convinced that this pious attitude would be well received.[81] It demonstrates that the feud between two factions was happening in a thoroughly Christian society, which is underlined by several other passages: King Magnús questions his conscience before his final battle and asks God for peace,[82] and King Sverrir at the end of his life forgives his enemies for the killing of his relatives and the speaking of *fullréttisorð* against him, with the hope for God's forgiveness in return.[83] This is no thin façade which merely screens the 'real' power play; it rather permeates it. In fact, Sverrir taunts his own men when they start kissing a church wall before a battle, as they are usually not especially pious.[84] The message is easily understood: *attritio*, compunction out of situational fear of death, does not signify an adequate understanding of one's sins.[85]

Sverris saga is no exception. *Morkinskinna*, which treats the time between St Óláfr and *Sverris saga* (1030–1177),[86] repeatedly shows kings and magnates in a state of compunction, or it deals with their conscience.[87] Haraldr Sigurðarson inn harðráði, one of the main characters (today often viewed as the last 'Viking' ruler), who fell in 1066 when he attempted to conquer England, spent about one decade in Byzantine military service. In this context, he was obviously sent to Jerusalem on a mission connected to the re-erection of the Church of the Holy Sepulchre in 1037.[88] The corroborating skaldic stanza from Harald's time is taken as a proof that Haraldr was a 'crusader', and the surrounding prose states that he went to Jerusalem to 'compensate for his crimes against God' ('at bœta sínar afgørðir við Guð'),[89] thus mirroring the later semantic framing of the real crusaders in verse and prose mentioned above.

King Eysteinn (1103–23), brother of Sigurðr the Crusader, is praised for his humility.[90] When he interprets a dream of Sigurðr in which St Óláfr appears and fetches the royal brothers one after the other but leaves out Sigurðr, he understands St Óláf's conduct in relation to his conscience. As the saint is gentle towards their youngest brother Óláfr, he will intercede on his behalf. The less gentle treatment of Eysteinn is understood as a result of the latter's 'afgørðir' (crimes) and 'boðorðabrot' (violation of God's commandments).[91] It looks even worse for Sigurðr, and that is underlined by his subsequent life: he goes insane and suffers from a lack of impulse control. When the old king Sigurðr deserts his wife and plans to marry another woman, Bishop Magni of Bergen strictly forbids this and does not relent, although the enraged king threatens him with his drawn sword. The bishop of Stavanger, however, turns the affair into a bargain. While he repeats that bigamy is against the law and the teachings of the church, he asks for a donation 'to thus compensate God and us' ('at bœta svá við Guð ok við oss'),[92] which results in Sigurðr giving him money so that he may marry the woman. Thus, a simoniacal practice – turning matters of sin and conscience into a monetary bargain – is vested in the established discourse.

Two points should be clear from this episodic look at the lesser-known *Konungasögur*. Firstly, the concept of sin, compunction, penance and forgiveness is present in several kings' lives in Old Norse from the beginning, on the level of action as well as its implicit evaluation. The dominance of *Heimskringla* in research on the 'saga society' may have obscured that fact. That Snorri Sturluson's workshop decided not to include any of the numerous aspects concerning the *homo interior* makes *Heimskringla* the exception, rather than the other way around.[93] Furthermore, it reveals Heimskringla's 'society' as a consciously crafted literary phenomenon, calling into question its reliability as an anthropological source and its qualification as a chief witness to political culture. In this case, the obtrusive absence of Latin erudition and theological knowledge is a proof of the author's familiarity with all the relevant concepts.[94] Secondly, it should be kept in mind that the Kings' Sagas were written in Iceland in the same places as the Family Sagas. It is highly likely that *Morkinskinna* was written at the monastery of Munkaþverá in North East Iceland, as were several Family Sagas.[95] The connections between power, conscience and compunction contain an Icelandic point of view.

Icelandic history: Compunction and forgiveness in the *Samtíðarsögur*

This Icelandic point of view is of course also found in Icelandic history proper. *Sturlunga saga* is a collection of Contemporary Sagas (*Samtíðarsögur*) on twelfth- and thirteenth-century history compiled around 1300. It provides us with a clear picture of the concentration of power in ever fewer hands, power struggles and the involvement of the Norwegian king in the acephalic society. It ends with the Icelandic acceptance of Norwegian royal control in 1262–64.[96] The sagas are arranged in a way that gives the impression of an escalation in conflicts among the magnates.[97] *Þorgils saga ok Hafliða* (written around 1240) serves as a sort of prelude, focusing as it does on a dangerous conflict between two *goðar* – big men and organizers of the local *þing* gatherings as well as the central annual *Alþingi* – from 1117 to 1121. The conflict is sparked by one of Hafliði's relatives and soon he and Þorgils find themselves on different sides as influential patrons. At the *Alþingi* in 1120, Hafliði takes an axe to the assembly site against his habit and the advice of his wife, and when Þorgils sees the weapon in his hand in the crowded gathering, he strikes at once with his axe, cutting off three of Hafliði's fingers. This breaking of the *þing* peace leads to a subsequent outlawry sentence against Þorgils,[98] which Hafliði would have to execute by formally seizing Þorgils's property. However, he cannot execute this act due to the absence of any central power. Advancing toward Þorgils's farm would mean war between equally strong magnates and their followers.[99] The situation at the Alþingi in 1121 is that Hafliði and his men want to deny Þorgils's party access to the assembly, as outlaws are not allowed, although they come to offer compensation and seek arbitration.[100] The risk of an escalation of violence between the two large groups is great, and the consequences in the long run are dire. In this situation, the bishop of Skálholt repeatedly tries to convince Hafliði to allow Þorgils and his retinue access to the þing. One argument is that God shall reward this.[101] Hafliði hides behind the law when he refuses, but it is quite clear that he feels his honour is at stake, as he will only accept a reconciliation if he is granted self-judgement in the case.

As the parties cannot agree and not even the threat of anathema has the desired effect, the priest Ketill tells a story from his own life, an *exemplum*, again applying legal terminology. After rumours had spread that his wife was unfaithful to him, the priest Ketill had attacked the man in question, and against all odds, his opponent was stronger and stabbed out one of his eyes. Ketil's attempt to have him outlawed came to nothing, and when the opponent offered compensation, he realized that 'whenever I thought about my honour (*mannvirðing*), no compensation (*bætr*) could be made which I would find honourable. So for the sake of God I decided to submit the whole case to him'[102] – which not only secured peace and friendship but also restored Ketil's honour. Hafliði is so impressed by this *exemplum* that he not only plans to have the priest elected as the next bishop of Hólar but also agrees to an arbitration, in which he obtains a conditional self-judgement. This results in a stable agreement, the highest compensation ever paid for three fingers in Icelandic history, and cooperation with Þorgils.[103] In this case, the reason for a change of mind and attitude is love for God, a central aspect of compunction. The reversal here lies in the altered view on honour, whose restoration doubtlessly remains central to the story, but which is now subordinate to a sense of equity informed by religion.

Compunction and conscience are definitely not dominant ideals, but they are the only reason why at this crucial point the escalation is averted – as opposed to later Icelandic history. The conflict constellation is clearly brought about by the 'game of honour' analysed by W. I. Miller. He states in an analysis based on the *Samtíðarsögur* and the Family Sagas:

> This is a world of shame and envy, the emotions of status, not of guilt and remorse, the emotions of conscience. The fact that saga people talked about shame more than they talked about guilt no doubt assists the perception of saga reserve and emotionlessness. Scholars who think that they see remorse and guilt usually attribute them to the effects of the Christian emotional style.[104]

This view, which is dominant in anthropological scholarship on Old Norse-Icelandic literature and Icelandic society, declares conscience and compunction irrelevant. It is revealing that from this perspective, figures like Bǫðvarr Ásbjarnarson become key witnesses of mentality. He dissuades Þorgils from attacking Hafliði at an earlier occasion on the morning of St Peter's Day after mass with religious arguments but later admits that this was only a pretence since he saw that Hafliði's men were more numerous and that he did not care a bit about religious or legal norms.[105] Religion in this view is only a tool, just like legal norms are. What is overlooked here is that characters like Bǫðvarr represent evil influence, as until the very end he tries to undermine a perfectly honourable reconciliation through interjections and insults, until Þorgils declares that he will not listen to this.[106] He is the poison in Þorgils's ear: his earlier advice led to Þorgils striking with his axe. Thus he is the negative counterpart to the priest Ketill and, ultimately, the powerless loser, the voice of an insatiable envy and hunger for honour.

It is not to be doubted that this hunger existed in numerous 'big' men and often led to peril, just as it does in *Guðmundar saga dýra*. It is one of the oldest *Samtíðarsögur*, written shortly after Guðmund's death in 1212, and it offers an apology for a hideous crime committed by its protagonist. Guðmundr came into a similar situation with his opponent Onundr Þorkelsson for similar reasons as Þorgils and Hafliði, although he was not attacked directly. Rather, Onundr encouraged one of his retainers to steal horses from Guðmundr which were paid as the result of a settlement. As Onund's sons and men then publicly mock the victim for his loss of honour and his inaptitude,[107] he retaliates by burning down Onund's farm with his opponent and his sons in it in 1197.[108] This excess is only explicable by the intricate rules of honour and the necessity of securing credibility by occasionally acting unpredictably.[109] After the burning, Guðmundr is able to reach arbitration but the settlement is broken by his opponents, and Guðmundr goes on to win the conflict and obtain self-judgement. Although he is the winner, however, he does not take it all but rather adheres to the old arbitrated settlement and ends his life in the monastery at Þingeyrar.[110] Compunction is not spelled out, but it is nevertheless an important facet of the story. It is clear from Guðmund's actions that no matter how necessary he and the monk who wrote the saga may have found his killings, he could not enjoy his success in the world. Ending one's life in penance becomes a recurrent motif in saga literature.[111]

In fact, the whole world of the Contemporary Sagas is not only permeated by escalating conflicts driven by envy and fear of dishonour, but also by penance, confession and the need for forgiveness.[112] In many key scenes, captives who are about to be executed ask for a *prestsfundr*, which gives them the opportunity to confess and this is usually granted even by the worst enemies, and in some cases, the status of the deceased is discussed, as in King Sverri's speech.[113] Church sanctuary is respected. The characters are intent on not sinning after their final confession, which is spelled out in a story of the two brothers Snorri and Þorsteinn in *Guðmundar saga dýra*. They took part in Guðmund's burning of Onund's farm and are later seized by Onund's surviving sons together with other perpetrators. After his confession, Snorri asks: 'I want to be killed before Þorsteinn because I trust him more to forgive (*fyrirgefa*) you, although he sees me killed.'[114]

From the anthropological perspective viewing Christendom as irrelevant to Icelandic mentality, this scene has been interpreted as exhibiting contempt for the other brother who will stand the sight without feeling rage.[115] This explanation rather overlooks the fact that the second brother does actually watch the bloody business with uncovered eyes and arguably faces the tougher task. Iceland is not a *civitas Dei* but if one does not apply a normative, anachronistic notion of Christendom, however, the picture becomes clearer. At the end of *Íslendinga saga*, the core of the *Samtíðarsögur* covering the decisive years between 1183 and 1264, Jarl Gizurr Þorvaldsson (1208–68), one of the central figures in the struggle for power and the Sturlungar's main adversary, gets hold of members of the Sturlungar collective, a certain Þórðr Andréasson and his brothers who had treacherously tried to kill him. Despite this attempt, he does not resort to vengeance against the whole family. Having allowed them to meet a priest, he is easily dissuaded from killing all the brothers and grants everyone quarter but Þórðr himself. Þórðr addresses Gizurr thus: 'This I will ask you, Gizurr, that you forgive me what I have done to you.'[116] The answer comes in laconic saga style and not without the grim humour of a man who had turned 'bitter and hard'[117] from decades of struggles during which his wife and sons had been murdered: 'This I shall do as soon as you are dead.'[118] This final scene in which Gizur's last enemy dies combines necessity for revenge and brutal assertiveness with Christian discourse, therein illustrating that the element of forgiveness had become indispensable in storytelling and death scenes. The concept of compunction is always present in the background and reliably breaks through the surface at crucial moments, before battles and at the moment before death, in the actions of the figures, if not in the voice of the narrator. With the final scene from *Íslendinga saga*, a circle closes which *Þorgils saga ok Hafliða* opens: *Sturlunga saga* as a collection is also a story of moral degeneration – prevented by the early characters in the name of God, compensated by penitent sinners like Guðmundr dýri, and finally brought about by power-obsessed magnates like Sturla Sigvatsson and Gizurr Þorvaldsson.

Epilogue: The silence of the Family Sagas

The Contemporary Sagas and their view of religious conduct among the characters have been criticized as a 'hollow accord' of 'pagan disposition to vengeance' and 'Christian magic'.[119] The 'outer apparatus' of Christendom is accused for having destroyed the purely Germanic, 'Viking lifestyle'[120] represented in the Family Sagas, which treat Icelandic history between c. 870 and 1030. This verdict by Andreas Heusler mirrors an understanding of the Family Sagas as the purest witnesses of a culture largely untouched by foreign influences and the alleged Christian obsession with sin.[121] This view constitutes an aesthetic verdict influenced by anti-Catholic sentiment and indignation at the fact that the *Samtíðarsögur* confront the beholder with ugly reality, broken heroes and the hybridity of culture. This romantic need for identification is still influential today, especially in research influenced by anthropological analysis. It regards the Family Sagas as reliable sources of mentalities and disputing strategies.[122] While it is impossible to do justice to the corpus of these c. 40 sagas in this context, it will be argued on the basis of the verse and prose corpus treated here that the 'saga world' and its mentality addressed in the introduction are first and foremost a literary phenomenon and the product of making sense of history through storytelling.

The *Íslendingasögur* are dealing with a time before and just after conversion to Christendom, which means that religious institutions are largely absent in their picture of history. Furthermore, the conversion is not particularly relevant to the narrations themselves, which is reflected in Snorri Sturluson's playing down of the change entailed by the conversion. All that means that in most cases, the visible actions connected to compunction which accompany the Contemporary Sagas as well as the Kings' Sagas are absent. But does that imply that compunction is irrelevant? The question becomes more urgent as the Family Sagas apply a discourse centred on action and heroic posture which emulates the style of the older eddic *Ereignislied*, which in turn precludes the insight into characters found in retrospective poems.[123]

Nevertheless, twelve *Íslendingasögur* contain the verb *iðrask*, and the occasional exception to the rule that feelings are not described reveals that it is a stylistic convention belonging to the construction of the 'saga age' as a heroic age. In other words, the narrator breaks character. This happens *en passant*, as demonstrated in *Ljósventinga saga*, a rather early text written shortly after 1220. In a protracted conflict situated after the conversion, the brother of one main character is killed in a melée. The slayer and his chief must leave Iceland and obtain passage on a ship, but the ship does not get favourable wind. They draw consecrated lots and fast for three days, after which it is revealed that a murderer is among the crew. After this ordeal, the murderer 'regretted' (*iðraðist*), left the ship and gave half of his belongings to the poor and the other half to the family of his victim.[124] The wind changes. This story serves to underline that the slayer Hallr and his chief Þorvarðr Hǫskuldsson are not abandoned by God, and although the *homo interior* of the protagonists is never laid open, the example demonstrates that the concept of compunction works just as well here as in the genres surrounding the *Íslendingasögur* and that it is safe to assume that Þorvarð's subsequent pilgrimage to Rome was motivated by his conscience.

In the great 'classics', the rarity of compunction as an explicit motif is even consciously employed to enhance the tragic effect. The second and main part of *Laxdœla saga*, which is comparatively open to courtly concepts and the expression of emotions,[125] deals with a famous love triangle between the foster brothers Kjartan and Bolli and Guðrún. While Kjartan is in love with Guðrún but stays at the Norwegian court longer than planned, Bolli marries her under the false pretence that Kjartan is in love with the king's daughter. The resulting mésalliance, clearly drawing on the model of the Vǫlsungs and Gjúkungs, leads to uneasiness and in the end an open conflict arises between the foster brothers and their wives. At the peak, Guðrún forces her husband Bolli to kill Kjartan, which he does.

> Bolli settisk þegar undir herðar honum ok andaðisk Kjartan í knám Bolla. Iðraðisk Bolli þegar verksins ok lýsti vígi á hendur sér.[126]
>
> Bolli sat down immediately and placed his legs under his shoulders, and Kjartan died on Bolli's knees. Bolli regretted his deed instantly and announced that he was the killer.

The *pietà*-like scene, appearing again between two enemies in *Vápnfirðinga saga*, serves to underline Bolli's bad conscience and his tragic situation: he could not avoid the deed if he wanted to keep his wife and his honour but in doing so he destroyed the lives of all the people involved. The fact that Guðrún (after Bolli's slaying at the hands of Kjartan's family and her revenge through her sons) ends her life as Iceland's first nun underlines this tragic structure from a Christian point of view. This perspective is prominent especially in the famous classics. When the wise Njáll of *Brennu-Njáls saga* is burned with his sons for the sons' crime, he tells them to trust in God with the words of Petrus Lombardus that He will not let them burn in this world and the next.[127] It is not only here that religious discourse comes to the fore. Some chapters before, Hǫskuldr, Njál's foster-son, is killed by Njál's sons, which is the reason for the burning. His last words are: 'Guð hjálpi mér, en fyrirgefi yðr' ('May God help me and forgive you').[128] It is precisely this mercy which Njáll hopes for later, knowing well that his sons committed a grievous sin and that they all would be killed.

These explicit passages are exceptions, but it may be inferred from them that pagan and early Christian characters could be haunted by their conscience. It would be interesting in this regard – though space does not allow me to do so here – to explore the connection between *harmr* (pain/grief), the longing for revenge and the decision to accept a settlement. Apart from envy, greed and a perceived loss of honour motivating the deeds of 'uneven' characters (*ójafnaðarmenn*), the grief felt at the loss of a close relative or friend is usually the cause of rage and the desire to take revenge (*reka harma*), even against nature and the Gods, as seen in Egill Skalla-Grímsson's poem *Sonatorrek* ('Loss of the Sons').[129] When characters who are described as wise and far-sighted decide not to listen to their *harmr* and do not include it into their demands for compensation, it may be that they have cautiously weighted their best options in the game of honour or have run out of violent options. But it may also imply that they regret what had happened. They want to prevent others from pursuing vengeance and at times do so by appealing to their conscience, as is the case in some early sagas. An example is found in *Reykdæla saga ok Víga-Skútu*, where the pagan *goði* Áskell dies like a saint and forbids revenge. Or again in *Heiðarvíga saga*, where one of the men who suffered most from the central conflict stresses the need not to let hate dictate the outcome and earns applause.[130] The structural similarity to *Þorgils saga ok Hafliða* and its *exemplum* is evident.

Besides its Christian semantics, *iðrask* is used occasionally in its secular meaning when characters regret a strategic decision or threaten others that they shall regret it if they do not act as they are supposed to do. One final aspect, nevertheless, underlines that the intended audience could infer emotional responses between sorrow and compunction from the saga action itself. Most of the occurrences are in future tense ('you/we shall regret'), are spoken by influential characters and serve as allusion to coming disaster, just as in *Vǫlsunga saga*. Thus, in *Egils saga Skalla-Grímssonar*, King Haraldr inn hárfagri of Norway warns his son Eiríkr that he shall regret befriending Þórólfr, the brother of Egill, and having him stay with him.[131] Similarly, Egill himself states that he shall regret parting with his brother before a battle in which Þórólfr actually falls.[132] Both predictions are true, as a long conflict arises between King Eiríkr blóðøx and Egill, which is also fuelled by Egil's mourning. In these and other cases, it is left to the audience to recognize the moment when the characters feel a sense of regret or even compunction.[133] The decisive scenes themselves are devoid of emotional vocabulary.

What we have traced so far from translations to poetry to the classical saga genres is an adaptation of a common European discourse. It is present in Old Norse in all its facets. As far as local and especially Icelandic history is concerned, however, it takes on a special form in highlighting the peculiarities of this local history, including the consciousness of a late conversion, of the political in an acephalic society and the aesthetics of inherited heroic legend. This contributed to the construction of a heroic age in which the look at the *homo interior* is consciously toned down in favour of action and posture. Textual surfaces are revealing with regard to these constructions of different pasts – the heroic and the recent. As a consequence, they are highly informative regarding questions of genre. But they can be misleading when it comes to defining the emotional potential of the societies they are supposed to represent. The 'emotional community' that unfolds in the famous Family Sagas is neither the one of thirteenth- to sixteenth-century Iceland nor that of the 'Viking' Age, but a community of skilful narrations adhering to a collective imagination of a past and its alleged properties. The sharp border between a saga age populated by figures plagued by grief and harm but without compunction, confession and forgiveness, and a recent past permeated by the concept of compunction and forgiveness at crucial moments, is as revealing as its eventual transgression. Compunction proves to be ubiquitous in Old Norse literature. In contrast to honour in the foreground, it constitutes a powerful concept in the background of saga action and character voice.

4

William of Auvergne and compunction: Describing the world through metaphors

Béatrice Delaurenti

In the 1230s, William of Auvergne wrote a treatise on penance in which he exposed his own interest in compunction, broadly understood as inner repentance. This was a highly anticipated exercise for a theologian. Indeed, confession and penance occupied an important place in doctrinal discourse and pastoral activity of the ministers of the Christian Church. They were topical issues both in ecclesial legislation, theological doctrine and pastoral admonition. On the legislative side, canon 21 'omnis utriusque sexus' of the Fourth Lateran Council of 1215 recommended that annual confession be practised across the whole Church. This prescription led to the standardization of earlier traditions of confession.[1] On the doctrinal side, penance and contrition were objects of renewed interest from the twelfth century onwards, first by secular theologians, then by members of the mendicants orders.[2] On the pastoral side, finally, the period was marked by clerical efforts to administer salvation to the faithful through predication and confession. A new literary genre destined for the clergy emerged, that of confessors' manuals, which were highly popular.[3] Such transformations accompanied a new attention paid towards 'man, his interiority, his emotions'.[4] William of Auvergne's treatise burgeoned in this doctrinal, pastoral and legislative landscape.

I am grateful to *Piroska* Nagy for her attentive reading and useful remarks.

At the crossroads of theology, pastoralism and natural philosophy

William of Auvergne was both a theologian and a philosopher. His writings were not limited to the theological and pastoral spheres, even those on penance and compunction. His intellectual production was nourished by other fields of knowledge, intermingling the study of the soul and the passions on the one hand, knowledge of nature and the human body on the other hand. William gave passions a place in his theological and pastoral discourse on penance, a peculiarity that has been studied in the context of the renewal of a cultural history of emotions.[5] The intersection he made between theology and natural philosophy is less known; this is what this article intends to examine.

William obtained the degree of master in theology from the University of Paris in 1225. Elected bishop of Paris three years later, he exercised this function until his death in 1249 and engaged in intense activities, at the same time pastoral, theological and diplomatic. He was a prolific author, both in theology and natural philosophy. These two areas of interest are perceptible in his intellectual output. He had in fact planned to compose an encyclopaedia which would have covered the whole field of natural philosophy and theology, as well as certain questions of logic and law. If the seven parts of this major work were written, they were never collated in a single volume, even though William had announced the project by entitling his work *Magisterium divinale sive sapientale*. If we are to believe William's hints, his encyclopaedia should have followed a ternary construction: first, a philosophical and demonstrative part would have gathered the treatises *De trinitate*, *De universo* and *De anima* together; followed by a transitional *Cur Deus Homo*; then a third part on faith, sacraments and moral theology, assembling the treatises *De fide et legibus*, *De virtutibus et moribus* and the treaty which we shall examine here, *De sacramentis*.[6]

The master's sources also reflect his interest in philosophy and natural science. He composed the texts of his *Magisterium* in 1228–31,[7] after the condemnation by the University of Paris of the teaching of Aristotle's *libri naturales* (1210 and 1215), and before these works were reintegrated into the curriculum of the Faculty of Arts (1255).[8] In this context of intellectual revolution, William's effort consisted in dealing with the massive inflow of texts by Aristotle and his Arab commentators, recently translated into Latin.[9] He presented his work as spearheading the glorification of faith and fighting the mistakes of his adversaries.[10] The result was a complex thought, vigorously combating Aristotle's and Avicenna's ideas, but also borrowing much from those he condemned in order to integrate them into the Christian tradition.

The discovery of this corpus of texts led William of Auvergne to take a close look at the natural world. Let us give just one example of this interest, taken from the first part of *De universo* on the corporeal universe. The master affirmed that the body is the soul's instrument for acting on the outside world:

> You must know that the spiritual substances attached to the bodies, as I told you regarding the human soul, have limited powers defined more or less ('quasi') by the limits and boundaries of their bodies, so that they can perform nothing beyond or outside them. But through the limbs of their bodies or through instruments applied to their limbs, it is manifest that many things are realised by [these spiritual substances], as it appears in building and in other arts.[11]

The contact between two bodies was considered a criterion that helped distinguish between the operations that proceed 'in a natural way' ('per modum naturae')[12] and others operations, pertaining to a demonic or divine causality. William incorporated the famous Aristotelian axiom – in every natural movement, the motor has to be together with the moved; there has to be contiguity between them[13] – and excluded the possibility of action at a distance. But the adjective *quasi* nuanced this stance: an action of the soul outside the body was made possible under certain conditions. William clarified this later by establishing a series of exceptions to the principle of contact, which formed 'the part of natural science called natural magic'.[14] By making this famous remark, he introduced the category of 'natural magic' in the Latin West.[15] It also demonstrates how much attention he paid to strange and unexplained phenomena that depart from the usual course of nature. Knowing the human body and its capacities was, for William, essential to explain the world.

Several of William's writings are devoted to the explanation of natural phenomena, *mirabilia* and mind-body relations. His positions on the subject have already been studied.[16] The question I wish to explore is different. Recent works questioning the boundaries of knowledge have shown how, in the Middle Ages, the fields of learning were permeable. Each field was built in interaction with the others.[17] William of Auvergne's conception of compunction should be viewed from this perspective. It constitutes a good vantage point to grasp how issues relating to the natural world and the human body emerged in a text in which they were quite unexpected. Thus, I would like to measure to what extent William of Auvergne's various interests interacted and were intertwined.

A singular position on penance and contrition

Two texts written by William of Auvergne deal with penance from both a theological and a pastoral perspective. The first work, *Tractatus novus de penitentia*,[18] was composed during William's youth (around 1223) before his graduation as a master in theology.[19] It contains two sections, the first of which, seventeen chapters on penance, is authentic; the second, some sort of confessor's manual in nine chapters, is not. The authentic section is mainly centred on confession (chap. 4–17) and tackles some of its different aspects, including its function, its phases, the different kinds of compensation due, the effect produced on the penitent's emotional state and the confessor's role. By contrast, the stage before confession in the process of penance is altogether disregarded, and no reference is made to contrition or to compunction.

The second text, *De sacramentis*, was to be part of his *Magisterium divinale sive sapientale*. It was composed later, around 1228, when the master in theology was ordained bishop. This treatise comprises three introductory chapters[20] and a separate part for each of the seven sacraments. The part devoted to penance is the longest one (21 chapters),[21] followed by those on ordination (13 chapters),[22] marriage (10 chapters)[23] and the Eucharist (7 chapters).[24] The parts on baptism (3 chapters),[25] confirmation (1 chapter)[26] and extreme unction (1 chapter)[27] are much shorter. On penance, the theologian this time adopted a tripartite model following the three great stages of the penitent conversion process: contrition (chap. 5–10), confession (chap. 12–19) and restitution (chap. 20–21).[28] The notion of compunction is evoked in a single passage of chapter 5 about contrition.

William of Auvergne's doctrine of penance was part of the 'theological systematisation of the sacrament of penance'[29] that characterized the first decades of the thirteenth century. In an article published in 1948, Paul Anciaux highlighted our author's main contributions to the subject.[30] William advocated a progressive conception of penance, the three stages (*contritio, confessio, restitutio* or *satisfactio*) laying a sequence that allowed a complete remission of sins. In the first stage, he integrated the twelfth century's distinction between two steps: attrition, an initial phase of repentance preparatory to the sacrament, and contrition, a culminating moment of destruction of sins with the direct intervention of divine grace. He also insisted on the priest's function and on the efficiency of his absolution.[31] These elements make of William of Auvergne an important milestone in a broader movement of theological and pastoral reflection on penance, even though his contribution, in substance, was traditional. His ideas on penance conformed to those of fellow theologians.

In some respects, however, William of Auvergne is a profoundly original author. His peculiarity does not lie in his theological analysis of contrition, but in two discursive characteristics which separate him from his contemporaries. First, William paid particular attention to the psychological aspects of penance. He offered a special treatment on the emotional movements involved in the process, especially in the central phase of contrition. He was certainly not alone to do so, for the act of penance constituted, throughout the thirteenth century, 'a sort of laboratory in which the geometry, dynamism and manifestations of passions could be observed and experimented'.[32] However, William's focus on the subject is remarkable. He implemented a 'pedagogy of passions' which gave his discourse the character of an actual 'sentimental education' for the faithful.[33]

William's conception of penance was also original by the very broad perspective that was adopted, 'an all-inclusive, rounded approach'[34] that distinguished him from his contemporaries. As Lesley Smith has shown, two levels were articulated: a theological analysis of contrition and a pastoral discourse aimed at regulating the conduct of people. This treatise was not only intended for fellow theologians and students of the Faculty of Theology, it was also a doctrinal guide for both priests and lay persons, i.e. for 'an educated, interested, devoted reading public, though not theologically trained'.[35] This positioning went hand in hand with a way of writing that strongly differed from the other penitential texts composed at the time. The tone was lively and straightforward. William of Auvergne used concrete, simple and evocative images to both surprise and convince his reader.[36] We shall see that his approach to compunction illustrates this very personal style, designed to reach different types of audience in different kinds of cultural backgrounds.

William of Auvergne's definition of compunction

Penance is the process by which the sinner passes from attrition to contrition, up to confession and finally to satisfaction. William of Auvergne set compunction in the second stage, that of contrition, 'the decisive phase of inner conversion'.[37] Contrition, William argued, consists of a violent, radical action of destruction of sins: 'the shattering, grinding, powdering of the old man'.[38] To enlighten the meaning of the word in all its implications, he inscribed it in a network of synonyms. Eight names were listed: contrition was qualified as compunction, reversal (*reversio*), conversion, baptism of fire, and was assimilated to the four great Christian feasts (Nativity, Easter, Pentecost and Ascension).[39]

Therefore, William did not study compunction in a specific way. He used the word as a conceptual tool for a reflection on the penitent's inner transformation, part of a network of terms linked together with the notion of contrition. But in this network, the emphasis was mainly placed on compunction. The term was the only one among the eight names of contrition to contain some consistency from the analysis, and the equivalence between contrition and compunction occupies more than a column of the 1674 edition.[40] William of Auvergne deemed the term highly as it made it possible to relate the central stage of contrition to a broader psychological and spiritual state, even if the definition of the term remained fuzzy.

In Christian theology, compunction is most often associated with tears. The expression *compunctio lacrimarum* (compunction of tears) reflects a strong correlation between compunction and the gift of tears, both in modern studies and in medieval texts.[41] Compunction, in this context, designates the psychological state that produces tears.[42] But the term also appears independently of the reference to weeping. It then has a much hazier meaning and refers to a 'sadness according to God' (*tristitia secundum Deum*), bearing a positive connotation.[43] It is, for example, the figure of the heart-broken man (*compunctus corde*) evoked in Psalm 108:17[44] and again in the Acts of the Apostles.[45] This last text was crucial in the history of the word *compunction* because it connected it anew to the sphere of penance and longing for salvation.

William of Auvergne used *compuncti* in this broad and vague meaning, with a penitential connotation. He referred explicitly to the Acts of the Apostles.[46] On the contrary, he made no allusion to the subsequent refinements of the notion by Latin patristics. He did not cite, for example, the subcategories of compunction made up by Gregory the Great, whose influence was considerable throughout the Middle Ages.[47] William adhered to a simple definition of the concept. This indicates, once more, that compunction was not at the core of his analysis. It was merely some prop on which to build his reflection on contrition. Primarily, it was contrition and not compunction that sparked his interest as a theologian.

Agricultural metaphors

To explain what compunction is, William of Auvergne implemented a very personal 'metaphorical game'.[48] Metaphors were inserted in his reasoning on a twofold level: compunction was an image of contrition, but it was also illustrated by a series of specific images in such a way that the metaphors were tightly embedded within each other. They related to two areas, i.e. the agricultural world and the human body.

Before analysing these metaphors, let us first remark that my purpose is not to discover what concrete reality each would specifically refer to in the author's mind. To a certain extent, William's metaphors function in his discourse 'without the metaphor', as Nicole Loraux puts it elsewhere.[49] Taking up this interpretation, I suggest reading William's metaphors through the lens of their actual textual function, rather than trying to uncover what they might be referring to. I argue that William's images cannot be reduced to a simple form of transfer, where the author merely replaces one thing with another, as allegedly happens with metaphors. The strangeness itself of these images carries meaning as a core component of the master's argumentation strategy.[50] They enhance the author's impact twofold by both grasping the reader's attention and clarifying his meaning. As a result, the question of what these images reflect is not relevant. Nor is it necessary to translate them. It seems best to 'hold on to the literality of the word for word'[51] and observe the impact of the reasoning. This option does not prevent us from appreciating William's network of images as multiple epiphanic layers meaningful to him. His metaphorical game informs the boundaries of his discourse and his implicit vision regarding knowledge.

At the beginning of chapter 5, before mentioning compunction, William of Auvergne introduced his study of contrition by comparing the penitent to a peasant: 'Penitents cultivate their lands like farmers cultivate salads. They drain out the extremely bitter juice or sap by contrition and rumination of anxious and profound memories. That is why, in the process, it at first tastes sweet, but tastes bitter later.'[52] The metaphor of cultivated land is common in the Bible, for example in Axa's story: having received a dry land as inheritance from her father Caleb, Axa asked him also to give her a source (3 Joshua 15, 18–19 and Judges 1:14–15). This biblical narrative was used by Gregory the Great in order to explain the different kinds of tears of compunction.[53] William took the same metaphor of cultivated land, but he used it in another direction. He did not refer to the story of Axa, nor to the tears as a source for the land. He rather employed the image with indications that created an effect of reality. The allusion to the bittersweet taste of salad was a way to underscore the role of sensations during the act of penance, a motive that was extended in the following chapter in connection with the passions of the soul.[54]

The first specific image of compunction we find in William's chapter is both botanical and animal. Contrition is a form of compunction, he said, because the sinner is stung by 'thorns and stings'. These are 'stuck into the bottom of the heart and in its intimate part'.⁵⁵ The image of the thorn (*spina*) that pierces the heart was explicitly found in Psalm 32,⁵⁶ but it came mainly from Augustine, who spoke of the 'thorns of penitential compunction'.⁵⁷ The sting (*aculeus*), on the other hand, seems to be William's contribution. Today's reader could picture a penitent-gardener, stung by a bee or a rose thorn as he cultivates his flowerbed. It is not certain that the thorn and the sting's metaphors summoned the same image associations for William of Auvergne's readers. We can assume, however, that this image, the thorn and the sting, was familiar to William's public both for its biblical and patristic resonances and for its concrete and experience-based character. We can perceive the theologian's efforts to adapt his discourse to his audience and his masterful art of storytelling.

A second agricultural image of compunction is proposed further:

> Or else, this is what compunction is, because the sinner is like an ox or a donkey mired in mud, or like a runaway horse, as it is commonly said. Just like stings or spurs are applied to an ox or a runaway horse, so that it may come out of the mud, likewise, God being most merciful, for He wishes sinners to come out of the fountain of misfortune and a waste mud, stings them so that they may set themselves upon the solid and firm stone of Christ our Lord and of the conversion of the saints.⁵⁸

The image of the ox or horse bogged down, pricked to be saved, is also evocative. It indicates that William of Auvergne did not consider compunction as a passive state of abandonment, but as a violent stimulation beginning with a passion, the sting, and evolving into movement. Compunction is a 'feeling in action'.⁵⁹

A third image dealt with the cultivation of myrrh and incense. Here, the reference was above all biblical, myrrh and incense being the Magi's gifts to the Christ newborn (Matthew 2:11). But William provided some botanical details:

> Moreover, we speak of compunction because, just as the trees of myrrh and incense are wounded by iron spikes and, because of this tear-like wound, they deliver the aroma of myrrh and incense – indeed incense and myrrh are the tears of these trees, but coagulated – likewise, the penitents' repentant hearts gush the incense of their prayers of devotion and the myrrh of their internal bitterness.⁶⁰

The allusion to tears of compunction is implicit here: the notched tree lets the incense or myrrh flow, as if it were weeping. The gesture is violent; it causes an injury, but it has a positive value because it allows men to collect a sweet and bitter fragrance. This metaphor must have struck thirteenth century's readers by establishing a bridge between different realities of everyday life: the biblical narrative, liturgical objects and cultivation techniques. Undoubtedly, between these three fields, the culture of myrrh and incense was the most alien to William's audience,[61] but the association between agriculture and Christian life was certainly evocative to medieval thinkers.

Indeed, the evocation of an aggressive gardening gesture with the positive results was used by other scholastic authors. Pruning and grafting, for example, were employed to signify the separation of the chosen from the damned and the conversion of the Jews. In these cases, the use of an image made it possible 'to undermine violence thanks to the serenity of arboriculture'.[62] William of Auvergne used the same rhetorical process: the poetry of the image and its trivial and innocuous character were meant to make the violence of penitence tolerable. For the sinner, compunction is certainly a painful moment, but a necessary one, bearable for its beneficial consequences.

These agricultural metaphors expressed the same motive in various ways, that of salutary pain. The sinner must accept the torments of compunction, for they are the promise of future benefits. William of Auvergne developed this reading in two directions. Firstly, pain was considered beneficial because it allowed the sinner to regain his lost sensitivity. The idea was already expressed in the *Tractatus novus de penitentia*, without any allusion to compunction: 'Dead limbs, certainly, do not feel their death nor the wounds. Therefore, if someone suffers violently, [it means that] the sense of touch will certainly be restored'.[63] To suffer is to be alive. Similarly, in *De sacramento penitentie*, the sting of the compunction was described as 'vivifying' (*vivifica*), in the literal sense: it gave life back to the 'amazed, or rather mortified and dead' heart of the sinner.[64] Without compunction, the wound of sin was not felt; the sinner remained dead, locked in a numb state. The awareness of having sinned made him feel alive.[65]

Secondly, William of Auvergne conflated pleasure and pain in the process of compunction. These were considered the two sides of the same reality 'for every sin is a double-edged sword'.[66] There are two kinds of prickle: the prickle of sin is made of honey; it deceives 'by [its] sweetness and [its] betrayal and [...] by [its] illusory and dreamy character'. Sinners with insensitive and numb hearts do not see this as something painful. They 'do not speak of being punished, pierced, or perforated, but of pleasure, gentleness and joy'.[67] Conversely, the prickle of compunction is experienced painfully, albeit it carries benefits. Indeed, 'it does destroy sins and because of this, the wound it causes is healthy. This sting expels all the poison of deadly pleasure'.[68]

The ambiguity and reversibility of the pain-pleasure association were illustrated by William of Auvergne when quoting Ovid:

The hand that wounded you will heal you.
The same soil often produces salutary and nefarious herbs
Nearby the rose grows the nettle
The injury inflicted unto the son of Hercules, his enemy,
The spear of Pelias itself healed it.[69]

Ovid enjoyed great popularity from the twelfth to the fourteenth century, and the period has even been named as an Ovidian era.[70] The *Remedia amoris* was included in a list of recommended books in Parisian schools for the study of liberal arts at the end of the twelfth century.[71] At the time of William of Auvergne, the poem had found its place in the collection of school texts called *Liber Catonianus*.[72] Thus, Ovid's quotation was an academic reference, but it was not specific to theological discourse. Ovid was known in scientific poetry, in encyclopaedias, in treatises of natural philosophy; it was quoted by such scholars as Albert the Great, Arnold of Villanova, Nicole Oresme or the Italian physician Peter of Abano.[73] William of Auvergne was fully in line with this scholastic environment, far beyond the fields of theology and pastoral ministry. His quotation of Ovid is the sign of a scientific culture that he developed in his other intellectual productions.

Pleasure and pain were thus two facets of the same active principle. William developed a similar analysis a few years later in a completely different context, in a chapter of *De Universo* devoted to the power of music. He explained that the force of music is twofold: a soothing remedy for pain, but also an exciting one helping the soul to defend itself.[74] This double quality was expressed by the verb *rapere*, which means 'to seduce, to delight, to carry away violently'.[75] The human souls, William said, 'are in a way torn away from themselves and seduced (*rapiuntur*) by the very sweetness of these harmonies'.[76] The rapture of the soul (*raptus animae*) was a gentle and violent action at the same time based on the seduction of harmonies and aiming at the brutal eradication of passions. Music thus had the power to create an inner salvific disorder made of sweetness and violence, enchantment and wrenching.[77] The compunction was based on the same alternation of pleasure and displeasure, to wrench the penitent free of his sins.

Bodily metaphors

William of Auvergne also proposed another set of images of compunction in chapter 5 of *De sacramento penitentie*. They were based on bodily realities and medical gestures. The health of the body and that of the soul were associated and compared. Just as surgical instruments incise the body to remove corrupted moods, so the prickle of compunction wounds the sinner to expel his sins and provide him spiritual relief.[78] This analogy was not an innovation in the thirteenth century. It was used in the Bible, in Patristic literature and even in the famous canon of the Fourth Lateran Council about annual confession: there, the parish priest was considered to be a doctor because both doctors and priests need caution and good judgment, and they both provide useful advice and remedies to restore health.[79] The theologian relayed Church's commonplace discourse on penance.[80]

However, William's conception of the priest's and the doctor's respective roles was possibly more elaborate than these few lines seem to show. In the chapter on music of *De universo*, we learn more about his vision of the boundary between medicine and religion. Doctors should be trained in musical art, he said, in order to counterbalance their incompetence in soul diseases:

> Many spiritual diseases are by chance cured by harmonies, by doctors who are unaware that these harmonies, or this kind of harmonies, are powerful. Indeed, if they had the aforementioned competence, there would hardly be any spiritual disease that would make them withdraw. [...] So you see how considerable doctors' deficiency is, especially in our time, with regard to spiritual diseases.[81]

William's regrets on doctors' failures concealed an attack against the medical profession's claim to bring mental illness treatment back into their field. That doctors began to treat the mentally ill was an innovation that still suffered pushback at the beginning of the thirteenth century. *De universo* echoed this tense situation and the priests' demand to maintain their priority in healing the soul's diseases.

This background of conflict and competition between the priestly and the medical profession was not directly referenced in relation to compunction, but William of Auvergne certainly had it in mind when he equated the priest's gesture with the physician's one. The 'pedagogy of passions'[82] that he implemented in the following chapter pursued the same objective: to make of priests the specialists of the soul, to give them a specific position in competition with that of doctors. William thus provided his fellow clerics with a fine knowledge of the soul's movements and gave them the means to relieve spiritual pain. Developments on compunction were part of the same enterprise. The mundane analogy between the priest and the doctor was therefore charged with topical issues. There is a social charge that underpinned the comparison. To perceive it, not only the theological and pastoral texts, but also the philosophical ones must be taken into account.

Another set of bodily metaphors is used in the chapter on contrition. They do not directly concern compunction, but they apply to one of the other eight names of contrition: conversion. William of Auvergne intended to show that contrition was a form of conversion, because it redresses the sinner into the right direction. The penitent literally has his body in a wrong position: 'He is inverted (*reversus*), having below what should be on top and conversely, that is to say that the spirit is below and the flesh on top, whereas it must be the opposite. And he is upset (*eversus*), having before him what should be behind him and conversely'.[83] The following images illustrated very concretely the effects of this confusion. The first concerned the five senses: the sinner's face is turned backwards, focused on worldly things. His eyes see nothing else; his ears hear nothing else.[84] His nose smells 'nothing sweet, only the manure of worldly things',[85] just like his mouth and palate.[86] Then, some metaphors referred to the position of the body and to its lateralization: the sinner 'has on his right what he should have on the left side and conversely'.[87] Finally, a series of images described the sinner as someone having outside what should be inside. For example, the sinner is rich outside, but he is poor inside.[88] Starting from this model, William gave a list of inside-outside oppositions: the lord and the slave, the man and the animal, the king and the thief, the monk and the libidinous, and so forth.[89] He multiplied striking expressions and symmetrical effects, like the tonsured cleric (*clericus tonsuratus*) vs the hairy layman (*laicus capillatus*), or the bearded man (*vir barbarus*) vs the hairless young man (*puer imberbis*). The result is a long and spectacular enumeration dealing with the social positions of individuals and the moral value associated with them.

Similar processes of enumeration were to be found in the Christian liturgy. In some medieval formulae of baptism, exorcism or curses, the different parts of the body were listed in detail, 'as if it were a scattered microcosm to be reunited'.[90] This was also the case in the anointing of the sick's formulae, which reflected the assimilation of possession with illness. In the same way, some medieval healing charms contained very precise anatomic lists.[91] The principle backing these performative formulae was to cure the person suffering by enumerating the different body parts concerned in order to expel the demon or the disease out from them and to fill the empty spaces left by this expulsion. Naming each part of the body allowed the restoration of a lost order by bringing the whole body together into the speech. As a bishop, William of Auvergne must have been familiar with these liturgical formulae. He also probably knew that incantations sometimes used the same lists: in another context, he more broadly analysed the power of words and the different kinds of efficiency between liturgical and magical formulae. So he was highly knowledgeable in the performative principle of enumeration. We can assume that it was some sort of model for him when he implemented a similar principle in his discourse. Indeed, the list he gave about contrition allowed him to encompass not only the Christian's body, but also Christian society as a whole in his speech. The physical body and the social body conflated into the same ideal of organization and ranking. Remorse and regret about sins appeared as a way to restore everyone back into their place and to reorder what had been topsy-turvy.

Thus, William of Auvergne's speech did not deliver an abstract theory but an embodied argumentation. The body served as a model of analysis with the double meaning of the sinner's body and of the Church's body.[92] This body could suffer from disorientation; it could feel false sensations and could be subject to incision and brutal operations in order to be turned over, renewed and healed. Such a profusion of images signals that the author, being a theologian, recognized the importance of the corporeal realities in everyday life. He did not ignore them but considered them relevant and even gave them a central place in his moral and theological discourse.

Conclusion

William of Auvergne eventually did not say much about compunction. He did not repeat former doctrinal distinctions between different kinds of compunction. He used the word only when examining contrition. However, the theologian's analysis sheds light on the relationship between contrition and compunction. On the one hand, compunction appeared as a diffuse feeling, a sorrow derived from the awareness of the sins committed. The term referred, in a vague and indeterminate way, to the emotional state of lamenting one's sins. On the other hand, contrition meant suffering too, based on the expression of repentance, but it fulfilled a precise function. It constituted the second and most important stage in the spiritual progression of the penitent, as it was the pivotal moment when sins are destroyed thanks to the penitent's virtuous movements, guided by divine grace. Contrition led then to a final stage, confession, whereby the penitent received absolution.[93] Thus, contrition was inscribed in a temporal process that made it necessary for the accomplishment of penance. This was not the case with compunction: the feeling did not play a clearly identified role in penance and did not intervene at a defined moment. On this point, William of Auvergne's thought fit the twelfth century's reflections on contrition. As in scholarly and monastic literature of the previous century, he considered that compunction was a broader, but also hazier notion than contrition.

This articulation demonstrates that compunction was not the most important in William's view. He knew the concept, he used it in his reasoning, but he did not ponder over it as such. It was reduced to the status of a metaphor of contrition. This relative lack of interest contrasts with previous centuries' developments on compunction. The motif was amply discussed in Patristic literature and during the High Middle Ages. The distinctions made by Gregory the Great were remarkably popular until Pierre Lombard. From the thirteenth century, however, the theme began to fell into disuse. Compunction was gradually abandoned in favour of contrition.[94] William of Auvergne's position epitomizes the premises of some transformations that can be observed both in scholastic theology of the thirteenth century, in Rhineland mysticism and, later, in various theological currents of the sixteenth century.[95] He was at the threshold of this movement. Such a position is consistent with that place occupied by William of Auvergne in scholastic debates on the power of words: some of his proposals on the power of music and sounds were endorsed and expanded by later authors such as Roger Bacon or Nicole Oresme.[96] Likewise, William's limited interest in compunction and his focus on contrition seemed to endorse transformations in penitential theology. In both cases, William of Auvergne played a pioneering role in formulating proposals that were subsequently taken up and extended.

So William of Auvergne said little about compunction. However, his voice was distinctive. The originality of his analysis lay, in particular, in his choice of concrete topics. These had to be articulated with pastoral concerns: examples enabled the preacher to adapt to his public and to be understood by them.[97] They revealed a man attentive to his contemporaries, a fine observer of the physical and corporeal realities of the world around him. Indeed, bodily and botanic metaphors structured William's discourse. They guided the analysis of contrition by embedding it in a network of images. The author constructed his own language to explain the world, the position of man within it and the way of behaving as a Christian. He considered the body and nature as the places where the transformation of the sinner into a penitent has to come into being, for contrition and compunction were reactions that concerned not only the soul, but also the body.[98] As a consequence, he obviously nourished his reflection with his own expertise on plants and the human body. His discourse had a scientific and anthropological tone.[99]

This use of images is finally telling of the way William of Auvergne conceived theological knowledge. The description of natural and human phenomena worked from within the theological reflection, with the help of metaphors, and helped conciliate different fields of experience.[100] The gap was reduced between theology and agriculture, physiological description and social hierarchy, because these different registers coexisted in the text. The literal and the figurative meanings were to be understood simultaneously. Their coexistence illustrates that William of Auvergne did not establish barriers between different forms of knowledge. Rather, he chose to embrace all aspects of human life together. The philosophical, scientific and theological ways of thinking were complementary in his writings. They both described the same reality, understood as a whole. Consequently, the very same author could account, on the one hand, for studying the penitential process in man and the place that contrition and compunction played in it, and on the other hand, for proposing a new analytical category, 'natural magic', to explain strange phenomena in a rational way. Moreover, the very same author could, in the same text, analyse the spiritual conduct of the faithful, the emotional states of human beings, mind-body interactions and the body's life. These different levels of meaning were present simultaneously in William of Auvergne's analysis of compunction. He integrated them into a kaleidoscopic discourse that captured man in all dimensions of his relationship to the world.

5

Seawater in flame: Compunction in the Lambeth and Trinity homilies

Ayoush Lazikani

In the New Testament Acts of the Apostles, Christ's followers are stung in their hearts (*compuncti sunt corde*):

> His autem auditis, compuncti sunt corde, et dixerunt ad Petrum, et ad reliquos Apostolos: Quid faciemus, viri fratres?
>
> (Now when they had heard these things, they had compunction in their heart, and said to Peter, and to the rest of the apostles: What shall we do, men and brethren?)[1]

Such 'compunction' permeates medieval affective reading practices. And yet, while medieval compassion has enjoyed a resurgence of interest in histories of emotion, compunction has been less prominent in this field – a fact redressed by the present essay collection.[2] One crucial area for investigation is compunctive emotion in early English sermonic materials, specifically the twelfth- and thirteenth-century Lambeth and Trinity homilies. Vernacular homilies have been left almost untapped in histories of emotion; they deserve more critical attention.[3] As will be seen, the Lambeth and Trinity homilists are committed to revealing compunctive richness and activity: they display the affectively composite nature of compunction, while also highlighting the potency of its stimulation in the heart. In 1937, P. Pourrat remarked that penitence is 'particularly fertile in affections', taking into its remit contrition, horror of sin and regret for the past.[4] The term *penitence* here can be replaced with *compunction*, for compunction embraces all these affective stirrings – along with the interconnected stirrings of love, longing and compassion. In its fertility, compunction is a forcible, at times even violent, affective shift.

Texts and audiences

The Lambeth and Trinity homilies are so named because of the two manuscripts in which they are found: London, Lambeth Palace Library, MS 487, datable to the first quarter of the thirteenth century; and Cambridge, Trinity College, MS 335 (B. 14. 52), datable to the second half of the twelfth.[5] Lambeth, in particular, has a complex textual history. Ralph Hanna has demonstrated that it is 'pieced together' from at least two 'existing books', though '[n]either appears to have been continuously available to the scribe'.[6] It contains seventeen homilies (fols 1r–59v), along with a copy of the *Poema Morale* (fols 59v–65r), all by one scribe. Appended to these is an unfinished copy of the *Wooing Group* meditation *On wel swuðe god ureisun of god almihti*, in the hand of another scribe, at a later, mid-thirteenth century, date (fols 65v–67r).[7] The Trinity manuscript contains thirty-four sermons, along with the *Poema Morale*.[8] Five homilies are found in both manuscripts: Lambeth 7/Trinity 4, Lambeth 17/Trinity 25, Lambeth 13/Trinity 26, Lambeth 16/Trinity 30 and Lambeth 15/Trinity 32. The language of the homilies and *Poema Morale* in Lambeth has been localized to the West Midlands, 'belonging somewhere near the border of Herefordshire and south Shropshire'.[9] Such localization associates these homilies with the *Ancrene Wisse* Group, and Bella Millett has made a case for a pastoral revival in the area.[10]

With their responsiveness to contemporary preaching practice, these homilies are strikingly innovative. This fact has been identified and studied by Millett, as encapsulated in her study on *distinctiones* in Lambeth 17 and *divisiones* in Lambeth 16.[11] The homilies' innovativeness has also been foregrounded in the source studies by Stephen Pelle.[12] Furthermore, the Lambeth and Trinity homilies were directed at a varied audience. According to Millett, whose insights are adopted here, these homilies seem to be indicative of 'supra-catechetical' preaching, 'more likely to have taken place, or at least been initiated, at diocesan than at parish level'.[13] As such, audiences may have been composed of laity (with varying levels of education), parish priests and cathedral clergy. Millett further proposes that the homilies may have been 'addressed either separately or as part of a mixed lay and clerical audience'.[14] An awareness of the diverse medieval audience allows modern readers to appreciate the multi-layered handling of compunction in the homilies, crafted for a spectrum of backgrounds and capacities.

Compunction: Terms and scholarship

The term *compunction* has an extensive scriptural and patristic history.[15] Its ultimate source is Christian Latin *compunctio*, from verb *compungere*: 'to prick sharply'.[16] Jean Leclercq has been a primary voice in the history of scholarship into medieval compunction. In his classic study *The Love of Learning and the Desire for God* (1961), he asserts famously that 'monastic literature is, in large part, a literature of compunction'.[17] He notes its dual causes, 'the existence of sin and our own tendency towards sin – *compunctio paenitentiae, timoris, formidinis* – and the existence of our desire for God and even our very possession of God'. As he continues, '"compunction of the heart," "of the soul" – *compunctio cordis, animi* – always tends to become a "compunction of love", "of delectation" and "of contemplation" – *compunctio amoris, dilectionis, contemplationis*'.[18] An especially evocative passage by Leclercq reads:

> Compunction is an act of God in us, an act by which God awakens us, a shock, a blow, a 'sting', a sort of burn. God goads us as if with a spear; He 'presses' us with insistence (*cum-pungere*), as if to pierce us. The love of the world lulls us; but, as if by a thunderstroke, the attention of the soul is recalled to God.[19]

With such affective range, the 'ultimate role of compunction is to bring to the soul a longing for Heaven'.[20] He also observes the composite nature of compunction in the two forms of tears:

> Two kinds of tears symbolize two forms of compunction: the lower stream, *irriguum inferius*, is the stream of repentance; the higher flood, *irriguum superius*, that of desire. Tears of love always accompany those of penitence; but more and more these are dominated by tears of joy.[21]

Leclercq further links compunction implicitly to kenosis: 'Compunction hollows us and thereby increases our capacity for God.'[22] Two key strands emerge in Leclercq's meditations. First, he signals the affective richness of compunction: it takes into its remit not only repentance for sin, but also love and longing. And, secondly, he exhibits the activity of compunctive feeling. Leclercq's discussion brims with verbs: to strike, to press, to hollow. Compunction is an inescapably dynamic process.

After Leclercq, the most major work on medieval compunction was undertaken by Sandra McEntire in the 1980s and 1990s, as embodied in an article of the *Mystical Traditions* series as well as her monograph, *The Doctrine of Compunction in Medieval England: Holy Tears*. As she observes, 'inner disposition is central to the grace': tears are only signs of the more significant affective shifts occurring beneath.[23] She suggests that, due to the influence of the Franciscans and Cistercians, the patristic sources on compunction became 'increasingly diffused and diluted'. As a 'vibrant grace', compunction 'was malleable to the imprints of later medieval pious practice and devotion, most particularly, the personalising of the suffering and death of Christ'.[24] She foregrounds the importance of joy within compunctive feeling, and she also makes a necessary distinction between compunction and other forms of 'sorrow': 'Compunction has nothing to do with natural mourning or sadness. It is the sting of remorse at the deep and existential realisation that one is a sinner.'[25]

Whereas 'compunction' has an expansive affective range, 'contrition' can more specifically define the perfect sorrow that enables the remission of sin during the penitential process.[26] It remains bonded with other affective stirrings, however. In the words of Paul Anciaux, contrition is 'repentance under the influence of justifying grace', and thus it cannot be 'separated' from *caritas* (charity, love).[27] Like compunction, it is also a vigorous affective activity. Thomas of Aquinas (d. 1274) describes contrition as a 'grinding down', basing it etymologically on *terendo* (wearing away, treading upon).[28] To quote Anciaux again: 'A body is said to be *contritus* when it has been reduced to tiny fragments, pulverized.' This is, according to Aquinas and in the words of Anciaux, unlike the less complete destruction of attrition: 'Contrition in the spiritual realm denotes [...] the act of repentance in which sin is destroyed inasmuch as the hardness of the will is broken.'[29]

Referencing Origen (d. 253), G. H. Gerrits also usefully posits a temporal difference between compunction and contrition. As he explains:

> [I]t was held that compunction must not be just a temporary sentiment necessary for the practice of penance, but that it must be an abiding one, an idea which appears for the first time in the writings of Origen. In patristic writing, therefore, the term compunction can refer to a permanent and abiding sorrow and repentance for sin, or to the repentance required for a fruitful reception of the sacrament of penance. [...] Origen introduced into Christian thought the concept of the desire for union with God experienced as an abiding, heartfelt sorrow and sadness because of man's separation from God in this life. This sentiment too was given the name compunction, and it frequently merged with compunction understood as sorrow and grief experienced on account of one's sins.[30]

It is thus not always feasible – at least on the level of terminology – to extract temporal and originary nuances. One term encompasses both an enduring compunction and a transient contrition formed only in a discrete moment of penitential practice. Furthermore, as Gerrits shows in accordance with Leclercq, the term *compunction* can conflate that generated from sin on the one hand with that generated from earth-bound longing on the other.

The preceding discussion on terminology has been informed by Latin texts. But what of the English language? The earliest recorded instance of 'compunction' in English is from the fourteenth century and thus does not have currency within our temporal framework.[31] 'Contrition' is also unusual in English before the fourteenth century.[32] In the Lambeth and Trinity homilies, the abstract noun for compunction/contrition is *bireusing(e)*, a term also used comparably in *Ancrene Wisse*. This term derives from Old English *behreowsung*, itself related to *hreow* – a term discussed by Daria Izdebska in the present volume.[33] In Lambeth 2, the related abstract noun *reowsumnesse* is used to indicate compunction/contrition.[34] There are also occurrences of *bireusing/reowsumnesse* in verb form: *bi-rewsien* in Lambeth 3, for example (p. 29). Alongside these terms are more generic nouns and adjectives for the feeling of 'sorrow' or 'pain' for sin, specifically *sore* and *sori*: 'heorte sar for þe monnes aʒene sunne' (heart sorrow for man's own sin, Lambeth 15/Trinity 32, p. 149), 'beo sari' (Lambeth 10) and 'sari in ure heorte' (Lambeth 5, p. 51).[35]

Affective richness of compunction

The Lambeth and Trinity homilies are significant sources for the affective richness of compunction in medieval devotional practices, enabling scholars to build upon the formative work of Leclercq, McEntire and Gerrits. Such richness is encoded in the compound *armhertnesse*, used in the Trinity 16 homily for Easter. Based on the Latin source, two garments are identified: firstly, innocence (*loðlesnesse*) through baptism and sin-satisfaction (*sinbote*),[36] and secondly *mildhertnesse* (mild-heartedness), which, the homilist says, 'is nemed ec armhertnesse' (is named also tender/poor-heartedness):

> Armheorted is þe man þe swiðere reoweð his sinne, and he hem forlet and bet and milce bit, alse ure drihten bad [...] Haue reoðe of þin ogen sovle, þenne likeste gode.
>
> (p. 95)

(Tender/poor-hearted is the man who thoroughly rues his sin, who forsakes them, amends them, and asks for mercy, as our Lord bade. [...] Have pity on your own self, and then you please God.)

There is a confluence of compassion and compunction in the verb *reuen* ('*reoweð*') in this passage; this one term is used to signal both, following Ecclesiasticus 30:24:[37]

> Miserere animae tuae placens Deo, et contine: congrega cor tuum in sanctitate ejus, et tristitiam longe repelle a te.
>
> (Have pity on thy own soul, pleasing God, and contain thyself: gather up thy heart in his holiness: and drive away sadness far from thee.)

The verb *miserere* here takes on the dual sense of compassion and compunction, a function also performed by *reuen* in this Trinity homily. As discussed elsewhere, this compound of *armhertnesse* (the only MED citation of which is from this Trinity homily) is modelled on Latin *miseri-cordia*, with the adjective of Old English origin, *arm*, meaning 'poor' or 'needy':[38]

> As the homilist explains with invocation of Ecclesiasticus 30:24, pitying sin ('reoweð his sinne') is an act of self-compassion: 'haue reoðe of þin ogen sovle'. Trinity 16's use of 'armhertnesse' is the only cited occurrence of the word in the *MED*. The dictionary gives the bare definition of 'contrition', with no other possible meanings provided. Morris translates the compound as 'tender-heartedness'; this dimension of 'tenderness' in the translation is important. The homilist attempts to provoke a softening or tenderness of affect in the audience, to facilitate genuine sorrow for sin, an authentic *contritio cordis* which can in turn effect sin-remission within the soul.[39]

Compunction is thus a composite affective process, taking into its remit both sorrow for sin and compassion for human souls.

Another essential demonstration of its affective richness is found in a homily shared between the two manuscripts, Lambeth 17/Trinity 25, dedicated to the person of St James in the Trinity manuscript. In this homily, compunction is linked to a range of affective stirrings: compassion, weariness or hatred for life, and longing for the hereafter. Compunction is thus not an isolated state; it is instead part of a broader affective nexus. The scriptural basis of this homily is Psalm 125:6: 'Euntes ibant et flebant, mittentes semina sua' (Going they went and wept, casting their seeds). From this foundation, the homilist lists the various kinds of tears, representing diverse affective stirrings – reminding us of Leclercq's observation on two types of tears cited earlier and comparable with Peter Comestor's (d. 1178) sermon for All Saints' Day.[40] The very first category is tears for compunction, defined as shedding hot tears for one's own sin ('scheden hate teres for hore aȝen sunnen'). This occurs when the act of sin is thought on ('biðohten þet heo isuneged hefden'); it involves the sinner painfully mourning the sin ('sare bimurneden') and praying for mercy ('milce beden') (pp. 155-7). The homilist subsequently develops an imagistic taxonomy, with each tear imaged as a particular form of water. In this classification, compunction becomes seawater. The Trinity version clarifies that such nomenclature emerges from its bitterness: 'Þe wop þe man wepeð for his agene sinne is swiðe biter alse saltwater and þere-fore is nemmed se water' (The tears/weeping that man weeps for his own sin are/is as bitter as saltwater and is therefore named 'sea water'). Mary Magdalene is celebrated as a perfect model for this 'seawater', followed by St Peter in the Trinity version (p. 145). Mary, the paragon of compunctive feeling, is further encountered in the preceding homily in the Trinity manuscript, Trinity 24.

In Trinity 24, a vivid case is made for the affective richness of compunction. The gospel narrative on 'Mary' (in fact the unnamed woman of Luke 7) is crystallized by the homilist into the opposing impulses of hate and love:

> ure drihten underfeng eadmodliche ane sinfulle wimman and forgiaf hire hire sinnen. for two þinge: an is muchel leððe to hire sunne; oðer muchel luue to him.
>
> (p. 141)

> (our lord received humbly a sinful woman, and forgave her her sins, for two reasons: one is the great hate towards her sin; the other the great love towards him.)

The composite Mary Magdalene formed in medieval exegetical traditions here becomes a paragon or example – a *forbisne* – of such affective polarization.[41] She loves and hates in equal measure, for the sins become very hateful to her: 'hire sinne hire bicome swiðe laðe' (p. 143). As Luke 7:47 reassures the devout soul, 'remittuntur ei peccata multa, quoniam dilexit multum' (Many sins are forgiven her, because she hath loved much). Trinity 24 responds implicitly to this verse in its suggestion that sins are forgiven her not only for great love, but also for great hate. Feeling sorrow for sin requires intense surges of hate towards the sin, a hatred that is inseparable from love for Christ.

The Magdalene's rich compunction finds its most perfect embodiment in the breaking of the alabaster box, a favourite image of medieval writers and readers:

> heo [...] nam ane box ȝemaked of marbelstone and hine fulde mid derewurðe smerieles. and cam þar he was and his holi fet ȝesohte. and sore hire sinne biwiep þat hie his fet lauede mid hire hote teres. and wipede hes þer after mid hire faire here and mid hire muðe custe, and þarafter smerede.
>
> (p. 145)

(she [...] took a box made of marble-stone/alabaster, and filled it with precious ointments, and she came where he was and sought his holy feet. And sorely she bewailed her sins so that his feet were laved with her hot tears. And she wiped them afterwards with her fair hair and kissed them with her mouth, and thereafter smeared them [with ointments])

It is possible to read this alabaster box as Mary's heart, overflowing with the precious delicacies of her love, her compunction, her longing, her hate for sin.[42] Compunctive richness becomes an incomparable gift that the audience must seek to give to Christ; they may fill their own alabaster hearts with exquisite fragrances, so that they too may hear the soothing balm of Christ's forgiving voice at the close of this homily: "'Wimman, þine sunnen þe beð forgiuene.' Swo beo us alle ure' (p. 145) ('Woman, your sins are forgiven you.' So may this be for us all).

A useful analogue to the Magdalene's affective response in Trinity 24 is an Anglo-Norman Passion verse narrative, found on ff. 74ra–80vb of Cambridge, Trinity College MS B. 14. 39 (323) (s.xiii¾). This is a trilingual manuscript, containing a range of devotional materials in prose and verse; the Anglo-Norman text in question has been editorially titled 'The Minstrels' Passion' by Tony Hunt and Jane Bliss. There is no evidence of direct influence of this text on the Trinity homilies, and in any case the later date of MS 323 indicates that this is unlikely. However, bringing these texts together – Trinity 24 and 25, and 'The Minstrels' Passion' – allows a comparative reading of three especially expressive accounts of the Magdalene's compunctive richness. 'The Minstrels' Passion' affirms that the compassionate and loving God himself mirrors human compunction, feeling sorrow for his sinful creation:

> E li pius Deus que tut saveit, / Qui pur nus salver i veneit, / De ses sainz ous prist a plurer / E de sun quor a suspirer. / 'Vai tei,' dit il, 'cité dolente, / Mut par as perdue ta entente / Qant tu ne cunuz tun seignur / Que wint morir pur tue amur. / Si tu saveies le turment / Que te vendrat hastivement, / Tu en aveies grant poür / E demenerés grant dolur'.[43]

> (And compassionate God who knows all, who had come here to save us, with his holy eyes began to weep and from his heart sigh: 'Woe to you', he said, 'sorrowful city, you have so lost your understanding that you do not know your lord who comes to die for love of you. If you knew the torment that will soon come to you, you would have great fear and lament in great sorrow'.)[44]

It is significant that this passage refers to 'Deus' rather than Christ: it is the Trinity, in hypostatic union, that undergoes such compassion/compunction –

God's own 'sting' – for humanity. Mary Magdalene, in turn, models her Lord's compassion by taking great pity ('prit [...] grant pitez') for Jesus's sore barefeet at the Last Supper. She is subsequently relieved from the weight ('pesance') of her sins as her compassionate shift is fused with her compunction:

> As pez Jesu se lait aler, / Forment començat a plurer. / Grant suspirs gette del parfund, / Tuz ses pecchez en lermes vunt. Dolur aveit de ses pecch[e]z, / Od ses lermes laveit ses pez.[45]
>
> (To the feet of Jesus she went and began to weep intensely. She sighed great deep sighs, and all her sins came out with her tears. She was sorrowful for her sins, and with her tears washed his feet.)[46]

Compassion and compunction become inseparable, inter-flowing waters that resist all attempts to divide them.

Affective potency of compunction

It is evident that compunction is multifaceted, a rich flow of affective stirrings. These homilies further evince its formidable potency. A key case in point is Lambeth 5, based on Jeremiah 38:6:

> Tulerunt ergo Jeremiam, et projecerunt eum in lacum Melchiae filii Amelech, qui erat in vestibulo carceris: et submiserunt Jeremiam funibus in lacum, in quo non erat aqua, sed lutum: descendit itaque Jeremias in coenum.
>
> (Then they took Jeremias and cast him into the dungeon of Melchias the son of Amelech, which was in the entry of the prison: and they let down Jeremias by ropes into the dungeon, wherein there was no water, but mire. And Jeremias sunk into the mire.)

Jeremiah's pit is read by the homilist as the abyss of sin. In its execution, the homily is highly conversant with contemporary preaching practice, with parallels found by Millett in the work of Odo of Cheriton (d. 1247) and James of Vitry (c. 1170–1240).[47] After an imagistic evocation of Jeremiah residing in the pit, the homily becomes resonant of confessional guidebooks. There is, indeed, a fundamental intimacy between confessional and homiletic modes, an intimacy that was bolstered by Canons 10 and 21 of the Fourth Lateran Council (1215).[48] The Lambeth 5 homilist details the three-fold nature of penitence: 'þurh heorte bireusunke, þurh muðes openunge, þurh dede wel endinge' (through contrition of heart, through opening of mouth, through good completion of deed, p. 50) – in other words, *contritio cordis*, *confessio oris* and *satisfactio operis*. The three elements are conveyed as different stages in a funerary process:

> þe we beoð sari in ure heorte þet we isuneged habbeð þenne slage we ure sunne; þene we to sunbote cumeð. þenne do we bi ure sunne al swa me deað bi þe deade. For efterþan þet þe mon bið dead me leið þene licome in þere þruh. Al swa þu leist þine sunne in þare þruh. Hwenne þu scrift underuongest of þe sunnen þe þu idon hauest to-geines godes wille. þenne þu hauest þine sunnen ibet; efter þines scriftes wissunge. þenne buriest þu þine sunnen and bringest heom ut of þine on–walde.
>
> (p. 51)

> (when we are sorrowful in our heart that we sinned, we have slain our sin. When we come to amendment of sin, then we do to our sin as one does to the dead: for after the man is dead one puts his body in the tomb. So you must lay your sins in the tomb. When you receive confession of the sins you have done against God's will, and when you have performed satisfaction for the sins according to the confessor's guidance, then you bury your sins and release them of their power over you.)

As suggested elsewhere on this passage, this homilist 'appears to ascribe to contritionist ideology': '[C]ontrition alone destroys sin in the soul, catalyzing the remission of sin. Confession is relegated to the sin's burial, and cannot be credited with its murder.'[49]

Compunction/contrition is shaped by a language of violence, analogous with Aquinas's etymology: it is a grinding down, a pulverizing of the will. Such violence in Lambeth 5 is comparable with Part V of *Ancrene Wisse*, the part on *schrift* (confession); this part was intended for a broad audience – beyond the anchoritic readers – from an early point in its transmission history, as declared by the *Ancrene Wisse* author himself.[50] The wide-reaching value of such confessional material is indicative of a post–Fourth Lateran (1215) date for this text.[51] In this part, the author employs the pseudo-biblical narrative of Judith to establish the close bond between contrition/compunction and confession. Whereas Judith signifies confession, Holofernes represents the devil lurking in souls:

> Ha hackede of his heaued ant seoððen com ant schawde hit to þe burh preostes. Þenne is þe feond ischend hwen me schaweð [i schrift] alle hise cweadschipes. His heaued is ihacket of ant he islein i þe mon sone se he eauer is riht sari for his sunnen ant haueð schrift on heorte. Ah he nis nawt þe-ȝet ischend hwil his heaued is ihulet – as dude on earst Iudith – ear hit beo ischawet: þet is, ear þe

muð i schrift do ut þe heaued sunne, nawt te sunne ane ah al þe biginnunge þrof ant te foreridles þe brohten in þe sunne.

(114: 13–20)

(She hacked off his head and then came and showed it to the city priests. Then the fiend is shamed when one shows in confession all his wiles. His head is hacked off and he is slain in the man as soon as he is truly sorrowful for his sin and has confession in heart. But he is not fully confounded while his head is concealed, as first did Judith, before it is shown: that is, before the mouth in confession does out with the main sin, not the sin alone but the beginning thereof and the initial preambles that brought in the sin.)

Holofernes is decapitated within the soul, but he can only be annihilated by the auricular act of confession. As noted earlier and elsewhere, the *Ancrene Wisse* author never uses the term *contritio*, but instead seems to employ the vernacular equivalent *heorte bireowsunge*, like the Lambeth and Trinity homilies.[52] Contrition is indicated in the above passage through the phrase 'riht sari for his sunnen' and is also alluded to through the terminology of an 'internal' vs an 'external' confession. Like Peter Lombard (d. 1160), a formative writer in the history of penance, the *Ancrene Wisse* author differentiates *confessio cordis* (confession of the heart) from *confessio oris* (confession of the mouth): 'schrift on heorte' vs 'schrift' from the 'muð'.[53] Linda Georgianna has demonstrated this shifting borderline between contrition and confession.[54] What is also unmistakable, however, is the sheer violence of this passage. In Lambeth 5, contrition/compunction is an act of murder; here in *Ancrene Wisse*, it is a decapitation of the devil, intensified with the aggressive past participle 'hackede': a verb with inescapable connotations of ferocity.[55] Such potency – with the disintegration of sin expressible only through acts of violence in both texts – is further discernible in the consuming flame of the Pentecost.

It is, in fact, the biblical account of the Pentecost itself that sees the use of the phrase *compuncti sunt corde* (Acts 2:37), quoted at the opening of this chapter. These words are connected immediately with the act of penance (*poenitentia*), effecting a remission of sins:

Petrus vero ad illos: Poenitentiam, inquit, agite, et baptizetur unusquisque vestrum in nomine Jesu Christi in remissionem peccatorum vestrorum: et accipietis donum Spiritus Sancti.

(Acts 2:38)

(But Peter said to them: Do penance, and be baptized every one of you in the name of Jesus Christ, for the remission of your sins: and you shall receive the gift of the Holy Ghost.)

As evident throughout Acts 2, the Pentecost was a moment at once celebratory and painful. The Spirit descends and unifies humanity, and there is a sudden efflorescence of shared meaning-making. Equally, however, the coming of the Spirit is haunted by the absence of Christ following his Crucifixion. It is also a time of acute awareness regarding humanity's sinfulness; it is a time when hearts must be pierced, flagrantly and exquisitely. As such, the Pentecostal homilies are essential in understanding the activity of compunctive feeling. Pentecostal homily Lambeth 9 first offers a biblical history alongside its instructive purpose:

> þes dei is ihaten pentecostes þet is þe fiftuða dei fram þan ester tid. þes dei wes on þere alde laȝe iset and ihalden.
>
> (p. 87)
>
> (this day is called 'Pentecost': that is, the fiftieth day from Easter time. This day was set and observed according to the Old Law).

The Old Law is elucidated for the composite audience. This allows the cultivation of compunction to be underpinned by sound scriptural understanding, with the Exodus narrative of the killing of the firstborns (p. 87). The day itself is clarified typologically:

> þet i-offrede lomb þet þe engel het offrian bitacneð cristes deðþe þet wes milde. and wiðutan gulte his feder i-offrad; for ure alesendnesse. Nu is his þrowunge and his ariste ure ester tid.
>
> (p. 87)
>
> (The sacrificial lamb offered by the angel signifies Christ's death, who was mild, without guilt, offered by his father for our redemption. Now is his suffering and his resurrection our Easter time.)

The homilist explains the position of the audience in relation to the three time periods outlined – before the law, after the law and after the advent of Christ.

Then, the compunctive core of the Pentecost after the advent of Christ emerges. The Lambeth 9 homilist calls on audiences to imagine themselves in the devil's bondage or service ('þewdome', p. 87). Scriptural references from 'Lucas þe godspellere' (Luke the evangelist) provide a biblical foothold. The Latin, in fact from Acts 2:1–3, resounds in the homilist's voice – and the words are then explicated for the audience.[56] But these are not the only terms for the day rendered 'on ure speche' (p. 89): it is the act of compunction itself that is given vernacular exposition. After all, verbal and affective translation together mark the Pentecost, with all languages made intelligible and the community made whole (pp. 89, 93). A celebration of healing ensues, evoking Acts 2:17 (p. 91).[57]

As healer, Peter's calls to compunction have special power, as he channels the Lord's own curative strengths:

> Ða and-wrde petrus. Bi-reowsiað eo[w]re sunnan and under|foð fuluht on cristes nome. þenne beoð eowre sunnen aleide and ȝe underfoð þene halie gast.
> (p. 91)

(Then answered Peter: 'Feel compunction for your sins and receive baptism in Christ's name. Then your sins will be ransomed and you will receive the Holy Ghost.')

The other Pentecostal homily, Trinity 20, does not concentrate as extensively as Lambeth 9 on the Old Testament's 'fiftieth day' and thus does not offer typological readings. But the hermeneutic activity of this homily is no less potent. It is an exercise in exegesis that is at once rousing and soothing, with exploration of Acts 2:1–4, among other crucial biblical verses. Compunction remains acutely painful, and yet there is continual remembrance from the outset on Christ the Comfort-Spirit, paralleling Lambeth 9's exposition of the Paraclete (p. 97). As will be seen, the Holy Spirit himself takes on compunctive feeling in Trinity 20, as was also witnessed earlier in the Anglo-Norman 'Minstrels' Passion'. Through invocation of John 14:1, there is a negation of sorrow and fear: 'Ne beo giuer heorte noht iðreued ne ofdred' (Do not let your hearts be troubled or afraid).[58] This is followed by assertion of Christ's comfort, his 'frefringe': 'ich wile giu senden þe heuenliche frefringe wið-innen a lit dages' (I will send you heavenly comfort within a few days).

Trinity 20, perhaps even more than Lambeth 9, emphasizes the complexity and potency of linguistic expression. We have the verbalization of praise, the intensely vocalized words of the Psalms. Furthermore, there is the aural reverberation, a cry of the horn, the dividing of Heaven: 'Þo com a dine of heuene, ase þeh it were to kidende þat þe holi gost com uppen þe apostles and filde ful þat hus þere hie inne seten' (Then came a din from Heaven, as though it were to announce that the Holy Ghost came upon the apostles and filled the house full in which they sat, p. 119). This din enables the miracle of shared speech, in a quotation ascribed by the homilist to Ambrose – though actually a reference to hymn 'Beata nobis gaudia' (These joys so blessed unto us).[59] The 'Ambrosian' Latin is then glossed: 'þat is on englis he hem makede fundie on worde' (which is, in English, he made them capable of words, p. 117). This gloss has the curious effect of asserting a shared language while simultaneously underscoring the linguistic divisions faced by contemporary audiences. With this charged vernacular explanation, the homilist continues: 'Swo þe holie gost hem fulde of him seluen and sette þe word on hem þe þere speken. and skilede on hem þat hie herden' (p. 119) (Thus the Holy Ghost filled them with himself and set the words in they that could speak there, and distinguished the words in those that heard them). The adverb 'sunderlepes' (separately, individually) had previously been used to indicate the distinct languages before the Spirit's coming – and the adverb remains a poignant reminder of the current audience's own linguistic barriers. In the Pentecost, however, separation and division are brought to nought, as the healing force of compunction closes the gap between sinner and Lord, human and divine.[60]

This unity is affiliated, crucially, with penitence. The homilist describes the powers of fire: 'Fir haueð on him þre mihtes: on to giuende hete; oðer to giuende liht; þridde to weldende elet to none þinge' (p. 119) (Fire has three strengths: one to give heat; the other to give light; the third to reduce oil to nothing). These three capacities of fire are mapped onto the Holy Spirit's activity within human souls:

> þese þre mihte notede þe holi gost on þe apostles, and þerefor com uppen hem on fires hewe alse ich er seide, and alihte hem of brihtere and of festere bileue þe hie hedden er, and maked hem hattere on soðe luue to gode and mannen, and welde here sinnes to none þinge, for gif anie hadden don he hem mid alle forgaf.
> (p. 119)

(The Holy Ghost applied these three capacities/strengths in the apostles, and therefore came upon them in fire's hue, as I before said, and lit them brighter and with more secure belief than they before had, and made them hotter in true love to God and men, and reduced their sins to nothing: for if they had done any sin he forgave them.)

The Flame-Lord burns in love, illuminates in belief and consumes in forgiveness. It is this consumptive, negating power of fire that is especially redolent of compunction. As is the ultimate goal of compunction, sin vanishes in an ardent and joyful erasure. Christ himself thus takes on the compunctive role in the Pentecost, acting within each desiring soul to expunge the marks of sin. As discussed earlier, the Anglo-Norman 'Minstrels' Passion' sees the Lord feel compunctive anguish on behalf of his creation. Here in Trinity 20, he performs the sin-cancellation that follows this anguish, just as fire reduces ('welde') oil to nothing.[61]

Conclusion

Medieval homiletic expressions of compunction need further and deeper research. The pioneering work of Leclercq, McEntire and Anciaux, among others, has highlighted the multifaceted nature of compunction. Its affective fecundity and intensity within vernacular homilies of the medieval centuries deserve more critical attention, however. The English twelfth- and thirteenth-century Lambeth and Trinity homilies, especially, still remain on the sidelines of scholarship on the histories of emotion. They deserve to be brought into brighter relief for their variegated treatments of compunctive feeling. Compunction in these texts is no straightforward 'sting' of the heart – its sting works on myriad affective levels; its affective reach is polychromatic and polysemous. In its piercing act, compunction binds sorrow with love, with compassion, with exilic longing, with hatred towards sin and with joy. With its affective richness, it also has a marked dynamism, flowing vigorously and even at times savagely in the heart. Yet always behind its pain is the Paraclete, the guiding Comfort Spirit who stimulates each tear, each fire's hue.[62]

6

The expression of remorse in Old and Middle French literature

Corinne Denoyelle
Translated by Emily Reed

The Middle Ages constituted a distinct civilization, removed from the Classical culture that it inherited and transformed under Christian influence. Over the course of this period, new values and a new vision of humanity emerged. Socrates's earlier assertion that 'nobody is knowingly immoral' was superseded by the knowledge of good and evil as presented in Genesis. The infernal punishments of the Ancients were met with the invention of Purgatory in the twelfth century.[1] It was in this context that repentance became a crucial value of Western civilization, which constructed religious rituals that orientated the life of the Christian. The shame that takes hold of an individual guilty of sin became an essential criterion for humanity:

> Cui conscïence ne reprent
> Plus tost au mal qu'au bien se prent.
> Cui conscïence ne remort
> Jor et nuit point contre sa mort.
> Sachiez por voir, n'en doutez mie,
> Cui conscïence ne chastie
> A nul mal faire ne s'areste.
> Ainz est bestïauz comme beste
> Hom qui n'a point de conscïence. (Gautier de Coinci,[2] *Miracles Notre-Dame*, t.1, p. 91)

This work has been undertaken as part of the research project FFI2013-41355-P 'Marqueurs pragmatiques et oralité en linguistique historique du français' (Pragmatic markers and markers of orality in French historical linguistics), funded by the *Ministerio de Economía y Competitividad*, Spain.

(He who is not taken over by his conscience gives himself up to evil rather than to good. He who is not continually bitten by his conscience, day and night, fights against his death. Know it in truth, do not doubt, he who is not chastised by his conscience never ceases to do wrong. He is bestial like an animal, the man who has no conscience.)

It is a conscience that 'reprent' (takes over), 'remort' (bites again), 'chastie' (chastises) that draws a clear distinction between man and beast.

This specific grief that a wrongdoer can feel, called *compunction* in the religious context, is more generally defined as *remorse* in a lay point of view.[3] In Old French, the word *compunction* is used nine times in the *Base du Français médiéval* (in a corpus of eighty texts in Old French) and only in a religious context: all examples are from either *Li Dialoge Gregoire lo Pape* (end of the twelfth century) or *Li Sermon Saint Bernart sor les Cantikes* (around 1300). The Old French Frantext[4] corpus gives three other examples, two in Pierre Abélard's letters and one in Gautier de Coinci's *Miracles de Notre Dame*, the only example which is a narrative work though still in a religious context.[5] Therefore, we can infer that the word was not of common usage and was strictly limited to clerical vocabulary, clearly directly transposed from Latin to French. Nevertheless, characters of medieval French narratives frequently express this feeling of shame and guilt without setting it in a religious context. Because of its specific background, *compunction* infers a meaning of repentance and conversion that *remors* – which seizes the wrongdoer without offering him the prospect of redemption – does not necessarily imply; it is *on remors* that I would like to focus in this chapter.

Unlike repentance, which has been the subject of much research, remorse has been relatively neglected. In 1967, in what has since become a significant reference work in France, *Le Motif du repentir dans la littérature française médiévale* (The Motif of Repentance in Medieval French Literature), Jean-Charles Payen described the twelfth century as a golden age of repentance.[6] Indeed, the Middle Ages developed an original theory of repentance that became fundamental in theology, morality and the conception of man. As a sinner in essence, a person can receive the grace to realize their sin and subsequently decide to change their ways. With its basis in human free will, this humanistic vision implies an awareness of one's sin, contrition (a sincere regret for having offended God), rejection of sin and resolution to never commit the offence again. The confession of sins to an intermediary of God and the satisfaction that ensues are secondary to the theologians of the twelfth century. Before the formalization of the practice of confession at the Fourth Lateran Council in 1215, the human capacity for change was configured and understood as a reason for hope in the twelfth century, and it lay at the heart of many medieval tales. This is evidenced, for example, by the tales of the *Chevalier au barisel* (The Knight and the Barrel) and *Robert le diable* (Robert the Devil), where two characters discover, in tears, that they have charted a wrong course in life.

Repentance is oriented towards the future: it 'implies the possibility for atonement'; it corresponds to an optimistic view of the human being, who is always able to convert and thereby save themselves. Repentance involves a trust and belief in forgiveness:

> Le repentir que nous peint la littérature médiévale n'est pas nécessairement le prélude au renoncement total; il n'est pas non plus un sentiment triste; il participe à sa manière de ces idéaux rayonnants qu'ont été la Joie, la Jouvence et la Promesse.[7]
>
> (Repentance, as portrayed to us in medieval literature, is not necessarily the prelude to total renunciation; nor is it an unhappy feeling; in its own way, it participates in these radiant ideas such as Joy, Rejuvenation and Promise.)

Remorse, conversely, as outlined by Vladimir Jankélévitch in his study on *La Valeur et signification de la mauvaise conscience* (The Value and Meaning of Bad Conscience), is

> une sorte de souvenir cancéreux, un souvenir qui accapare toute la place, qui veut être seul et qui intéresse non plus telle plus telle portion superficielle et régionale de mon expérience mais la totalité de la personne et son essence la plus intime.[8]
>
> (a kind of cancerous memory, a memory that occupies all space, that wants to be alone and that is interested not in some superficial and localised portion of my experience, but the totality of the person and its most intimate essence.)

Remorse is a violent shame felt before, or in the absence of, any prospect of redemption. The verb *remordre* in Old French retains the physical sense of 'bite again', and, carried over into the moral sense, it reflects the very real violence of a guilty individual's disgrace.

This feeling rarely occurs alone in the Middle Ages, and it is often considered only as the first step of repentance, though the verb *remordre* is less frequently used in Old French than *repentir*. There are only four occurrences of the word *remordre* in a moral sense in the *Base du Français médiéval* while in the same corpus, there are 250 occurrences of *repentir*. The division between the two is aptly described in the narrative of the King of Hungary, who wanted to marry his own daughter and then put her to death:

Se furent li.ix. an passés.
Mais adonques fu il assés
Par **repentance** qui li vint
Et du grand mesfait li souvint
Qu'il fist faire sa fille a tort.
Ceste pensee mout le **mort**
Si tost comme il fu repentans
Qu'il ne fu semaine passans
Qu'il ne plourast pour le pecié
Dont il se sent si entechié
[…] Tante fois li ot remembree
Que li rois se repenti
A poi li cuers ne li menti
Quant l'en souvint, par mout de fois. (*La Manekine*, v. 6705–14)[9]

(He did not repent for more than nine years. Remembering the crime committed against his daughter, he was plagued by remorse. This thought overwhelmed him to the point that as soon as he repented he did not spend a week without crying because of the sin by which he felt overwhelmed. […] These frequent reminders led the king to repent and to remember his daughter, his heart failing him several times.)

Repentance begins with the memory: 'Et du grand mesfait li souvint' (literally 'and he remembered the great sin'). The author insists upon this several times by using the verb *souvenir* (to remember) or *remembrer*. This memory does not pass, coming back 'par mout de fois' (many times) and it is also cruel: 'ceste pensee mout le mort' (this thought excessively bit him). The author here uses the verb *mordre* (to bite), the derivatives of which, *remordre* or *remords*, are not yet fixed. It is from this recurring and biting memory that contrition and compunction are established, in tears and with the desire for redemption.

In this chapter, as we want to focus specifically on that feeling of shame that may, or may not, precede repentance, we will use *remorse* rather than *compunction*. If repentance and compunction can indeed involve a phase of remorse, the same is not true and vice versa; remorse does not necessarily work towards repentance if the character is regarded as beyond all redemption.

Repentance has a strong narrative function in medieval literature in Old French, to the point of being described as a *motif* by Jean-Charles Payen: a character repents, is forgiven, becomes a convert, changes his life; his destiny is thus fundamentally transformed, and the fictional plot consequently experiences an essential shift. Remorse, on the other hand, is less narratively fruitful for the character, locked in the constant rehashing of their fault: remorse either transforms into repentance and opens up the possibility of conversion and salvation, or it leads to despair and death, considered to be the only escape. However, this distinct pattern is especially conducive to speech: the authors of verse texts in particular are fond of long, plaintive or desperate speeches where remorse is expressed and renewed in rhetorical clichés. If the feeling of remorse, such as presented by V. Jankélévitch, is a drawn-out and all-encompassing suffering, writers of the Middle Ages express it as an articulated and discursive form, which necessarily implies a literary elaboration. Remorse creates the possibility for both subtle psychological analysis and literary brilliance. Indeed, the verbal expression of remorse always needs to be renewed and revitalized in order to both maintain its biting violence and escape the emotive erosion associated with overuse of certain words and phrases. As a result, the literary expression of remorse suggests a whole rhetoric that never freezes into stereotyped formulae.

We will here adapt the theoretical concepts of J. P. Martin, developed initially for *chansons de geste*, but which can perhaps be more loosely adapted to novelistic texts. Like him, we will consider that a narrative motif is expressed in the form of commonplaces or rhetorical clichés, themselves structured around formulae.

> Le *cliché rhétorique* désignera donc *la substance de l'expression* à laquelle la *formule* donnera *forme*. Et de même que le cliché se fonde sur un noyau sémémique, la formule est caractérisée par un noyau lexématique à partir duquel elle se modèle et se développe plus ou moins largement.[10]

> (The *rhetorical cliché* will therefore designate *the substance of expression* to which the *formula* will give *shape*. And in the same way that the cliché is based on a sememic core, the formula is characterised by a lexematic core from which it is modeled and developed more or less widely.)

The discourse of remorse is a psychological analysis of the present ethical implications of a past act: presented in texts as a monologue or integrated into a dialogue, it can be broken down into rhetorical clichés mostly related to the passage of time. We will designate three essential clichés: (1) Remorse implies a given speaker's introspection and self-analysis that equates to self-loathing. (2) It moreover requires an admission of fault that goes through a narrative phase and which does not permit justification. (3) Finally, remorse predicates on a relationship to time which opposes the 'innocent' lost past to the suffering of the present and a deadly future.

These various pictures constitute 'matrices', the frames upon which the speech of character (who are victims of remorse) is articulated. Some matrices will be more developed than others depending on the particular situation of the character and narrative development. While the motif of remorse leads to significant developments in poetic narratives, it is less common in prose fiction of the thirteenth century, where it is limited to a thought expressed in narrative speech or a few exclamatory sentences. The prose texts and adaptations of the late Middle Ages give remorse a more central position, cultivated by the contributions of the contemporary lyric. Without limiting ourselves to a specific period or a genre, we will observe speeches of remorse in various literary texts.

Self-loathing

Remorse is, in the first instance, the awareness of a fault. It implies the recognition of being in a sinful state, resulting in a self-evaluation as one who is at fault.

> C'est une conscience qui s'accuse elle-même, qui a horreur de soi. […]; et comme elle ne peut ni se regarder en face, ni se détourner de cette vue, elle est tourmentée par la honte et les regrets.[11]
>
> (It is a conscience that blames itself, that experiences a horror of itself. […]; and as it can neither face up to itself, nor turn away, it is tormented by shame and regret.)

The cliché of self-condemnation is often expressed by recurrent formulae consisting of either qualifiers used as subject complements or as self-addressed vocatives or interjections. This last construction implies that it is the enunciator who defines themselves by a deprecatory term of address, which is absolutely not mimetic. The importance of terms of address in medieval texts is well known. They have long been considered as the opening markers of direct speech for characters;[12] they are used here to open a monologue of introspection by indicating immediately the *ethos* from which the enunciator speaks. This simple fact prevents us from seeking authentic formulae in these speeches of remorse.

This hatred is expressed mostly through formulae constructed around the adjectives *las, lasse* (wretched), and/or *chetif* (*caitif*) (miserable), which are maintained for several centuries:

> Quant cil voit cele aventure, il est tant esbahiz com nus plus, si dit: 'Ha ! las, honiz sui qui ai fait morir par mon orguel la plus preude dame dou monde.' (the son of King Clodovex in *Tristan* en prose, T.1 éd. Curtis,[13] p. 121)
>
> (When he sees what he has just done, he is the most astounded in the world and says: 'Ah! wretched and lost am I, who made the best lady of the word die of my pride.')

> Las moy chetis, com sui dampnés!
> Quant mon seigneur ai la mort livree!
> [...] Las chetiz, com sui esperdus,
> De pechié morz et confondus! (Judas' monologue in *Passion du Palatinus*[14])
>
> (Wretched, miserable that I am, I am damned! Since I delivered my master to his death! [...] Wretched and miserable, I am lost, dead and confounded by sin!)

This construction is also found in indirect speech:

> Si se claime lasse chaitive et dit que ele est la plus chaitive feme qui el monde soit quant ele a fait metre a mort la demoisele del monde qui plus li avoit fait d'onor. (Yseut in *Tristan* en prose t. 2, éd. Curtis p. 96)[15]
>
> (She laments herself as wretched and miserable and says that she is the most miserable woman in the world since she had the maiden who, out of anybody else, had done her the most honor put to death.)

Las et *chaitif* are not limited to the expression of remorse. They can express any situation of suffering and misfortune. Their use in this context is interesting because it means that the individual in the grip of remorse considers themselves as first and foremost unfortunate and only then as a sinner. Indeed, the offender is not far from identifying themselves as a victim. This hesitation is recurrent in other expressions that are used to designate an enunciator beset by remorse. One could therefore classify the speakers' self-directed address terms according to whether they lean more towards the seme of suffering or that of detestation.

Aligning towards the seme of suffering, one finds: 'lasse moy' (wretched me); 'meschante chetive, lasse; tremaleuree dame, povre femme' (wretched, unfortunate prisoner; very unhappy lady, poor woman); 'O que chetive fenme me puis je repputer!' (Oh that I could comprehend myself such a wretched woman!) (Enide in *L'Histoire d'Erec* en prose,[16] p. 195).

Under the seme of detestation, one finds a series of disparaging qualifiers, often reinforced within hyperbolic constructions that describe the person who committed the act, more than the act itself:

> Sire, mout ai esté proisie,
> Mes je sui fausse et renoïe.
> [...] C'estoit je, qui los avoie,
> Mes mout mavese fame estoie. (the wife in *Chevalier qui fit sa fame confesse*)
>
> (Father, I was highly esteemed but I am cunning and perverse. [...] It was I who received praise, but I was a very wicked woman.)

> Ha, Diex! Quel damage, quel perte del plus preudome del monde qui mors est por le plus vil chevalier et por le plus malvés qui onques fust! (Lancelot in *Lancelot* en prose, éd. Micha, t. 2, §10[17])

> (Ah! My God! What shame, the loss of the best man in the world, who died for the most vile and wicked knight there ever was!)

> Que fel feisoie et desleaus
> Et traïtres et foresenez! (Galoain in *Erec et Enide*, 3635–56)

> (How much I acted like a felon, like a disloyal man, treacherous and without sense!)

The qualifier *déloyal* (disloyal) appears to be the most common. In fact, the sin most commonly committed in these stories is either a breach of faith or the rules of *fiance* (trust) which governed feudal society. At the same time that the shameful speaker discredits themselves, they value their victim. Hence, the speech of remorse often has a eulogy phase, also hyperbolic, extolling the merits of the one who suffered the offence or injury.

Later narratives in Middle French, strongly influenced by allegorical developments, use metonymic expressions that also contribute to creating a distance between the sinner and their sin. For instance, Enide in the prose adaptation of Chrétien's text talks about her 'mall bouce procureresse et administreresse de ce grant meschief' (evil mouth that brought about and administered this great disaster). Elsewhere, in the *Roman de Perceforest*, Marmona complains about her 'outrecuidié' (arrogant/conceited) heart, 'adollé, foible et aneanty' (afflicted, weak and destroyed):

> Ha! cuer, foible et aneanty, beney soit le presoir qui le puant venin d'orguel et d'oultrecuidance a fait de toy partir par destrainte de bonté. [...] Ha! cuer outrecuidié, comment me osas tu enhorter de prendre guerre contre Amours a qui oncques n'eus pouoir? Quoy m'as tu fait gaignier fors grant homte et blasme, paine et traveil tant que mon cuer n'en peut plus porter? (Marmona in *Perceforest*,[18] V, 1, p. 151–2)

> (Ah! weak and destroyed heart, blessed be the press that has extracted the stinking poison of pride and arrogance from you, by the constraint of his goodness [...] Ah, arrogant heart, how could you advise me to make war against Love, against which you have never had power? What have you made me gain if not such great shame, blame, pain and suffering that my heart cannot stand it anymore?)

This stylistic process inscribes the speech of complaint into a lyrical and allegorical tradition that renders even the most culpable character a victim.

The duty of condemnation

Remorse is a judgment caused by a conscience that stands as judge. The rhetorical cliché of this sentence is based on formulae of duty. Speech acts as a court that assesses a given situation according to higher standards, never explicitly specified, but based on a Christian and feudal morality. The characters' speech is therefore articulated between the impersonal expression of a higher duty and the assessment of their own villainy, generally marked by the verb *devoir* (to be obligated). In *Yvain* we find this obligation to self-hate, expressed by a gradation between *blasmer* (condemning) and *despire* (despising) and then *haïr* (hating), itself reduplicated in a slight variation between *haïr de mort* (hating to death) and *haïr et occhire* (hating and killing):

> Et mout blasmer et mout despire
> Me doi, voir, molt, et je si fas.
> Qui pert la joie et le soulas
> Par son meffait et par son tort
> Mout se doit bien haïr de mort.
> Haïr et ochirre se doit. (Yvain in *Le Chevalier au lion*,[19] v. 3536–41)

(I have many things to blame myself for and I must greatly despise myself, if not infinitely, and that is what I am doing. When one loses the source of his joy and pleasure by his own fault and his own wrong, one must hate oneself to death. One must hate and kill oneself.)

This passage is based on a process that moves from a general condemnation to its personal application. After a first movement, couched within the remit of duty and articulated by a statement of a higher internalized moral authority ('Et mout blasmer et mout despire Me doi', 'And I must blame and despise myself'), verse 3537 ends with this commitment 'et je si fas' (and I do so), strongly emphasized by the separation of the personal pronoun from the verb by the adverb *si*. However, some time is necessary for Yvain to fully assume the first person: immediately afterwards, he returns to an impersonal and gnomic construction, with a relative substantive, 'Qui pert la joie et le soulas / Par son meffait et par son tort' (literally, (he) who loses joy and pleasure / by his own fault and his own wrong), passing judgement condemning the culprit to death.

This suffering is not considered abnormal. There is no revolt in remorse and no challenge to the rules of the world. The characters are aware of their fault and accept it. They moreover hope for punishment in line with an imminent and transcendent justice, which establishes another cliché:

> An mon orguel avrai damage
> Quant je ai dit si grant outrage
> Et bien est droiz que je l'i aie. (Enide in *Erec et Enide*, v. 2607–09)
>
> (My pride will cause my damnation as my words have been offensive, and I will have only what I deserve.)

> Mais quant le dieu [des Desiriers] vey ma requeste soullie d'orgueil, il me donna penitance grieve et anuieuse, combien que plus en avoie deservi, dont je le remercye humblement, car par sa criminelle verge de penitance il a fait saillir de moy le vil et puant orgueil dont le cuer avoit enfflé. (Marmona in *Perceforest*, V, 1, p. 150)
>
> (But when the god [of Desires] saw that my request was defiled with pride, he gave me a heavy and painful penance, although I deserved far worse, for which I thank him humbly, because by his cruel rod of penance he has purged from me the vile and stinking pride with which my heart was inflamed.)

The culmination of this sentence is death. Certainly, the most flagrant rhetorical cliché is one that propels remorseful characters into the temptation of death, being the only escape from the pain of remorse. The speech of Partonopeu, after having broken a taboo that Mélior had imposed upon him, plays entirely on this cliché that compels the young man to beg for death in seeking forgiveness. Death is seen here as the only possible release:

> Dame, merci !
> J'ai mort u noaus deservi.
> [...] N'ai droit en menbre ne vie
> Laissiés me ocire as cevaliers
> Qui m'ocireont si volentiers.
> N'en querés onques jugement,
> Car j'ai vescu trop longement.
> [...] Ma doce dame, por ce pri
> Que vos aiés de moi merci
> Si que demain je soie ocis.
> Plus avrai joie mors que vis. (Partonopeu in *Partonopeu de Blois*,[20] 4766–804)
>
> (Lady, pity me! I deserved death or worse. [...] The admission of my felony deprives me of any right to live. Deliver me to the prompt vengeance of your knights. There is no need for judgment since I have lived too long. [...] My sweet lady, for pity's sake, I beg you to kill me tomorrow. The idea of dying rejoices me more than living.)

Even hardened criminals, knowing their probable damnation, will also claim the punishment that they deserve in the hope that it will ease the inevitable divine punishment.

> Por ce vos requier, por Deu, que vos de cest cheitif de cors qui tant est traitres et desloiaus prengiez venjance tele que jamés nus n'en oie parler qui ost si grant traison enprendre a faire. Et si en sera, si come je croi, m'ame alegie, car de tant come li cors sofferra en cest siecle greignor torment, de tant avra l'ame en l'autre siecle mains de mal. (Bertelai in *Lancelot du Lac*, éd. Mosès, t.3, p. 316)

> (For this reason, I pray you for the love of God: take from my miserable body, so disloyal and so treacherous, a vengeance so great that no one hears about it without being terror-stricken at the mere thought of committing such a crime. My soul, I believe, will be alleviated all the more because all the punishments that my body will suffer in this world will be spared in the other.)

These instances operate on the perspective that repentance, more so than remorse, works towards a better future, even post-mortem. Other characters, however, choose suicide, which was linked in the Middle Ages to the sin of despair.[21] Such characters crave death or try to bring it upon themselves:

> Pour son encombrier et tresdollant infortune morir me fault. Je veul la mort. (Enide in *L'Histoire d'Erec* en prose, pp. 195–6)

> (For the shame and the cruel misfortune he has received, I must die. I want death.)

The lover of the Châtelaine de Vergy declares before piercing his heart with a sword:

> Més je ferai de moi justise
> Por la trahison que j'ai fete. (the lover in *Châtelaine de Vergy*,[22] 894–6)

> (So will I do justice to myself
> for the betrayal I committed.)

This movement toward suicide is the most blatant difference between remorse and compunction. As explained by Jankélévitch, remorse is confinement without an escape from suffering, whereas compunction is open to a future:

> Nous savons d'instinct qu'une âme mutilée ne regénère pas, et nous devinons, malgré notre désir d'éterniser en nous l'innocence ou le bonheur, tout ce qu'il y a d'inhumain dans l'idée d'une réparation littérale. Pourtant c'est là, à y bien réfléchir, une représentation si insupportable que les hommes s'en détournent le plus possible; afin de la rendre inutile, la religion et la morale ont inventé le *Repentir*.[23]

(We know instinctively that a mutilated soul does not regenerate, and we sense, despite our desire to eternalize innocence or happiness in ourselves, all that is inhuman in the idea of a literal reparation. However, there is, upon consideration, a representation so insupportable that men turn away from it as much as possible; to render it useless, religion and morality invented *Repentance*.)

The admission of sin

The character beset by remorse is, first and foremost, fundamentally guilty. As a result, the evocation of the fault returns constantly; it constitutes a narrative that often occupies a large proportion of the characters' speech. This account serves several narrative functions: in a dialogue of revelation or confession, in which the remorseful character recounts their wrongdoing, the story acts as a carrier of information to the reader. Indeed, the concerns of the narrative are often prioritized over the representation of the psychological subject matter. Yet in many cases, in monologues where there is either no need to inform a potential addressee or the addressee is already aware, the recounting of transgression has no other function than to manifest the sudden awareness of the misdeed or to demonstrate the rehashing of one's conscience in an endless remembrance. However, the speakers hesitate between a direct confession and bias mediated by the third person.

As confession developed after the Lateran Council, admission became an essential component, and many texts display its importance. Admission involves a developed account of misdeeds that offers to the sinner the ability to erase their sin. Nevertheless, even outside of the framework of repentance, admission is the act that structures the discourse, just as the fault committed tends to structure the guilty individual as a whole.

The admission of a fault is expressed in formulae using the first person, and by a perfect-tense verb, representing the accomplished act; it constitutes a speech act that engages the speaker in the recognition of their responsibility:

> 'Biax tres douz pere Jhesucrist,
> Onques mençonge ne deïs.
> Or t'ai renoié trois fois,
> Encor n'a mie chanté le quoc'.
> [li quoc chante] (Peter in *Passion du Palatinus*, 537–44)

('Sweet Father, Jesus Christ, you never said a lie and now I have denied you three times before the rooster crows.' The rooster crows.)

> Je meïsmes ay aprestee
> la mort dont ele s'est occise!
> [...] Je vous ai morte voirement
> Mais ne l'ay fait a escïent.
> Je fis ce que me commandastes;
> [...] Je vous ai fait moult las service
> Car par mon fait estes occise. (Anna in *Roman d d'Eneas*, v. 2169–86)

(I myself have prepared the death she gave herself! [...] I killed you in truth, but I did not do it willingly. I did what you ordered me. [...] I served you badly, because by my fault you are dead.)

The admission is highlighted stylistically by supporting formulae, adverbs or pronouns. Even Anna, the sister of the unfortunate Dido, who is only indirectly guilty of the queen's suicide (for which she prepared the woodstove without knowing what it was intended for and could therefore reasonably justify herself), uses very strong formulae to designate her guilt: the first-person pronoun is reinforced by the adverb *meïsmes* (self) or placed at the beginning of verse in a rather insistent way and then resumed again by 'par mon fait' (by my fault).

The first person is essential because, as Jankélévitch posits, remorse is founded on the full awareness of one's responsibility:

> Le malheur du regret est simplement dans l'impossibilité du retour au passé: le temps seul est coupable, mais non pas *moi*. Le tragique du remords réside en ceci que je suis moi-même l'artisan de cette impossibilité. (p. 55)

(The hardship of regret lies in the impossibility of returning to the past: time alone is guilty, but not *me*. The tragedy of remorse lies in the fact that I am myself the architect of this impossibility.)

Remorse has been defined as a 'moral emotion' by D. Konstan,[24] whereas regret only concerns the feeling of the irrevocable passage of time. Because of that moral point of view, it directly implies the character's responsibility while regret could be more general and could address other than oneself. Yet some characters experience trouble in formulating this personal responsibility. In *Erec and Enide*, the movement that directs the young woman towards a declarative sentence in the first person is rather sinuous: she first confesses her fault in an interrogative form, which tends to seek a justification for guilt.

> Deus! et por quoi fui je tant ose
> Que tel forsenage osai dire? (*Erec et Enide*, 2591–2)

(God! What audacity led me to make such foolish remarks?)

Later, it is her pride that is accused of having urged her to speak.

> Mes trop m'a orguiauz sozlevee:
> An mon orguel avrai damage
> Quant je ai dit si grant outrage. (*Erec et Enide*, 2606–08)

> (But pride has turned my head: my pride will cause my loss as my words have been offensive.)

While pride itself is not a separate and autonomous entity, this is an indirect and metonymic way to refer to oneself. Nevertheless, we must read through several more misfortunes before she states explicitly, in the first person, the burden of her culpability:

> Mes qu'ai je dit! Trop ai mespris,
> Qui la parole ai maintenue
> Don mes sire a mort receüe,
> La mortel parole antoschiee
> Qui me doit estre reprochiee;
> Et je reconois et otroi
> Que nus n'i a coupes fors moi;
> Je sole an doi estre blasmee. (*Erec et Enide*, 4644–51)

> (But what did I say! I have done too much harm, I who uttered these words which caused the death of my husband, these words carrying a deadly poison that must be reproached; I acknowledge and confess that the fault is all mine; I alone must be blamed.)

At a time when personal pronouns are not obligatory, the use of the preverbal *je* (I) twice formalizes this declaration of guilt, reinforced by the opposition between *nus* (nobody) and *fors moi* (except me), and by the adjective *sole* (alone), further emphasized by the brevity of the proposition.

Similarly, the first verses of Yvain's monologue exemplify this movement where subjectivity struggles to be fixed onto an 'I':

> Que fait il qu'il ne se tue,
> Cis las qui joie s'est tolue?
> Que fais je, las, qui ne m'ochi? (*Le Chevalier au lion*, 3527–9)

> (Why does he wait to kill himself, this wretch who has taken all joy? What am I waiting for, a miserable wretch, to put an end to my life?)

After a distancing utterance constructed using the third person 'que fait cis las qui … ' (literally, what does this wretch, who …), Yvain again takes the same syntactic structure and finally articulates it in the first person, 'que fais je, qui … ' (literally, what do I, who …).

Accounts of admission, with the liberating value of confession, alongside the violence of recognizing responsibility, do not allow for an escape. In many cases, the characters would have mitigating circumstances in our eyes. But at a time when this concept was not invented, confession was also an acceptance of sin in a full and complete way, without justification. Partonopeu also expresses this responsibility to utter an admission that would condemn him.

> Vers vos sui guencis de ma foi,
> Mais certes ne l'ai fait par moi.
> Et cui caut, quant je por altrui
> ne vos deüsce querre anui?
> Ne puis desfendre par raison
> Que n'aie faite traïsson
> Quant le counois et je l'ai faite,
> Ma vien en ai vers vos forfaite.
> Quant je connois ma felonie
> N'ai droit en menbre ne en vie. (*Partonopeu de Blois*, v. 4769–80)

(I broke my word, but I did not really do it of my own accord. What does it matter, however, since I did not have to persuade myself to harm you? I cannot reasonably deny my betrayal. In admitting my crime, I condemn myself to your eyes. The confession of my felony deprives me of all right to live.)

Partonopeu could acquit himself by invoking his maternal influence, but not only does he choose to take responsibility for this decision, but he also understands the weight of his word: admission compels the confessor as much as their initial misdeed. There is an irreversibility in confession, in the same way as exists in the original sin.

The perpetual present of remorse

Transgression, eradicating past happiness, leaves only a detestable present, placed entirely under the sign of the sin committed, from which it is impossible to escape, the future being limited to the weight of this fault. This is one of the rhetorical clichés that we find in the discourse of remorse. This is expressed by a specific relation to time: on the one hand, the eternal present of a sin continually renewed; on the other hand, the definitive and irremediable rupture with the past. 'Le remords au contraire est une présence, une présence obsédante et qui nous harcèle sans pitié'[25] (on the contrary, remorse is a presence, a haunting presence, that harasses us without mercy).

The suffering of remorse is founded on the impossibility of escaping from the permanence of the fault, which King Mark expresses very well here:

> Rois March, fait li cevaliers, oïs tu onques parler de Taulas de la Montaingne, le merveilleus gaiant ki tant a fait de mal en Cornuaille? – Oïl voir, fait li rois. Je en ai maintes fois plus oï parler que je ne vausisse. Encore n'a pas un mois entier k'il ochist deus de mes cevaliers, teus preudomes que je mout amoie et prisoie, dont il me poise mout cierement et pesera toutes les fois k'il m'en souvenra mais. (*Tristan* en prose, éd. Ménard t. 1[26])

> (King Mark, said the knight, have you heard of Taulas of the Mountain, the formidable giant who has wrought so much destruction in Cornwall? – Yes, the king answers. I have heard about it more often than I would have liked. It has not yet been a month since he killed two of my knights, two good men whom I liked and esteemed a lot, which greatly saddens me and will sadden me always whenever I remember.)

The memory of the horrific death of two knights, at the hands of Taulas the giant, is a memory that does not pass: its significance permeates the present, and indeed, it never passes from the present into the future. As Jankélévitch explains, remorse is locked in the permanent resurrection of the fault:

> Se le rappeler, c'est le revivre, le refaire; en sorte que la mauvaise conscience se sent pour ainsi dire pécher continuellement. C'est à mon avis, l'essence même du remords que cette continuation d'une faute qui ressuscite littéralement, qui à tous moments se renouvelle dans mon cœur. Il n'y a donc ici aucune différence entre la matière et le représenté: c'est la mauvaise action qui se transporte telle quelle, toute vivante et brûlante au milieu de notre présent. Entre la faute originale et son remords, quelle est donc la différence ? La différence est justement dans cet anachronisme paradoxal d'un passé qui s'éternise et qui refuse de mourir. [...] Là où le regret et la mémoire essaient de retenir, le remords voudrait au contraire dissoudre. Pourtant le remords se souviendra quoi qu'il fasse. Cette impuissance est sa marque propre et, si l'on peut dire, sa signature. (pp. 57–8)

> (To remember is to relive, to redo; so that a bad conscience feels, so to speak, as if it is sinning continually. It is, in my opinion, the very essence of remorse: this continuation of a fault that literally resurrects itself, which at every moment is renewed in my heart. So, there is no difference here between matter and its representation: it is the misdeed which is transported as it is, alive and burning in the midst of our present. Between the original fault and a person's remorse, what is the difference? The difference is precisely in this paradoxical anachronism of a

past that goes on forever and refuses to die. [...] Where regret and memory try to hold back, remorse would rather dissolve. Yet remorse will be remembered no matter what it does. This impotence is its mark and, one could say, its signature.)

This impotence is fittingly described by Partonopeu after he transgresses the prohibition that had prevented him from seeing Melior in the light:

> Tant ai forfait que jo confort
> N'en puis avoir devant la mort.
> Con onques plus durra ma vie,
> Plus comperrai ma felonie.
> Je sui plus morts et plus honis
> Et plus tués et plus traïs
> Que n'est li leres cui on pent,
> Car cil passe son duel briement;
> Li miens ne vait qu'il ne reveigne,
> Ne me guerpist qu'il ne tiegne,
> Car se j'ai de repos une eure,
> lors me racorra mes diols seure. (*Partonopeu de Blois*, 4787–898)

(My crime will not afford me any rest before death. The longer I live, the more I will blame myself. My condemnation, my shame, my martyrdom and my infamy are worse than those of the thief who is led to the gallows, because if his torment does not last long, mine only stops to resume with greater intensity; it has scarcely gone before it is back. At the slightest truce, it assails me again.)

Partonopeu expresses the philosophy of remorse very well as an 'anachronistic' pain that does not pass or diminish with time: 'Con onques plus durra ma vie, / Plus comperrai ma felonie' (The longer I live, the more I will pay dearly for my misdeed). This pain incessantly imposes itself onto the conscience in back-and-forth movement staged by the binary parallelism between centrifugal motion verbs ('li miens ne vait [...] ne me guerpist', 'mine does not go [...] does not leave me') and the centripetal verb of motion ('qu'il ne reveigne', 'only to return'). This coming and going ends on the static verb *tenir* (to hold) in 'qu'il ne teigne' (only to hold) which marks this confinement in memory which cannot disperse, preventing, in quasi-Pascalian terms, any diversion: 'Car se j'ai de repos une eure, / lors me racorra mes diols seure' (Indeed, even if I have rest for an hour, my afflictions will surely run back to me). Partonopeu's hyperbolic comparison with the thief condemned to death insists on the perpetuity of pain, always in the present. It is a 'survivance' (survival) (p. 56), says Jankélévitch, 'notre présent tout vif et encore chaud' (of our present, alive and still hot).

The description of the present state, the intensification of suffering

The present state of a sinner may be described using a wide range of expressions that denote suffering. The present regret for the transgression committed is expressed in a rather neutral way by the verb *peser* (to weigh) in the expression 'telle chose *me poise*' (such a thing weighs me down):

> Ha sire, fait il, un chetis, un maleros. Artus ai non, si ai esté une piece rois de Bretagne, ce doit moi peser, car je muir en si malvais point come cil qui assez mal fait a la terre et pis a m'ame. (Arthur in *Lancelot* du lac, t.3, éd. Mosès, p. 304)

> (Ah my father, he answers, a wretch, a wretch. My name is Arthur, and I was king of the Britons for a long time, which must sadden/[which weighs on me] me because I am dying in such a bad way as the one who has subjected the world to many damages and even more to his own soul.)

The same metaphor of weight is found in the fabliau of the *Chevalier qui fit sa fame confesse* (the knight who made his lady confess) when the lady explains a sin that *grève* (strains) her body:

> Dont li miens cors est mout grevez
> Et la moie ame en grant freor. (*Le Chevalier qui fit sa fame confesse*, 164–5)

> (From which my body is much strained
> And my soul in much fear.)

Conversely repentance is lightness; it removes what weighs down:

> Se vous en requier penitence
> Pour oster m'ame de grevance. (the King of Hungary in *Manekine*, v. 7123–4)

> (I come to ask you for penitance to lift from my soul this weight.)

The lady of Landuc, in beseeching the Knight of the lion to free himself from the weight of his sin, asks him to give up this weight *(pesance)* and his anger *(ire)*.

> Or alez donc a Deu, biaus sire,
> Qui vostre pesance et vostre ire,
> Se lui plest, vos atort a joie! (*Le Chevalier au Lion*, v. 4621–3)

> (Now go, good lord! God bless you! If it pleases Him, may He turn your weight and anger into joy.)

But the verb *peser* (to weigh) is the minimum degree of suffering, often considered too weak to adequately render the strong violence of remorse. There are also more physical and warlike formulae. We have seen the use of the verb *(re)mordre* (to bite (again)); Partonopeu used the verb *acorer* (literally, to tear out the heart).

The verb *poindre* (to sting) can also be used in this sense, which metaphorically gives a physical element to remorse as a fight between evil and the soul:

> Trop durement me sui mefais.
> Dix, s'il Li plaist, le me pardoinst
> Car c'est la riens qui plus me point. (the King of Hungary in *Manekine*, v. 6758-60)

(I have committed too grave a sin. God, if it is His will, forgive me! Because that's what stings me the most.)

Characters attacked by remorse describe their physical and bodily pain, essentially by the verb *doloir* (to suffer) or the related adjective *doulans*.

> Sy remés en vostre voulenté mon corps et tous mes bien, repentant et tresdoulant de ce que je puis avoir commis a l'encontre de vostre majesté. Parquoy veez moy icy tout prest pour l'amender de mon corps et veez cy mon espee dont vous me pouez occire ou laissier vivre, s'il vous plaist, combien que avant toute oeuvre je vous requiers mercy de mon meffait comme tres doulant que j'en suis. (Dryant dans *Perceforest*, III, 1)

(I put myself and all my property in your good will, repentant and suffering for the acts I committed against your majesty. So, here am I here ready to amend with my body and here is my sword with which you can kill me or let me live, please, although above all, I beg you mercy for my misdeeds as the wretch that I am.)

> Que ele est noïe en la mer
> Dont je me puis dolans clamer[27]
> Car sans raisons et a grant tort
> Et pour bien faire ai mise a mort
> Ma fille. (the King of Hungary in *Manekine*, v. 7111-15)

(She drowned in the sea; and I can say that I am suffering because it is I who without reason, unjustly, even though she had acted well, put to death my own daughter.)

The present is a source of distress because it is haunted by a transgression that does not pass, that stings, bites, devours or simply weighs like a heavy burden on the conscience.

The opposition between past and present

Remorse is an oscillation between the present and the past, originating in the initial misdeed that makes felt the weight of irreversibility. One of the rhetorical clichés, fundamental although not systematically expressed, is that of the lost past, or the paradise of innocence, which is placed under the sign of perfection and fullness:

> Par ce passé coupable et qui nous tourmente parce qu'en somme il est notre présent tout vif et encore chaud, nous regrettons un vrai passé qui est celui-là, notre innocence perdue; par opposition au passé de la faute, le plus-que-passé de l'innocence est un souvenir très cher et qui me semble à jamais disparu. (Jankélévitch, p. 63)

> (By this culpable past that torments us because it is our present, alive and still hot, we come to grieve for a true past that is our lost innocence; as opposed to the past of the fault, the 'more-than-past' of innocence is a very dear memory and one that seems lost to me forever.)

In this way, Dido paints a picture of herself as a virtuous woman:

> Tant fui ainçois et preus et saige
> Que me donnast Amor la raige,
> Et moult fuisse bonne eüree
> Se ne venist en ma contree
> Li troÿens qui m'a traÿe. (*Roman d'Eneas*, 2142–6)

> (I was full of virtue and wisdom before Love inspired me with this rage, and I would have been very happy if this Trojan had not come to my country, who has betrayed me.)

The young Cortois d'Arras, the prodigal son, recounts the simple pleasure of feeding himself the meagre straw-filled bread crusts, which he must now eat while keeping the pigs.

> Quant je regart ceste croute,
> C'est merveille que nus en gouste;
> Tant par est fet de pute blee.
> Et s'est ja bien nonne passee!
> Jeüns ne sueil estre a ceste eure.
> Hé Diex ! Com ma char se desveure,
> Qui soloit mengier devant prime! (*Cortois d'Arras*, v. 523–9)

> (When I look at this crust, I am surprised that one can savour it, so contaminated is the flour by which it is made. And it's already past three o'clock! I am not used to fasting at this time. My God, how my body suffers, as one who was accustomed to eat in the morning.)

It is the experience of hunger that echoes throughout the speech, increasing over the course of the verses. The satiety that characterizes the past is opposed to this fierce hunger of the present.

The monologue of Enide displays a confinement in regret of the past by playing with repetitions and hyperboles:

> Or estoie je trop a eise,
> Qu'il ne me faloit nule chose.
> [...] don ne m'amoit trop mes sires?
> An foi, lasse, trop m'amoit il.
> Or m'estuet aller en essil!
> Mais de ce ai je duel greignor
> Que je ne verrai mon seignor
> Qui tant m'amoit de grant meniere
> Que nule rien n'avoit tant chiere.
> [...] Nule chose ne me faloit:
> Moult estoie buene eüree. (*Erec et Enide*, 2590–605)

(I was too comfortable, I did not lack anything. [...] Did not my husband love me passionately? Ah yes, wretched woman, he loved me with too much passion. Now I must go into exile! But what afflicts me the most is that I will no longer see my husband who loved me so dearly, who loved me more than anything. I did not want for anything: what happiness was mine!)

Her monologue is framed by two verses that make a chiasm: 'Qu'il ne me faloit nule chose.' / 'Nule chose ne me faloit' (I did not lack a thing / nothing to me was lacking); the past turns and returns constantly in the memory as the time of abundance, signified by the quantity adverbs *trop, moult, tant*. This lost prosperity and innocence works in opposition to the present in the same way that 'Or estoie je trop a eise' (then I was too comfortable) echoes and opposes 'Or m'estuet aler an essil!' (Now I must go into exile!). The beginning of the two verses is a quasi-paronomasis, but in one case the first person is subject;[28] in the other, she is subject to an impersonal verb of obligation. In the first verse, the stability of past happiness is signified by the stative verb *estre* (to be); in the second, the pain of the present is set in motion, indicated by the verb *aler* (to go).

A few centuries after Chrétien, when a writer of the Burgundian Court reworked *Erec and Enide* into prose, the figure of Fortune and her wheel became key features in the literary psyche in order to adapt the work to the tastes of his audience. The prose writer uses it here to understand the reversal of Enide's situation:

> J'estoie trop aise et en trop grant habondance de biens. Du bas, j'estoie eslevee par bonne adventure quant soubdainement descendre m'en fault. [...] Fortune m'avoit trop bonnement adrescie, et en trop grande excellence j'estoie honnouree quant par ung soubit admonnestement de verité estre exillee me convendra certez. (Enide, dans *l'Histoire d'Erec* en prose, p. 172)

(I was too happy and in too much abundance of goods. From the bottom, I had been raised by happy adventure when suddenly, I must fall back. Fortune had favored me too much, and I was excellently honored when, by a sudden warning of truth, I must now be exiled.)

O tresmalheuree dame, qui du hault au tresbas es admenee par ung des trebuchets de Fortune. (*id.* p. 195)

(Oh, very unhappy lady, who falls from the top to the lowest on one of the trebuchets of Fortune.)

This figure is more elaborate and refers to a rich intertext. However, it loses the harsh recognition of the irreversibility of time and almost entirely dismisses Enide's responsibility.

The past is indeed permanently cut off from the present: 'ce que la mauvaise conscience "regrette", ce n'est pas *la chose même*, mais l'état qui précédait cette chose et que cette chose a détruite' (what the guilty conscience 'regrets' is *not the very act*, but the state which preceded that act and what it has subsequently destroyed), explains Jankélévitch (p. 64). Irreversibility is evident in the use of hypotheticals that regularly return in speeches of remorse:

Si fust droiture
Que sor moi tornast l'aventure
Si que vous n'en eüssiez mal. (the lover in *La Châtelaine de Vergy*, 889–91)

(It would have been right for this misfortune to fall on me, and for you to not suffer.)

Sur mon ame, je eusse ainçois arrachiee la langue a bons poings qu'elle eust profferré la malheuree parolle! (Enide in *L'Histoire d'Erec* en prose, p. 194)

(By my soul, I would rather have torn out my tongue than [allow my mouth] to utter this unhappy speech!)

desja vouldroi je estre morte et mon seigneur fust vivant encores. (Enide in *L'Histoire d'Erec* en prose, p. 194)

(I wish I was dead and that my husband was still alive.)

Such hypothetical utterances thus create another reality which would have prevented the misdeed and its consequences, as Jankélévitch states:

Le malheur de l'irréversibilité est donc un double malheur; nous regrettons d'une part l'acte irréparable qui s'est accompli, et d'autre part les possibles dont cet acte nous a privés à jamais; car la même faute qui s'installe irrévocablement exclut l'innocence sans retour. Il y a donc dans la douleur du remords tout ensemble un plein et un vide: le plein de la mauvaise action dont nous ne pouvons nous défaire, et le vide de notre ancienne pureté, dont la faute à jamais nous sépare. (p. 64)

(The tragedy of irreversibility is therefore a double misfortune; we regret on the one hand the irreparable act that has been accomplished, and, on the other hand, the possibilities that this act has forever deprived from us; for the same fault which takes place irrevocably excludes innocence, without return. There is then, in the pain of remorse, together a 'fullness' and an 'emptiness': the fullness of the wicked deed from which we cannot escape, and the emptiness of our former purity, from which we are forever separated by the fault.)

Another thing could have happened, which disappears at the same time that the irreversibility of the sin is made permanent.

The uncertainty of the future

When the present is painful, and the past irretrievably lost, the future appears to signal no escape. The rhetorical cliché of suicide is also manifested in the negation of the future. The desperate subject sees no way out of their suffering. Characters in remorse hesitate between questions about their future, like Enide after Erec's death:

> Lasse moy comment me advendra de celle grant perte que le monde fait ou corpz de ce gentil chevalier! De quel mort serai adjugie, de quelle penance serai je chergie pour la recompensacion de ce dur meschief par moy mesmes advenu? (*L'Histoire d'Erec* en prose, p. 194)

> (Unhappy that I am, what will happen to me from this great loss suffered by the world in the person of this noble knight? What death will I be sentenced to? What penance will I be charged to compensate for this hard fee for which I am responsible?)

And total negations:

> Quant ne m'avra cist a moilllier
> Yray je dont autre proier
> Ou ceulz que ne veul a seignor?
> Fferay je dont tel deshoneur?
> Quant il voudrent, je ne daignay
> Or derechief lor priëray?
> Non feray voir, mielz vel morir
> quant autrement ne puis garir. (Dido in *Roman d'Eneas*, v. 2084–91)

(Since he will not have me for a wife, shall I go and pray to another, or to those whom I have rejected? Shall I conduct myself so shamefully? When they wanted to marry me, I despised them, and now I would solicit them in my turn? No, I prefer to die since there is no other way out.)

To the very real question of her future as sovereign, Dido choses to refuse all the humiliating alternatives. There is apparently no future for this pagan in the world.

Conclusion

The moral suffering of remorse is extensively discursive. It is expressed in lengthy monologues that testify to a well-established literary tradition. Without being completely fixed, the formulae that express the rhetorical clichés that comprise such speeches are founded in the semantic fields of pain, misery and in formulae of duty and condemnation. Whether it is conceived as a step prior to repentance, or a feeling of shame that invades a guilty individual without hope of salvation, remorse is for many authors an occasion for long and expressive speeches wherein characters articulate the hatred they feel for their sin, and especially for their own person, and call out for a harsh judgment against themselves. Remorse is based on a relationship to the time when the misdeed committed, the confession of which reveals horror, has irreversibly corrupted the present and makes the past a lost happiness, thereby compromising any future.

7

Peter's three tears

Véronique Plesch

On a fresco in the pilgrimage sanctuary of Notre-Dame des Fontaines in La Brigue in the southern French Alps, as the apostle Peter realizes he has denied his Master, he sheds three tears, one for each of his denials (Figures 1 and 2). This detail is part of the Passion cycle completed in 1492 by Giovanni Canavesio, a Piedmontese artist who was also a priest. Taking as point of departure Peter's three tears, a detail I believe has gone unnoticed, this chapter considers how this particular scene contributes to the frescoes' message(s) and enters in a dialogue with other scenes and characters, articulating a rich discourse on compunction, contrition and penance.

Peter's Denial and its aftermath

The titulus[1] that runs below the fresco announces: 'Capitulum X. Qualiter Petrus percussus voce ancille hostiarie[2] negavit Christum' (Chapter X. How Peter, having been struck by the voice of the innkeeper's maid, denied Christ). The panel is divided in two successive scenes, to be read, like the rest of the cycle, from left to right. First, we see Peter warming himself at a fireplace and being recognized by a maid, who points him out to a soldier who seizes him by the neck. In the second half, Peter exits through a door and weeps. Behind him on a low wall, the rooster crows, as predicted by Christ at the Last Supper (Matthew 26:34, Mark 14:30, Luke 22:34 and John 13:38). Between the rooster and Peter's

---

I am grateful to Allen Jenkins for drawing my attention to Peter's three tears during our visit to Notre-Dame des Fontaines in October 2017. As always for all things Brigasque, my gratitude goes to my friends in La Brigue, in particular to Liliane Pastorelli, to whose memory this essay is dedicated. I also wish to thank Charlotte Steenbrugge and Graham Williams for inviting me to contribute to this book, the anonymous readers for their excellent suggestions and my research assistant Annie Muller for her help.

head is an inscription that reads, 'Petrus flevit amare' (Peter cried bitterly), a literal quotation from the Gospel of Luke (22:62) that complements the titulus below by referring to the aftermath of the Denial.[3]

Although following the established iconographic tradition, Canavesio's rendition of the Denial is nonetheless remarkable on account of its complexity, achieving, to borrow George Henderson's felicitous phrase, a 'pictorial Gospel harmony'.[4] According to all four canonical Gospels (Matthew 26:69–75, Mark 14:66–72, Luke 22:55–61, John 18:25–7), Peter denied Christ three times while he was warming himself at a fire in Caiaphas's courtyard. In pictorial cycles, the three denials are generally reduced to a single representation with a preference given to the maid, who all four Gospels agree was the first person to recognize the apostle[5] – and this is typically the case in the extant cycles produced in the Duchy of Savoy, where Canavesio was trained and where he was primarily active.[6] For the second and third denials, the Gospels diverge. For Matthew, the protagonists of the last two denials are another maid and bystanders; for Mark, it is again the same maid as in the first denial and some bystanders; for Luke, it is two men; John, on the other hand, speaks of 'servants and ministers'[7] and a male servant of the high priest. Canavesio follows the pictorial tradition and represents the maid, but remarkably he also includes enough figures as to encompass all four diverging versions of the two remaining denials. We see Matthew's second maid standing in the doorway and enough male figures for all the other versions (Matthew's 'bystanders', Luke's two men or John's 'servants and ministers').

The decision to include the second moment, when the rooster crows and Peter sheds tears as he realizes what has just happened, is noteworthy. In that panel's second part, Canavesio closely follows the Gospels of Matthew and Luke, who both report that Peter exited and wept 'bitterly' ('amare'). As a separate scene, Peter's Weeping is by far less common than the Denial itself,[8] and it is even rarer to find both scenes together in a single cycle, as they occur at La Brigue: Notre-Dame des Fontaines, in fact, is the only case in the Savoyard tradition known to me.

Canavesio fleshes out his rendition of the Denial's aftermath with a few details that at first glance might seem gratuitous. As Peter realizes Christ's prophecy of his betrayal, he wipes his tears with a white kerchief, a motif that finds a visual echo in the white cloth hanging from a balcony directly above him (and right next to the rooster). One is reminded of the presence of similar immaculate fabrics in Netherlandish paintings where such elements of 'disguised symbolism' allude to the Virgin Mary's purity.[9] At La Brigue, yet another cloth appears in the

Crowning with thorns, in the hand of a maid who stands at a balcony overlooking the scene (Figure 3) while in the Mocking of Christ (Figure 4) we see another maid engaged in housekeeping, this time carrying a bucket on her head: she ascends a staircase on the left of the composition. That this motif is pregnant with meaning is supported by the fact that it appears in earlier Savoyard fresco cycles, for instance in the chapel of San Fiorenzo at Bastia (Figure 5), where it is inserted into the same narrative context of the Mocking. Further proof of the detail's significance for Canavesio is proven by its presence in the diminutive chapel of the White Penitents at Peillon, where the pictorial programme had to be reduced to the essential. Very tellingly, Canavesio went out of his way to keep the motif. The scene in which the maid in the staircase appears at La Brigue, the Mocking, is not included in Peillon's short cycle of eleven scenes, so Canavesio moved it to the appearance of Christ before Caiaphas (Figure 6). On the panel's left side, a similar woman, this time without bucket but wearing a white apron, stands facing the viewer at the top of a staircase. As Canavesio multiplies these details, he drives home an equation between cleaning and cleansing from one's sins: the Original Sin purified through Christ's sufferings and Peter cleansing the sin he has just committed through his tears.[10]

In many ways the structuring of Canavesio's pictorial discourse bears witness to his training as a priest.[11] We can see in these domestic details the visual equivalent to the metaphors that were an important tool for the late medieval and early modern preacher. As a matter of fact, house-cleaning was a very common homiletic trope for confession.[12] Peter's wiping of his tears calls to mind the statement by the famous fifteenth-century preacher, Olivier Maillard, that 'confession washes with tears, true contrition dries them with a linen cloth'.[13]

Repentance at Notre-Dame des Fontaines

The faithful attending mass at Notre-Dame des Fontaines would see Peter's Denial and Weeping on her right-hand side, at the centre of the lower register of the frescoes on the south side of the nave. On the opposite wall, on the sinister side, is another scene of contrition: Judas Returning the Thirty Pieces of Silver (Figure 7). In La Brigue's Passion cycle, as could be expected, Christ is present in most of the twenty-six scenes, but two figures are afforded special prominence: Peter and Judas, who appear in the panels in which Christ is absent. As we have seen, this occurs in Peter's Denial and Remorse (Figure 8) and this is also the case for Judas in his Pact (Figure 8) and his Suicide (Figure 9). Remarkably, two of these panels are subdivided into two secondary scenes and as a result each figure (Judas and Peter) appears twice, conferring further importance on them.

As it turns out, at La Brigue Judas is the most important *dramatis persona* after Christ. An extremely dynamic figure, he is here the real motor of the drama, propelling the action by the restless positions he adopts throughout the cycle. He appears in the cycle a total of eight times – or even nine if we count his soul in the Suicide (Figure 9) – and his story is narrated in an unusually thorough manner (it is uncommon to find all three scenes of his Pact, Remorse and Suicide). With the division into two episodes of the panel devoted to his Pact, there are no fewer than six scenes that tell in a continuous manner the first part of his role in the Passion: beginning at the Last Supper and up to the climactic Arrest of Christ, Judas is always present. In all these panels, the traitor appears wearing consistently the same yellow robe with a green cape draped over it. He is endowed with distinctive features that ensure that the viewer will recognize him and perceive the panels as a succession of interrelated moments: red hair and beard, hooked nose, sunken cheeks and elongated eyes.[14] The scenes in which Judas dominates (and from which Christ is absent) clearly separate his story into two moments: one appears on each nave wall. The first 'act' of the drama is centred on the Pact (Figure 8), preceded and prepared by his presence among the apostles in the Last Supper and Christ washing the feet of the Apostles (Figure 10) and followed by its consequence: the Arrest of Christ. In the second 'act', on the north wall, we become witnesses to the dramatic unravelling of his life when, regretting his actions, he returns the money (Figure 7) and hangs himself (Figure 9). His story is therefore presented as a two-act drama, in which sin leads to repentance, but also to death. The dénouement, the Suicide, is a memorable image: it is the only panel in the cycle devoted to a single figure and it grabs the beholder's attention by its violent expression, its elongated format, different from the rest of the cycle, and by the monumental way in which the body fills the pictorial field and seems to project into the viewer's space.[15]

Of all the scenes featuring Judas, his Remorse (Figure 7) is by far the least common and its inclusion in the cycle contributes to highlighting the character's significance. As the traitor returns the money, we see Christ being led: but if both are present, they do not interact and, significantly enough, Jesus appears only in the background, his body cut off by the frame, leaving centre stage for Judas.[16] The importance Canavesio confers upon the figure of Judas and in particular on the moment of his remorse finds a literary parallel in a contemporary play, Jean Michel's *Passion*, which was performed in Angers in 1486. Jean Michel based his text on an earlier Passion play by Arnoul Greban (believed to have been written shortly before 1452), to which he added, according to his own expression, 'addicions et corrections'.[17] Maurice Accarie has shown that the *remaniement* by Jean Michel of Greban's text consists primarily in the development of episodes of the public life of Christ and of the past life of certain protagonists destined to repentance and conversion, such as Mary Magdalen, Judas and Lazarus.[18] I am not suggesting any direct relationship between Canavesio and Jean Michel, but rather wish to point out that their works – completed only six years apart – betray similar interests. In their edifying purpose, both breathe life and humanity into figures who sin and repent. That Judas's motivation for returning the money was repentance is already forcefully stated by Matthew 27:3 when he recounts how Judas was 'poenitentia ductus' (Douay-Rheims translates 'repenting himself' but I find 'driven by repentance' more vivid).

La Brigue's frescoes offer other several exemplars of repentance. One such figure is the good thief Dismas, whose last-minute conversion as he dies crucified next to Christ[19] enables him to stand behind Christ in the Descent into Limbo (Figure 11), suggesting that he gained immediate access to paradise. Canavesio's choice to include Dismas in that scene, a rather uncommon detail,[20] but one that illustrates the rewards of repentance, also finds echoes in the moral message in Jean Michel's *Passion* as well as in another contemporary play, the *Passion* of Revello.[21] Both plays develop the stories of the thieves: in Revello, for instance, they appear as early as the first *Giornata*, during the flight into Egypt. Gestas, the bad thief, wants to rob the Holy Family, but Dismas persuades him not to, for he is convinced that the baby is the Son of God.[22]

Given the importance of repentance in Notre-Dame's paintings, several other protagonists, even though traditionally present in Passion scenes, are invested with a supplementary dimension in Canavesio's cycle that causes them to reinforce the penitential message. Among these figures is Longinus, who pierces Christ's side at the Crucifixion and is miraculously cured of his blindness (to be understood both physically and spiritually): in effect, the blood that streams from Jesus's pierced side cleanses Longinus's sins (Figure 12). Also present at the Crucifixion is the Roman centurion, who recognizes Jesus as 'vere filius Dei' and Mary Magdalen at the foot of the cross (who later witnesses the Deposition and the Entombment). There are also the apostles who abandon Christ by falling asleep while Christ prays during the Agony in the Garden and who run away at the Arrest[23] – powerfully summarized by one of them, John, Christ's favourite, whom we see at the extreme right of La Brigue's Arrest, trying to flee and being seized by a soldier. All of these, on some level, are figures who sin or have sinned, who repent and are forgiven by Christ, or who convert by recognizing Jesus's divinity. There is also Simon of Cyrene, whose bearing of Christ's cross brings to mind the phrase recorded by Hervé Martin of 'croix de pénitence' (cross of penance)[24] and whom we see engaged in an action itself re-enacted in penitential rituals.[25]

The sacrament of penance

In its development and structure, the second act of Canavesio's telling of Judas's story at La Brigue recalls the workings of the sacrament of penance. Moved by contrition, the feeling the sinner experiences when he realizes he has sinned and regrets it, the traitor confesses his sin to the priests: confession's speech act is materialized by the speech scroll with the opening words 'Pec[c]avi' (I have sinned; Figure 7). Simultaneously to this utterance, Judas raises the moneybag in his right hand, as he is about to throw it to the priests; in so doing, as he returns these ill-gotten gains, he achieves satisfaction.[26] The *Passion* of Greban makes it clear that at that moment he has fulfilled all the requirements for the sacrament of penance:

> J'ay fait confession
> en tant que je dis *peccavi*,
> puis ay fait satisfacion
> en tant que les deniers rendy,
> et puis en tel contricion
> qu'a peu le cueur me fendy.
>
> (I confessed,
> by saying *peccavi*.
> Then I made restitution
> by returning the money,
> and then felt such contrition
> that my heart almost burst.)[27]

Remarkably, in La Brigue's Pact of Judas (Figure 8), i.e. the moment in which Judas commits the very sin he later confesses (Figure 7), we see him speaking through a speech scroll. In the cycle, only four panels are enhanced with such textual insertions and their presence contributes to highlighting crucial moments in the narrative. In the Pact, Judas says: 'Quid vultis mihi dare et ego eum vobis tradam' (What will you give me, and I will deliver him unto you).

When Judas returns the money, he tells the priests: 'Pec[c]avi tradens sanguinem iustum' (I have sinned in betraying innocent blood). In the Ecce Homo, the scroll near Pilate, now illegible, most likely contained the words 'Ecce Homo' (Behold the man). Finally, in the Crucifixion (Figure 12), the Centurion affirms, pointing to Christ: 'Vere filius Dei erat iste' (Indeed this was the Son of God).[28] The last two utterances – in the Ecce Homo and the Crucifixion – are part of these scenes' established iconography and therefore not really noteworthy, but the two former ones, containing words spoken by Judas, are extremely rare.[29]

In these two Judas scenes, the presence of the speech scrolls singles them out amidst the rest of the cycle, reinforcing the sense of pairing that we have characterized as a two-act drama, but which, in light of their visual mirroring of one another, might also be thought of as a diptych, in which repentance follows sin. Elsewhere in the cycle, we find a similarly meaningful juxtaposition of sin, contrition and, in this case, an allusion to the workings of the sacrament of penance. The panel with the Denial of Peter and his tears of contrition appears directly below the one in which Christ washes the apostles' feet (Figure 13). As the ritual washing of the feet was considered the institution of the sacrament of penance,[30] the juxtaposition of these two panels, when read from bottom to top, demonstrates that penance's cleansing is available to all, as for instance to Peter, who is seen below sinning and then crying in contrition. The Washing of the Feet (Figure 10) deserves further attention for the way in which it contributes to articulating the opposition between Peter and Judas, who are depicted next to each other. Peter is seated in the foreground as Christ, his sleeves rolled up, kneels and washes his feet, while the rest of the apostles stand on both sides. On the extreme right, Judas, putting on a sandal, is about to exit the scene, implying that he was the first to have had his feet washed.[31] The interaction between Peter and Christ is alluded to by the gesture of the apostle, who lifts his right hand to his forehead. In John 13:8 the apostle protests ('Thou shalt never wash my feet'), but after Jesus responds, 'If I wash thee not, thou shalt have no part with me,' Peter says: 'Lord, not only my feet, but also my hands and my head.'[32]

The ritual washing of the feet is rich in implications for the figure of Judas as well – and even more so here given his preferential treatment. The act of humility performed by Christ at the Washing of the Feet is indeed directly related to his treachery; it functions as a *repoussoir* increasing the infamy of his sin. In fact, when in the *Passione di Revello* Judas realizes the full impact of his act – Barabbas has been released and Christ condemned – he breaks into a *planctus*, a lament, in which he remembers the scene:

> El myo Signore cum tanta humilitate
> li mey piedy ch'el m'abia lavato
> ensì tratamente l'abia ingannato.³³
>
> (My lord, who with so much humility
> washed my feet
> I betrayed so treacherously.)

The sins committed by La Brigue's repenting figures are often associated in devotional literature and art. For instance, in Francesco Suriano's 1485 *Il Trattato di Terra Santa e dell'Oriente*: 'Iuda lo ha tradito e venduto per trenta denari; Pietro lo ha renegato tre volte; li altri discipoli lo hanno lassato solo, e tutti sono fugiti'³⁴ (Judas betrayed him and sold him for thirty deniers; Peter denied him three times; the other disciples left him alone, and all fled). In a French book of hours in the style of the Rohan Master, the kiss of Judas occupies the central part of the page, flanked on each side by secondary depictions of Peter's Denial and Remorse, with below an apostle fleeing and abandoning his mantle.³⁵

But if their sins are indeed comparable, their outcome is not the same. In the monumental Last Judgement that concludes La Brigue's pictorial decoration, we see Peter in heaven, seated with the other apostles but at the place of honour, the closest to Christ's right, while Judas is in hell (Figures 14 and 15). The banner placed above the latter explains the reasons for his damnation: he is in a section reserved to the 'traditori e desperati' (traitors and despairers).³⁶ In fact, he appears directly to the right of the apostles, a reminder of his former status. And the gesture of the last apostle, who points to him and addresses his neighbour, ensures that the viewer will not miss him. But as we know, Judas's betrayal is not the reason for his damnation; after all, Notre-Dame's paintings convincingly affirm contrition's redeeming might. Judas's real sin is to have despaired of Christ's forgiveness and despair was the impetus for his suicide.³⁷ It is therefore logical that among the personifications of the vices and virtues on the dado of the Arena Chapel Giotto depicted *desperatio* as a hanged woman.³⁸ The association of despair and suicide by hanging is no doubt linked to the figure of Judas – the archetypal suicide – but is probably also supported by the fact that in the Middle Ages hanging was by far the most favoured form of suicide.³⁹

Passion plays compellingly elaborate on Judas's despair and subsequent suicide, with several instances in which the traitor affirms that despair is the impetus for his suicide.⁴⁰ Writing his *Passion* in the fifteenth century, Arnoul Greban takes the idea a step further, creating a new character to personify the sin: *Desesperance*, Lucifer's daughter, who comes to persuade the traitor to give up hope and commit suicide. Her intervention compels Judas to vehemently repent and affirm his belief that Christ could still grant him mercy, but Desesperance convinces him that it is impossible.[41] As Judas realizes that he is losing the battle, he cries: 'Je me repens, je me repens / et Desesperance me larde'[42] (I repent, I repent, and Despair harms me).

When eventually Desesperance has the upper hand, Judas concludes:

> Puisque desesperer me fault
> et priver de toute esperance
> et que le don d'espoir me fault.
>
> (Since despair I must
> and be deprived of all hope,
> and I lack the gift of hope.)[43]

He then asks Desesperance to help him die.

Judas repented and still hoped for divine mercy – until the moment despair personified in Desesperance won him over. Here no middle road is possible, for in the medieval conception, 'penance and suicide were mutually exclusive'.[44] The solution adopted by Greban, with the intervention of Desesperance, is an original one: the scene of Judas's despair indeed varies somewhat from play to play. In the *Passion de Semur*, for instance, Judas meets with Mary after he returns the money, and to the traitor's declaration that his sin is beyond mercy, she asserts that 'Par repentance peulx avoir sauvement'[45] (Through repentance you can gain salvation). Whichever way the *fatistes* chose to present the suicide, it is always clear that Judas despaired of obtaining forgiveness, but also that forgiveness was still available to him.

Efficacious tears

Just like Judas, who could potentially be forgiven after his betrayal of Christ, the faithful could obtain forgiveness through the sacrament of penance, whose three steps – contrition, confession and satisfaction – are all alluded to in La Brigue's Remorse of Judas. And yet, as we saw, despite having successfully gone through the required steps, Judas succumbs to despair and damns himself by committing suicide in the next panel. On the other hand, the shedding of tears absolves Peter of the sin he committed by denying Christ. The efficacy of tears, simultaneous expression of contrition and confession, but also effecting satisfaction, is the proof for Pierre Abélard, who invokes Peter's example, that confession is not always indispensable.⁴⁶ In the Middle Ages, tears were indeed profoundly linked to repentance: one only needs to think of Mary Magdalen, the repentant sinner still today associated with tears in common speech: 'pleurer comme une Madeleine' in French or 'maudlin' in English.⁴⁷

As Piroska Nagy explains, what in the Middle Ages was called the 'gift of tears' (*gratia lacrymarum* or *donum lacrymarum*) was seen as a manifestation of God endowed with the ability 'to wash away one's sins'.⁴⁸ In Christian thought, weeping was believed to come directly from the heart or the soul and thus to convey inner truths, while also manifesting inner transformation. Nagy suggests that towards the end of the Middle Ages the shedding of such tears became an 'intimate ritual' and that in this process of purification of the soul, weeping came to be seen as a second baptism, opposed to the first, exterior (and public) one.

The identification of penitential tears as a second baptism appears in a passage from Guillaume de Deguileville's *Pèlerinage de vie humaine*. The personification of Grace shows the pilgrim a rock with an eye from which tears drop unto a tub. She explains that the rock is the hardened heart 'de celi qui a / A escient aussi com tu / Laissie la voie de salu' (of someone who knowingly left the way of salvation, as you have).⁴⁹ As the eye, beholding the heart's state, started weeping bitterly, Grace set the tub to collect the tears. Grace tells the pilgrim that bathing in it 'est [un] baptesme secondaire / Dont Penitance set [bien] faire / Sa lexive et sa buee' (is a second Baptism, and Penance can make her laundry and her wash-water from it)⁵⁰ and that, long ago, Mary Magdalene and St Peter bathed in it, concluding that 'tu veux, dedens ester lavez / Te faut, c'est un grant purgement' (you must be washed in it, for it is a great purifier).⁵¹

The remarkable cleansing and healing powers of the water of tears so compellingly illustrated in this passage echo what we have seen in Canavesio's paintings, with details that contribute to fleshing out a discourse on cleaning, visual metaphors for the cleansing of sins, which go beyond simple references to the Psalmist's words: 'Wash me yet more from my iniquity, and cleanse me from my sin',⁵² to weave vivid metaphors drawn from the lowly domestic realm, just like Deguileville's Penance who does her laundry.

Pilgrimage, tears and water

Deguileville's casting of human life as a pilgrimage is most relevant as we reflect upon a pilgrimage site like Notre-Dame des Fontaines. In the late Middle Ages, religious tears were integrated into specific penitential rituals, and William

Christian observed, 'People went to certain places and did certain things in order to weep.'[53] Among these 'certain places' were those visited by pilgrims. It should be stressed that Notre-Dame's paintings are informed by a distinct expiatory dimension as is proven by the unusual weight given to the representation of Christ's sufferings.[54] This emphasis should not come as a surprise in the pictorial decoration of a pilgrimage sanctuary, a building at the service of an eminently penitential practice.[55]

Furthermore, given the importance given in Deguileville's text as in Canavesio's paintings of the washing of sins, it is surely meaningful that La Brigue's sanctuary is linked to water, which, just like the tears in the *Pèlerinage*, emerge from rocks, right below the building (Figure 16). The local tradition recounting the establishment of the cult might be purely legendary but is nevertheless profoundly meaningful. As the story goes, at an unspecified point in history, the springs, a vital source of water for the town, ran dry. La Brigue's population sought the aid of the Virgin, vowing to build a chapel as a thank-offering for her intercession. When the springs began to flow again, construction of the votive chapel started at a chosen site near the town. But what was built during the day was mysteriously and miraculously destroyed during the night. The population understood that the Virgin did not want the chapel in that place but, rather, next to the springs; thus they moved construction to the chapel's present location. This time, work was carried without any further negative intervention from the Virgin; on the contrary, with her help, every day at lunch, the springs were transformed into wine – without nonetheless allowing excesses: the miraculous wine had to be consumed in situ or it was changed again into water! At La Brigue, miraculous spring waters thus become a metaphor for the purification achieved through pilgrimage, reminiscent of the beautiful lines Alphonse Dupront wrote about the 'chthonic implantation' of pilgrimage sites.[56] Although an isolated building, four kilometres from the town of La Brigue, Notre-Dame des Fontaines lies at the crossroads of 'routes muletières' (mule paths), linking La Brigue to villages that depended from it and allowing traffic between the county of Nice and Piedmont and to Provence and Lombardy,[57] but the truly defining features are the springs,[58] which give the sanctuary its name, the Madonna of the Fountains, in French *Notre-Dame des Fontaines* and in Italian *Madonna del Fontan* or *del Sorgente*.

These reflections on the experience of the pilgrim visiting the votive chapel erected at the miraculous springs bring us inevitably back to Peter's three tears. I am struck by the fact that as the apostle, his heart pricked by compunction,[59] weeps in contrition, he is alone. In contrast to the other repenting characters at

Notre-Dame, he does not communicate with Christ or with other figures (as does, for instance, Judas when he returns the thirty pieces of silver to the priests; Figures 1 and 7). Only later, his penance fulfilled and his sin purged by his tears, will he be seen again among the apostles in heaven (Figure 14). Nagy explains that the development of weeping as a private ritual establishing a direct contact with God somehow circumvented 'the social, the Church, and the community'.[60] The same can be said of the function of Peter's tears at Notre-Dame: we see him redeeming himself (and earning Paradise) by his tears alone. He does not need Christ to voice forgiveness, as in the case of Dismas, for instance, who makes a public statement and gets an answer from Jesus, promising him to be in paradise with him that very day.[61]

Not only is Peter alone when he weeps, but at this very moment the outcome of his contrition, of whether his tears will prove efficacious in purging his sin, is still unclear. Will he despair like Judas and damn himself? That denial can lead to despair and to damnation is forcefully expressed in Notre-Dame des Fontaines' Last Judgment, where, as already mentioned, the section reserved to *ira* (wrath) contains sinners who have despaired and denied (Figure 16). This uncertainty might be the reason why in early representations of Peter Weeping, the apostle very often appears seated, resting his cheek on his hand, in the pose of the melancholic.[62] Not surprisingly, Alexander Murray highlights the link between melancholy and suicide.[63] At Notre-Dame des Fontaines, though, Peter does not sit like a melancholic figure but is rather in motion and sheds his tears in an expressive manner (Figures 1 and 2). In their introduction, Charlotte Steenbrugge and Graham Williams ponder the role of facial expressions in the social and artistic performance and depiction of compunction. We can wonder with them whether compunction generates 'an independent facial expression distinguishable from other forms of sadness' – in other words, is it a specific emotion? – and, more specifically for us, what exact 'inward feeling' does the apostle's face reflect at this particular moment?[64] One detail might help us consider this question: as the apostle sheds his three tears and wipes his face with the white cloth, his mouth is open and shows his upper teeth (Figure 2). The baring of teeth is a detail that Ruth Mellinkoff includes among the distortions and deformities that signal the evil character of Christ's enemies, their animal-like savagery and 'barbaric cruelty'.[65] At La Brigue, we see indeed many evil figures – far too many to list here![66] – adopting such a facial expression. It is remarkable, though, that a few of the 'good' figures as well show their teeth. That is the case for Christ when he gives up the ghost at the Crucifixion and for Mary in the Descent of the Cross: moments of physical and emotional agony.[67] Not surprisingly then, the motif, as an expression of intense distress, is found again in the Last Judgment (Figures 14 and 15).

Without being able to pinpoint what exactly Peter feels as he experiences compunction, we can agree that the detail of his open mouth with visible teeth contributes to strengthening the intensity – if not the violence[68] – of his emotions at this crucial moment, one in which the apostle is suspended between sin and atonement, indeed, 'betwixt and between' two states, to borrow the phrase Victor Turner used to refer to liminal phenomena, among which is the practice of pilgrimage.[69] A universal phenomenon that appears in all religions, pilgrimage is nothing but travel undertaken with the goal of transformation, be it the expiation of sins or the curing of illness. Turner studied the practice by developing the ideas first expounded by Arnold van Gennep in his study of rites of passage.[70] Such rituals, which occur at times of change and transition, are composed of a succession of three stages: a preliminary one, characterized by rites of separation; a transitional one in which the subject is suspended in a liminal state; and finally a postliminary stage in which rites of aggregation or incorporation take place.[71] Turner chose to focus on the central moment in Gennep's rites of passage and noted that 'liminality is not only *transition* but also *potentiality*'.[72] For the pilgrim and/or the penitent, Peter's example shows that Christ's forgiveness is *possible* and that, unlike Judas, he should not despair.

Gennep noted that a 'territorial passage' is part and parcel of rites of passage, a physical movement that translates the idea that one exits a former world to enter into a new one.[73] Liminal, the name Gennep chose for the rites' central moment, is rooted in the Latin word for 'threshold' (*limen*), for indeed the zone through which one transits as one changes status could be 'a simple stone, a beam, or a threshold'.[74] Gennep further elaborates that it is not just the threshold but the entire door or gate that becomes charged with efficacious meaning.[75] Such an architectural feature simultaneously marks the leaving behind of an old status (through rites of separation) and the reintegration into society (through rites of aggregation). At La Brigue, we see Peter shedding his tears as he steps out of an arched gateway, caught in the transformative moment of his weeping.[76] Gennep talks about the importance – and the recurrence – of the motif of the 'passage sous un portique' (passage under a portal) sometimes to be understood in a symbolic manner, but more often than not, involving an actual archway.[77] Canavesio's depiction of Peter exiting the building where the sin took place, although grounded in the Gospel text (but rare enough to be remarkable), echoes what Corinne Denoyelle, drawing on Vladimir Jankélévitch, writes in this volume, how remorse without repentance is equal to confinement.⁷⁸ Is it then a coincidence, that after Judas remorsefully returns the silver coins, he heads towards an enclosed space that is accessed through an arched entryway (Figure 7)?

Thus the three tears Peter sheds at Notre-Dame des Fontaines not only represent each of his sinful denials; they also mark the salvific nature of this moment, their number recalling the tripartite structure of the rites of passage and of the sacrament of penance.⁷⁹ Within the remarkable and innovative narrative structure of Canavesio's frescoes at La Brigue, Peter's three tears, caused by compunction, constitute a wordless confession of his sin that achieves satisfaction and earns the apostle access to Heaven.

Figure 1 Giovanni Canavesio, Denial of Peter, 1492, Notre-Dame des Fontaines, La Brigue (Photo: author).

Figure 2 Giovanni Canavesio, Denial of Peter (detail), Notre-Dame des Fontaines, La Brigue (Photo: author).

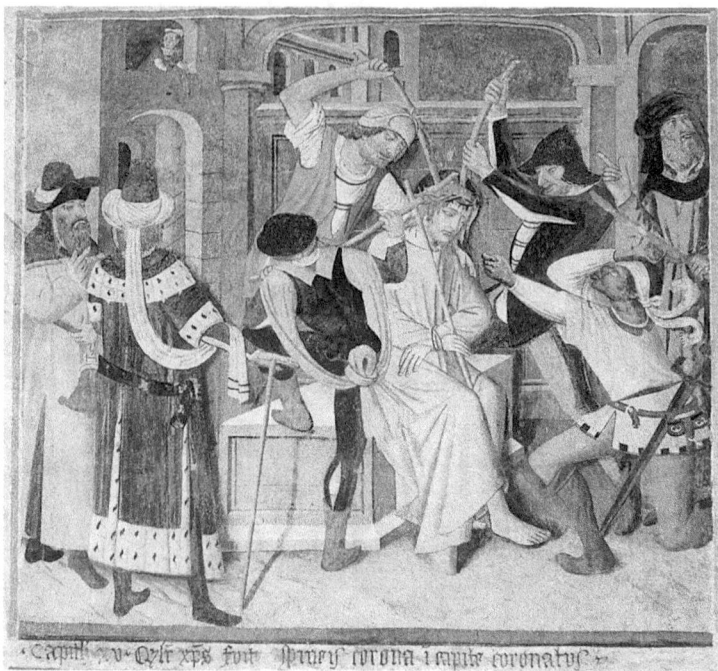

Figure 3 Giovanni Canavesio, Crowning with Thorns, 1492, Notre-Dame des Fontaines, La Brigue (Photo: author).

Figure 4 Giovanni Canavesio, Mocking of Christ, 1492, Notre-Dame des Fontaines, La Brigue (Photo: author).

Figure 5 Mocking of Christ, 1472, chapel of San Fiorenzo, Bastia Mondovì (Photo: author).

Figure 6 Giovanni Canavesio, Christ before Caiaphas, after 1492, chapel of Notre-Dame des Douleurs des Pénitents Blancs, Peillon (Photo: author).

Figure 7 Giovanni Canavesio, Remorse of Judas, 1492, Notre-Dame des Fontaines, La Brigue (Photo: author).

Figure 8 Giovanni Canavesio, Pact of Judas, 1492, Notre-Dame des Fontaines, La Brigue (Photo: author).

Figure 9 Giovanni Canavesio, Suicide of Judas, 1492, Notre-Dame des Fontaines, La Brigue (Photo: author).

Figure 10 Giovanni Canavesio, Christ Washing the Feet of the Apostles, 1492, Notre-Dame des Fontaines, La Brigue (Photo: author).

Figure 11 Giovanni Canavesio, Descent into Limbo, 1492, Notre-Dame des Fontaines, La Brigue (Photo: author).

Figure 12 Giovanni Canavesio, Crucifixion, 1492, Notre-Dame des Fontaines, La Brigue (Photo: author).

Figure 13 Giovanni Canavesio, Christ Washing the Feet of the Apostles (upper register) and Denial of Peter (lower register), 1492, Notre-Dame des Fontaines, La Brigue (Photo: author).

164 Cultures of Compunction in the Medieval World

Figure 14 Giovanni Canavesio, Last Judgment, 1492, west wall, Notre-Dame des Fontaines, La Brigue (Photo: author).

Figure 15 Giovanni Canavesio, Last Judgment, detail: traitors and despairers, 1492, west wall, Notre-Dame des Fontaines, La Brigue (Photo: author).

Figure 16 Arches and springs below the sanctuary of Notre-Dame des Fontaines, La Brigue (Photo: author).

Notes

Introduction

1. Charlotte Steenbrugge, *Drama and Sermon in Late Medieval England: Performance, Authority, Devotion* (Kalamazoo: Medieval Institute Publications, 2017), esp. Chapter 6.
2. Graham Williams, *Sincerity in Medieval English Language and Literature* (London: Palgrave, 2018), esp. Chapter 4.
3. Most notably Sandra McEntire, *The Doctrine of Compunction in Medieval England: Holy Tears* (Lewiston, NY: Edwin Mellen Press, 1991).
4. Sarah McNamer, *Affective Meditation and the Invention of Medieval Compassion* (Philadelphia: University of Pennsylvania Press, 2010); Anne McTaggart (now Schuurman), *Shame and Guilt in Chaucer* (Basingstoke: Palgrave, 2012).
5. Peter Biller and Alastair J. Minnis, *Handling Sin: Confession in the Middle Ages* (York: York Medieval Press, 1998); Rob Meens, *Penance in Europe, 600–1200* (Cambridge: Cambridge University Press, 2014).
6. William M. Reddy, *The Making of Romantic Love: Longing and Sexuality in Europe, South Asia and Japan, 900–1200 CE* (Chicago and London: University of Chicago Press, 2012); McNamer, *Affective Meditation*.
7. Ibid.
8. For a hearty academic response to this phenomenon, see Deirdre N. McCloskey, *The Bourgeois Virtues: Ethics for an Age of Commerce* (Chicago: University of Chicago Press, 2006).
9. Angela Jane Weisl, 'Confession, Contrition, and the Rhetoric of Tears: Medievalism and Reality Television', in *Medieval Afterlives in Popular Culture*, ed. G. Ashton and D. T. Kline (New York: Palgrave, 2012), p. 140.
10. The opening sentence of L. P. Hartley's *The Go-Between* (London: Hamish Hamilton, 1953).
11. P. Ekman and W. V. Friesen, *Unmasking the Face: A Guide to Recognizing Emotions from Facial Clues* (Englewood Cliffs, NJ: Prentice-Hall, 1975); cf. C. E. Izard, *Human Emotions* (New York: Springer, 1977).
12. Margery Kempe, *The Book of Margery Kempe*, ed. Sanford Brown Meech (London: Early English Text Society, 1997), Prologue, p. 2.
13. Ibid., Chapter 14, p. 31.

14 However, cf. Anna Wierzbicka, *Imprisoned in English: The Hazards of English as a Default Language* (Oxford, 2013), Chapter 7, for an important discussion of Anglocentricism in the vocabulary used in emotion studies.
15 Ralph B. Hupka, Alison P. Lenton and Keith A. Hutchison, 'Universal Development of Emotion Categories in Natural Language', *Journal of Personality and Social Psychology* 77, no. 2 (1999), p.259.
16 *The Oxford Dictionary of the Christian Church*, ed. F. L. Cross and E. A. Livingstone (Oxford, 1983), pp. 341–2.
17 The textbase forms part of the database associated with the *Anglo-Norman Dictionary* (AND). Available at http://www.anglo-norman.net/gate/ (accessed 20 November 2019).
18 The text here is taken from the *Corpus of Middle English Prose and Verse* (CMEPV). Available at https://quod.lib.umich.edu/c/cme/ (accessed 20 November 2019).
19 All Chaucer citations are from *The Riverside Chaucer*, ed. Larry D. Benson (Oxford, 1988).
20 Woodburn O. Ross, ed., *Middle English Sermons, Edited from British Museum MS. Royal 18 B. xxiii* (London, 1940), p. 141.
21 Ibid., p. 105.
22 Stephen Morrison, ed., *A Late Fifteenth-century Dominical Sermon Cycle, Edited from Bodleian Library MS E Museo 180 and Other Manuscripts*, 2 vols (Oxford: 2012 for 2011), p. 102.
23 See the explanatory notes from the *Riverside Chaucer*.
24 Ralph Hanna and Sarah Wood, eds., *Richard Morris's Prick of Conscience: A Corrected and Amplified Reading Text* (Oxford, 2013).
25 Nicholas Love, *The Mirror of the Blessed Life of Jesus Christ: A Reading Text*, ed. M. G. Sargent (Exeter, 2004). See Sargent's introduction for fuller contextualization of this significant text.
26 OED online.
27 Mark Davies, *The TV Corpus: 325 Million Words, 1950–2018*. Available at https://www.english-corpora.org/tv/ (accessed 20 November 2019).
28 Mark Davies, *The 14 Billion Word iWeb Corpus*. Available at https://www.english-corpora.org/iWeb/ (accessed 20 November 2019).

Chapter 1

1 The period of fasting before Easter is called 'Great Lent' to distinguish it from other Lenten seasons in the Byzantine liturgical calendar. For example, the period before the Nativity of Christ is a Lenten season.
2 Κατάνυξις is the Greek word for compunction in Byzantium. See G. W. H. Lampe, *Patristic Greek Lexicon* (Oxford: Clarendon Press, 1961), p. 713. The Greek

word is not found in any writings from antiquity but makes its first appearance in the Septuagint. See, for example, Isaiah 29:10 or Psalm 59:5. On the biblical understanding of compunction and its transformation into a Christian concept, see Marguerite Harl, 'Les Origines Grecques du Mot et de la Notion de Componction dans la Septante et chez ses Commentateurs', *Revue des Études Augustiniennes* 32 (1986), pp. 3–21. On compunction as a liturgical emotion, see Andrew Mellas, *Liturgy and the Emotions in Byzantium: Compunction and Hymnody* (Cambridge: Cambridge University Press, 2020).

3   An earlier form of Byzantine hymnography, a *kontakion* is a chanted sermon that celebrated a major feast or commemorated a saint. It comprises a prelude, a number of stanzas and a recurring refrain, which was repeated by the congregation. See Elizabeth M. Jeffreys, 'Kontakion', in *ODB*, 1148.

4   Dionysius the Areopagite, *The Celestial Hierarchy* 1.3. The Greek text is from Günter Heil and Adolf Martin Ritter, eds., *Corpus Dionysiacum II: Pseudo-Dionysius Areopagita. De Coelesti Hierarchia, De Ecclesiastica Hierarchia, De Mystica Theologia, Epistulae*, Patristische Texte Und Studien (Berlin: De Gruyter, 2012), p. 9. The English translation is my own.

5   Dionysius the Areopagite, *Ecclesiastical Hierarchy* 1.5, ibid., 84. See also Andrew of Crete's homily *On the Palms*, which describes how the earthborn sing with the Seraphim and the heavenly chorus so that the faithful might dance with the angels. PG 97, 996D–997A.

6   In the works of the early Church Fathers and in the Byzantine tradition, the spiritual pedagogy of the faithful, their initiation into divine mysteries, was often described as 'mystagogy'. See Paul van Geest, 'Studying the Mystagogy of the Fathers: An Introduction', in *Seeing through the Eyes of Faith: New Approaches to the Mystagogy of the Church Fathers*, ed. Paul van Geest (Leuven: Peeters, 2016), pp. 3–22.

7   *Homily on the Apostolic Saying That States: But Know This, That in the Last Days Perilous Times Will Come*, chapter 6. PG 56, 277.

8   Cyril of Alexandria, *Commentary on the Gospel of John*, chapter 7 (on John 11:33), PG 74, 53A.

9   Cyril of Alexandria, *The Twelve Chapters*, Anathema 12.

10 For an introduction to the Byzantine liturgy, see Kallistos Ware, 'The Meaning of the Divine Liturgy for the Byzantine Worshipper', in *Church and People in Byzantium*, ed. Rosemary Morris (Birmingham: Centre for Byzantine, Ottoman and Modern Greek Studies, University of Birmingham, 1990), pp. 7–28; Robert F. Taft, *Through Their Own Eyes: Liturgy as the Byzantines Saw It* (Berkeley: InterOrthodox Press, 2006).

11 Sarah McNamer, 'The Literariness of Literature and the History of Emotion', *PMLA* 130, no. 5 (2015), p. 1436.

12　The notion of affective and intimate scripts (though not in a Byzantine context) is canvassed in McNamer, *Affective Meditation and the Invention of Medieval Compassion* (Philadelphia: University of Pennsylvania Press, 2010), pp. 1–21.
13　See William M. Reddy, *The Navigation of Feeling: A Framework for the History of Emotions* (Cambridge: Cambridge University Press, 2001), pp. 173–210.
14　Oliver J. T. Harris and Tim Flohr Sørensen, 'Rethinking Emotion and Material Culture', *Archaeological Dialogues* 17, no. 2 (2010), pp. 150–1.
15　Pascha is the festival of Easter, though it can also refer to the climactic events in the life of Christ: the Crucifixion, Resurrection and Ascension. See John Behr, *John the Theologian and His Paschal Gospel: A Prologue to Theology* (Oxford: Oxford University Press, 2019), p. ix.
16　The other two Sundays were the Sunday of the Last Judgment (or Meat-Fare Sunday), which was centred on Matthew 25:31–46, and the Sunday of the Exile from Paradise (or Cheese-Fare Sunday), which juxtaposed the tears Adam and Eve wept by the gate of paradise with the hope of redemption. For a more detailed analysis of this liturgical cycle, see Job Getcha, *The Typikon Decoded: An Explanation of Byzantine Liturgical Practice* (Yonkers, NY: St Vladimir's Seminary Press, 2012), pp. 141–232; Kallistos Ware and Mother Mary, *The Lenten Triodion* (Boston: Faber, 1978), pp. 44–64.
17　Juan Mateos, *Le Typicon de la Grande Église: Tome II, Le Cycle des Fêtes Mobiles.* OCA 166 (Rome: Pontificum Institutum Orientalium Studiorum, 1963), p. 2.
18　Sinai Graecus 734–5, fol. 3r. This is also the prelude to a *kontakion* that Romanos the Melodist may have composed but which scholars consider to be dubious. See Paul Maas and C. A. Trypanis, *Sancti Romani Melodi Cantica Dubia* (Berlin: Walter De Gruyter, 1970), p. 181.
19　The English translation is partly my own and partly an unpublished translation by the late Archimandrite Ephrem Lash.
20　Luke 15:17. The Greek text from the Old Testament will be cited from Alfred Rahlfs, *Septuaginta: Id est Vetus Testamentum Graece iuxta LXX Interpretes* (Stuttgart: Privilegierte Württembergische Bibelanstalt, 1935). English translations are based on or follow the translations in Albert Pietersma and Benjamin G. Wright, *A New English Translation of the Septuagint* (New York: Oxford University Press, 2007). The Greek text of the New Testament is *The Greek New Testament*, ed. Barbara Aland, et al. (Stuttgart: Deutsche Bibelgesellschaft, 1994). English translations generally follow the New King James Version in *The Orthodox Study Bible* (Nashville: Thomas Nelson, 2008).
21　See Guy D. Nave, Jr., *The Role and Function of Repentance in Luke-Acts* (Leiden: Brill, 2002).
22　An excellent introduction to the significance of repentance for Eastern Christendom and how the early church fathers interpreted the scriptural meaning

of repentance is Kallistos Ware, 'The Orthodox Experience of Repentance', *Sobornost* 2 (1980), pp. 18–28. For notions of repentance in monastic literature, see Brouria Bitton-Ashkelony, 'Penitence in Late Antique Monastic Literature', in *Transformations of the Inner Self in Ancient Religions*, ed. Jan Assmann and Guy G. Stroumsa (Leiden: Brill, 1999), pp. 179–94.

23 Alexis Torrance, *Repentance in Late Antiquity: Eastern Asceticism and the Framing of the Christian Life* (Oxford: Oxford University Press, 2012), p. 2.
24 Lampe, *Patristic Greek Lexicon*, pp. 855–8.
25 Torrance, *Repentance in Late Antiquity*, p. 9.
26 Sinai Graecus 734–5, fol. 5v.
27 The English translation is by Ephrem Lash (unpublished).
28 A *kanon* is a set of eight or nine odes that rose to prominence as a popular form of Byzantine hymnography. These odes were sung during the office of matins.
29 On the authorship, text and context of this *kanon*, see Derek Krueger, 'Authorial Voice and Self-presentation in a 9th-century Hymn on the Prodigal Son', in *The Author in Middle Byzantine Literature: Modes, Functions, and Identities*, ed. Aglae Pizzone (Berlin: De Gruyter, 2014), pp. 105–18.
30 Psalm 4:5.
31 Brian Daley, 'Finding the Right Key: The Aims and Strategies of Early Christian Interpretation of the Psalms', in *Psalms in Community*, ed. Attridge and Fassler, p. 189.
32 After Peter's homily leaves the crowd '"feeling compunction in the heart" (κατενύγησαν τὴν καρδίαν)', the Apostle calls on his listeners to '"repent" (μετανοήσατε)'.
33 On Origen and Gregory of Nyssa, see Ilaria Ramelli, 'Tears of Pathos, Repentance and Bliss: Crying and Salvation in Origen and Gregory of Nyssa', in *Tears in the Graeco-Roman World*, ed. Thorsten Fögen (Berlin: De Gruyter), pp. 367–96. For Chrysostom see Francis Leduc, 'Penthos et Larmes dans l'œuvre de Saint Jean Chrysostome', *Proche-Orient Chrétien* 41 (1991), pp. 220–57; Laurence Brottier, *Propos sur la Contrition de Jean Chrysostome: Le Destin d'Écrits de Jeunesse Méconnus* (Paris: Éditions du Cerf, 2010).
34 See the exploration of his *Homily on the Sinful Woman* (an exegesis of Luke 7:36–50) in Hannah Hunt, 'The Tears of the Sinful Woman: A Theology of Redemption in the Homilies of St. Ephraim and His Followers', *Hugoye: Journal of Syriac Studies* 1, no. 2 (1998), pp. 165–84.
35 Kallistos Ware, '"An Obscure Matter": The Mystery of Tears in Orthodox Spirituality', in *Holy Tears: Weeping in the Religious Imagination*, ed. Kimberley Christine Patton and John Stratton Hawley (Princeton: Princeton University Press, 2005), pp. 242–54.
36 *To Demetrius*, chapter 7. See PG 47, 404 and John Chrysostom, *A Companion for the Sincere Penitent: Or, a Treatise on the Compunction of the Heart. In Two Books*, trans. John Veneer (London: Judge's-Head, St. Dunstan's Church, 1728), p. 35.

37 'Now it's especially a time for tears and compunction, and for a prepared soul and much zeal and much firmness of purpose', *On the Statues*, homily 17, *John Chrysostom*, trans. Wendy Mayer and Pauline Allen (New York: Routledge, 2000), p. 106. See also *Homilies on the Gospel of St Matthew*, homily 55 on Matthew 16: 24: 'And after this hymn, being filled with much compunction, and with many and fervent tears, so they proceed to sleep, snatching just so much of it as a little to refresh themselves.' St John Chrysostom, *The Homilies of S. John Chrysostom, Archbishop of Constantinople, on the Gospel of St. Matthew, Translated with Notes and Indices. Part 2. Hom. 26–58* (Oxford: John Henry Parker, 1844, p. 754). And *Homilies on the Epistles of Paul to the Corinthians*, homily 7 on 1 Corinthians 2: 6, 7: 'For their call was from fornication unto chastity; from love of life unto sundry kinds of death; from drunkenness unto fasting; from laughter unto tears and compunction', John Chrysostom, *Saint Chrysostom: Homilies on the Epistles of Paul to the Corinthians*, trans. Philip Schaff (New York: Christian Literature Company, 1899), p. 74.

38 See, for example, letters 343 and 461 in *Barsanuphius and John: Letters*, trans. Chryssavgis, vol. 1 (Washington, DC: Catholic University of America Press, 2006), pp. 314; *Letters*, vol. 2, 75. The Greek text is in *Barsanuphe et Jean de Gaza: Correspondance*, ed. François Neyt and Paula de Angelis-Noah. SC 450–51 (Paris: Éditions du Cerf, 2000–2).

39 See Hannah Hunt, 'The Monk as Mourner: St. Isaac the Syrian & Monastic Identity in the 7th C. & Beyond', in *Orthodox Monasticism Past and Present*, ed. John A. McGuckin (Piscataway, NJ: Gorgias Press, 2015), pp. 331–42.

40 *On the Consecration of Hagia Sophia*, strophe 16, in Constantine Trypanis, *Fourteen Early Byzantine Cantica* (Vienna: Böhlau in Kommission, 1968), p. 146. The English translation is my own.

41 *On the Prodigal* was a '"compunctious *kontakion*" (κοντάκιον κατανυκτικόν)' that was chanted either during the Second Sunday of Great Lent – according to the Patmiacus 213 manuscript – or on the first of the three preparatory Sundays preceding Lent – according to the Athous Vatopedinus 1041 manuscript. As I have not examined Athous Vatopedinus 1041, it is worth noting that whereas Grosdidier de Matons indicates that this manuscript assigns the hymn to 'the Sunday of the Prodigal Son' (which he equates with the first of the three preparatory Sundays before Lent), Lash and Krueger suggest that this manuscript makes no assignment. See Romanos le Mélode, *Hymnes. Tome III: Nouveau Testament*, ed. Grosdidier de Matons. SC 114 (Paris: Éditions du Cerf, 1965), p. 235; *On the Life of Christ: Chanted Sermons by the Great Sixth-Century Poet and Singer St. Romanos*, trans. Ephrem Lash (Lanham, MD: AltaMira Press, 1998), p. 100; Derek Krueger, *Liturgical Subjects: Christian Ritual, Biblical Narrative and the Formation of Self in Byzantium* (Philadelphia: University of Pennsylvania Press, 2014), p. 177. For the

Greek text of the hymn, see Romanos le Mélode, *Hymnes. Tome III*, 234–60. For the English translation, see Lash, *On the Life of Christ*, 101–11.

42 For an analysis of the biographical sources available on Romanos, see José Grosdidier de Matons, *Romanos le Mélode et les Origines de la Poésie Religieuse à Byzance* (Paris: Beauchesne, 1977), pp. 159–98.

43 'The Liturgical Place of the Kontakion in Constantinople', 53. The crusade did not simply ransack the city; it devastated the Byzantine Empire. The Latin conquest ushered in a period of decline and decadence, ending Byzantium's reign as a political and economic superpower. See Steven Runciman, *The Last Byzantine Renaissance* (Cambridge: Cambridge University Press, 1970), pp. 1–23.

44 Frank, 'Romanos and the Night Vigil in the Sixth Century', 63.

45 These details appear at the beginning of each *kontakion* in Grosdidier de Matons's multi-volume critical edition of Romanos's hymns.

46 This chapter alludes to how Byzantine hymnody approached this biblical narrative. For Middle English evocations of this Gospel story, see the chapter by Ayoush Lazikani in this volume.

47 See Taft, *Through Their Own Eyes*, pp. 148–54; Catherine Brown Tkacz, 'Singing Women's Words as Sacramental Mimesis', *Recherches de Théologie et Philosophie Médiévales* 70, no. 2 (2003), pp. 275–328; Derek Krueger, 'Romanos the Melodist and the Early Christian Self', in *Proceedings of the 21st International Congress of Byzantine Studies: London, 21–26 August 2006*, ed. Elizabeth Jeffreys (Aldershot: Ashgate, 2006), pp. 255–74.

48 On the intersubjective dimension of Byzantine worship in sixth-century Constantinople, see Nadine Schibille, *Hagia Sophia and the Byzantine Aesthetic Experience* (Farnham: Ashgate, 2014), pp. 32–7. *and the Byzantine Aesthetic Experience*, 32–7.

49 Getcha, *The Typikon Decoded*, p. 189.

50 Mateos, *Le Typicon de la Grande Église: Tome II*, p. 30. Instead, the passage from Mark 2:1–12 (the healing of the paralytic) is prescribed. It is only the Hagiopolite tradition and its lectionaries emerging from Jerusalem that assigns this passage to the Second Sunday of Great Lent. See Getcha, *The Typikon Decoded*, p. 146.

51 Mateos, *Le Typicon de la Grande Église: Tome II*, p. 2.

52 See Sinai Graecus 734–5, fol. 3 r–v, and Vaticanus Graecus 771, fol. 9 r–v.

53 Romanos le Mélode, *Hymnes. Tome III*, p. 234.

54 Luke 15:17.

55 Prelude 2, Romanos le Mélode, *Hymnes. Tome III*, p. 234.

56 Prelude 1, ibid.

57 The English translation is my own.

58 Prelude 2, line 1, ibid., p. 77; Romanos le Mélode, *Hymnes. Tome III*, p. 20.

59 Strophe 4, *Hymnes. Tome III*, p. 26.

60 The English translation is my own.
61 See Sinai Graecus 734-5, fol. 159r-v; the eleventh-century Vaticanus Graecus 771, fol. 162v; and the late eleventh-, early twelfth-century Grottaferrata Δβ I, fol. 161r. On Kassia, see Anna M. Silvas, 'Kassia the Nun c. 810-c. 865: An Appreciation', in *Byzantine Women: Varieties of Experience AD 800-1200*, ed. Lynda Garland (Aldershot: Ashgate, 2006), p. 17.
62 Romanos le Mélode, *Hymnes. Tome III*, p. 236; Lash, *On the Life of Christ*, pp. 101-2.
63 Strophe 4, Romanos le Mélode, *Hymnes. Tome III*, p. 238; Lash, *On the Life of Christ*, p. 103.
64 Genesis 3:21. Indeed, as noted in the previous section, the worshipping faithful heard passages from Genesis during Lenten vespers, so the narrative of the exile from Eden was a recurring theme during Great Lent.
65 Galatians 3:27.
66 Romanos intimates in the first strophe that the father of the prodigal son is 'the Father of all humankind'. Lash, *On the Life of Christ*, p. 101.
67 Strophe 5, Romanos le Mélode, *Hymnes. Tome III*, p. 240.
68 The English translation is my own. The phrase 'my divine image' is a clear allusion to Genesis 1:26.
69 Strophe 8, Romanos le Mélode, *Hymnes. Tome III*, p. 244.
70 The English translation is my own.
71 For an exploration of how Romanos's *On the Prodigal* imagined the Eucharist and invited the faithful to taste the bliss of the repentant son, see Bissera V. Pentcheva, *Hagia Sophia. Sound, Space and Spirit in Byzantium* (Pennsylvania: Pennsylvania State University Press, 2017), pp. 166-9.
72 Strophe 9, Romanos le Mélode, *Hymnes. Tome III*, p. 246; Lash, *On the Life of Christ*, p. 105. The word 'ἔδεσμα' literally means 'meat' but I have decided not to alter Lash's translation.
73 Strophe 10, Romanos le Mélode, *Hymnes. Tome III*, p. 246.
74 The English translation is my own. 'Taste and see that the Lord is good' (Psalm 33:9) is arguably the earliest communion hymn of the Byzantine liturgy. See Dimitri E. Conomos, *The Late Byzantine and Slavonic Communion Cycle: Liturgy and Music* (Washington, DC: Dumbarton Oaks, 1985), pp. 6-16.
75 Strophe 10, Romanos le Mélode, *Hymnes. Tome III*, p. 246.
76 Lash, *On the Life of Christ*, p. 106.
77 Strophe 22, ibid., p. 111.
78 Strophe 21, Romanos le Mélode, *Hymnes. Tome III*, p. 258; Lash, *On the Life of Christ*, p. 110.
79 Alexander Lingas, 'From Earth to Heaven: The Changing Musical Soundscape of the Byzantine Liturgy', in *Experiencing Byzantium: Papers from the 44th Spring*

Symposium of Byzantine Studies, Newcastle and Durham, April 2011, ed. Claire Nesbitt and Mark Jackson (Farnham: Ashgate, 2013), p. 315.

80 Carol Harrison, 'Enchanting the Soul: The Music of the Psalms', in *Meditations of the Heart: The Psalms in Early Christian Thought and Practice. Essays in Honour of Andrew Louth*, ed. Andreas Andreopoulos, Augustine Casiday, and Carol Harrison (Turnhout: Brepols, 2011), pp. 205–24; Amy Papalexandrou, 'Perceptions of Sound and Sonic Environment across the Byzantine Acoustic Horizon', in *Knowing Bodies, Passionate Souls: Sense Perceptions in Byzantium*, ed. Susan Ashbrook Harvey and Margaret Mullett (Washington, DC: Dumbarton Oaks Research Library and Collection, 2017), pp. 67–85; Bissera V. Pentcheva, ed., *Aural Architecture in Byzantium: Music, Acoustics, and Ritual* (New York: Routledge, 2017).

81 Carol Harrison, 'Augustine and the Art of Music', in *Resonant Witness: Conversations between Music and Theology*, ed. Jeremy S. Begbie and Steven R. Guthrie (Grand Rapids, MI: Eerdmans, 2011), p. 31. On the possible influence of Augustine in Byzantium, see Aristotle Papanikolaou and George E. Demacopoulos, 'Augustine and the Orthodox: The "West" in the East', in *Orthodox Readings of Augustine*, ed. Aristotle Papanikolaou and George E. Demacopoulos (Crestwood, NY: St Vladimir's Seminary Press, 2008), pp. 11–40.

82 Augustine expressed this view on sacred chant moving the soul and eliciting devotion in *Confessions* 10.33.49, which is quoted in Harrison, 'Augustine and the Art of Music', p. 42.

83 See Johannes Quasten, *Music and Worship in Pagan and Christian Antiquity*, trans. Ramsay Boniface (Washington, DC: National Association of Pastoral Musicians, 1983), pp. 35–9, 137–9; Lukas Richter, 'Antike Überlieferungen in der Byzantinischen Musiktheorie', *Acta Musicologica* 70, no. 2 (1998), pp. 133–208; Alexander Lingas, 'Music', in *Encyclopedia of Ancient Greece*, ed. Nigel Wilson (New York: Routledge, 2010), p. 485. Aristotle's view of music as an ethical force that embodied emotion in sound and rhythm is reflected in the writings of the Cappadocian Fathers on music. See the relevant catalogue of texts in James McKinnon, ed., *Music in Early Christian Literature* (Cambridge: Cambridge University Press, 1987), pp. 64–74. See also the Platonic resonance in Gregory of Nyssa's *On the Inscriptions of the Psalms* 1.3 in Ronald E. Heine, ed., *Gregory of Nyssa's Treatise on the Inscriptions of the Psalms* (Oxford: Oxford University Press, 1995), pp. 88–92. On a theoretical level, Aristides Quintilianus states, '[T]he ancients saw that we do not turn to singing for a single reason, rather some sing in contentment accompanying pleasure, others in vexation accompanying pain, and still others sing occupied by divine impulse and inspiration accompanying divine suffusion; or even when these are mixed one with another by certain chances and circumstances, or when children, because of their age, or even those advanced in age, because of weakness of nature, are led on by such passions.' Thomas J.

Mathiesen, ed. *Aristides Quintilianus: On Music, In Three Books* (New Haven and London: Yale University Press, 1983), p. 120. Bryennius also explored the relationship between melody and feeling. See G. H. Jonker, ed. *The Harmonics of Manuel Bryennius* (Netherlands: Gröningen, 1970), pp. 123, 365.

84 PG 37, p. 1332.
85 The English translation is my own.
86 *Letter to Marcellinus on the Interpretation of the Psalms* 10 in PG 27, 20D. For an English translation of the Greek text, see Athanasius of Alexandria, *The Life of Antony and the Letter to Marcellinus*, trans. Robert C. Gregg (New York: Paulist Press, 1980), pp. 101–30. The English translations that follow are my own but are based on those of Gregg.
87 *Letter to Marcellinus* 11, PG 27, 21C.
88 *Letter to Marcellinus* 12, PG 27, 24BC.
89 First ode, penultimate strophe of the Great Kanon by Andrew of Crete in Sinai Graecus 734–5, fol. 70r.
90 Jerome Neu, *A Tear Is an Intellectual Thing: The Meanings of Emotion* (New York: Oxford University Press, 2000), pp. 2, 14–40.
91 Isaac the Syrian, *Discourses* 2, 'Concerning Renunciation of the World'. Quoted in Archbishop Stylianos Harkianakis, *On Prayer* (Athens: Armos, 1999), p. 96.
92 John Klimakos, *Ladder of Divine Ascent*, chapter 7, PG 88, 812A. The English translation is my own.
93 Isaac the Syrian, *Homilies* 35 [37] and 14. Quoted in Ware, '"An Obscure Matter": The Mystery of Tears in Orthodox Spirituality', in *Holy Tears*, ed. Patton and Hawley, p. 250.

Chapter 2

1 British National Corpus XML Edition (BNC) (Oxford, 2007). Available at http://www.natcorp.ox.ac.uk/corpus/index.xml (accessed 15 November 2018).
2 The wpm (word per million) count is conventionally used to measure token frequency in a corpus or subcorpus and indicates how many occurrences on average of the search term can be found per 1 million tokens.
3 The wildcard search would include such variants as *remorseful*, *remorse*, but also *remorseless*.
4 Similarly, *regret*, *regretful*, *regrets*, *regretting*.
5 BNC: EFV 1492.
6 BNC: FAB 3278.
7 Latin definitions are either from *Dictionary of Medieval Latin from British Sources* (DMBS) or Lewis-Short, accessed via Logeion. Available at https://logeion.uchicago.edu

(accessed 20 November 2019). *Dictionary of Medieval Latin from British Sources* (Oxford, 2012). Available at http://www.dmlbs.ox.ac.uk/web/welcome.html (accessed 20 November 2019); Lewis, T. Charlton and Charles Short, *A Latin Dictionary, Founded on Andrews' Edition of Freund's Latin Dictionary* (Oxford: Clarendon Press, 1975); Philip Posner, Ethan Della Rocca, and Josh Day, *Logeion* (Chicago, 2018). Available at https://logeion.uchicago.edu (accessed 15 November 2018).

8   *Oxford English Dictionary Online* (OED) (Oxford University Press, 2019). Available at www.oed.com (accessed 30 October 2019). 'contrite, adj. and n., sense 1', Johnson's Dictionary 1755 gives *contrite* as 'bruised, much worn'.

9   Stephen J. Morse, 'Commentary: Reflections on remorse', *Journal of American Academy of Psychiatry Law* 42 (2014), pp. 49–55, 52.

10 OED.

11 Alessia Celeghin, Matteo Diano, Arianna Bagnis, Marco Viola, and Marco Tamietto, 'Basic emotions in human neuroscience: Neuroimaging and beyond', *Frontiers in Psychology* 8, no. 1432 (2017), pp. 1–13, 2. '[They] emerge from the dynamic interactions of large-scale brain networks […] fear, joy, attention, working memory, and other psychological constructs cannot be mapped to isolated brain regions because no one region is both necessary and sufficient' (Hadas Okon-Singer, Talma Hendler, Luiz Pessoa, and Alexander J. Shackman, 'The Neurobiology of Emotion–Cognition Interactions: Fundamental Questions and Strategies for Future Research', *Frontiers of Human Neuroscience* 9, no. 58 (2015), pp. 1–14, 58).

12 Ibid.

13 For a review, see Daria Izdebska, 'The Curious Case of *TORN*: The Importance of Lexical-semantic Approaches to the Study of Emotions in Old English', in *Anglo-Saxon Emotions: Reading the Heart in Old English Language, Literature and Culture*, ed. A. Jorgensen, F. McCormack, and J. Wilcox (Burlington: Ashgate, 2015), pp. 53–74.

14 Though some of his claims have been debated over the years, Paul Ekman was a pioneer of work on basic emotions and facial expressions. Ekman Paul 'Facial Expression and Emotion', *American Psychologist* 48 (1993), pp. 384–92 or 'Basic emotions', in *The Handbook of Cognition and Emotion*, ed. T. Dalgleish and M. Power (Chichester: John Wiley & Sons, 1999), pp. 45–60.

15 P. Shaver, J. Schwartz, D. Kirson, and C. O'Connor, 'Emotional Knowledge: Further Exploration of a Prototype Approach', in *Emotions in Social Psychology: Essential Readings*, ed. G. Parrott (Philadelphia, PA: Psychology Press, 2001), pp. 26–56.

16 Marcel Zeelenberg, 'Anticipated Regret: A Prospective Emotion about the Future Past', in *The Psychology of Thinking about the Future*, ed. Gabriele Oettingen, A. Timur Sevincer and Peter M. Golliwitzer (London: Guildford Press, 2018), pp. 276–95, 277.

17 Giorgio Coricelli, Raymond J. Dolan, and Angela Sirigu, 'Brain, Emotion and Decision Making: The Paradigmatic Example of Regret', *Trends in Cognitive Sciences* 11, no. 6 (2007), pp. 258–65, 258.

18 Jonathan Culpeper and Michael Haugh, *Pragmatics and the English Language* (Basingstoke: Red Globe Press, 2003), p. 176.
19 Dominika Baran, *Language in Immigrant America* (Cambridge: Cambridge University Press, 2017), p. 287.
20 See ibid. and also Mary Besemeres, 'Language and Emotional Experience. The Voice of Translingual Memoir', in *Bilingual Minds: Emotional Experience, Expression and Representation*, ed. A. Pavlenko (Clevedon: Multilingual Matters, 2006), pp. 34–58, in particular on pp. 41–4, and 'Between żal and *Emotional Blackmail*: Ways of Being in Polish and English', in *Translating Lives: Living with Two Languages and Cultures*, ed. M. Besemeres and A. Wierzbicka (St Lucia, Queensland, University of Queensland Press, 2007), pp. 128–38.
21 Graham Williams, *Sincerity in Medieval English Language and Literature*. New Approaches to English Historical Linguistics (London: Palgrave Macmillan, 2018).
22 Thomas Kohnen, 'Anglo-Saxon Expressives: Automatic Historical Speech-act Analysis and Philological Intervention', *Anglistik: International Journal of English Studies* 28, no. 1 (March 2017), pp. 43–56, 54.
23 Ibid.
24 Fulkerson, Laurel, *No Regrets: Remorse in Classical Antiquity* (Oxford: Oxford University Press, 2013), p. 6.
25 Ibid., p. 213.
26 Eric Gerald Stanley, 'Did the Anglo-Saxons Have a Social Conscience Like Us?' *Anglia. Journal of English Philology* 121, no. 2 (2003), pp. 238–64.
27 Rafael J. Pascual, 'Material Monsters and Semantic Shifts', in *The Dating of Beowulf. A Reassessment*, ed. L. Neidorf (Woodbridge: D.S. Brewer, 2014), pp. 202–18, 201.
28 *The Historical Thesaurus of English* (HTE), version 4.21. 2017. (Glasgow, 2017). Available at http://historicalthesaurus.arts.gla.ac.uk/ (accessed 30 October 2018).
29 The mapping of senses for specific words as either central/core or relegated to the fuzzy boundary or alternatively words in a category follows the prototype theory from cognitive semantics, which was first introduced in cognitive psychology by Eleanor Rosch. For a general overview of prototype theory see Dirk Geeraerts, *Theories of Lexical Semantics* (Oxford, 2009), pp. 183–202.
30 Simon Nicholson, 'The Expression of Emotional Distress in Old English Prose and Verse', *Culture, Medicine and Psychiatry* 19, no. 3 (1995), pp. 327–38.
31 Sandra J. McEntire, *The Doctrine of Compunction in Medieval England: Holy Tears* (Lewiston: E. Mellen Press, 1990).
32 Ibid., p. 11.
33 Ibid., pp. 22–3.
34 Tracey-Anne Cooper, 'Chapter 9: The Shedding of Tears in Late Anglo-Saxon England', in *Crying in the Middle Ages: Tears of History*, ed. E. Gertsman (New York: Routledge, 2012), pp. 175–92.

35 McEntire, *The Doctrine of Compunction in Medieval England*, pp. 89–90.
36 Frances McCormack, 'Those Bloody Trees: The Affectivity of *Christ*', in *Anglo-Saxon Emotions: Reading the Heart in Old English Language, Literature and Culture*, ed. A. Jorgensen, F. McCormack, and J. Wilcox (Burlington: Ashgate, 2015), pp. 143–61.
37 See McCormack, 'Those Bloody Trees', Cooper, 'Chapter 9: The Shedding of Tears in Late Anglo-Saxon England', and James. M. Palmer, 'Compunction and the Heart in the OE Poem *The Wanderer*', *Neophilologus* 88 (2004), pp. 447–60.
38 McEntire, *The Doctrine of Compunction in Medieval England*, p. 52.
39 Here, particularly, Allan Frantzen, *The Literature of Penance in Anglo-Saxon England* (New Brunswick, NJ: Rutgers University Press, 1983) and 'The Tradition of Penitentials in Anglo-Saxon England', *Anglo-Saxon England* 11 (1982), pp. 23–56, but see also Alice Jorgensen, '"It Shames Me to Say It": Ælfric and the Concept and Vocabulary of Shame', *Anglo-Saxon England* 41 (2012), pp. 249–76, and Helen Foxhall Forbes, 'Affective Piety and the Practice of Penance in Late-eleventh-century Worcester: The Address to the Penitent in Oxford, Bodleian Library, Junius 121', *Anglo-Saxon England* 44 (2015), pp. 309–45, among others.
40 Frantzen, *The Literature of Penance*, pp. 8–9, 116, 117.
41 Frantzen, 'The Tradition of Penitentials', pp. 23–56.
42 *A Thesaurus of Old English* (Glasgow, 2007). Available at http://oldenglishthesaurus.arts.gla.ac.uk/ (accessed 30 October 2018).
43 Though compunction, contrition, repentance and penitence are not equivalent emotions in the analysed material, the term compunction (in small caps) will be used in this chapter as a superordinate conceptual category name to refer to all of these.
44 For more information about the rationale behind these structures, see Marc Alexander and Christian Kay, 'Classification', *About the Historical Thesaurus of English* (Glasgow, 2017). Available at https://ht.ac.uk/classification/ (accessed 30 October 2018) and also Jane Roberts and Christian Kay, *About a Thesaurus of Old English* (Glasgow, 2017). Available at http://oldenglishthesaurus.arts.gla.ac.uk/classification (accessed 30 October 2018).
45 Roberts and Kay, 'Classification'.
46 Izdebska, 'Curious Case', and Daria Izdebska, *The Semantic Field of ANGER in Old English*. University of Glasgow, 2014 (unpublished PhD thesis). See also Caroline Gevaert, 'The Evolution of the Lexical and Conceptual Field of ANGER in Old and Middle English', in *A Changing World of Words: Studies in English Historical Lexicography, Lexicology and Semantics*, ed. J. E. D. Vera (Amsterdam: Rodopi, 2002), pp. 275–99 and Hans-Juergen Diller, 'ANGER and TÊNE in Middle English', in *Middle and Modern English Corpus Linguistics: A Multidimensional Approach*, ed. M. Markus, Y. Iyeiri, and R. Heuberger (Amsterdam: John Benjamins, 2012), pp. 109–24.

47 Diller uses the term *word-families*; Díaz-Vera refers to these as 'expressions' in Javier E. Díaz-Vera, 'On Saying Two Things at Once: The Historical Semantics and Pragmatics of Old English Emotion Words', *Folia Linguistica Historica* 35, no. 1 (2014), pp. 101–34.

48 *Dictionary of Old English Web Corpus* (DOEC), compiled by Antonette diPaolo Healey with John Price Wilkin and Xin Xiang (Toronto, 2009).

49 The words omitted from analysis entirely are *gehnyst* (only one occurrence) and *geswicenness* ('repentance' appears to be an incidental meaning for this word).

50 Regarding the conventions of representing words in Old English, I have chosen to include length marks when the (more abstract) lexeme or lexicographic forms are discussed but did not include length marks in direct citations from Old English texts (whether on a word, phrase or sentence level).

51 Where the lexeme in question falls in the fascicle between A and I, the most recent edition of the Dictionary of Old English was consulted, i.e. Angus Cameron, Ashley Crandell Amos, Antonette diPaolo Healey et al., eds., *Dictionary of Old English: A to I Online* (Toronto, 2018). Available at http://www.doe.utoronto.ca (accessed 30 October 2019). Senses for words starting with letters after I were taken from Joseph Bosworth and T. Northcote Toller, *An Anglo-Saxon Dictionary Based on the Manuscript Collections of the Late Joseph Bosworth* (London: Oxford University Press, 1898).

52 Ælfric's use of *behreowsung* as typical of his style has been discussed by L. G. Hallander, *Old English Verbs in '-sian': A Semantic and Derivational Study* (Stockholm: Almqvist & Wiksell, 1966) and Walter Hofstetter, 'Winchester and the Standardization of Old English Vocabulary', *Anglo-Saxon England* 17 (1988), pp. 139–62. *Behreowsung* appears to be a typically West Saxon or Winchesterian feature (see also Hugh Magennis, 'Contrasting Features in the Non-Ælfrician Lives in the Old English *Lives of Saints*', *Anglia* 104 (1986), pp. 316–48, and Inge B. Milfull, *The Hymns of the Anglo-Saxon Church: A Study and Edition of the 'Durham Hymnal'* (Cambridge: Cambridge University Press, 1996), as opposed to *hrēow* which is considered Anglian (Patrizia Lendinara, 'The Kentish Laws', in *The Anglo-Saxons from the Migration Period to the Eighth Century*, ed. J. Hines (Woodbridge: Boydell Press, 2003), pp. 211–30); Javier Martin Arista analyses derivational patterns on the example of *hrēow* ('Projections and Constructions in Functional Morphology: The Case of Old English HRĒOW', *Language and Linguistics* 12, no. 2 (2011), pp. 393–425). In his study, Arista also includes such words as *wælhreow* 'cruel, bloodthirsty' and *hrēownes* 'turbulence, storm, turmoil', as the *hreow* spelling could suggest they belong to the same family. These are derived from *hreoh, hreow, reow* 'cruel, fierce'. In the entry for *hreoh* in DOE we read that 'Hrēoh and rēow are sometimes regarded as separate words. Because the etymology of both adjectives is obscure, and since the variant forms never suggest any discernible difference in

sense, examples beginning *hreoh-*, *hreow-*, *reow-*, etc. have been treated here as if forms of the same word.' However, the adjective *hreow* 'sorrowful' is treated as a separate lexeme in the DOE, so it is likely a case of homonymy.
53 *Hreuwa, hreuwan, hreuwon, hriulik, hriuliko, hriuwi, hriuwig, hriuwiglik, hriuwigliko, hriuwigmod, hriuwon* (Gerhard Köbler, *Indogermanisches Wörterbuch*. 5th ed. (2014). Available at https://www.koeblergerhard.de/idgwbhin.html (accessed 25 November 2019)).
54 Vladimir Orel, *A Handbook of Germanic Etymology* (Leiden: Brill, 2003).
55 Guus Kroonen, *An Etymological Dictionary of Proto-Germanic* (Leiden: Brill, 2013).
56 Wolfgang Pfeifer, *Etymologisches Wörterbuch des Deutschen* (Berlin: Akademie Verlag, 1992).
57 Ibid.
58 Richard Cleasby and Gudbrand Vígfusson, *An Icelandic-English Dictionary*. 2nd ed. (Oxford, 1957).
59 Laurel Joy Lied, *A Meeting of Worlds. An Investigation into the Development of a Christian Vocabulary Set within the Old Norse Language Using a New Statistical Methodology* (Oslo, 2016) University of Oslo. Master Thesis, p. 123.
60 Ibid., p. 133. Interestingly, in Old Norse the compound coined to translate the concepts of *poenitentia* works with the same base as Old English (i.e. *bōt*), though Old Norse chooses to modify it with the prefix *yfir-* 'over, above'. *Compunctio* is also translated with a coined *viðrkomning*, while *iðrun*, which is used for both *contritio* and *paenitentia*, references metaphorically the inward movement of the bowels (Cleasby/Vígfusson). See also the contribution by Scheel in the present volume.
61 See Orel, *A Handbook of Germanic Etymology*, Pfeifer, *Etymologisches Wörterbuch des Deutschen*, Kroonen, *An Etymological Dictionary of Proto-Germanic*. In Polish, the noun *skrucha*, used predominantly in Christian contexts, has the sense of 'contrition, remorse' and is derived from the verb *skruszyć* 'to grind, break apart'.
62 OED 3 ed., Orel, *A Handbook of Germanic Etymology*.
63 See Izdebska, 'Curious Case', for the discussion of TORN, which has similar physical, embodied motivation.
64 In much more practical terms, the corpus search was performed only on *dædbēt** and *dædbōt**, as extending it to various forms of *bētan* would have affected both recall and precision of the query, due to a greater likelihood of homonymy, and would considerably extend the scope of this study (e.g. a search for *bet** could also bring up *betweonan* 'between', and a search for *betst* (2nd p sg pres of *bētan*) could also be a superlative adjective meaning 'best').
65 See Dieter Kastovsky, 'Old English Word-format and Loan Translations', in *Convergent Approaches to Mediaeval English Language and Literature. Selected Papers from the 22nd Conference of SELIM*, ed. J. Martín Arista, R. Torre Alonso, A. Canga Alonso, and I. Medina Barco (Cambridge: Cambridge Scholars, 2012),

pp. 29–43 for a good overview of the semantic loans, loan translations and word-formation processes between Latin and Old English. The de-verbal nouns can be treated as loan translations, where the Old English formations with the suffix *-nes* reflect the Latin suffix *-tio*. However, the words can also be considered as semantic loans, where the sense of existing OE words is expanded to include the additional senses of the Latin equivalents.

66 DOE '*for-*'.
67 Lewis and Short.
68 Kastovsky, Old English Word-format and Loan Translations, 39.
69 The letters A-D correspond to the broad division of texts in the DOEC corpus.
70 The Psalter glosses are an excellent tool to investigate dialectal and, to some extent, diachronic variety, representing e.g. Mercian and early and late West Saxon. See for instance, Michiko Ogura, 'The Variety and Conformity of Old English Psalter Glosses', *English Studies* 83, no. 1 (2003), pp. 1–8 and Peter Kitson, 'Topography, Dialect and the Relation of Old English Psalter-glosses (I)', *English Studies* 83, no. 6 (2002), pp. 474–503.
71 One of the examples of such 'affective' usage is the phrase *dēoplic dǣdbōt* 'a deep repentance', which occurs in the *Handbook for the Use of a Confessor*, a later Old English text (DOEC Short Title: Conf4). It may very well be that the later the text in which it appears, the more likely *dǣdbōt* is to denote an emotional state, though there are also some suggestions of dialectal differences, with West Saxon texts preferring *dǣdbōt* over *hrēow* (see Lendinara, 'The Kentish Laws'); future research could trace the development of senses for *dǣdbōt* in more detail.
72 s.v. *bētan* (DOE).
73 There are parallels of such systems of fines in earlier Germanic laws. Anglo-Saxon legislative writing has been compared to its continental counterparts (for instance, Lombard law) and these comparisons have often been quite illuminating. See in particular Hough, An Ald Reht, p. 158; and for an overview: Karl Shoemaker, 'Germanic Law', in *The Oxford Handbook of European Legal History*, ed. H. Pihlajamäki, M. D. Dubber and M. Godfrey (Oxford: Oxford University Press, 2018), pp. 249–63.
74 Carole Hough, 'Legal and Documentary Writings', in *Companion to Anglo-Saxon Literature*, ed. P. Pulsiano and E. Treharne (Oxford: Blackwell, 2001), pp. 170–87. Reprinted in Carole Hough, *An Ald Reht: Essays on Anglo-Saxon Law* (Cambridge: Cambridge Scholars, 2014).
75 Lisi Olivier, 'Æthelberht's Code'. *Early English Laws* (London, 2020). Available at https://earlyenglishlaws.ac.uk/laws/texts/Abt/ (accessed 7 January 2020).
76 Hough, 'Legal and Documentary Writings'.
77 The text of Æthelberht's code is available through *Early English Laws* (London, 2020). Available at http://www.earlyenglishlaws.ac.uk/laws/texts/abt/view/#edition-9/translation-10 (accessed 20 November 2019).

78 Carole Hough, 'Penitential Literature and Secular Law in Anglo-Saxon England', *Anglo-Saxon Studies in Archaeology and History* 11 (2001), pp. 133–41. Reprinted in Hough, *An Ald Reht*.
79 Ibid., p. 35.
80 Morse, 'Commentary'. Morse discusses the difficulties in determining remorse of the accused or normalizing it for standardized, but stresses this is often part of practice and judicial discretion.
81 Carole Hough, 'Alfred's *domboc* and the Language of Rape: A Reconsideration of Alfred', *Medium Aevum* 66, no. 1 (1997), pp. 1–27. Reprinted in Hough, *An Ald Reht*, pp. 187–8.
82 Ibid.
83 Williams, *Sincerity in Medieval English*, p. 56.
84 Carole Hough, 'Penitential Literature and Secular Law in Anglo-Saxon England', *Anglo-Saxon Studies in Archaeology and History* 11 (2001), pp. 133–41, p. 33, draws attention to II, Edmund ch. 4: *he hæbbe godcunde bote underfangen 7 wið þa mægðer gebet on bote begangen* (he has undergone ecclesiastical penance and undertaken the prescribed compensation to the kindred).
85 Ibid., pp. 43–4.
86 ÞRÆST seems to break this pattern only in the glosses to Aldhelm's *De Virginitate*, where the Latin equivalents focus mostly on physically threatening and obstructive actions (*arto* 'press, contract', *obstrunco* 'kill, slaughter', *attero* 'grind, rub' and *suffoco* 'choke, strangle'), but also include *addico* 'resign', *compello* 'compel, urge' and *mancipo* 'sell' – possibly with some metaphorical extension.
87 The abbreviations used for all Old English texts follow the 'Short Title' designations set by the Dictionary of Old English Corpus, detailed information on which, including editions used, can be found and searched for in 'List of texts (all)' on the Dictionary website. Available at https://tapor.library.utoronto.ca/doe/ (accessed 20 November 2019).
88 For more on translation practices, particularly those produced at the time of King Alfred, see Janet M. Bately 'Old English Prose before and during the Reign of Alfred', *Anglo-Saxon England* 17 (1988), pp. 93–138, and Andreas Lemke, *The Old English Translation of Bede's 'Historia Ecclesiastica Gentis Anglorum' in Its Historical and Cultural Context*. Göttinger Schriften zur Englischen Philologie, vol. 8. (Göttingen: Universitätsverlag Göttingen, 2015); for translation equivalence see Haruko Momma, 'The Old English Metrical Psalms: Practice and Theory of Translation', in *Early English Poetic Culture and Meter: The Influence of G.R. Russom*, ed. L. Brady, and M. J. Toswell (Kalamazoo: Medieval Institute Publications, 2016), pp. 93–110, and for the issue of bilingualism in Anglo-Saxon England, see Olga Timofeeva, 'Anglo-Latin Bilingualism before 1066: Prospects and Limitations', in *Interfaces between Language and Culture in Medieval England: A Festschrift for Mattio Kilpio*, ed. A. Hall, O. Timofeeva, A. Kiricsi, and B. Fox. The Northern World 48. (Leiden: Brill, 2010), pp. 1–36, 'Anglo-Latin and Old English. A Case

for Integrated Bilingual Corpus Studies of Anglo-Saxon Registers', in *New Methods in Historical Corpora*, ed. P. Bennett, M. Durrell, S. Scheible, and R. J. Whitt (Tübingen: Narr verlag, 2013), pp. 195–204, and 'Latin Loans in Old English and Finnish Loans in Modern English: Can We Distinguish Statistics from Myth?' in *Selected Proceedings of the 2012 Symposium on New Approaches in English Historical Lexis (HEL-LEX 3)*, ed. R. W. McConchie (Somerville, MA: Cascadilla Proceedings, 2013), pp. 166–76.

89 Doublets or synonymous pairs (see Kastovsky, 'Old English word-format' and Bately, 'Old English prose', among others) can serve as clarification, but also as rhetoric amplification (Sherman Kuhn, 'Synonyms in the Old English Bede', *The Journal of English and Germanic Philology* 46, no. 2 (1947), pp. 168–76) and Lemke, *Old English Translation*, discusses the influence of rhetoric on the translation of Bede's *Historia Ecclesiastica* where he reports that doublets may have been used for stylistic reasons 'as hinted at by Waite, Hart and Van Draat' (p. 197).

90 This sample size provides us with a confidence level of 95 per cent and a confidence interval of 8.5.

91 As the particulars of dating of each poem are not as important as broad diachronic look for my purposes, I shall adopt Fulk's division of poems, based on metrical and linguistic evidence, into four groups from his *A History of Old English Meter*. This would consist of an (1) early 'Caedmonian' group (*Genesis A, Exodus, Daniel, Beowulf, Guthlac A*), (2) the 'Cynewulfian' group (signed poems of Cynewulf, *Guthlac B, Andreas, The Phoenix*), a (3) Alfredian group (*Meters of Boethius, Judith*), and (4) a late group including *Battle of Maldon* and the Paris Psalter. See R. D. Fulk, 'Cynewulf: Canon, Dialect, and Date', in *The Cynewulf Reader*, ed. R. E. Bjork (London: Routledge, 2001), p. 17. We could also add *Genesis B*, an Old English 'transliteration' of the Saxon Genesis to group (3) and date it roughly to c.850 (Michael Fox, 'Feðerhama and hæleðhelm: The Equipment of Devils', *Florilegium* 26 (2009), pp. 133–57, p. 132); The dating of *Beowulf* has been the subject of ongoing debate for almost two centuries, producing a breadth of scholarship that has been assessing and reassessing evidence and coming up with disparate dates; see the most recent edited collection by Leonard Neidorf, *The Dating of Beowulf. A Reassessment* (Woodbridge: D.S. Brewer, 2014).

92 R. D. Fulk, 'Cynewulf: Canon, Dialect, and Date'.

93 Izdebska, *Semantic Field*.

94 The conceptual metaphor sadness is darkness is pervasive in Old English and visible in such words as *geswearcian* 'to darken, to grow troubled'.

95 The same pattern of behaviour can be seen elsewhere with other sadness/grief emotions and has been discussed at length.

96 Cooper, 'Chapter 9: The Shedding of Tears in Late Anglo-Saxon England', p. 186. But also Williams, *Sincerity in Medieval English*, on grief.

97 B-T has 'fearful'.

98 Robert Rice, 'Hreowcearig "penitent, contrite"', *English Language Notes* 12, no. 4 (June 1975), pp. 243–50.

99 For some of these words and senses, see *PWN-Oxford English-Polish Dictionary* (Warszawa, 2004). Available at https://oxford.pwn.pl/about_the_dictionary.html (accessed 5 January 2020) or *Pons.eu* (Stuttgart, 2020). Available at https://en.pons.com/translate?q=%C5%BCal&l=enpl&in=&lf=pl#dict (accessed 5 January 2020).

100 This is why, for instance, Nicholson, 'The Expression of Emotional Distress in Old English Prose and Verse'. when analysing the vocabulary for negative affective states in the Old English translation of Boethius does not include *hreow* seeing it as 'repentance', though he acknowledges that it is 'used elsewhere to signify a negative affective state akin to sorrow' (p. 331).

101 MtGl (Ru) [0512 (15.32)].

102 PsCaI (Lindelöf) [010000 (7(6).36)].

103 RegCGl (Kornexl).

104 PsCaG (Rosier).

105 PsGlI (Lindelöf) [0030 (4.5)].

106 Stanley, 'Did the Anglo-Saxons Have a Social Conscience Like Us?' p. 246.

107 Syntactically, there is some evidence that Latin may have influenced the constructions where for verbs of emotion the prepositional or adverbial complement represents the target of the emotion, as in *him hrywth*. See Ruth Möhlig-Falke, *The Early English Impersonal Construction. An Analysis of Verbal and Constructional Meaning* (Oxford, 2012), p. 141, who discusses *hreowan* in this context.

Chapter 3

1 For an overview, see Vésteinn Ólason, *Dialogues with the Viking Age. Narration and Representation in the Sagas of Icelanders* (Reykjavík: Heimskringla, 1998), pp. 63–94, 135–79. For the representation of feud and honour, see Jesse L. Byock, *Feud in the Icelandic Saga* (Berkeley/London: University of California Press, 1982), pp. 24–62; William I. Miller, *Bloodtaking and Peacemaking. Feud, Law and Society in Saga Iceland* (Chicago: The University of Chicago Press, 1990), pp. 179–220; Preben Meulengracht Sørensen, *Fortælling og ære. Studier i islændingesagaerne* (Aarhus: Aarhus University Press, 1993), pp. 187–248.

2 Dorothee Frölich, 'Eddische Heroische Elegie und *Laxdæla saga*. Bemerkungen zu einigen motivischen und formalen Verbindungslinien', in *Studien zur Isländersaga. Festschrift für Rolf Heller*, ed. H. Beck (Berlin/New York: De Gruyter, 2000) (Reallexikon der Germanischen Altertumskunde. Ergänzungsband 24), pp. 51–71;

Vésteinn Ólason, 'Gísli Súrsson – A Flawless or a Flawed Hero?' in *Die Aktualität der Saga. Festschrift für Hans Schottmann*, ed. S. Toftgaard Andersen (Berlin/New York: De Gruyter, 1999) (Reallexikon der Germanischen Altertumskunde. Ergänzungsband 21), pp. 163–75.

3   Christopher Crocker, 'Emotions', in *The Routledge Research Companion to the Medieval Icelandic Sagas*, ed. Ármann Jakobsson and Sverrir Jakobsson (London/New York: Routledge, 2017), pp. 240–52; William I. Miller, 'Emotions and the Sagas', in *From Sagas to Society: Comparative Approaches to Early Iceland*, ed. Gísli Pálsson (Enfield Lock: Hisarlik Press, 1992), pp. 89–109; Kirsten Wolf, 'Body Language in Medieval Iceland. A Study of Gesticulation in the Sagas and Tales of Icelanders', *Scripta Islandica* 64 (2013), pp. 99–122; Eadem, 'Somatic Semiotics: Emotion and the Human Face in the Sagas and *þættir* of Icelanders', *Traditio* 69 (2014), pp. 125–45; Sif Rikhardsdottir, *Emotion in Old Norse Literature. Translations, Voices, Contexts* (Cambridge: Brewer, 2017), pp. 62–4.

4   Michael Argyle, *Bodily Communication* (London: Methuen, 1975), p. 213f.

5   See also note 3 and esp. Wolf, 'Somatic Semiotics', p. 143f.

6   William I. Miller, *Humiliation. And Other Essays on Honor, Social Discomfort, and Violence* (Ithaca, NY/London: Cornell University Press, 1993), pp. 93–130; Preben Meulengracht Sørensen, *Fortælling og ære*, pp. 291–327. For older research, see the overview in Theodore M. Andersson, 'The Displacement of the Heroic Ideal in the Family Sagas', *Speculum* 45 (1970), pp. 575–93. Haki Antonsson, *Damnation and Salvation in Old Norse Literature* (Cambridge: Brewer, 2018) appeared after this study was finished. It provides an instructive and pioneering analysis of these contexts in Old Norse hagiography and historiography.

7   The access to the field is based upon Ernst Walter, *Lexikalisches Lehngut im Altwestnordischen. Untersuchungen zum Lehngut im ethisch-moralischen Wortschatz der frühen lateinisch-altwestnordischen Übersetzungsliteratur* (Berlin: Akademie-Verlag, 1976) (Abhandlungen der Sächsischen Akademie der Wissenschaften zu Leipzig. Philologisch-Historische Klasse 66, 2), pp. 107–30.

8   For this anthropological approach and its justification, see Kirsten Hastrup, *Culture and Society in Medieval Iceland. An Anthropological Analysis of Structure and Change* (Oxford: Clarendon Press, 1985), pp. 1–14; Sverre Bagge, 'Icelandic Uniqueness or a Common European Culture? The Case of the Kings' Sagas', *Scandinavian Studies* 69, no. 4 (1997), pp. 418–42; Kim Esmark and Hans J. Orning, 'General Introduction', in *Disputing Strategies in Medieval Scandinavia*, ed. K. Esmark et al. (Leiden/Boston: Brill, 2013) (Medieval Law and Its Practice 16), pp. 1–28, here pp. 13–28.

9   The question of genuineness and the role of oral tradition vs literary models is one of the main conflicts in saga research; Gísli Sigurðsson, *The Medieval Icelandic Saga and Oral Tradition. A Discourse on Method* (Cambridge, MA/London:

Harvard University Press, 2004) (Publications of the Milman Parry Collection of Oral Literature 2), pp. 1–48; Chris Callow, 'Dating and Origins', in *The Routledge Research Companion to the Medieval Icelandic Sagas*, ed. Ármann Jakobsson and Sverrir Jakobsson (London/New York: Routledge, 2017), pp. 15–33.

10 Þórir Óskarsson, 'Rhetoric and Style', in *A Companion to Old Norse-Icelandic Literature and Culture*, ed. R. McTurk (Malden, MA/Oxford: Blackwell, 2005), pp. 354–71, here pp. 366–8.

11 See the stylistic unity of *Moðruvallabok* (AM 132 fol.) from the middle of the fourteenth century, the biggest medieval collection of *Íslendingasögur*, which also dominates the modern editions. Other redactions of the contained sagas betray a greater variation in style and licence especially with regard to the narrator.

12 Barbara Rosenwein, *Emotional Communities in the Early Middle Ages* (Ithaca, NY/London: Cornell University Press, 2006), pp. 20–9, esp. p. 25 and 27, where it is stressed that 'the constraints of genre admittedly pose a problem' and that this is addressed by 'drawing together different kinds of sources'.

13 The database *Íslenskt textasafn. Stofnun Árna Magnússonar í íslenskum fræðum*. Available at http://corpus.arnastofnun.is/leit.pl?hreinsaform=N%C3%BD+leit (accessed 24 July 2020) provides an uncontrolled corpus of digitized medieval texts. Html versions of non-critical editions of the 'classics' are available in modern Icelandic via *Netútgáfan*. Available at https://www.snerpa.is/net/fornrit.htm (accessed 24 July 2020). I would like to cordially thank Ármann Jakobsson (Reykjavík) for providing me with an electronic version of his edition of *Morkinskinna*.

14 *Ordbog over det norrøne prosasprog*. Available at https://onp.ku.dk/ (accessed 24 July 2020).

15 AM 619 4to (Walter, *Lexikalisches Lehngut*, p. 108f.).

16 *Ordbog over det norrøne prosasprog*, s.v. *iðra* and *iðrun*.

17 Albert Eßer, 'Reue II: Philosophisch-ethisch', in *Theologische Realenzyklopädie 29*, ed. H. Balz et al. (Berlin/New York: De Gruyter, 1998), pp. 101–3, here p. 102f.

18 Cf. Astrid Salvesen, *Studies in the Vocabulary of the Old Norse Elucidarium* (Oslo: Universitetsforlaget, 1968), pp. 20–8, 62–9.

19 *The Old Norse Elucidarius. Original Text and Translation*, ed. E. Scherabon Firchow (Columbia: Camden House, 1992), 2.68f., p. 68. Quotations are taken from the mildly normalized edition. Translation of all quotations from Old Norse are my own unless otherwise stated. Cf. *Elucidarius in Old Norse Translation*, ed. E. Scherabon Firchow and K. Grimstad (Reykjavík: Stofnun Árna Magnússonar, 1989) (Stofnun Árna Magnússonar á Íslandi. Rit 36), p. 110.

20 *The Old Norse Elucidarius*, ed. E. Scherabon Firchow 3.60–2, p. 88. See also *Elucidarius*, ed. E. Scherabon Firchow and K. Grimstad, p. 132.

21 *Ordbog over det norrøne prosasprog*, s.v. *iðrun*.

22 Gabriel Turville-Petre, *Origins of Icelandic Literature* (Oxford: Clarendon Press, 1953), pp. 109–42; Þórir Óskarsson, 'Rhetoric and Style', pp. 360–6.

23 Karen Wagner, 'Cum aliquis venerit ad sacerdotem: Penitential Experience in the Central Middle Ages', in *A New History of Penance*, ed. A. Firey (Leiden/Boston: Brill, 2008) (Brill's Companion to the Christian Tradition 14), pp. 201–18; Gustav L. Benrath, 'Buße V. Historisch', in *Theologische Realenzyklopädie 7*, ed. H. Balz et al. (Berlin/New York: De Gruyter, 1981), pp. 452–73; Haki Antonsson, *Damnation and Salvation*, pp. 23–33.

24 Reinhart Koselleck, 'Hinweise auf die temporalen Strukturen begriffsgeschichtlichen Wandels', in *Begriffsgeschichten. Studien zur Semantik und Pragmatik der politischen und sozialen Sprache* (Frankfurt am Main: Suhrkamp Verlag, 2006), pp. 86–98, here pp. 95–8.

25 Stefanie Würth, 'Die mittelalterliche Übersetzung im Spannungsfeld von lateinischsprachiger und volkssprachiger Literaturproduktion. Das Beispiel der Veraldar saga', in *Übersetzen im skandinavischen Mittelalter*, ed. V. Johanterwage and S. Würth (Wien: Fassbaender, 2007) (Studia medievalia septentrionalia 14), pp. 11–32, here p. 19f; Roland Scheel, 'Byzantium – Rome – Denmark – Iceland: Dealing with Imperial Concepts in the North', in *Transcultural Approaches to the Concept of Imperial Rule in the Middle Ages*, ed. C. Scholl, T. R. Gebhardt and J. Clauß (Frankfurt am Main et al: Peter Lang, 2017), pp. 245–94, here p. 263f.

26 *Veraldar saga*, ed. Jakob Benediktsson (København: Luno, 1944) (Samfund til Udgivelse af gammel nordisk Litteratur 61), p. 11.

27 This aspect dominates the meaning of compunction in the Old Testament in the time before exile: Jörg Jeremias, 'Reue I: Biblisch', in *Theologische Realenzyklopädie 29*, ed. H. Balz et al. (Berlin/New York: De Gruyter, 1998), pp. 99–101, here p. 99f.

28 *Ordbog over det norrøne prosasprog*, s.v. iðra.

29 Jan de Vries, *Altnordisches etymologisches Wörterbuch*. 2. verbesserte Aufl. (Leiden: Brill, 1977), p. 283.

30 Walter, *Lexikalisches Lehngut*, p. 107f.

31 Snorri Sturluson, *Heimskringla*, ed. Bjarni Aðalbjarnarson, 3 vols (Reykjavík: Hið íslenzka fornritafélag, 1941–51) (Íslenzk fornrit 26–28), vol. 1, p. 7; Klaus von See, 'Skaldenstrophe und Sagaprosa. Ein Beitrag zum Problem der mündlichen Überlieferung in der altnordischen Literatur', in K. von See *Edda, Saga, Skaldendichtung. Aufsätze zur skandinavischen Literatur des Mittelalters* (Heidelberg: Winter, 1981) (Skandinavistische Arbeiten 6), pp. 461–85.

32 Finnur Jónsson and Sveinbjörn Egilsson, *Lexicon poeticum antiquæ lingæ septentrionalis. Ordbog over det norsk-islandske Skjaldesprog* (København: Møller, 1931) and *The Skaldic Project*. Available at http://skaldic.abdn.ac.uk/db.php?if=default&table=home (accessed 20 November 2019), which however is not yet comprehensive.

33 Ulrike Sprenger, *Die altnordische heroische Elegie* (Berlin/New York: De Gruyter, 1992) (Ergänzungsbände zum Reallexikon der germanischen Altertumskunde 6), especially pp. 311–50. The relative dating on the basis of represented emotions has been cast into doubt; see Daniel Sävborg, *Sorg och elegi i Eddans hjältediktning*

(Stockholm: Almqvist & Wiksell International, 1997) (Acta Universitatis Stockholmiensis. Stockholm Studies in History of Literature 36), especially pp. 7–59, 450–65, and the answer by Theodore M. Andersson, 'Is There a History of Emotions in Eddic Heroic Poetry? Daniel Sävborg's Critique of Eddic Chronology', in *Codierungen von Emotionen im Mittelalter. Emotions and Sensibilities in the Middle Ages*, ed. C. S. Jaeger and I. Kasten (Berlin/New York: De Gruyter, 2003) (Trends in Medieval Philology 1), pp. 193–202 as well as Sif Rikhardsdottir, *Emotion*, pp. 97–102, who stresses the functional coexistence of the elegies and the action-centred poems in manuscript tradition.

34 Klaus von See et al., *Kommentar zu den Liedern der Edda 6. […]*. (Heidelberg: Winter, 2009), pp. 309–17; Klaus von See et al., *Kommentar zu den Liedern der Edda 7. […]*. (Heidelberg: Winter, 2012), pp. 398–400, 412–21.

35 Von See et al., *Kommentar zu den Liedern der Edda 6*, p. 317.

36 *Vǫlsunga saga. The Saga of the Volsungs. The Icelandic Text according to MS Nks 1824 b, 4°. With an English Translation, Introduction and Notes by Kaaren Grimstad*, ed. K. Grimstad (Saarbrücken: AQ-Verlag, 2000) (Bibliotheca Germanica. Series Nova 3), ch. 22, p. 154, ch. 25, p. 160.

37 *Edda. Die Lieder des Codex regius nebst verwandten Denkmälern 1. Text*, ed. G. Neckel and H. Kuhn. 4. umgearb. Aufl. (Heidelberg: Winter, 1962), p. 207f.

38 Ibid., p. 208.

39 Sprenger, *Elegie*, pp. 273–5.

40 *Edda*, ed. G. Neckel and H. Kuhn, st. 2, p. 219.

41 On Brynhildr see Sprenger, *Elegie*, pp. 171–89, 307–9. Brynhild's avoidance of admitting to guilt after the insight into her conscience brings the concept of guilt and the heroic together.

42 80,4: 'vacþir vá micla, er þú vátt brœðr mína.' (*Edda*, ed. G. Neckel and H. Kuhn, p. 259; cf. 69,2, p. 257).

43 See also below, pp. 81–84.

44 Von See et al., *Kommentar zu den Liedern der Edda 7*, pp. 405–21; cf. above, note 33.

45 *Vǫlsunga saga*, ed. K. Grimstad, ch. 30, p. 176: 'yðrazt muntv ef þv giorir þat' ('you shall regret it if you do so').

46 Von See et al., *Kommentar zu den Liedern der Edda 7*, pp. 405–12; Andersson, 'Is There a History', pp. 196–9.

47 Andersson, 'Is There a History', pp. 200–2.

48 Retrieved through the combination of occurrences noted in Finnur Jónsson and Sveinbjörn Egilsson, *Lexicon poeticum*, and *The Skaldic Project* database (note 32).

49 'Sigvatr Þórðarson, Erfidrápa Óláfs helga', ed. J. Jesch, in *Poetry from the Kings' Sagas 1,2*, ed. D. Whaley (Turnhout: Brepols, 2012) (Skaldic Poetry of the Scandinavian Middle Ages 1), pp. 663–98, here st. 11, p. 678.

50 Theodoricus monachus, 'Historia de antiquitate regum Norwagiensium', in *Monumenta historica Norvegiæ. Latinske Kildeskrifter til Norges Historie i Middelalderen*, ed. G. Storm (Kristiania: Brøgger, 1880), pp. 3–68, here ch. 21, p. 44.

51 'Ágrip af Nóregskonunga sǫgum', in *Ágrip af Nóregskonunga sǫgum. Fagrskinna – Nóregs konunga tal*, ed. Bjarni Einarsson (Reykjavík: Hið íslenzka fornritafélag, 1985) (Íslenzk fornrit 29), pp. 1–54, here ch. 33, p. 32.

52 *Morkinskinna*, ed. Ármann Jakobsson and Þórður Ingi Guðjónsson, 2 vols (Reykjavík: Hið íslenzka fornritafélag, 2011) (Íslenzk fornrit 23–24), ch. 1, vol. I, p. 18.

53 Heinrich Beck, *Wortschatz der altisländischen Grágás (Konungsbók)* (Göttingen: Vandenhoeck & Ruprecht, 1993) (Abhandlungen der Akademie der Wissenschaften in Göttingen. Philologisch-historische Klasse. 3. Folge 205), s.v. *bœta, glǫp, illvirki, misrœða*.

54 Sigvatr Þórðarson, 'Erfidrápa', st. 11, p. 678.

55 An exception is grief for the lord who has died in memorial poems.

56 Lars Boje Mortensen, 'The Anchin Manuscript of Passio Olavi (Douai 295), William of Jumièges, and Theodoricus Monachus. New Evidence for Intellectual Relations between Norway and France in the 12th Century', *Symbolae Osloenses* 75, no. 1 (2000), pp. 165–89, here p. 170.

57 Haki Antonsson, *Damnation and Salvation*, esp. pp. 44–95, 183–209, 229f.

58 'Þórarinn loftunga, Glælognskviða', ed. M. Townend, in *Poetry from the Kings' Sagas 1,2*, ed. D. Whaley (Turnhout: Brepols, 2012) (Skaldic Poetry of the Scandinavian Middle Ages 1), pp. 863–7, here st. 7, p. 872f. The poem is from the 1030s.

59 'Hallfreðr vandræðaskáld Óttarsson, Erfidrápa Óláfs Tryggvasonar', ed. K. Heslop, in *Poetry from the Kings' Sagas 1,1*, ed. D. Whaley (Turnhout: Brepols, 2012) (Skaldic Poetry of the Scandinavian Middle Ages 1), pp. 400–41, here st. 27, p. 439f. The poem is from the time shortly after the death of the missionary king Óláfr Tryggvason in AD 1000 and stresses that 'Christ may have the soul of the wise king' ('hafi Kristr [...] ǫnd kœns konungs').

60 'Markús Skeggjason, Eiríksdrápa', ed. J. Carroll, in *Poetry from the Kings' Sagas 2,1*, ed. M. Clunies Ross (Turnhout: Brepols, 2009) (Skaldic Poetry of the Scandinavian Middle Ages 2), pp. 432–60, here st. 26, p. 455f.

61 'Ívarr Ingimundarson, Sigurðarbálkr', ed. K. E. Gade, in *Poetry from the Kings' Sagas 2,2*, ed. M. Clunies Ross (Turnhout: Brepols, 2009) (Skaldic Poetry of the Scandinavian Middle Ages 2), pp. 501–27, here st. 8–9, p. 506f. On the context, cf. Haki Antonsson, *Damnation and Salvation*, pp. 57–9.

62 'Þórarinn stuttfeldr, Stuttfeldardrápa', ed. K. E. Gade, in *Poetry from the Kings' Sagas 2,2*, ed. M. Clunies Ross (Turnhout: Brepols, 2009) (Skaldic Poetry of the Scandinavian Middle Ages 2), pp. 473–9, here st. 1, p. 474 compares Sigurðr and his fleet to the mythological king Hrólfr kraki and his retinue.

63 Thus the Danish magnate Esbern Snare in an exhortation speech for a crusade as reaction to the papal bull *Audita tremendi* from 1187: 'Historia de profectione Danorum in Hierosolymam', in *Scriptores minores historiae Danicae medii ævi 2*, ed. M. C. Gertz (København: Gad, 1918–22), pp. 457–92, here ch. 5, pp. 465–7.
64 *Morkinskinna*, ed. Ármann Jakobsson and Þórður Ingi Guðjónsson, ch. 64, vol. 2, p. 71.
65 Cf. Snorri Sturluson, *Heimskringla*, ed. Bjarni Aðalbjarnarson, Magnússona saga ch. 1, vol. 3, p. 238.
66 These are mainly hagiographic or edifying poems (*Heilags anda drápa, Kátrínardrápa, Líknarbraut, Lilja, Drápa af Maríugrát, Maríuvísur, Heilagra meyja drápa, Pétrsdrápa*).
67 'Gamli kanóki, Harmsól', ed. K. Attwood, in *Poetry on Christian Subjects 1. The Twelfth and Thirteenth Centuries*, ed. M. Clunies Ross (Turnhout: Brepols, 2007) (Skaldic Poetry of the Scandinavian Middle Ages 7), pp. 70–132, here st. 25, p. 94f. On penitential poems, cf. Haki Antonsson, *Damnation and Salvation*, pp. 33–43.
68 Ibid., 93. Cf. Attwood's commentary ibid., p. 95.
69 St. 42, ibid., p. 109f. The 'man'-kenning here ('Óðinn of the Miðgarðsormr') is again taken from mythology. There are three occurrences of *bœta* (st. 42, p. 109f; st. 47, p. 114; st. 62, p. 128f.).
70 *Grágás 1*, ed. Vilhjálmur Finsen, p. 12; 'Den ældre Eidsivathings-Christenret', in *Norges gamle Love indtil 1387 1. Norges Love ældre end Kong Magnus Haakonssöns Regjerings-Tiltrædelse i 1263*, ed. R. Keyser and P. A. Munch (Christiania: Gröndahl, 1846), pp. 373–406, here 391, 405; 'Nyere Christenret, udgiven af Erkebiskop Jon den Yngre', in *Norges gamle Love indtil 1387 2. Lovgivningen under Kong Magnus Haakonssöns Regjeringstid fra 1263 til 1280, tilligemed et Supplement til förste Bind*, ed. R. Keyser and P. A. Munch (Christiania: Gröndahl, 1848), pp. 339–86, here p. 384.
71 Knut Helle, *Gulatinget og Gulatingslova* (Leikanger: Skald, 2001), pp. 20–3; Lars Boje Mortensen, 'Den formative dialog mellem latinsk og folkesproglig litteratur, ca. 600–1250. Udkast til en dynamisk model', in *Reykholt som makt- og lærdomssenter i den islandske og nordiske kontekst*, ed. E. Mundal (Reykholt: Snorrastofa, 2006) (Snorrastofa. Rit 3), pp. 239–71, here p. 255f.
72 'Den ældre Gulathings-Lov', in *Norges gamle Love indtil 1387 1. Norges Love ældre end Kong Magnus Haakonssöns Regjerings-Tiltrædelse i 1263*, ed. R. Keyser and P. A. Munch (Christiania: Gröndahl, 1846), pp. 1–118, here p. 70.
73 'Den nyere Lands-Lov. Udgiven af Kong Magnus Haakonssön', in *Norges gamle Love indtil 1387 2. Lovgivningen under Kong Magnus Haakonssöns Regjeringstid fra 1263 til 1280, tilligemed et Supplement til förste Bind*, ed. R. Keyser and P. A. Munch (Christiania: Gröndahl, 1848), pp. 1–178, here pp. 14, 31, 56, 62, 126; *Jónsbók. Kong Magnus Hakonssons Lovbog for Island vedtaget paa Altinget 1281 og Réttarbœtr. De for Island givne Retterbøder af 1294, 1305 og 1314*, ed. Ólafur Halldórsson (København: Møller, 1904), here pp. 5, 8, 24, 28, 46, 155, 166.

74 'Ágrip af Nóregskonunga sǫgum', ed. Bjarni Einarsson, ch. 6, p. 11.
75 On the textual history see Julia Zernack, 'Vorläufer und Vollender. Olaf Tryggvason und Olaf der Heilige im Geschichtsdenken des Oddr Snorrason Munkr', *Arkiv för nordisk filologi* 113 (1998), pp. 77–95, here pp. 83–92.
76 Oddr Snorrason, 'Óláfs saga Tryggvasonar', in *Færeyinga saga. Óláfs saga Tryggvasonar eptir Odd munk Snorrason*, ed. Ólafur Halldórsson (Reykjavík: Hið íslenzka fornritafélag, 2006) (Íslenzk fornrit 25), pp. 123–380, here ch. A49, p. 286, the story on pp. 283–6.
77 *Orkneyinga saga.* [...], ed. Finnbogi Guðmundsson (Reykjavík: Hið íslenzka fornritafélag, 1965) (Íslenzk fornrit 34), ch. 48–50, pp. 107–11 (the trap and the killing); ch. 51, p. 111 (Hákon denies the burial); ch. 52, p. 112f. (Hákon's tears and pilgrimage).
78 Knut Helle, *Norge blir en stat, 1130–1319* (Bergen/Oslo/Tromsø: Universitetsforlaget, 1974), pp. 53–85 (Handbok i Norges historie 3); Sverre Bagge, 'Den heroiske tid – kirkereform og kirkekamp 1153–1214', in *Ecclesia Nidrosiensis 1153–1537. Søkelys på Nidaroskirkens og Nidarosprovinsens historie*, ed. S. Imsen (Trondheim: Tapir Akademisk Forlag, 2003) (Senter for Middelalderstudier. Skrifter 15), pp. 51–80.
79 Hans-Werner Löbner, *Reden und Träume als strategische Elemente der Geschichtsschreibung des Mittelalters. Eine Untersuchung am Beispiel der Reden und Träume der Sverris-Saga* (Freiburg: [n. p.], 1992), pp. 107–42; Ármann Jakobsson, 'King Sverrir of Norway and the Foundations of His Power: Kingship Ideology and Narrative in Sverris saga', *Medium Ævum* 84 (2015), pp. 109–35.
80 *Sverris saga*, ed. Þorleifur Hauksson (Reykjavík: Hið íslenzka fornritafélag, 2007) (Íslenzk fornrit 30), ch. 38, p. 63.
81 See also the argument by Haki Antonsson, *Damnation and Salvation*, p. 202, on the basis of other passages from the saga.
82 Ibid., ch. 89, p. 138f.
83 *Sverris saga*, ed. Þorleifur Hauksson, ch. 179, p. 277: 'Nú vil ek þat fyrirgefa þeim fyrir Guðs sakir ok vænta þar á mót af honum fyrirgefningar þess er ek hefi honum á móti gǫrt.' 'Now I will forgive them for the sake of God and hope in return for His forgiveness for what I have done against His will.' See Haki Antonsson, *Damnation and Salvation*, pp. 198–202.
84 *Sverris saga*, ed. Þorleifur Hauksson, ch. 164, p. 258.
85 Benrath, 'Buße', pp. 458–65.
86 The preserved text ends earlier due to missing leaves in the MS. Cf. *Morkinskinna*, ed. Ármann Jakobsson and Þórður Ingi Guðjónsson, vol. 1, pp. VI–XXXIV.
87 Cf. the reasons for accepting St Óláf's son Magnús (above, p. 70). The royal ideal and the ideal of conduct in *Morkinskinna* are treated by Ármann Jakobsson, *A Sense of Belonging. Morkinskinna and Icelandic Identity, c. 1220* (Odense: University Press of Southern Denmark, 2014) (The Viking Collection 22), pp. 229–74.

88 Daniel Föller, 'Wikinger als Pilger. Drei norwegische Könige, zwei Runensteine und der Wiederaufbau der Grabeskirche', in *Konflikt und Bewältigung. Die Zerstörung der Grabeskirche zu Jerusalem im Jahre 1009*, ed. T. Pratsch (Berlin/Boston: De Gruyter, 2012) (Millennium-Studien 32), pp. 281–99, here pp. 294–7, and Roland Scheel, *Skandinavien und Byzanz. Bedingungen und Konsequenzen mittelalterlicher Kulturbeziehungen*, 2 vols (Göttingen: Vandenhoeck & Ruprecht, 2015) (Historische Semantik 23), pp. 298–321, 1021–23.

89 *Morkinskinna*, ed. Ármann Jakobsson and Þórður Ingi Guðjónsson, ch. 15, vol. 1, p. 106.

90 Ibid., ch. 71, vol. 2, p. 102.

91 Ibid., ch. 74, vol. 2, pp. 106–8, the quotation on p. 108.

92 Ibid., ch. 87, vol. 2, p. 150f., the quotation on p. 151.

93 A similar phenomenon occurs at the end of the life of King Magnús inn góði (Haki Antonsson, *Damnation and Salvation*, pp. 97–9).

94 On Snorri's political goals, see Kevin J. Wanner, *Snorri Sturluson and the Edda. The Conversion of Cultural Capital in Medieval Scandinavia* (Toronto: University of Toronto Press, 2008), pp. 154–61; Klaus von See, 'Snorris Konzeption einer nordischen Sonderkultur', in *Snorri Sturluson. Kolloquium anläßlich der 750. Wiederkehr seines Todestages*, ed. A. Wolf (Tübingen: Narr, 1993) (ScriptOralia 51), pp. 141–77; Scheel, *Skandinavien und Byzanz*, pp. 340–9.

95 Theodore M. Andersson, 'Snorri Sturluson and the Saga School at Munkaþverá', in *Snorri Sturluson. Kolloquium anläßlich der 750. Wiederkehr seines Todestages*, ed. A. Wolf (Tübingen: Narr, 1993) (ScriptOralia 51), pp. 9–25; Theodore M. Andersson, 'Víga-Glúms saga and the Birth of Saga Writing', *Scripta Islandica* 57 (2006), pp. 5–39.

96 Jón Viðar Sigurðsson, *Chieftains and Power in the Icelandic Commonwealth* (Odense: Odense University Press, 1999), pp. 62–83.

97 Guðrún Nordal, 'The Contemporary Sagas and Their Social Context', in *Old Icelandic Literature and Society*, ed. M. Clunies Ross (Cambridge: Cambridge University Press, 2000) (Cambridge Studies in Medieval Literature 42), pp. 221–41, here pp. 221–31; Úlfar Bragason, *On the Poetics of Sturlunga* (Ann Arbor, MI: University Microfilms International, 1986), pp. 124–8.

98 'Þorgils saga ok Hafliða', in *Sturlunga saga. Fyrra bindi*, ed. Jón Jóhannesson, Magnús Finnbogason and K. Eldjárn (Reykjavík: Sturlungaútgáfan, 1946), pp. 12–50, here ch. 18, p. 34f.

99 Ibid., ch. 19, p. 36f.

100 Ibid., ch. 22–8, pp. 39–47.

101 Ibid., ch. 22, p. 39f, ch. 28, p. 46.

102 Ibid., ch. 29, p. 47f., the quotation from p. 48: 'Fann ek þá þat, alls ek hugða þá at mannvirðinginni, at ekki myndi þær bætr fyrir koma, er myndi at sæmð verða. Gerða ek þá fyrir guðs sakir at gefa honum upp allt málit.'

103 Ibid., ch. 31f., p. 49f.
104 Miller, *Humiliation*, p. 123.
105 'Þorgils saga ok Hafliða', ed. Jón Jóhannesson et al., ch. 16, p. 32f. See Miller, *Bloodtaking and Peacemaking*, here p. 194f. and his attempt to reduce the religious argument in Ketil's *exemplum* to a purely rhetorical strategy (ibid., p. 269f.), simply serving to remind Hafliði that the outcome of a case is never certain and vesting this in theological *parole*. In his attempt to explain away religious motivation, Miller does not take into account that the restauration of Ketil's honour is explicitly linked to God's mercy. He further conceals the opposition between Ketil's good advice founded in moral ethics and Bǫðvar's bad advice which denies the relevance of any moral or religious norms. This illustrates a general weakness in an anthropological approach which does not take narrative structure and its semantics into account but isolates single scenes from their surroundings and uses them as 'raw data'.
106 'Þorgils saga ok Hafliða', ed. Jón Jóhannesson et al., ch. 31, p. 50.
107 'Guðmundar saga dýra', in *Sturlunga saga. Fyrra bindi*, ed. Jón Jóhannesson, Magnús Finnbogason and K. Eldjárn (Reykjavík: Sturlungaútgáfan, 1946), pp. 160–212, here ch. 12, pp. 183–5.
108 Ibid., ch. 14f., pp. 189–94.
109 Hans J. Orning, *Unpredictability and Presence. Norwegian Kingship in the High Middle Ages* (Leiden: Brill, 2008) (The Northern World 38), esp. pp. 314–19; Knut Görich, *Die Ehre Friedrich Barbarossas. Kommunikation, Konflikt und politisches Handeln im 12. Jahrhundert* (Darmstadt: Wissenschaftliche Buchgesellschaft, 2001), pp. 364–77.
110 'Guðmundar saga dýra', ed. Jón Jóhannesson et al., ch. 23, p. 209 and ch. 25f., p. 212.
111 It is found again for instance in *Grettis saga*, *Dámusta saga* and *Gibbons saga*.
112 Guðrún Nordal, *Ethics and Action in Thirteenth-century Iceland* (Odense: Odense University Press, 1998) (The Viking Collection 11), pp. 182–219 for a more comprehensive study of ethics and conscience in the *Samtíðarsögur*. Haki Antonsson, *Damnation and Salvation*, pp. 27–33, 100–14, discusses the *Samtíðarsögur* and preparations for death (pp. 183–209) extensively.
113 *Prestsfundr*: 'Guðmundar saga dýra', ed. Jón Jóhannesson et al., ch. 10, p. 180; ch. 18, p. 198. 'Íslendinga saga', in *Sturlunga saga. Fyrra bindi*, ed. Jón Jóhannesson, Magnús Finnbogason and K. Eldjárn (Reykjavík: Sturlungaútgáfan, 1946), pp. 160–212, here ch. 21, p. 248; ch. 96, p. 369f; ch. 107, p. 383f; ch. 138, p. 435; ch. 200, p. 532; 'Þórðar saga kakala', in *Sturlunga saga. Síðara bindi*, ed. Jón Jóhannesson, Magnús Finnbogason and K. Eldjárn (Reykjavík: Sturlungaútgáfan, 1946), pp. 1–86, here ch. 20, p. 40. Status of deceased who fell *án iðran ok lausn*

('without compunction and absolution'): 'Íslendinga saga', ed. Jón Jóhannesson et al., ch. 23, p. 253.

114 "'Þat vilda ek,' segir hann, "at ek væra fyrr af lífi tekinn en Þorsteinn, því at ek treystumst honum betr, at hann muni fyrirgefa yðr, þótt hann sjái mik af lífi tekinn.'" ('Guðmundar saga dýra', ed. Jón Jóhannesson et al., ch. 18, p. 198.

115 Miller, *Bloodtaking and Peacemaking*, here p. 191f. He follows Andreas Heusler, *Zum isländischen Fehdewesen in der Sturlungenzeit* (Berlin: Verlag der Königlichen Akademie der Wissenschaften, 1912) (Abhandlungen der Königlich Preußischen Akademie der Wissenschaften, Philosophisch-Historische Classe 1912, 4), p. 30f.

116 'Íslendinga saga', ed. Jón Jóhannesson et al., ch. 200, p. 534: 'Þess vil ek biðja þik, Gizurr jarl, at þú fyrirgefir mér þat, er ek hefi af gert við þik.'

117 *Beiskr ok harðr*: ibid., ch. 199, p. 532.

118 Ibid., ch. 200, p. 534: 'Þat vil ek gera, þegar þú ert dauðr.'

119 Heusler, *Fehdewesen*, p. 16.

120 Ibid., p. 12.

121 It is revealing that Nietzsche is evoked in this context: by Andreas Heusler, *Germanentum. Vom Lebens- und Formgefühl der alten Germanen* (Heidelberg: Winter, 1934), pp. 64–76 (Kultur und Sprache 8) in a chapter on 'Herrenethik', but also by Miller, *Humiliation*, pp. 127–30. The principle permeates research in the Family Sagas in so far as the majority has operated with an opposition of 'old' and 'new' values within the sagas; see also the overview in Meulengracht Sørensen, *Fortælling og ære*, pp. 291–327; Andersson, 'Displacement'.

122 See above, note 8.

123 Andersson, 'Is There a History', pp. 200–2.

124 'Ljósvetninga saga', in *Ljósvetninga saga [...]*, ed. Björn Sigfússon (Reykjavík: Hið íslenzka fornritafélag, 1940) (Íslenzk fornrit 10), pp. 1–106, here ch. 18, p. 93f.

125 Sif Rikhardsdottir, *Emotions*, p. 125f.

126 'Laxdœla saga', in *Laxdœla saga. Halldórs þættir Snorrasonar. Stúfs þáttr*, ed. Björn Sigfússon (Reykjavík: Hið íslenzka fornritafélag, 1934) (Íslenzk fornrit 5), pp. 1–248, here ch. 49, p. 154.

127 *Brennu-Njáls saga*, ed. Einar Ólafur Sveinsson (Reykjavík, 1954) (Íslenzk fornrit 12), ch. 129, p. 328f. See Thomas Hill, 'Njáll's Comforting Words: *Brennu-Njáls saga*, Chapter 129', *Saga-Book of the Viking Society* 41 (2017), pp. 71–8; Haki Antonsson, *Damnation and Salvation*, pp. 217–21.

128 *Brennu-Njáls saga*, ed. Einar Ólafur Sveinsson, ch. 111, p. 281.

129 *Sonatorrek*, st. 8 states that Egill would like to kill Ægir and to draw his sword against the waves in order to take revenge for his drowned son Bǫðvarr: *Den norsk-islandske Skjaldedigtning B. Rettet Tekst 1. 800–1200*, ed. Finnur Jónsson (København: Gyldendal, 1912), p. 35.

130 'Reykdœla saga ok Víga-Skútu', in *Ljósvetninga saga [...]*, ed. Björn Sigfússon, (Reykjavík: Hið íslenzka fornritafélag, 1940) (Íslenzk fornrit 10), pp. 149–243, here ch. 16, pp. 197–203; 'Heiðarvíga saga', in *Borgfirðinga sǫgur. [...]*, ed. Sigurður Nordal (Reykjavík: Hið íslenzka fornritafélag, 1938) (Íslenzk fornrit 3), pp. 213–328, here ch. 36f., pp. 316-19.
131 *Egils saga Skalla-Grímssonar*, ed. Sigurður Nordal (Reykjavík: Hið íslenzka fornritafélag, 1933) (Íslenzk fornrit 2), ch. 36, p. 92f.
132 Ibid., ch. 54, p. 140. Cf. also 'Laxdœla saga', ed. Björn Sigfússon, ch. 48, p. 151.
133 The only exception to the rule is 'Hrafnkels saga Freysgoða', in *Austfirðinga sǫgur. [...]*, ed. Jón Jóhannesson (Reykjavík, 1950) (Íslenzk fornrit 11), pp. 95–133. Here, the farmer Sámr secures the help of influential magnates who help to have his powerful adversary Hrafnkell outlawed. When Sámr does not want to kill Hrafnkell, his supporters state that he shall regret this (ch. 5, p. 121). When Hrafnkell later returns, Sám's helpers withdraw their support and call to mind their prediction that he would *þess mest iðrask* (ch. 10, p. 132). See the discussion of the extensive research on Hrafnkatla's implied ethics in Theodore M. Andersson, *The Growth of the Medieval Icelandic Sagas (1180–1280)* (Ithaca, NY/ London: Cornell University Press, 2006), pp. 175–82.

Chapter 4

1 See Peter Biller, 'Confession in the Middle Ages: Introduction', in *Handling Sin: Confession in the Middle Ages*, ed. P. Biller and A. J. Minnis (York, 1998), pp. 1–35; Nicole Bériou, 'Autour de Latran IV (1215): la naissance de la confession moderne et sa diffusion', in *Pratiques de la confession, des Pères de l'église à Vatican II. Quinze études d'histoire*, ed. Groupe de la Bussière (Paris, 1983), pp. 73–92.
2 Biller, 'Confession'; Paul Adnés, 'Pénitence. V. La doctrine médiévale du sacrement de la pénitence', *Dictionnaire de Spiritualité Ascétique et Mystique* XII, no. 1 (Paris, 1984), pp. 970–80.
3 Pierre Michaud-Quantin, *Sommes de casuistique et manuels de confession au moyen âge, XIIe–XVIe siècles*, (Louvain, Lille, Montréal, 1962). See also Biller, 'Confession'; Roberto Rusconi, 'De la prédication à la confession: Transmission et contrôle de modèles de comportements au XIIIe s.' in *Faire croire. Modalités de la diffusion et de la réception des messages religieux du XIIe au XVe siècle. Actes de table ronde de Rome (22-23 juin 1979)* (Rome, 1981), pp. 67–85.
4 Piroska Nagy, *Le don des larmes au Moyen Âge* (Paris, 2000), p. 380.
5 On William of Auvergne's conception on the passions of the soul, see Carla Casagrande, 'Guglielmo d'Auverne e il buon uso delle passioni nella penitenzia' and Silviana Vecchio, '*Passio, affectus, virtus*: il sistema delle passioni nei trattati morali

di Guglielmo d'Auverne', in *Autour de Guillaume d'Auvergne*, ed. F. Morenzoni and J. Y. Tilliette (Turnhout, 2005), pp. 189–201 and pp. 173–87. On the taking into account of emotions in theological and pastoral discourses of the scholastic period, see Alain Boureau, 'Un sujet agité. Le statut nouveau des passions de l'âme au XIIIe siècle', in *Le Sujet des émotions au Moyen Âge*, ed. P. Nagy and D. Boquet (Paris, 2009), pp. 187–200; Damien Boquet, Piroska Nagy, *Sensible Moyen Âge. Une histoire des émotions dans l'Occident médiéval* (Paris, 2015), pp. 211–24 and pp. 333–46.

6   For a presentation of the *Magisterium divinale ac sapientiale*, with an update of the historiographical debates surrounding it, see Jean-Baptiste Brenet, 'Introduction traduction et notes', in *De anima, VII, 1–9*, ed. Guillaume d'Auvergne (Paris, 1998), pp. 72–80.

7   Iosef Kramp, 'Des Wilhelm von Auvergne *Magisterium divinale*', *Gregorianum*, II (1921), pp. 42–78 (Latin version pp. 79–114), gave a summary of the dates of the *Magisterium*'s different items: see p. 78 (in German) and p. 103 (in Latin).

8   For an update on anti-Aristotelian procedures in the thirteenth century at the University of Paris, see Catherine König-Pralong, *L'Avènement de l'aristotélisme en terre chrétienne* (Paris, 2005), pp. 15–24.

9   On William of Auvergne's sources, see Brenet, 'Introduction traduction et notes', pp. 73–80. On his relation to Avicenna, see Roland Teske 'William of Auvergne's Debt to Avicenna', in *Avicenna and His Heritage. Acts of the International Colloquium, Leuven-Louvain la neuve, 8–11 Sept 1999*, ed. J. L. Janssens and D. de Smet (Leuven, 2002), pp. 153–70.

10 As William says in *De Trinitate*'s prologue, often considered as the prologue of the whole *Magisterium*. See also Roland J. Teske, *Guillaume d'Auvergne, The Universe of Creatures* (Milwaukee, 1998).

11 William of Auvergne, *De universo*, I, i, cap. 43, *Opera omnia* (Orléans-Paris, 1674, repr. Frankfurt a M., 1963), vol. I, p. 648aFG: 'Sciendum autem est tibi quia substantiae spirituales quae alligationem habent cum corporibus, ut dixi tibi de anima humana, limitatas habent virtutes et diffinitas quasi limitibus et terminis corporum suorum, ut ultra ea vel extra ea per seipsas nihil operetur. Per organa vero membrorum corporum suorum, vel per instrumenta membris eorum applicata multa manifestum est eas operari, sicut apparet in aedificiis et aliis artificiis'.

12 The expression occurs in another chapter of the *De Universo*: William of Auvergne, *De Universo*, I, i, cap. 46, p. 663aA: 'Operationes enim corporales per modum naturae per contactum sunt aut mediatum aut immediatum, quod est dicere quia corpus virtute sua corporali non agit, nisi vel in corpus, quod contingit, vel in aliud contingens illud'.

13 Aristote, *Physica*, VII, 2, 243a 333–35, in F. Bossier and J. Brams, eds., *Physica, translatio vetus* (*Aristoteles latinus*, VII/2) (Leyde/New York, 1990), p. 103: 'Movens

[...] est simul cum eo quod movetur. Simul autem dico, quia nichil ipsorum medium est; hoc enim in omni moto et movente est'. On the medieval reception of this text, see Nicolas Weill-Parot, *Points aveugles de la nature: la rationalité scientifique médiévale face à l'occulte, l'attraction magnétique et l'horreur du vide (XIIIe-milieu du XVe siècle)* (Paris, 2013), pp. 140–4. On medieval discussions about remote action, see Béatrice Delaurenti, 'L'action à distance est-elle pensable? Dynamiques discursives et créativité conceptuelle au XIIIe siècle', in *Histoires pragmatiques* ed. F. Chateauraynaud and Y. Cohen (Paris, 2016), pp. 149–78, and Nicolas Weill-Parot, 'Pouvoirs lointains de l'âme et des corps: éléments de réflexion sur l'action à distance entre philosophie et magie, entre Moyen Âge et Renaissance', *Lo Sguardo* 10, no. III (2012), pp. 85–98.

14 William of Auvergne, *De universo*, I, i, cap. 43, p. 648aFG: 'Forsitan anima basilici et animae quorundam aliorum animalium et quaedam animae humanae multa operantur, et mira valde extra corpora sua. Et illa nominanda sunt et numeranda in ea parte naturalis scientiae, quae vocatur magica naturalis.'

15 See Jean-Patrice Boudet, *Entre science et nigromance. Astrologie, divination et magie dans l'Occident médiéval (XIIe-XVe siècle)* (Paris, 2006), p. 128, who traces the genesis of the notion of 'natural magic' and considers this text of William of Auvergne as an essential stage in the process of theorizations of learned magic during the twelfth and the thirteenth centuries.

16 Cf. Steven P. Marrone, 'Magic and the Physical World in the Thirteenth-century Scholasticism', in *Evidence and Interpretation in Studies on Early Science and Medicine. Essays in Honor of John E. Murdoch*, ed. E. Sylla and W. Newman (Leiden, 2009), pp. 158–85; Steven P. Marrone, 'The Philosophy of Nature in Early Thirteenth Century', in *Albertus Magnus und die Anfänge der Aristoteles-Rezeption im lateinischen Mittelalter von Richardus Rufus bis zu Franciscus de Mayronis / Albertus Magnus and the Beginnings of Aristotle Reception in the Latin West from Richardus Rufus to Franciscus de Mayronis*, ed. L. Honnefelder, R. Wood, M. Dreyer, and M.-A. Aris (Münster, 2005), pp. 115–58; Béatrice Delaurenti, *La puissance des mots: 'virtus verborum'. Débats doctrinaux sur les incantations au Moyen Âge* (Paris, 2007), pp. 108–11 and pp. 202–30; Nicolas Weill-Parot, *Les 'images astrologiques' au Moyen Âge et à la Renaissance. Spéculations intellectuelles et pratiques magiques (XIIe-XVe siècle)* (Paris, 2002), pp. 175–212; Steven P. Marrone, 'William of Auvergne on Magic in Natural Philosophy and Theology', in *Wast ist Philosophie im Mittelalter?* ed. J. A. Aersten and A. Speer (Berlin, 1998), pp. 741–8.

17 See Joël Chandelier and Aurélien Robert, eds., *Frontières des savoirs en Italie à l'époque des premières universités (XIIIe-XVe siècles)* (Rome, 2015), especially Joël Chandelier and Aurélien Robert's introduction, pp. 1–13. On the intersecting between theology and medicine, see Aurélien Robert, 'Médecine et théologie à la cour angevine de Naples', in *Frontières des savoirs*, ed. Robert and Chandelier,

pp. 285–349; Peter Biller, 'Confessor's Manuals and Avoiding Offsprings', in *Handling Sin*, ed. Minnis and Biller, pp. 165–87, esp. pp. 177–82; Nicole Bériou, 'La confession dans les écrits théologiques et pastoraux du XIIIe siècle: médication de l'âme ou démarche judiciaire?' in *L'Aveu, Antiquité et Moyen Âge. Actes de la table ronde de Rome (28–30 mars 1984)* (Rome, 1986), pp. 261–82, esp. pp. 269–73.

18 William of Auvergne, *Tractatus novus de poenitentia* (Orléans-Paris, 1674, repr. Frankfurt a M., 1963), I, pp. 570b–592b.

19 Palémon Glorieux's datation in *Répertoire des maîtres de théologie de Paris du XIIIe siècle* (Paris, 1933), I, pp. 315–20 (p. 317).

20 William of Auvergne, *De sacramentis* (Orléans-Paris, 1674, repr. Frankfurt a M., 1963), I, pp. 407–16.

21 Ibid., pp. 451–512.

22 Ibid., pp. 528–53.

23 Ibid., pp. 512–28.

24 Ibid., pp. 429–51.

25 Ibid., pp. 416–26.

26 Ibid., pp. 426–29.

27 Ibid., pp. 553–5.

28 William of Auvergne, *De sacramento penitentie* (Orléans-Paris, 1674, repr. Frankfurt a M., 1963): introduction (cap. 1–4, pp. 451–62), *Tractatum de contritione* (cap. 5–10, pp. 463–82), *Tractatum de confessione* (cap. 12–19, pp. 482–504) and *Tractatum de restitutione* (cap. 20–21, pp. 505–12). On the organization of the treatise *De sacramento penitentie*, see Lesley Smith, 'William of Auvergne and Confession', in *Handling Sin*, ed. Minnis and Biller, pp. 95–107 (p. 99).

29 Cf. Paul Anciaux, 'Le sacrement de pénitence chez Guillaume d'Auvergne', *Ephemeride Theologicae Lovanienses*, 24 (1948) pp. 98–118 (cit. p. 98).

30 Ibid.

31 SeePaul Anciaux, 'Le sacrement de pénitence'; Casagrande, 'Guglielmo d'Auverne e il buon uso'.

32 Casagrande, 'Guglielmo d'Auverne e il buon uso', p. 190: 'una specie di laboratorio nel quale è possibilie osservare e sperimentare geometrie, dinamiche e manifestazioni della passioni'.

33 Ibid., p. 191: 'Guglielmo d'Auvergne è uno degli autori più attenti al problema delle passioni nella penitenza. Un attenzione che si traduce in une vera e propria pedagogia della passioni'; and p. 199: 'La penitenza si presenta come une stroaordinaria occasione di educazione sentimentale, une spazio ideale per apprendere l'arte di governare e usare l'affetivita'.

34 Smith, 'William of Auvergne and Confession', pp. 100–1 (cit. p. 100).

35 Ibid., p. 107. On the double statuto of these texts, see also Casagrande, 'Guglielmo d'Auverne e il buon uso', p. 191.

36 On William of Auvergne's style and mode of argumentation, see Anciaux, 'Le sacrement de pénitence', pp. 98-9; Casagrande, 'Guglielmo d'Auverne e il buon uso', pp. 190-4. See also Smith, 'William of Auvergne and Confession', p. 103: 'William never divorces the theology from the everyday, nor the "ignorant" questions from the theology.' As Etienne Gilson has shown, William was influenced by Avicenna's style in his choice of a continuous and personal speech, with some addresses to the reader and many digressions: cf. Etienne Gilson, 'Avicenne en Occident au Moyen Âge', *Archives d'Histoire Doctrinale et Littéraire du Moyen Âge*, 36 (1969) pp. 89-121, esp. pp. 91-2. On William's sense of humour, see Jacques Berlioz, 'La voix de l'évêque Guillaume d'Auvergne dans les *exempla* (XIIIe-XVe s.)', in *Autour de Guillaume d'Auvergne*, ed. Morenzoni and Tilliette, pp. 9-34.

37 Casagrande, 'Guglielmo d'Auverne e il buon uso', p. 193: '*contritio*, seconda e decisiva fase della conversione interiore prevista dalla penitenza'.

38 William of Auvergne, *De sacramento penitentie*, cap. 5, p. 462bH: 'Contritio est confractio et comminutio et quasi pulverem redactio veteris hominis'. See also cap. 6, p. 465bD: 'Contritio est violenta divisio, partium allisione, et collisione, et percussione facta'. On this conception of contrition, see Casagrande, 'Guglielmo d'Auverne e il buon uso', pp. 193-4.

39 Ibid., cap. 5, pp. 463aA-464bE: 'Nominatur etiam compunctio [...]. Nominatur etiam reversio [...]. Nominatur etiam conversio [...]. Sunt et aliae nominationes ipsius contritionis [...]. Prima est, quam dicitur baptismus in Spiritu Sancto, sive in igne. [...] Nominatur etiam nominibus quatuor festivitatum. Dicitur enim Natale [...]. Dicitur etiam Pascha [...]. Dicitur Pentecoste [...]. Dicitur etiam Ascensio'. On this argumentation, see Casagrande, 'Guglielmo d'Auverne e il buon uso', p. 294, and Anciaux, 'Le sacrement de pénitence', p. 110.

40 William of Auvergne, *De sacramento penitentie*, cap. 5, pp. 463aA-463bA.

41 On this correlation, see Nagy, *Le don des larmes*, 'Annexe: Définition, historique. Componction et don des larmes', pp. 421-30.

42 Nagy, *Le don des larmes*, p. 425.

43 On the history of the word 'compunction' and its various meanings in Christian spirituality, see Joseph Pegon, 'Componction' in *Dictionnaire de Spiritualité ascétique et mystique*, III (Paris, 1953), pp. 1312-21; Pie-Raymond Régamey, 'La componction du cœur', in *Portrait spirituel du chrétien* (Paris, 1963), pp. 67-116; Nagy, *Le don des larmes*, pp. 421-30.

44 Ps 108, 17 (109, 16): 'Et persecutus est virum inopem et pauperem et conpunctum corde ut interficeret'.

45 Actes, 2, 37: 'His auditis, compuncti sunt corde'. On this text, see Régamey, 'La componction du cœur', pp. 74-6.

46 William of Auvergne, *De sacramento penitentie*, cap. 5, p. 463aA.

47 On Gregory the Great and compunction, see Nagy, *Le don des larmes*, pp. 124-33; Régamey, 'La componction du cœur', pp. 83-96; Pegon, 'Componction'.

48 Casagrande, 'Guglielmo d'Auvergne e il buon uso', p. 1194: 'il gioco metaforico'.
49 Nicole Loraux, 'La métaphore sans métaphore: à propos de l'Orestie', *Revue philosophique de la France et de l'Etranger* 180, no. 2 (1990), pp. 247–68.
50 Ibid., p. 248: 'On ne saurait se passer impunément de l'étrangeté'.
51 Ibid., p. 254: 'Il faut coûte que coûte s'en tenir à la littéralité du mot à mot, avec cet énoncé tout en hiatus où la discontinuité glisse des silences dans l'entendre, où l'oreille construit du sens sur le heurt des visions arrêtées aussitôt qu'ébauchées. [...] Ni surtraduction, ni localisation trop précise. Rien d'autre que les mots, rien hors les mots, que leur enchaînement réponde ou non aux critères admis de la cohérence.'
52 William of Auvergne, *De sacramento penitentie*, cap. 5, p. 462bH: 'Poenitentes autem ea conterunt sicut lactucas agrestes, et jus sive succum amarissimum qui in eis latebat, ipsa contritione et ruminatione recognitionum solicitissimarum aut profundissimarum inde exprimunt; propter quod cum primum eis dulce sperent, dum ea faciebant, nunc amarum eisdem sapiunt.'
53 On this commentary of Gregory the Great, see Nagy, *Le donc des larmes*, pp. 127–9.
54 The scope of chapter 6, however, is different. It is less focused on sensations than on emotions: William questioned human emotional sensibility. Cf. Casagrande, 'Guglielmo d'Auvergne e il buon uso', p. 197.
55 William of Auvergne, *De sacramento penitentie*, cap. 5, pp. 462bH–462aA: 'Nominatur etiam compunctio sive propter illud, quia tunc primo sentiuntur spinae et aculei peccatorum [...], sive quia tunc in imo cordis et in intimo cordis infinguntur.'
56 Ps 32 (31), 4: 'Conversus sum in ærumna mea, dum configitur spina'.
57 Pegon, 'Componction'.
58 William of Auvergne, *De sacramento penitentie*, cap. 5, p. 463aD: 'Vel propter hoc compunctio, quia peccator est sicut bos et asinus in lutum mersus, vel sicut equus qui vulgo dicitur infugatus. Quemadmodum bos vel equo infugato aculei vel calcaria adhibentur, ut de luto exiliat, si elementissimus Deus peccatores de lacu miseriae et de luto faecis educeis volens, compungit ut supra petram Christum dominum vel sanctae conversionis soliditatem sei firmitatem exiliant'.
59 Nagy, *Le don des larmes*, p. 425.
60 William of Auvergne, *De sacramento penitentie*, cap. 5, p. 463bA: 'Vel ideo dicitur compunctio quia quemadmodum arbores thuris et mirrhae sudibus ferreis vulnerantur, et ipsa vulneratione velut lachrimatae, aromata mirrhae et thuris proferunt, thus enim et mirrha lachrimae sunt hujusmodi arborum, sed coagulatae; sic compuncta corda poenitentium thus devotae orationis et mirrham internae amaricationnis emittunt'.
61 This is a conjecture. I have not been able to find any information about cultivating myrrh and incense during the Middle Ages.

62 Cf. Alain Boureau, 'Élaguer et greffer. Un discours chrétien bien planté', *Penser/Rêver*, 11 (printemps 2007), pp. 95–109, cit. pp. 105–6: 'faire passer la violence sous la sérénité de l'arboriculture'.
63 William of Auvergne, *Tractatus novus de poenitentia*, cap. 12, p. 586bG: 'Mortui quippe membra mortem suam et vulnera sentire non possunt. Si itaque vehementer dolet, tactum ei restitutum certum erit.'
64 William of Auvergne, *De sacramento penitentie*, cap. 5, p. 463aA: 'Ante adventum ejus et vivificam ejusdem visitationem corde stupido, vel potius mortificato et mortuo, nec vulnus peccati, nec ferrum in vulnere sentiebatur, nec aculei peccatorum, nec punctiones ipsorum.'
65 On the motive of salutary pain in William of Auvergne's writings, see Esther Cohen, *The Modulated Scream: Pain in Late Medieval Culture* (Chicago, 2010), pp. 28–37.
66 Ibid.: 'Quia omne peccatum est gladius biceps'.
67 Ibid.: 'Alterum acumen habet quasi amorosum atque mellitum fallacissima suavitate ac proditiosa, et (ut veritius loquar) phantasmatica et somniali. [...] Et propter hoc punitio, non transfixio, nec transverberatio nominatur a stultis et corde insensibilibus, sed delectatio atque suavitas et gaudium.'
68 Ibid., p. 463aB: 'Aliud vero acumen peccata sensibiliter laedit et vulnerat et propter hoc salubriter. Totum enim virus mortiferae delectationis acumen istud expellit.'
69 Ovid, *Remedia amoris*, I, v. 44–8, ed. Henri Bornecque (Paris, 1961), p. 12: 'Una manus uobis uulnus opemque feret. / Terra salutares herbas eademque nocentes / Nutrit et urticae proxima saepe rosa est. / Vulnus in Herculeo quae quondam fecerat hoste, / Vulneris auxilium Pelias hasta tulit'. William of Auvergne cited only one verse and replaced Hercules's name by Achilles's. William of Auvergne, *De sacramento penitentie*, cap. 5, p. 463aA: 'Visus est Poeta: Vulnus Achilleo que quondam fecerat hosti. Vulneris auxilium Pelias hasta tulit'.
70 Cf. Ludwig Traube, *Vorlesungen und Abhandlungen* (München, 1911), vol. II, p. 113.
71 Cf. Charles H. Haskins, 'A List of Texts-books from the Close of the XIIth Century', *Harvard Studies in Classical Philology* 20 (1909), pp. 75–94.
72 Elisabeth Pellegrin, 'Les *Remedia amoris* d'Ovide, texte scolaire médiéval', *Bibliothèque de l'Ecole des Chartes* 115 (1957) pp. 172–9.
73 On Ovid's popularity in the twelfth and the thirteenth centuries, see Simone Viarre, *La survie d'Ovide dans la littérature scientifique des XIIe et XIIIe siècles* (Poitiers, 1966), esp. pp. 68–9 and pp. 131–4 on medical allusions to Ovid by William of Auvergne. On Peter of Abano's citation of Ovid, see Delaurenti, *La puissance des mots*, 'Ovide contre les incantations', pp. 276–82.
74 William of Auvergne, *De universo*, II, iii, cap. 21, p. 1056bH: 'Nemini intelligenti dubium est, musica esse virtutem harmoniarum ad mitigandos dolores animarum

humanarum, et ad incuti(e)ndos eosdem, similiter ad laetificandas ipsas, et ad omnes passiones ingerendas eisdem'.

75 In classical Latin, *rapere* means 'to trigger, to take away by force, to thrill' (Grand Gaffiot). In medieval Latin, *raptus* refers to a violent act perpetrated on a woman (Du Cange, Niermeyer).

76 William of Auvergne, *De universo*, II, iii, chap. 21, p. 1057aA: 'Animas humanas [...] a semetipsis quodammodo abstrahuntur, et in ipsam harmoniarum suavitatem rapiuntur.'

77 On the power of music in William of Auvergne's writings, see Delaurenti, *La puissance des mots*, pp. 217-30; Brenno Boccadoro, 'La musique, les passions, l'âme et le corps', in *Autour de Guillaume d'Auvergne*, ed. Morenzoni and Tilliette, pp. 75-92.

78 William of Auvergne, *De sacramento penitentie*, cap. 5, p. 463aD: 'Undique enim transfigendum est cor ferro medicinali, ut unique mors spiritualis in eo moriatur, et unique virus ac sanies effluat peccatorum'.

79 Canon 21 ('*Omnis utriusque sexus*'), Fourth Lateran Council (1215), in *Conciliorum oecumenicorum generaliumque decreta*, ed. Giuseppe Alberigo and Alberto Melloni (Turnhout, 2013), II/1 p. 178, l. 521-5: 'Sacerdos autem sit discretus et cautus, ut more periti medici superinfundat vinum et oleum vulneribus sauciati, diligenter inquirens et peccatoris circumstantias et peccati, per quas prudenter intelligat quale illi debeat prebere consilium et cuiusmodi remedium adhibere, diversis experimentis utendo ad sanandum aegrotum'. On this text, see Bériou, 'La confession dans les écrits théologiques et pastoraux du XIIIe siècle', pp. 261-2.

80 On the use of the analogy between the priest and the doctor in thirteenth-century theology, see Bériou, 'La confession dans les écrits théologiques et pastoraux du XIIIe siècle', pp. 269-73. For previous examples of this analogy in Patristic literature and in Christian penitentials, see Rudolph Arbesmann, 'The Concept of *christus medicus* in St Augustine', *Traditio* 10 (1954), pp. 1-28 and John T. Mc Neill, 'Medicine for Sin as Prescribed in the Penitentials', *Church History* 1 (1932), pp. 14-26.

81 William of Auvergne, *De universo*, II, iii, cap. 21, pp. 1057aB-1057aC: 'Forte igitur, et fortuito curati sunt multi morbi spirituales per harmonias a nescientibus medicis, quae, vel quales harmoniae virtutem istam habent. Verum si praenominata peritia prediti essent, vix eos effugeret aliquis morbus spiritualis. [...] Vides igitur quantus defectus est in medicis, tempore isto potissimus, quantum ad morbos spirituales.' On this text, see Delaurenti, *La puissance des mots*, pp. 228-30, 'Médecine et musique, les enjeux d'une confrontation'.

82 Casagrande, 'Guglielmo d'Auverne e il buon uso'.

83 William of Auvergne, *De sacramento penitentie*, cap. 5, p. 463bD: 'Peccator, dum in peccatis est, subversus est, habens sub quod deberet habere supra et econverso,

videlicet spiritum habet sub et carnem supra, cum esse debeat exonverso, et eversus est, habens ante se quod deberet habere retro et econverso.'

84 Ibid.: 'Habet enim faciem ad posteriora, hoc est temporalia seu terrena, si quidem oculos habet ad illa, ut alia non videat. [...] Similiter et aures habet ad illa, ut alia audire non possit'.

85 Ibid.: 'Nares [...] nihil ei redoleat suave, nisi stercora temporalium.'

86 Ibid.: 'Sic fauces et palatum non habet, nisi illa, et propter hoc non comedit et saporat, nisi illa.'

87 Ibid.: 'Similiter et everius est habens in dextera quod debet habere in sinistra, et econverso.'

88 Ibid.: 'Et est eversus habens extra quod debet habere intra et econverso.'

89 Ibid., pp. 463bD–464aE: 'Est enim extra plenus et intus vacuus; extra dives, intus paupes; extra vestitus, intra nudus; extra nitidus, intus sordidus; extra dominus, intus servus; extra eques, intus jumentum diaboli; et iterum extra homo, intus brutum; et interdum extra sanctus, intus execrabilis, extra monachus sive claustralis, intus autem omni lascivia et inordinatione saecularis; et iterum, extra Rex coronatus, intus autem latro spirituali suspendio damnatus; et extra Episcopus pontificalibus onamentis decoratus, intus autem diabolica turpitudinis insigniis deturpatus; extra Sacerdos insulatus, intus autem monstri scelerum contaminatus; et iterum extra clericus tonsuratus, intus laicus capillatus; et item extra vir barbarus, intus vero puer imberbis, vel quod deterius est, mulier imbecillis et omnino imbellis.'

90 See Florence Chave-Mahir, *L'exorcisme des possédés dans l'Eglise d'Occident (X^e–XIVe siècle)* (Turnhout, 2011), pp. 104–9 (cit. p. 106).

91 This was the object of Jacqueline Borsje's keynote lecture: 'Lettering down formulae and anatomic lists in verbal remedies for fevers and headache: A long-term and broad perspective' (unpublished), during the conference *Interdisciplinary Approaches to the Study of Healing Charms and Medicine* (Harvard University, 6–8 April 2018). See also Béatrice Delaurenti, 'La pratique incantatoire à l'époque scolastique. Charmes et formules des réceptaires médicaux en latin et en langues romanes (XIIIe–XVe siècle)', in *La formule au Moyen Âge, II. Actes du colloque de Nancy et Metz, 7–9 juin 2012*, ed. I. Draelants and C. Balouzat-Loubet (Turnhout, 2015), pp. 473–94.

92 For another bodily metaphor in another chapter of William of Auvergne's treatise on penance, see Smith, 'William of Auvergne and Confession': in chapter 12, confession is compared to vomiting. William of Auvergne, *De sacramento penitentie*, cap. 12, p. 487aB.

93 On the articulation of these stages, see Casagrande, 'Guglielmo d'Auverne e il buon uso', pp. 193–9.

94 Cf. Pegon, 'Componction'.

95 Ibid.
96 Delaurenti, *La Puissance des mots*, esp. p. 201, p. 230, pp. 455–61.
97 On William's adaptation to his audience, see Smith, 'William of Auvergne and Confession'; Jacques Berlioz, 'Pouvoirs et contrôle de la croyance: la question de la procréation démoniaque chez Guillaume d'Auvergne', *Razo* 9 (1989), pp. 5–27.
98 For a similar appreciation of pain, located both in the soul and in the body, in others authors, see Cohen, *The Modulated Scream*, pp. 28–32: 'The entire tradition of penitential literature deliberately did not differentiate between physical and emotional pain in this context' (p. 29); Robert, 'Médecine et théologie à la cour angevine de Naples', pp. 333–5.
99 The same intermingling was perceptible in the scholastic discourses on the gift of tears that became from the thirteenth century more scientific than devotional. Cf. Nagy, *Le don des larmes*, p. 384.
100 This interpretation of William's metaphorical game is inspired by Loraux, 'La métaphore sans métaphore', esp. her remarks on the recurrent coexistence of two meanings and on the double regime of words (p. 263 and p. 267). See, for example, p. 253: '[la métaphore est] une accumulation de sauts – c'est-à-dire étrangement de heurts – entre champs d'expérience différents, voie inconciliables, mais dont seul l'entrechoquement produit [...] cet énoncé singulier'.

Chapter 5

1 Acts of the Apostles 2:37. Biblical references are to the Douay-Rheims version along with Latin Vulgate text (online), Available at *www.drbo.org* (accessed 29 June 2018).
2 On compassion, see, for example, *Studies on Medieval Empathies*, ed. Karl F. Morrison and Rudolph M. Bell (Turnhout, 2013), especially the chapters by Rachel Fulton Brown (pp. 115–38) and Barbara Newman (pp. 189–212); and Sarah McNamer, *Affective Meditation and the Invention of Medieval Compassion* (Philadelphia, 2010), especially pp. 1–22. See also the more recent work by Daniel McCann in his *Soul-Health: Therapeutic Reading in Later Medieval England* (Cardiff, 2018), especially pp. 93–7.
3 For a recent interrogation of the state of the 'history of emotions' field (including the contention that 'both the history of emotions and contemporary affect theory are insufficient for dealing with the complexity and nuance of medieval renderings'), see Glenn D. Burger and Holly A. Crocker, 'Introduction', in *Medieval Affect, Feeling, and Emotion*, ed. Glenn D. Burger and Holly A. Crocker (Cambridge, 2019), pp. 1–24 (for quotation see 12). See also the introduction to *Emotion and Textual Media*, ed. Mary Catherine Flannery (Turnhout, 2018), pp. 1–18.

4   'Particulièrement fertile en affections': P. Pourrat, 'Affections', in *Dictionnaire de spiritualité: ascetique et mystique, doctrine et histoire*, ed. Marcel Viller et al., 17 vols, I (Paris, 1937), 235–40 (237).
5   See Margaret Laing and Angus McIntosh, 'Cambridge, Trinity College, MS 335: Its Texts and Their Transmission', in *New Science out of Old Books: Studies in Manuscripts and Early Printed Books in Honour of A. I. Doyle*, ed. Richard Beadle and A. J. Piper (Aldershot, 1995), pp. 14–52 (14); and Bella Millett, 'The Pastoral Context of the Trinity and Lambeth Homilies', in *Essays in Manuscript Geography: Vernacular Manuscripts of the English West Midlands from the Conquest to the Sixteenth Century*, ed. Wendy Scase (Turnhout, 2007), pp. 43–64 (44–5).
6   Ralph Hanna, 'Lambeth Palace Library, MS 487: Some Problems of Early Thirteenth-century Textual Transmission', in *Texts and Traditions of Medieval Pastoral Care: Essays in Honour of Bella Millett*, ed. Cate Gunn and Catherine Innes-Parker (York, 2009), pp. 78–88 (84–5).
7   See further: Sarah M. O'Brien, 'An Edition of Seven Homilies from Lambeth Palace Library MS. 487' (unpublished doctoral thesis, University of Oxford, 1985); Millett, 'The Pastoral Context', p. 63; Hanna, 'Lambeth Palace Library, MS 487', p. 79; and Laing and McIntosh, 'Cambridge, Trinity College, MS 335', p. 14.
8   On this manuscript, see further Jerome Oetgen, 'The Trinity College Ascension Sermon: Sources and Structure', *Medieval Studies* 45 (1983), 410–17.
9   Laing and McIntosh, 'Cambridge, Trinity College, MS 335', p. 39.
10 Millett, 'The Pastoral Context', p. 61.
11 Bella Millett, 'The Discontinuity of English Prose: Structural Innovation in the Trinity and Lambeth Homilies', in *Text and Language in Medieval English Prose: A Festschrift for Tadao Kubouchi*, ed. Akin Oizumi, Jacek Fiscal and John Scahill (Frankfurt, 2005), pp. 129–50 (especially pp. 130, 134–35, 139).
12 See especially Stephen Pelle, 'Source Studies in the Lambeth Homilies', *Journal of English and Germanic Philology* 113 (2014), 34–72.
13 Millett, 'The Pastoral Context' p. 58.
14 Ibid., p. 60.
15 See Sandra McEntire, *The Doctrine of Compunction in Medieval England: Holy Tears* (Lewiston, 1990), especially chapter 2 ('Scriptural and Historical Context'), pp. 11–31.
16 See 'compunction (n.)' in *The Oxford English Dictionary* (Online) (Entry not fully updated since 1891; accessed 30 June 2018).
17 Jean Leclercq, *The Love of Learning and the Desire of God*, trans. Catharine Misrahi (NY, 1961), p. 66.
18 Ibid., pp. 29–30.
19 Ibid., pp. 38–9.
20 Ibid., p. 30.

21 Ibid.
22 Ibid., p. 31.
23 Sandra McEntire, 'The Doctrine of Compunction from Bede to Margery Kempe', in *The Medieval Mystical Tradition in England IV*, ed. Marion Glasscoe (Cambridge, 1987), pp. 77–90 (78).
24 McEntire, 'The Doctrine of Compunction from Bede to Margery Kempe', pp. 84, 88.
25 On joy, see McEntire, *The Doctrine of Compunction in Medieval England: Holy Tears*, pp. 75–6. On compunction in contrast to other kinds of mourning, see McEntire, 'The Doctrine of Compunction from Bede to Margery Kempe', p. 78.
26 Pierre Adnès, 'Pénitence', in *Dictionnaire de spiritualité ascétique et mystique: doctrine et histoire*, ed. Marcel Viller et al., vol xii (1) (Paris, 1984), 943–1010 (971).
27 Paul Anciaux, *The Sacrament of Penance* (London, 1962), p. 93.
28 See *In IV Sententiarum*, distinctio 17, quaestio 2, articulus 1, quaestiuncula 2, argumentum 3: cited from Library of Latin Texts Series A (Online) (accessed 19 October 2019). Thomas Aquinas is cited here as an important contributor to the devotional climates of the thirteenth century and not as a direct source for the Lambeth and Trinity homilies.
29 Anciaux, *The Sacrament of Penance*, pp. 94–5.
30 G. H. Gerrits, *Inter Timorem et Spem: A Study of the Theological Thought of Gerard Zerbolt of Zutphen (1367–1398)* (Leiden, 1986), p. 179.
31 See *The Oxford Dictionary of English Etymology*, ed. C. T. Onions (Oxford, 1966), p. 199.
32 See entry for 'contrite', in *The Oxford Dictionary of English Etymology*, ed. Onions, p. 210, which cites an occurrence in the *Cursor Mundi* from the thirteenth century. See also 'contrition (n.)' in *The Oxford English Dictionary* (Online); the earliest citation given here is Chaucer's *Parson's Tale, c.* 1386. (Entry not updated fully since 1893; accessed 30 June 2018.)
33 See entry for 'bireusing(e), -ung (n.)' in the *Middle English Dictionary*, ed. Hans Kurath and S. M. Kuhn (Online). Available at http://quod.lib.umich.edu/m/med/ (accessed 21 October 2019).
34 *Old English Homilies*, First Series, ed. Richard Morris. EETS O.S. 29, 34 (London, 1867–1868), p. 21. All subsequent references to the Lambeth homilies are to this edition; punctuation has been slightly modernized, as Morris provides a heavily diplomatic edition. Translations are my own.
35 See entries for 'sor(e n.(1)' and 'sori adj.' and in the *Middle English Dictionary* (Online) (accessed 21 October 2019).
36 *Old English Homilies*, Second Series, ed. Richard Morris, EETS O.S. 53 (London, 1873), p. 95; all subsequent references to the Trinity homilies are to this edition; punctuation has been slightly modernized, as Morris provides a heavily diplomatic edition. Translations are my own.

37 See 'reuen v.(1)' in the *Middle English Dictionary* (Online) (accessed 19 October 2019).
38 See the entry 'armhertnesse (n.)' in the *Middle English Dictionary* (Online) (accessed 29 June 2018).
39 A. S. Lazikani, *Cultivating the Heart: Feeling and Emotion in Twelfth- and Thirteenth-century Religious Texts* (Cardiff, 2015), p. 41.
40 This is identified and discussed in Millett, 'The Discontinuity of English Prose', pp. 134–5.
41 On the creation of 'Mary Magdalene' in medieval exegesis, see further Benedicta Ward, *Harlots of the Desert: A Study of Repentance in Early Monastic Sources* (London, 1987), p. 15.
42 The alabaster box is read as a devout heart in Aelred of Rievualx's (d. 1167) *De institutione inclusarum: Aelredi Rievallensis Opera Omnia: 1 Opera Ascetica*, ed. Anselm Hoste and Charles H. Talbot, Corpus Christianorum Continuatio Mediaevalis, i (Turnhout, 1971, 667). For a translation of this text, see 'A Rule for the Life of a Recluse', trans. Mary Paul Macpherson, in *Treatises: The Pastoral Prayer*, ed. M. Basil Pennington (Kalamazoo, MI, 1982), pp. 41–102.
43 '*Cher alme*': *Texts of Anglo-Norman Piety*, ed. Tony Hunt and trans. Jane Bliss (Tempe, AZ, 2010), pp. 202–3, ll. 71–82.
44 Translation my own.
45 *Cher alme*, ed. Hunt and Bliss, pp. 204–7, ll. 160–1, 167–8, and 183–8.
46 Translation my own.
47 See further Millett, 'The Discontinuity of English Prose', p. 139, and p. 147 n. 72.
48 See further D. L. d'Avray, *The Preaching of the Friars: Sermons Diffused before 1300* (Oxford, 1985), pp. 47, 51; M. Michèle Mulchahey '*First the Bow Is Bent in Study*': *Dominican Education before 1350* (Toronto, 1998), p. 527; and P. H. Tibber, 'The Origins of the Scholastic Sermon, c. 1130–c. 1210' (unpublished doctoral thesis, University of Oxford, 1983), p. 192.
49 Lazikani, *Cultivating the Heart*, p. 36.
50 See *Ancrene Wisse: A Corrected Edition of the Text in Cambridge, Corpus Christi College, MS 402 with Variants from Other Manuscripts*, ed. Bella Millett, 2 vols. EETS O.S. 325 and 326 (London, 2005–06), I, 129: 595–7; all subsequent references are to this edition. Millett and Kirchberger have both remarked on Part V's wide audience. See Bella Millett, '*Ancrene Wisse* and the Conditions of Confession', *English Studies* 80 (1999), pp. 193–215 (193); and Clare Kirchberger, 'Some Notes on the *Ancrene Riwle*', *Dominican Studies* 7 (1954), 215–38 (231).
51 See further Millett, ed., *Ancrene Wisse*, II, xi–xiii. See also T. P. Dolan, 'The Date of *Ancrene Wisse*: A Corroborative Note', *Queries and Notes* 219 (1974), 322–3.
52 See, for example, 'heorte bireowsunge' (139: 303), translated by Millett as 'contrition of heart' (*Guide for Anchoresses: A Translation Based on Cambridge, Corpus Christi College, MS 402* (Exeter, 2009), p. 139).

53 Peter Lombard, *Sententiae in IV libris distinctae*, 2 vols (Rome, 1971–81), II, 345. The Lombard is not cited as a direct source for the English material. He was, however, an indispensable contributor to the development of the sacrament of penance (see especially Adnès, 'Pénitence', p. 970). For the Lombard's sacramental definitions, see Alister E. McGrath, *Iustitia Dei: A History of the Christian Doctrine of Justification* (Cambridge, 1998), p. 93.

54 Linda Georgianna, *The Solitary Self: Individuality in Ancrene Wisse* (Cambridge, MA, 1981), p. 107.

55 See entry 'hakken (v.)' in the *Middle English Dictionary* (Online) (accessed 30 June 2018).

56 'Et cum complerentur dies Pentecostes, erant omnes pariter in eodem loco et factus est repente de caelo sonus, tamquam advenientis spiritus vehementis, et replevit totam domum ubi erant sedentes. Et apparuerunt illis dispertitae linguae tamquam ignis, seditque supra singulos eorum' (Acts 2:1–3) (And when the days of the Pentecost were accomplished, they were all together in one place: And suddenly there came a sound from heaven, as of a mighty wind coming, and it filled the whole house where they were sitting. And there appeared to them parted tongues as it were of fire, and it sat upon every one of them).

57 'Et erit in novissimis diebus, dicit Dominus, effundam de Spiritu meo super omnem carnem: et prophetabunt filii vestri, et filiae vestrae, et juvenes vestri visiones videbunt, et seniores vestri somnia somniabunt' (Acts 2:17) (And it shall come to pass, in the last days, (saith the Lord,) I will pour out of my Spirit upon all flesh: and your sons and your daughters shall prophesy, and your young men shall see visions, and your old men shall dream dreams).

58 'Non turbetur cor vestrum. Creditis in Deum, et in me credite' (John 14:1) (Let not your heart be troubled. You believe in God, believe also in me).

59 See further Lazikani, *Cultivating the Heart*, p. 45.

60 See entry 'sonder-lepes (adv.)' in the *Middle English Dictionary* (Online) (accessed 30 June 2018).

61 See especially Trinity 20:

Ðus þe holie apostles were gadered on ane stede. and þus þe holi gost com uppen hem and fulde hem of him seluen. and freurede hem of sorege. and tehte hem speken eches londes speche. and lihte hem of rihte bileue and makede hem hattere on soðe [luue] to gode and to men. and clensede hem alle of þe hore of alle sinnes. (p. 119)

(Thus the holy apostles were gathered in one place, and thus the Holy Ghost came upon them and filled them with himself, and comforted them of their sorrow, and taught them to speak in each land's speech, and enlightened them with true belief and made them the hotter in true love to God and to man – and cleansed them of all their sins.)

62 See Acts of the Apostles 2:3: 'Et apparuerunt illis dispertitae linguae tamquam ignis, seditque supra singulos eorum' (And there appeared to them parted tongues as it were of fire, and it sat upon every one of them).

Chapter 6

1 For more information about the conception of repentance in the Antiquity, see D. Konstan, 'From Regret to Remorse: The Origins of a Moral Emotion', in *Understanding Emotions in Early Europe*, M. Champion and A. Lynch (dir.) (Turnhout: Brepols, 2015), pp. 3–23.
2 G. de Coinci, *Les Miracles de Nostre Dame*, ed. V. F. Koenig (Geneva; Lille, Droz: Giard, 1955).
3 In today's French, *compunction* has taken the meaning of 'gravity, seriousness'. It is almost only used in the specific expression *avec componction* meaning 'with gravity or with seriousness', these two words being often used with it. However nowadays very few people do really understand its meaning without using a dictionary. Paradoxically, it is still in use as the corpus of contemporary French texts from Frantext counts it fifty times (almost always in the expression *avec componction*) whereas *remorse*, that everybody can certainly define, is only to be found five times in the same corpus.
4 Which contains fifty-nine texts, some belonging to both.
5 « De plorer ses pechiez ne fine Ne jor ne nuit, ne tart ne tempre. Sainz Esperites li atempre Si devote devocïon Et si poingnant compunctïon Dedens son cuer que sanz sejor Ses pechiez pleure nuit et jor » (724–30) Gautier de Coinci, *Le Miracle de Théophile*, ed. Annette Garnier (Paris: Champion, 1998).
6 J.-C. Payen, *Le Motif du repentir dans la littérature française médiévale* (Geneva: Droz, 1967), p. 18.
7 Ibid., p. 594.
8 V. Jankélévitch, *Valeur et signification de la mauvaise conscience* (Paris: F. Alcan, 1933), p. 56.
9 Philippe de Remi, *La Manekine*, ed. M.-M. Castellani (Paris: H. Champion, 2012).
10 J.-P. martin, *Les motifs dans la chanson de geste: définition et utilisation*, Villeneuve d'Ascq, Centre d'Études Médiévales et Dialectales, Univ. de Lille III, 1992, pp. 326–7.
11 v. jankélévitch, *Valeur et signification de la mauvaise conscience* (Paris: F. Alcan, 1933), p. 32.
12 See B. cerquiglini, *La Parole médiévale: discours, syntaxe, texte* (Paris: les Éditions de Minuit, 1981). His position has been very much nuancé par D. Lagorgette, in particular: lagorgette D., « Termes d'adresse, insultes et notion de détachement en diachronie » *Cahiers de praxématique*, 40, « Linguistique du détachement », F.

Neveu éd., 2003, «; 43–69 et lagorgette D., « Termes d'adresse et verbes de parole en moyen français: approche pragmatique », dans *Le Discours rapporté dans tous ses états*, éd. J. M. López-Muñoz, S. Marnette et L. Rosier (Paris: L'Harmattan, 2004), 194–203.

13   *Le Roman de Tristan en prose*, ed. R. L. Curtis (München: M. Hueber Verlag, 1963).
14   *La Passion du Palatinus*, ed. G. Frank (Paris: H. Champion, 1992).
15   This expression is repeated later when the servants, sent by Yseut to retrieve Bragain's body, arrive into a valley devoid of any trace of the young woman: 'Et quant il ne la troverent ne morte ne vive, il se clamerent las chaitif, car il cuident vraiement que les bestes l'aient devoree et qu'eles aient de li mangié et chair et os; (And when they find her neither dead nor alive, they lament themselves as wretched and miserable, because they truly believe that the animals have devoured her and that they have eaten her flesh and bone) (ibid., p. 98) or p. 106, p. 109, p. 138. *Le Roman de Tristan en prose*, ed. R. L. Curtis (Woodbridge, Suffolk: D.S. Brewer, 1985).
16   *L' Histoire d'Erec en prose: roman du xve siècle*, ed. M. Colombo Timelli (Geneva: Droz, 2000).
17   *Lancelot*, ed. A. Micha (Geneva; Paris: Librairie Droz, 1978).
18   *Perceforest*, ed. G. Roussineau (Geneva: Droz, 2012).
19   chrétien de Troyes, *Le Chevalier au lion*, ed. D. F. Hult (Paris, Libr: Générale Française, 2009).
20   *Le Roman de Partonopeu de Blois*, ed. A. Paris (Paris: Librairie générale française, 2005).
21   See also the beautiful dialogue between Judas and Despair in Gréban's *Passion*, in which their debate concerns the possibility of forgiveness. Where Judas persists in hoping for divine forgiveness, Despair one by one closes the doors of hope and pushes him to suicide. (Arnoul Gréban, *Le Mystère de la Passion Nostre Seigneur*, éd. O Jodogne, Troisième journée, v. 21, 747–21, 856).
22   *La Châtelaine de Vergy*, ed. J. Dufournet et L. Dulac (Paris: Gallimard, 1997).
23   v. jankélévitch, *Valeur et signification de la mauvaise conscience* (Paris: F. Alcan, 1933), p. 72.
24   Konstan, 'From regret to remorse', p. 6. D. Konstan uses and quotes R. Kaster, *Emotion, Restraint, and Community in Ancient Rome* (Oxford: Oxford, University Press, 2005), p. 80.
25   Ibid., p. 54.
26   *Le Roman de Tristan en prose*, ed. Ph. Ménard (Geneva: Droz, 1987).
27   Same expression in verses 6758–60: 'Mais ele est noïe en la mer / Se je m'en doi las, dolent, clamer' (But she has drowned in the sea / And I must declare myself as wretched and suffering).
28   The happiness described in this monologue remains a very passive happiness: Enide mourns her status as a beloved wife and her lost 'eise' (ease). She presents herself here as the object of love. It is, of course, true that she herself continues to love.

Chapter 7

1. See Véronique Plesch, *Painter and Priest: Giovanni Canavesio's Visual Rhetoric and the Passion Cycle at La Brigue* (Notre Dame, 2006), p. 230 for the rarity of fifteenth-century passion cycles with tituli. On pp. 245–7, I discuss how comparing Notre-Dame des Fontaines' set of tituli with the few cycles that possess a similar textual apparatus reveals its unusual scope and complexity.
2. The way the woman is referred to closely follows John 18:17, which designates the woman as 'ancilla ostiaria' (the maid therefore that was portress). All biblical citations are from the Vulgate and the Douay-Rheims version. Unless noted, all translations are by the author.
3. The full verse reads: 'Et egressus foras Petrus flevit amare' (And Peter going out, wept bitterly). Matthew 26:75: 'Et egressus foras, flevit amare' (And going forth, he wept bitterly) is very close.
4. George Henderson, 'Narrative Illustration and Theological Exposition in Medieval Art', in *Religion and Humanism*, ed. Keith Robbins (Oxford, 1981), p. 25. Henderson used the term in the context of twelfth- and thirteenth-century manuscript illumination.
5. Louis Réau, *Iconographie de l'art chrétien*, 3 vols (Paris, 1955–9), II/2, p. 439.
6. For instance in the paintings by Guglielmetto Fantini (c. 1432) in the baptistery of Chieri's cathedral, in addition to the maid, there is a soldier behind Peter who leans forward to the apostle and points to Christ; similarly, in the chapel of the castle at La Manta (c. 1427–before 1435), both the maid and a man who is warming himself at the fire address the apostle. At the chapel of Saint-Sébastien in Lanslevillard (1490–1500) and, as much as the state of the fresco allows to see, in the chapel of San Sebastiano at Bastia Mondovì (1472), two denials are staged (during Christ's appearances before Annas and Caiaphas for the first and Caiaphas and Herod for the latter). For bibliography on these cycles, see Plesch, *Painter and Priest* and *Le Christ peint: Le Cycle de la Passion dans les chapelles peintes du XVe siècle dans les États de Savoie* (Chambéry: Société Savoisienne d'Histoire et d'Archéologie, 2004).
7. John 18:25 simply writes 'they said' ('dixerunt') but refers to the 'servants and ministers' warming by the fire who are mentioned in verse 18.
8. A search in the Index of Medieval Art yields forty-four entries for 'Apostle Peter, Weeping' against 192 for 'Apostle Peter, Denial' (with some overlaps). Although the online database only represents approximately 30 per cent of the paper files in this archive of medieval art through the sixteenth century, these results still give a good sense of how much more common the Denial is compared to its aftermath. See examples in Gertrud Schiller, *Iconography of Christian Art* (London, 1968), vol. 2, pp. 58–60 and figures 198–200. As Schiller (ibid., p. 60), Réau (*Iconographie*, II/2, p. 440) and other authors have noted, the representation of Peter's Remorse gained

popularity during the Counter-Reformation and the Baroque age, when it becomes associated with the sacrament of penance.

9 Margaret B. Freeman, 'The Iconography of the Merode Altarpiece', *The Metropolitan Museum of Art Bulletin* 16, no. 6 (1957), pp. 130–9, discusses the motif of the hanging towel in this early and influential instance. The concept of disguised symbolism was first introduced by Erwin Panofsky in 'Jan van Eyck's *Arnolfini* Portrait', *Burlington Magazine* 64 (1934), pp. 117–27 and fully developed in *Early Netherlandish Painting* (Cambridge, MA, 1953), in particular chapter 5 'Reality and Symbol in Early Netherlandish Painting: "Spiritualia sub Metaphoris Corporalium"', pp. 131–48. For a recap and assessment of Panofsky, see, for instance, John L. Ward, 'Disguised Symbolism as Enactive Symbolism in Van Eyck's Paintings', *Artibus et Historiae* 15, no. 29 (1994), pp. 9–53.

10 The motif of the bucket appears in Jean de Journy's *Dîme de pénitence*, in which penance is compared to a well. The lowering of the bucket is a metaphor for the sinner's humility and its lifting his redemption. The length of the rope holding the bucket expresses the need for perseverance. See Jean-Charles Payen, *Le Motif du repentir dans la littérature française médiévale (des origines à 1230)* (Geneva, 1967), p. 570. Journy's metaphor might help understand the presence of a staircase in our painting: the descending motion of the bucket would gesture towards the sinner's humility and the ascending his redemption.

11 See Plesch, *Painter and Priest, passim*.

12 Hervé Martin, *Le Métier de prédicateur à la fin du moyen âge (1350–1520)* (Paris, 1988), pp. 392, 448–52, 451 and G. R. Owst, *Literature and Pulpit in Medieval England*, 2d ed. rev. (New York, 1961), pp. 35–6. In 1215, the Fourth Lateran Council made confession obligatory at least once a year. As Canon 21 explained, the goal was that they may 'receive the sacrament of Eucharist at least at Easter' (quoted in John W. Baldwin, 'From the Ordeal to Confession: In Search of Lay Religion in Early Thirteenth-century France', in *Handling Sin: Confession in the Middle Ages*, ed. Peter Biller and A. J. Minnis (York, 1998), p. 202. Since Lateran IV, one of the main purposes of preaching has been to encourage confession. For Alan of Lille, *The Art of Preaching*, trans. Gillian R. Evans (Kalamazoo, 1981), pp. 19–20, a good sermon should 'move the spirits of its hearers, stir up the mind, and encourage repentance'. Canavesio aims at the same target and the means he uses to promote confession are similar.

13 Quoted by Larissa Juliet Taylor, *Soldiers of Christ: Preaching in Late Medieval and Reformation France* (New York/ Oxford, 1992), p. 127. In a similar metaphor, Huon de Méry writes in the *Tournoiement Antéchrist* that Devotion washes the sinners' wounds with tears of Compunction, and Penance dries them with the cloth of Satisfaction; see Payen, *Le Motif*, p. 510. William A. Christian, Jr, 'Provoked Religious Weeping in Early Modern Spain', in *Religious Organization and Religious*

Experience, ed. John Davis (London, 1982), p. 100, mentions the 'long tradition of medieval preachers and celebrants who provoked tears' among which was St Vincent Ferrer, who, coincidentally, preached in La Brigue.

14　On Judas's physiognomy and its relationship to anti-Jewish rhetoric, see Plesch, *Painter and Priest*, p. 278ff.

15　Not surprisingly, Judas's Suicide is the most frequently reproduced panel from Notre-Dame. On the iconography of the Suicide of Judas (with a review of the literature on the subject), see Benjamin Russell Zweig, 'Depicting the Unforgivable Sin: Images of Suicide in Medieval Art', PhD dissertation Boston University, 2014, in particular pp. 55–148.

16　For other ways in which Canavesio singles out Judas and gives relief to his story; see Plesch, *Painter and Priest*, passim.

17　Jean Michel, *Le Mystère de la Passion (Angers 1486)*, ed. Omer Jodogne (Gembloux, 1959), before v. 889.

18　Maurice Accarie, *Le Théâtre sacré de la fin du moyen âge. Étude sur le sens moral de la Passion de Jean Michel* (Geneva, 1979).

19　Luke (23:39–43) is the only evangelist who distinguishes between a good and a bad thief. During the Crucifixion the good thief reproves his colleague who rails at Christ ('Neither doest thou fear God'), declares that they deserve their penalty ('And we indeed justly, for we receive the due reward of our deeds'), affirms his faith in Christ's innocence, and finally asks Jesus: 'Lord, remember me when thou shalt come into thy kingdom.' Christ answers, '[T]his day thou shalt be with me in paradise.' Matthew 27:38 and Mark 15:27 only recount that Christ was crucified between two 'latrones' (thieves), and John 19:18 is even less specific: 'alios duos' (two others).

20　See Plesch, *Painter and Priest*, pp. 213–16.

21　The play derives its name from a *petizione* at the beginning of the only extant manuscript (Florence, Biblioteca Laurenziana, ms Fondo Ashburnham 1190), addressed to Revello's officials. Revello is some forty kilometres southwest of Turin and only thirty kilometres south of Canavesio's town of Pinerolo. The manuscript bears an *explicit* date of 1490, which is only two years before the completion of La Brigue's cycle. Anna Cornagliotti, *La Passione di Revello: sacra rappresentazione quattrocentesca di ignoto piemontese* (Turin, 1976) estimates that the play was written between 1479 and 1482.

22　Revello I.3, 102–22. On the apocryphal sources for the episode, see Cornagliotti in *La Passione di Revello*, pp. 216–17. For the development of the figure of the thieves in Jean Michel, see Accarie, *Jean Michel*, pp. 115, 421 and 429. Just as Judas stands as counterpoint to Peter, the two thieves are opposed: see Mitchell B. Merback, *The Thief, the Cross and the Wheel. Pain and the Spectacle of Punishment in Medieval and Renaissance Europe* (Chicago, 1998), in particular Chapter 7 'Dysmas and Gestas: Model and Anti-model'.

23 On the expression of regret and repentance by the apostles after their flight and of Peter after his Denial in Jean Michel's *Passion*, see Eldegard DuBruck, 'Changes of Taste and Audience Expectation in Fifteenth-century Religious Drama', *Fifteenth-century Studies* 6 (1983), pp. 72–5.
24 Cited by Martin, *Le Métier*, p. 390, in his analysis of *Penitentia*'s semantic field.
25 Another scene closely connected to penitential practices is of course the Flagellation, which remarkably appears in La Brigue's cycle in an unusually early place and might therefore suggest that Christ was scourged twice; for this and examples of cycles with more than one depiction of the episode, see Plesch, *Painter and Priest*, p. 160.
26 As St Bonaventure put it: 'Ipsius autem partes integrales sunt *contritio* in animo, *confessio* in verbo et *satisfactio* in facto' (my emphasis). St Bonaventure, 'Breviloquium', pars vi, cap. x, in *Tria Opuscula*, Ad Claras Aquas (Quaracchi, 1911, 3rd ed.), p. 235. Quoted in Accarie, *Jean Michel*, p. 261, note 83. On confession, see Thomas Tentler, *Sin and Confession on the Eve of the Reformation* (Princeton, 1977) and Biller and Minnis, *Handling Sin*.
27 Arnoul Greban, *Le Mystère de la Passion d'Arnoul Gréban*, ed. Omer Jodogne (Bruxelles, 1965).
28 For scrolls at La Brigue, see Plesch, *Painter and Priest*, pp. 247–52; on p. 249 I give the sources – all textual – for these scrolls.
29 A search in the Index of Medieval Art yields no examples with such speech scrolls. Remarkably, Canavesio also included these scrolls in his earlier Passion cycle at San Bernardo in Pigna; see Plesch, *Painter and Priest*, pp. 251–2.
30 Jean-Pierre Bordier, *Le Jeu de la Passion. Le message chrétien et le théâtre français (XIIIe–XVIe s.)* (Paris, 1998), p. 466.
31 For previous assessments of Judas's pose, see Plesch, *Painter and Priest*, p. 52 n. 82. See also pp. 77–9 for a discussion of how Judas's stances and placement in the compositions contribute to dynamically linking the scenes. On pp. 178–9, I cite examples drawn from the visual arts and theatre in which Judas is given the place of honour in the ritual of the washing of the feet.
32 John 13:9.
33 Revello II.360–3.
34 Quoted in Santino Langé and Alberto Pensa, *Il Sacro Monte. Esperienza del reale e spazio virtuale nell'iconografia della Passione a Varallo* (Milan, 1991), p. 22.
35 The manuscript is dated c. 1425–30 (Princeton University Library, Garrett MS 48). See Dorothy Miner, *Illuminated Books of the Middle Ages and Renaissance* (Baltimore, 1949), no. 97, and *The Taste of Maryland. Art Collecting in Maryland, 1800–1934* (Baltimore, 1984), no. 51.
36 For Judas in hell, see Zweig, 'Depicting the Unforgivable Sin', pp. 110–12 and Alexander Murray, *Suicide in the Middle Ages*, 2 vols (Oxford, 1998), 'Judas the Damned', vol. II, pp. 331–4.

37 For a discussion of texts on Judas's despair, see Plesch, *Painter and Priest*, pp. 224–8 and Zweig, 'Depicting the Unforgivable Sin', pp. 65–6 and 120–4. See Murray, *Suicide in the Middle Ages, passim* for the connection between despair, suicide and Judas.
38 See Jean-Claude Schmitt, 'Le Suicide au moyen âge', *Annales. Economies, Sociétés, Civilisations* 31, no. 1 (1976), pp. 14–15.
39 Ibid., p. 5: suicide by hanging represents 60 per cent of the suicides, followed far behind by drowning, only 22 per cent. Still in the early nineteenth century, Victor Orsel, in his large symbolic ensemble *Le Bien et le Mal* (1932, Musée des Beaux-Arts de Lyon), depicted Despair as a hanged woman: see Jan Białostocki, 'The Dichotomy of Good and Evil in the Visual Arts: Remarks on Some aspects', in *The Verbal and the Visual: Essays in the Honor of William Sebastian Heckscher*, ed. Karl-Ludwig Selig and Elizabeth Sears (New York, 1990), Figure 1.
40 For examples, see Plesch, *Painter and Priest*, p. 227.
41 Bordier, *Le Jeu de la Passion*, p. 597 noted how the character of Desesperance assisted the spectators in grasping the abstract concepts of sin and despair.
42 Gréban, *Passion*, vv. 21, 853–4.
43 Gréban, *Passion*, vv. 21, 899–901.
44 Schmitt, 'Le Suicide, p. 16: 'pénitence et suicide s'excluaient mutuellement'.
45 Émile Roy, *Le Mystère de la Passion en France du XIVe au XVIe siècle* (Dijon, 1903–04, reprint, Geneva, 1974), v. 6, 651. The same statement is made in the thirteenth- or fourteenth-century Anglo-Norman verse tale of Judas: 'Mes si il eust crié, "Merci," uncore avereit pardon.' Friedrich Ohly, *The Damned and the Elect: Guilt in Western Culture*, trans. Linda Archibald (Cambridge, 1992), p. 57, who translates: 'But if he had cried "Mercy," he would still have had forgiveness.'
46 'En ce qui concerne la confession, Abélard, sans contester que les prêtres ne soient pas les seuls à détenir le pouvoir des clés, soutient que la confession n'est pas toujours nécessaire: Pierre n'a-t-il pas satisfait en pleurant?' Payen, *Le Motif*, 61–2, referring to Abélard, *Ethica*, p. 634 in Victor Cousin (ed.), *Petri Abaelardi Opera*, vol. 2 (Paris, 1859); Payen also mentions p. 492 Guichard de Beaulieu's sermon, who similarly affirms that Peter's tears gained him Christ's forgiveness. For the importance of tears in the context of repentance, see the great number of entries in Payen's 'Index des notions et des termes', p. 601. Tears also appear in the semantic field of *penitentia* as analysed by Martin, *Le Métier*, pp. 389–92, in late medieval sermons.
47 On Mary Magdalen see Susan Haskins, *Mary Magdalen: Myth and Metaphor* (London, 1993) and Katherine Ludwig Jansen, *The Making of the Magdalen: Preaching and Popular Devotion in the Later Middle Ages* (Princeton, 2000). For Mary Magdalen, tears and contrition, see in particular Jansen, pp. 207–12 and 215–16.

48 'Religious Weeping as Ritual in the Medieval West', *Social Analysis: The International Journal of Social and Cultural Practice* 48 (2004), pp. 110–37, quote p. 119. For the purification process through tears in medieval religious writers, see also her *Le Don des larmes au Moyen Âge* (Paris, 2000), pp. 421–30.

49 Vv. 11, 256–8. Guillaume de Deguileville, *Le Pèlerinage de vie humaine*, ed. J. J. Stürzinger (London, 1893) and *The Pilgrimage of Human Life (Le Pèlerinage de la vie humaine)*, trans. Eugene Clasby (New York and London, 1992), p. 153.

50 Vv. 11, 281–3.

51 Vv. 11, 2492–3.

52 Psalm 50 (51), v. 4.

53 Christian, 'Provoked Religious Weeping', p. 97.

54 See Plesch, *Painter and Priest*, for instance, pp. 154–5: all the scenes of torments inflicted on Christ are represented: the Mocking, the Flagellation and the Crowning with Thorns, along with a fourth scene.

55 On pilgrimage, see 'Pèlerinages', in Marcel Viller et al., *Dictionnaire de Spiritualité ascétique et mystique. Doctrine et Histoire* (Paris, 1984), vol. 12, in part, P. A. Sigal, 'Moyen âge occidental', cols 918–29 and 'Le Pèlerinage comme pénitence', cols 919–20. On pilgrimage in general, see Alphonse Dupront, 'Pèlerinages et lieux sacrés', in *Du Sacré. Croisades et pèlerinages. Images et langages* (Paris, 1987), pp. 366–415.

56 Dupront, 'Pèlerinages et lieux sacrés', p. 37.

57 One of these roads was particularly important as it was used by the dukes of Savoy for the transport of salt. See Plesch, *Painter and Priest*, p. 12.

58 These are intermittent springs, maybe as many as a dozen; see Plesch, *Painter and Priest*, p. 14, For details on the pilgrimages made to the sanctuary, see ibid., p. 17.

59 The sword that, in a rather skewed perspectival effect, reaches out to his figure could offer the preacher a nice opportunity for elaboration!

60 Nagy, 'Religious Weeping', p. 130.

61 Luke 23:43.

62 See, for instance, figure 200 in Schiller II/2, an illumination from the Golden Gospels of Heinrich III, 1043–6, Real Biblioteca del Monasterio de San Lorenzo del Escorial, Cod. Vitrinas 17.

63 Murray, *Suicide in the Middle Ages*; see for instance, the section on 'Religious Melancholiacs: Suicides', vol. I, pp. 339–47.

64 Introduction, p. 5.

65 Ruth Mellinkoff, *Outcasts: Signs of Otherness in Northern European Art of the Late Middle Ages* (Berkeley/Los Angeles/Oxford, 1994), p. 122.

66 In the illustrations to this chapter, see Figure 1 (a man who recognizes Peter), Figure 4 (two men, one on the left and one on the right, the latter with a single tooth) and several figures in Figure 12.

67 The pairing of Christ and Mary through this detail might convey the idea of Mary's compassion – her suffering in her heart a passion parallel to that of her son. See the classic article by Otto G. von Simson, '*Compassio* and *Co-Redemptio* in Roger van der Weyden's *Descent from the Cross*', *Art Bulletin* 35, no. 1 (1953), pp. 9–16.

68 See Ayoush S. Lazikani's chapter in this volume and what she writes about the violent dimension of compunction.

69 Victor Turner, 'Pilgrimage as a Liminoid Phenomenon', in *Image and Pilgrimage in Christian Culture: Anthropological Perspectives*, ed. Victor Turner and Edith Turner (New York, 1978), p. 2.

70 Arnold van Gennep, *Les Rites de passage* (Paris, 1909, augmented edition, 1969, Paris, 1981); *The Rites of Passage*, trans. Monika B. Vizedom and Gabrielle L. Caffee (London, 1960).

71 Gennep, *Les Rites de passage*, p. 14.

72 Turner, 'Pilgrimage as a Liminoid Phenomenon', p. 3; his emphasis. See also Victor Turner, *The Ritual Process: Structure and Anti-structure* (Chicago, 1969).

73 See Gennep, *Les Rites de passage*, chapter II, 'Le Passage materiel', pp. 19–33 and *The Rites of Passage*, 'The Territorial Passage', pp. 15–25.

74 Ibid., p. 19.

75 Gennep, *Les Rites de passage*, p. 26.

76 The idea that contrition is not so much an emotion as an action with a transformative dimension appears in many of this book's chapters. As we noted earlier, the actual depiction of Peter's tears is rare before the Council of Trent; among the few instances where the apostle is in motion (and not seated like a melancholic), a few are worth noting as we see him exiting through a similar archway: a leaf with scenes from the Passion of Christ from the Eadwine psalter, illuminated in Canterbury c. 1140 (London, Victoria and Albert Museum, available at http://collections.vam.ac.uk/item/O86305/leaf-from-a-psalter-eadwine-manuscript-unknown/, accessed 13 October 2019) and in another English manuscript, the Holkham Bible Picture Book, 1327–35 (London, British Library, Add MS 47682, fol. 29v, available at http://www.bl.uk/manuscripts/FullDisplay.aspx?ref=Add_MS_47682, accessed 13 October 2019). It is worth noting that on the facing page (30r), we see Judas returning the silver coins and hanging himself. As early as the Carolingian Stuttgart Psalter, 820–30 (Stuttgart, Württembergische Landesbibliothek, Cod.bibl.fol.23, fol. 49r, available at http://digital.wlb-stuttgart.de/purl/bsz307047059, accessed 13 October 2019) there is an arch behind the apostle as he warms himself at a fire and is recognized by the maid, before we then see him exiting, on the other side of this arch (with the rooster standing on it).

77 Gennep, *Les Rites de passage*, p. 276; *The Rites of Passage*, p. 192.

78 Corinne Denoyelle, 'The Expression of Remorse in Old and Middle French Literature', p. 129.

79 Given the trenchant and eloquent opposition that Canavesio sets between Peter and Judas, Peter's three tears could be opposed to Judas's noose, which for Alexander Murray is made of three symbolical strands. Murray explains that 'the association of Judas and suicide, suicide with the sin of despair, and the sin of despair with Judas are three separate ideas', which he sees implied in an illuminated frontispiece of Gregory IX's *Decretals* by Nicolas of Bologna (1354, Milan, Bibl. Ambrosiana, ms B 42 Inf., fol. 1) in which 'Judas desperatus', a noose around his neck, appears below the virtue of *Spes* (Hope) (Murray, *Suicide in the Middle Ages*, vol. II, figure 8 and p. 325).

Bibliography

Accarie, Maurice, *Le Théâtre sacré de la fin du moyen âge. Étude sur le sens moral de la Passion de Jean Michel* (Geneva, 1979).

Adnés, Paul, 'Pénitence. V. La doctrine médiévale du sacrement de la pénitence', *Dictionnaire de Spiritualité Ascétique et Mystique* XII, no. 1 (Paris, 1984), pp. 970-80.

Adnès, Pierre, 'Pénitence', in Marcel Viller et al. (ed.), *Dictionnaire de spiritualité ascétique et mystique: doctrine et histoire*, 17 vols, XII (Paris, 1984), pp. 943-1010.

Aelred of Rievaulx, *De institutione inclusarum*, *De institutione inclusarum: Aelredi Rievallensis Opera Omnia: 1 Opera Ascetica*, ed. Anselm Hoste and Charles H. Talbot, Corpus Christianorum Continuatio Mediaevalis, i (Turnhout, 1971).

'Ágrip af Nóregskonunga sǫgum', in Bjarni Einarsson (ed.), *Ágrip af Nóregskonunga sǫgum. Fagrskinna - Nóregs konunga tal* (Reykjavík: Hið íslenzka fornritafélag, 1985) (Íslenzk fornrit 29), pp. 1-54.

Alan of Lille, *The Art of Preaching*, trans. Gillian R. Evans (Kalamazoo, 1981).

Alexander, Marc, and Christian Kay, 'Classification', *About the Historical Thesaurus of English* (Glasgow, 2017). Available at https://ht.ac.uk/classification/ (accessed 30 October 2018).

Anciaux, Paul, 'Le sacrement de pénitence chez Guillaume d'Auvergne', *Ephemeride Theologicae Lovanienses* 24 (1948) pp. 98-118.

Anciaux, Paul, *The Sacrament of Penance* (London, 1962).

Ancrene Wisse: A Corrected Edition of the Text in Cambridge, Corpus Christi College, MS 402 with Variants from Other Manuscripts, ed. Bella Millett, 2 vols. EETS O.S. 325 and 326 (London, 2005-06).

Andersson, Theodore M., 'The Displacement of the Heroic Ideal in the Family Sagas', *Speculum* 45 (1970), pp. 575-93.

Andersson, Theodore M., *The Growth of the Medieval Icelandic Sagas (1180-1280)* (Ithaca, NY/London: Cornell University Press, 2006).

Andersson, Theodore M., 'Is There a History of Emotions in Eddic Heroic Poetry? Daniel Sävborg's Critique of Eddic Chronology', in C. S. Jaeger and I. Kasten (eds.), *Codierungen von Emotionen im Mittelalter. Emotions and Sensibilities in the Middle Ages* (Berlin/New York: De Gruyter, 2003) (Trends in Medieval Philology 1), pp. 193-202.

Andersson, Theodore M., 'Snorri Sturluson and the Saga School at Munkaþverá', in A. Wolf (ed.), *Snorri Sturluson. Kolloquium anläßlich der 750. Wiederkehr seines Todestages* (Tübingen: Narr, 1993) (ScriptOralia 51), pp. 9-25.

Andersson, Theodore M., 'Víga-Glúms Saga and the Birth of Saga Writing', *Scripta Islandica* 57 (2006), pp. 5-39.

Aquinas, Thomas, 'In IV Sententiarum', in Library of Latin Texts: Series A (Turnhout, 2015). Available at http://apps.brepolis.net/BrepolisPortal/ (accessed 20 November 2019).

Arbesmann, Rudolph, 'The Concept of *christus medicus* in St Augustine', *Traditio*, 10 (1954), pp. 1–28.

Archimandrite Vasileios, *Hymn of Entry: Liturgy and Life in the Orthodox Church*, trans. Elizabeth Briere (New York: St Vladimir's Seminary Press, 1984).

Argyle, Michael, *Bodily Communication* (London: Methuen, 1975).

Arista, Javier Martín, 'Adjective Formation and Lexical Layers in Old English', *English Studies* 92, no. 3 (2011), pp. 323–44.

Arista, Javier Martín, 'Recursivity, Derivational Depth and the Search for Old English Lexical Primes', *Studia Neophilologica* 85, no. 1 (2013), pp. 1–21. doi: 10.1080/00393274.2013.771829.

Arista, Javier Martín, 'Projections and Constructions in Functional Morphology: The Case of Old English *HRĒOW*', *Language and Linguistics* 12, no. 2 (2011), pp. 393–425.

Aristote, Physica, in F. Bossier and J. Brams (eds.), *Physica, translatio vetus* (Aristoteles latinus, VII/2) (Leyde/New York, 1990).

Arranz, Miguel, 'N.D. Uspensky: The Office of the All-night Vigil in the Greek Church and in the Russian Church', *St. Vladimir's Theological Quarterly* 24 (1980), pp. 69–95, 83–113.

Austin, J. L., *How to Do Things with Words* (Oxford: Clarendon Press, 1975).

Bagge, Sverre, 'Den heroiske tid – kirkereform og kirkekamp 1153–1214', in S. Imsen (ed.), *Ecclesia Nidrosiensis 1153–1537. Søkelys på Nidaroskirkens og Nidarosprovinsens historie* (Trondheim: Tapir Akademisk Forlag, 2003) (Senter for Middelalderstudier. Skrifter 15), pp. 51–80.

Bagge, Sverre, 'Icelandic Uniqueness or a Common European Culture? The Case of the Kings' Sagas', *Scandinavian Studies* 69, no. 4 (1997), pp. 418–42.

Baldwin, John W., 'From the Ordeal to Confession: In Search of Lay Religion in Early Thirteenth-century France', in Peter Biller and A. J. Minnis (eds.), *Handling Sin: Confession in the Middle Ages* (York, 1998), pp. 191–209.

Baran, Dominika, *Language in Immigrant America* (Cambridge: Cambridge University Press, 2017).

Barsanuphios and John, *Letters*, trans. John Chryssavgis. 2 vols (Washington, DC: Catholic University of America Press, 2006–07).

Barsanuphios and John, *Letters. Barsanuphe et Jean de Gaza: Correspondance*, ed. François Neyt and Paula de Angelis-Noah. 5 vols. SC 426–7, 450–1, 468 (Paris: Éditions du Cerf, 1997–2002).

Bately, Janet M., 'Old English Prose before and during the Reign of Alfred', *Anglo-Saxon England* 17 (1988), pp. 93–138.

Beck, Heinrich, *Wortschatz der altisländischen Grágás (Konungsbók)* (Göttingen, 1993) (Abhandlungen der Akademie der Wissenschaften in Göttingen: Vandenhoeck & Ruprecht. Philologisch-historische Klasse. 3. Folge 205).

Behr, John, *John the Theologian and His Paschal Gospel: A Prologue to Theology* (Oxford: Oxford University Press, 2019).

Benrath, Gustav L., 'Buße V. Historisch', in H. Balz et al. (eds.), *Theologische Realenzyklopädie 7* (Berlin/New York: De Gruyter, 1981), pp. 452–73.

Bériou, Nicole, 'Autour de Latran IV (1215): la naissance de la confession moderne et sa diffusion', in Groupe de la Bussière (ed.), *Pratiques de la confession, des Pères de l'église à Vatican II. Quinze études d'histoire* (Paris, 1983), pp. 73–92.

Bériou, Nicole, 'La confession dans les écrits théologiques et pastoraux du XIIIe siècle: médication de l'âme ou démarche judiciaire ?' in *L'Aveu, Antiquité et Moyen Âge. Actes de la table ronde de Rome (28-30 mars 1984)* (Rome, 1986), pp. 261–82.

Berlioz, Jacques, 'La voix de l'évêque Guillaume d'Auvergne dans les *exempla* (XIIIe–XVe s.)', in F. Morenzoni and J. Y. Tilliette (eds.), *Autour de Guillaume d'Auvergne* (Turnhout, 2005), pp. 9–34.

Berlioz, Jacques, 'Pouvoirs et contrôle de la croyance: la question de la procréation démoniaque chez Guillaume d'Auvergne', *Razo* 9 (1989), pp. 5–27.

Besemeres, Mary, 'Between *Żal* and *Emotional Blackmail*: Ways of Being in Polish and English', in M. Besemeres and A. Wierzbicka (eds.), *Translating Lives: Living with Two Languages and Cultures* (St Lucia, Queensland: University of Queensland Press, 2007), pp. 128–38.

Besemeres, Mary, 'Language and Emotional Experience. The Voice of Translingual Memoir', in A. Pavlenko (ed.), *Bilingual Minds: Emotional Experience, Expression and Representation* (Clevedon: Multilingual Matters, 2006), pp. 34–58.

Białostocki, Jan, 'The Dichotomy of Good and Evil in the Visual Arts: Remarks on Some Aspects', in Karl-Ludwig Selig and Elizabeth Sears (eds.), *The Verbal and the Visual: Essays in the Honor of William Sebastian Heckscher* (New York, 1990), pp. 23–40.

Biblia Sacra iuxta Vulgatam Clementinan, ed. Albero Colunga and Laurentio Turrado, 6th ed. (Madrid, 1982).

Biller, Peter, 'Confession in the Middle Ages: Introduction', in P. Biller, A. J. Minnis (eds.), *Handling Sin: Confession in the Middle Ages* (York, 1998), pp. 1–35.

Biller, Peter, 'Confessor's Manuals and Avoiding Offsprings', in P. Biller and A. J. Minnis (eds.), *Handling Sin: Confession in the Middle Ages* (York, 1998), pp. 165–87.

Biller, Peter, and Alastair J. Minnis (eds.), *Handling Sin: Confession in the Middle Ages* (York, 1998).

Boccadoro, Brenno, 'La musique, les passions, l'âme et le corps', in F. Morenzoni and J. Y. Tilliette (eds.), *Autour de Guillaume d'Auvergne* (Turnhout, 2005), pp. 75–92.

Boje Mortensen, Lars, 'The Anchin Manuscript of Passio Olavi (Douai 295), William of Jumièges, and Theodoricus Monachus. New Evidence for Intellectual Relations between Norway and France in the 12th Century', *Symbolae Osloenses* 75, no. 1 (2000), pp. 165–89.

Boje Mortensen, Lars, 'Den formative dialog mellem latinsk og folkesproglig litteratur, ca. 600–1250. Udkast til en dynamisk model', in E. Mundal (ed.), *Reykholt som makt- og lærdomssenter i den islandske og nordiske kontekst* (Reykholt: Snorrastofa, 2006) (Snorrastofa. Rit 3), pp. 239–71.

Bonaventure, St, 'Breviloquium', pars vi, cap. x, in *Tria Opuscula*, Ad Claras Aquas, 3rd ed. (Quaracchi, 1911).

Boquet, Damien and Piroska Nagy, *Sensible Moyen Âge. Une histoire des émotions dans l'Occident médiéval* (Paris, 2015).

Bordier, Jean-Pierre, *Le Jeu de la Passion. Le message chrétien et le théâtre français (XIIIe–XVIe s.)* (Paris, 1998).

Boudet, Jean-Patrice, *Entre science et nigromance. Astrologie, divination et magie dans l'Occident médiéval (XIIe–XVe siècle)* (Paris, 2006).

Boureau, Alain, 'Élaguer et greffer. Un discours chrétien bien planté', *Penser/Rêver*, 11 (printemps 2007), pp. 95–109.

Boureau, Alain, 'Un sujet agité. Le statut nouveau des passions de l'âme au XIIIe siècle', in P. Nagy, D. Boquet (eds.), *Le Sujet des émotions au Moyen Âge* (Paris, 2009), pp. 187–200.

Bradshaw, Paul F., and Maxwell E. Johnson, *The Origins of Feasts, Fasts and Seasons in Early Christianity* (Collegeville, MN: Liturgical Press, 2011).

Brenet, Jean-Baptiste, 'Introduction traduction et notes', in Guillaume d'Auvergne (ed.), *De anima, VII, 1–9* (Paris, 1998).

Brennu-Njáls saga, ed. Einar Ólafur Sveinsson (Reykjavík: Hið íslenzka fornritafélag, 1954) (Íslenzk fornrit 12).

Breugelmans, Seger M., Marcel Zeelenberg, Thomas Gilovich, Wen-Hsien Huang, and Yaniv Shani, 'Generality and Cultural Variation in the Experience of Regret', *Emotion* 14, no. 6 (2014), pp. 1037–48. doi: 10.1037/a0038221.

Brottier, Laurence, *Propos sur la Contrition de Jean Chrysostome: Le Destin d'Écrits de Jeunesse Méconnus* (Paris: Éditions du Cerf, 2010).

Burger, Glenn D., and Holly A. Crocker (eds.), 'Introduction', in Glenn D. Burger and Holly A. Crocker (eds.), *Medieval Affect, Feeling, and Emotion* (Cambridge, 2019), pp. 1–24.

Byock, Jesse L., *Feud in the Icelandic Saga* (Berkeley/London: University of California Press, 1982).

Callow, Chris, 'Dating and Origins', in Ármann Jakobsson and Sverrir Jakobsson (eds.), *The Routledge Research Companion to the Medieval Icelandic Sagas* (London/New York: Routledge, 2017), pp. 15–33.

Casagrande, Carla, 'Guglielmo d'Auverne e il buon uso delle passioni nella penitenzia', in F. Morenzoni and J. Y. Tilliette (eds.), *Autour de Guillaume d'Auvergne* (Turnhout, 2005), pp. 189–201.

Celeghin, Alessia, Matteo Diano, Arianna Bagnis, Marco Viola, and Marco Tamietto, 'Basic Emotions in Human Neuroscience: Neuroimaging and Beyond', *Frontiers in Psychology* 8, no. 1432 (2017), pp. 1–13. doi: 10.3389/fpsyg.2017.01432.

Chandelier, Joël and Aurélien Robert, 'Introduction', in J. Chandelier, A. Robert (eds.), *Frontières des savoirs en Italie à l'époque des premières universités (XIIIe–XVe siècles)* (Rome, 2015), pp. 1–31.

Chaucer, Geoffrey, *The Riverside Chaucer*, ed. Larry D. Benson (Oxford, 1988).
Chave-Mahir, Florence, *L'exorcisme des possédés dans l'Eglise d'Occident (X^e–XIVe siècle)* (Turnhout, 2011).
'*Cher alme*': *Texts of Anglo-Norman Piety*, ed. Tony Hunt and trans. Jane Bliss (Tempe, AZ, 2010).
chrétien de troyes, *Erec et Enide*, ed. M. Rousse (Paris, Flammarion, 1994).
chrétien de troyes, *Le Chevalier au lion*, ed. D. F. Hult (Paris, Libr. Générale Française, coll. « Le livre de poche Lettres gothiques », 2009.
Christian, William A. Jr, 'Provoked Religious Weeping in Early Modern Spain', in John Davis (ed.), *Religious Organization and Religious Experience* (London, 1982), pp. 97–112.
Chryssavgis, John, *Ascent to Heaven. The Theology of the Human Person According to Saint John of the Ladder*, Brookline, MA: Holy Cross Orthodox Press, 1989.
Chryssavgis, John, *John Climacus: From the Egyptian Desert to the Sinaite Mountain*. Aldershot: Ashgate, 2004.
Chryssavgis, John, 'Κατάνυξις: Compunction as the Context for the Theology of Tears in St. John Climacus', *Κληρονομία* 17, no. 2 (1985), pp. 131–6.
Chryssavgis, John. 'A Spirituality of Imperfection: The Way of Tears in Saint John Climacus', *Cistercian Studies Quarterly* 37, no. 4 (2002): 359–71.
Cohen, Esther, *The Modulated Scream: Pain in Late Medieval Culture* (Chicago, 2010).
Conomos, Dimitri E., *Byzantine Hymnography and Byzantine Chant* (Brookline, MA: Hellenic College Press, 1984).
Cooper, Tracey-Anne, 'Chapter 9: The Shedding of Tears in Late Anglo-Saxon England', in E. Gertsman (ed.), *Crying in the Middle Ages: Tears of History* (New York: Routledge, 2012), pp. 175–92.
Coricelli, Giorgio, Raymond J. Dolan, and Angela Sirigu, 'Brain, Emotion and Decision Making: The Paradigmatic Example of Regret', *Trends in Cognitive Sciences* 11, no. 6 (2007), pp. 258–65.
Cornagliotti, Anna, *La Passione di Revello: sacra rappresentazione quattrocentesca di ignoto piemontese* (Turin, 1976).
Courtois d'Arras: l'Enfant prodigue, ed. J. Dufournet (Paris, Flammarion, coll. « GF Bilingue », 1995).
Cousin, Victor (ed.), *Petri Abaelardi Opera*, vol. 2 (Paris, 1859).
Crocker, Christopher, 'Emotions', in Ármann Jakobsson and Sverrir Jakobsson (eds.), *The Routledge Research Companion to the Medieval Icelandic Sagas* (London/New York: Routledge, 2017), pp. 240–52.
Cubitt, Catherine, 'Bishops, Priests and Penance in Late Anglo-Saxon England', *Early Medieval Europe* 14, no. 1 (2006), pp. 41–63.
Culpeper, Jonathan and Michael Haugh, *Pragmatics and the English Language* (Basingstoke: Red Globe Press, 2003).
Cunningham, Mary, 'Dramatic Device or Didactic Tool? The Function of Dialogue in Byzantine Preaching', in Elizabeth Jeffreys (ed.), *Rhetoric in Byzantium: Papers from the Thirty-fifth Spring Symposium of Byzantine Studies, Exeter College, University of Oxford, March 2001* (Aldershot: Ashgate, 2001), pp. 101–13.

Cunningham, Mary, 'The Reception of Romanos in Middle Byzantine Homiletics and Hymnography', *DOP* 62 (2008), pp. 251–60.

Cyril of Alexandria, *Commentary on the Gospel of John*, 7–8. PG 74, 9–104.

Cyril of Alexandria, *Cyril of Alexandria*, trans. Norman Russell (London: Routledge, 2000).

Cyril of Alexandria, *Explanation of the Twelve Chapters*. PG 76, 293–312.

d'Avray, D. L., *The Preaching of the Friars: Sermons Diffused before 1300* (Oxford, 1985).

Dailey, Patricia, 'The Body and Its Senses', in Amy Hollywood and Patricia Z. Beckman (eds.), *The Cambridge Companion to Christian Mysticism* (Cambridge: Cambridge University Press, 2012), pp. 264–76.

Daley, Brian, 'Finding the Right Key: The Aims and Strategies of Early Christian Interpretation of the Psalms', in Harold W. Attridge and Margot Elsbeth Fassler (eds.), *Psalms in Community: Jewish and Christian Textual, Liturgical, and Artistic Traditions* (Leiden: Brill, 2004), pp. 189–205.

Davies, Mark, *The 14 Billion Word iWeb Corpus* (2018–). Available at https://www.english-corpora.org/iWeb/ (accessed 20 November 2019).

Davies, Mark, *The TV Corpus: 325 Million Words, 1950–2018* (2019–). Available at https://www.english-corpora.org/tv/ (accessed 20 November 2019).

Davies, Stephen, 'Emotions Expressed and Aroused by Music', in Patrik N. Juslin and John A. Sloboda (eds.), *Handbook of Music and Emotion: Theory, Research, Applications* (Oxford: Oxford University Press, 2010), pp. 15–43.

Deguileville, Guillaume de, *Le Pèlerinage de vie humaine*, ed. J. J. Stürzinger (London, 1893).

Deguileville, Guillaume de, *The Pilgrimage of Human Life (Le Pèlerinage de la vie humaine)*, trans. Eugene Clasby (New York and London, 1992).

Delaurenti, Béatrice, 'L'action à distance est-elle pensable? Dynamiques discursives et créativité conceptuelle au XIIIe siècle', in F. Chateauraynaud and Y. Cohen (eds.), *Histoires pragmatiques* (Paris, 2016), pp. 149–78.

Delaurenti, Béatrice, 'La pratique incantatoire à l'époque scolastique. Charmes et formules des réceptaires médicaux en latin et en langues romanes (XIIIe –XVe siècle)', in I. Draelants, C. Balouzat-Loubet (eds.), *La formule au Moyen Âge*, II. *Actes du colloque de Nancy et Metz, 7-9 juin 2012* (Turnhout, 2015), pp. 473–94.

Delaurenti, Béatrice, *La puissance des mots: 'virtus verborum'. Débats doctrinaux sur les incantations au Moyen Âge* (Paris, 2007).

'Den ældre Eidsivathings-Christenret', in R. Keyser and P. A. Munch (eds.), *Norges gamle Love indtil 1387 1. Norges Love ældre end Kong Magnus Haakonssöns Regjerings-Tiltrædelse i 1263* (Christiania: Gröndahl, 1846), pp. 373–406.

'Den ældre Gulathings-Lov', in R. Keyser and P. A. Munch (eds.), *Norges gamle Love indtil 1387 1. Norges Love ældre end Kong Magnus Haakonssöns Regjerings-Tiltrædelse i 1263* (Christiania: Gröndahl, 1846), pp. 1–118.

Den norsk-islandske Skjaldedigtning B. Rettet Tekst 1. 800–1200, ed. Finnur Jónsson (København: Gyldendal, 1912).

'Den nyere Lands-Lov. Udgiven af Kong Magnus Haakonssön', in R. Keyser and P. A. Munch (eds.), *Norges gamle Love indtil 1387 2. Lovgivningen under Kong Magnus Haakonssöns Regjeringstid fra 1263 til 1280, tilligemed et Supplement til förste Bind* (Christiania: Gröndahl, 1848), pp. 1–178.

Desby, Frank, 'The Modes and Tunings in Neo-Byzantine Chant'. PhD diss., University of Southern California, 1974.

Díaz-Vera, Javier E., 'On Saying Two Things at Once: The Historical Semantics and Pragmatics of Old English Emotion Words', *Folia Linguistica Historica* 35, no. 1 (2014), pp. 101–34. doi: https://doi.org/10.1515/flih.2014.003 (accessed 20 November 2019).

Diller, Hans-Juergen, 'ANGER and TÊNE in Middle English', in M. Markus, Y. Iyeiri, and R. Heuberger (eds.), *Middle and Modern English Corpus Linguistics: A Multidimensional Approach* (Amsterdam: John Benjamins, 2012), pp. 109–24.

Dionysius the Areopagite, *Corpus Dionysiacum II: Pseudo-Dionysius Areopagita. De Coelesti Hierarchia, De Ecclesiastica Hierarchia, De Mystica Theologia, Epistulae*, ed. Günter Heil and Adolf Martin Ritter, Patristische Texte Und Studien (Berlin: De Gruyter, 2012).

Dixon, Thomas, *From Passions to Emotions: The Creation of a Secular Psychological Category* (Cambridge: Cambridge University Press, 2003).

Dixon, Thomas, 'Revolting Passions'. *Modern Theology* 27, no. 2 (2011), pp. 298–312.

Driscoll, Michael S., 'Compunction', in Michael Downey (ed.), *Catholic Dictionary of Spirituality* (Collegeville, MN: Liturgical Press, 1995), p. 193.

Du Chevalier qui fist sa fame confesse, dans W. Noomen et N. van den Boogaard, *Nouveau recueil complet des fabliaux*, tome 4, Maastricht, Van Gorcum, 1988, pp. 236–43.

Dubowchik, Rosemary, 'Singing with the Angels: Foundation Documents as Evidence for Musical Life in Monasteries of the Byzantine Empire', *DOP* 56 (2002), pp. 277–96.

DuBruck, Eldegard, 'Changes of Taste and Audience Expectation in Fifteenth-century Religious Drama', *Fifteenth-century Studies* 6 (1983), pp. 59–91.

Dupront, Alphonse, 'Pèlerinages et lieux sacrés', in *Du Sacré. Croisades et pèlerinages. Images et langages* (Paris, 1987).

Edda. Die Lieder des Codex regius nebst verwandten Denkmälern 1. Text, ed. G. Neckel and H. Kuhn. 4. umgearb. Aufl. (Heidelberg: Winter, 1962).

Egils saga Skalla-Grímssonar, ed. S. Nordal (Reykjavík: Hið íslenzka fornritafélag, 1933) (Íslenzk fornrit 2).

Ekman, P., and W. V. Friesen, *Unmasking the Face: A Guide to Recognizing Emotions from Facial Clues* (Englewood Cliffs, NJ, 1975).

Ekman, Paul, 'Basic Emotions', in T. Dalgleish and M. Power (eds.), *The Handbook of Cognition and Emotion* (Chichester: John Wiley & Sons, 1999), pp. 45–60.

Ekman, Paul, 'Facial Expression and Emotion', *American Psychologist* 48 (1993), pp. 384–92.

Elucidarius in Old Norse Translation, ed. E. Scherabon Firchow and K. Grimstad (Reykjavík: Stofnun Árna Magnússonar, 1989) (Stofnun Árna Magnússonar á Íslandi. Rit 36).

Esmark, Kim and Orning, Hans J., 'General Introduction', in K. Esmark et al. (eds.), *Disputing Strategies in Medieval Scandinavia* (Leiden/Boston: Brill, 2013) (Medieval Law and Its Practice 16), pp. 1–28.

Essary, Kirk, 'Passions, Emotions, or Affections? On the Ambiguity of 16th-century Terminology', *Emotion Review* 9, no. 4 (2017), pp. 367–74.

Eßer, Albert, 'Reue II: Philosphisch-ethisch', in H. Balz et al. (eds.), *Theologische Realenzyklopädie 29* (Berlin/New York: De Gruyter, 1998), pp. 101–3.

Færeyinga saga. Óláfs saga Tryggvasonar eptir Odd munk Snorrason, ed. Ólafur Halldórsson (Reykjavík: Hið íslenzka fornritafélag, 2006) (Íslenzk fornrit 25).

Fernández, Tomás, 'Byzantine Tears: A Pseudo-chrysostomic Fragment on Weeping in the *Florilegium Coislinianum*', in Peter Van Deun and Caroline Macé (eds.), *Encyclopedic Trends in Byzantium?: Proceedings of the International Conference Held in Leuven 6–8 May 2009* (Leuven: Peeters, 2011), pp. 125–42.

Finnur Jónsson and Sveinbjörn Egilsson, *Lexicon poeticum antiquæ lingæ septentrionalis. Ordbog over det norsk-islandske Skjaldesprog* (København: Møller, 1931).

Flannery, Mary Catherine (ed.), *Emotion and Textual Media* (Turnhout, 2018).

Florovsky, Georges. *Aspects of Church History: Volume Four in the Collected Works of Georges Florovsky*. Belmont: Nordland Publishing Company, 1975.

Föller, Daniel, 'Wikinger als Pilger. Drei norwegische Könige, zwei Runensteine und der Wiederaufbau der Grabeskirche', in T. Pratsch (ed.), *Konflikt und Bewältigung. Die Zerstörung der Grabeskirche zu Jerusalem im Jahre 1009* (Berlin/Boston: De Gruyter, 2012) (Millennium-Studien 32), pp. 281–99.

Fox, Michael, '*Feðerhama* and *hæleðhelm*: The Equipment of Devils', *Florilegium* 26 (2009), pp. 133–57.

Foxhall Forbes, Helen, 'Affective Piety and the Practice of Penance in Late-eleventh-century Worcester: The Address to the Penitent in Oxford, Bodleian Library, Junius 121', *Anglo-Saxon England* 44 (2015), pp. 309–45.

Frank, Georgia, 'Dialogue and Deliberation: The Sensory Self in the Hymns of Romanos the Melodist', in David Brakke, M. L. Satlow and S. Wetzman (eds.), *Religion and the Self in Antiquity* (Indianapolis: Bloomington, 2005), pp. 163–79.

Frank, Georgia, 'The Memory Palace of Marcellinus: Athanasius and the Mirror of the Psalms', in Blake Leyerle and Robin Darling Young (eds.), *Ascetic Culture: Essays in Honour of Philip Rousseau* (Notre Dame, IN: University of Notre Dame Press, 2013), pp. 97–124.

Frank, Georgia, 'Romanos and the Night Vigil in the Sixth Century', in Derek Krueger (ed.), *Byzantine Christianity: A People's History of Christianity* (Minneapolis: Fortress Press, 2006), pp. 59–78.

Frantzen, Allen J., *The Literature of Penance in Anglo-Saxon England* (New Brunswick, NJ: Rutgers University Press, 1983).

Frantzen, Allen J., 'The Tradition of Penitentials in Anglo-Saxon England', *Anglo-Saxon England* 11 (1982), pp. 23–56.

Freeman, Margaret B., 'The Iconography of the Merode Altarpiece', *The Metropolitan Museum of Art Bulletin* 16, no. 6 (1957), pp. 130–9.

Frölich, Dorothee, 'Eddische Heroische Elegie und *Laxdœla saga*. Bemerkungen zu einigen motivischen und formalen Verbindungslinien', in H. Beck (ed.), *Studien zur Isländersaga. Festschrift für Rolf Heller* (Berlin/New York: De Gruyter, 2000) (Reallexikon der Germanischen Altertumskunde. Ergänzungsband 24), pp. 51–71.

Frøyshov, Stig Simeon Ragnvald, 'The Early Development of the Liturgical Eight-mode System in Jerusalem'. *St. Vladimir's Theological Quarterly* 51 (2007), pp. 139–78.

Frøyshov, Stig Simeon Ragnvald, 'The Georgian Witness to the Jerusalem Liturgy: New Sources and Studies', in Bert Groen, Steven Hawkes-Teeples and Stefanos Alexopoulos (eds.), *Inquiries into Eastern Christian Worship: Selected Papers of the Second International Congress of the Society of Oriental Liturgies, Rome, 17–21 September 2008* (Leuven: Peeters, 2012), pp. 227–67.

Fulk, R. D., 'Cynewulf: Canon, Dialect, and Date', in R. E. Bjork (ed.), *The Cynewulf Reader* (London: Routledge, 2001).

Fulkerson, Laurel, *No Regrets: Remorse in Classical Antiquity* (Oxford: Oxford University Press, 2013).

Gador-Whyte, Sarah, 'Rhetoric and Ideas in the Kontakia of Romanos the Melodist'. PhD diss., University of Melbourne, 2011.

Gador-Whyte, Sarah, *Theology and Poetry in Early Byzantium: The Kontakia of Romanos the Melodist* (Cambridge: Cambridge University Press, 2017).

Galadza, Daniel, *Liturgy and Byzantinization in Jerusalem* (Oxford: Oxford University Press, 2017).

'Gamli kanóki, Harmsól', ed. K. Attwood, in M. Clunies Ross (ed.), *Poetry on Christian Subjects 1. The Twelfth and Thirteenth Centuries* (Turnhout: Brepols, 2007) (Skaldic Poetry of the Scandinavian Middle Ages 7), pp. 70–132.

Gautier de Coinci, *Les Miracles de Nostre Dame*, V. F. Koenig (éd.) (Geneva; Lille, Droz: Giard, 1955).

Geeraerts, Dirk, *Theories of Lexical Semantics* (Oxford, 2009).

Geest, Paul van, 'Studying the Mystagogy of the Fathers: An Introduction', in Paul van Geest (eds.), *Seeing through the Eyes of Faith: New Approaches to the Mystagogy of the Church Fathers* (Leuven: Peeters, 2016), pp. 3–22.

Gennep, Arnold van, *Les Rites de passage* (Paris, 1909, augmented edition, 1969, Paris, 1981).

Gennep, Arnold van, *The Rites of Passage*, trans. Monika B. Vizedom and Gabrielle L. Caffee (London, 1960).

Georgianna, Linda, *The Solitary Self: Individuality in Ancrene Wisse* (Cambridge, MA, 1981).

Gerrits, G. H., *Inter Timorem et Spem: A Study of the Theological Thought of Gerard Zerbolt of Zutphen (1367–1398)* (Leiden, 1986).

Gertsman, Elina (ed.), *Crying in the Middle Ages: Tears of History* (Abingdon: Routledge, 2011).

Getcha, Job, *The Typikon Decoded: An Explanation of Byzantine Liturgical Practice* (Yonkers, NY: St Vladimir's Seminary Press, 2012).

Gevaert, Caroline, 'The Evolution of the Lexical and Conceptual Field of ANGER in Old and Middle English', in J. E. D. Vera (ed.), *A Changing World of Words: Studies in English Historical Lexicography, Lexicology and Semantics* (Amsterdam: Rodopi, 2002), pp. 275–99.

Giannouli, Antonia, 'Catanyctic Religious Poetry: A Survey', in Antonio Rigo, Pavel Ermilov and Michele Trizio (eds.), *Theologica Minora: The Minor Genres of Byzantine Theological Literature* (Turnhout: Brepols, 2013, pp. 86–109.

Giannouli, Antonia, 'Die Tränen der Zerknirschung. Zur katanyktischen Kirchendichtung als Heilmittel', in Paolo Odorico, Panagiotis A. Agapitos and Martin Hinterberger (eds.), *'Doux remède …'. Poésie et Poétique à Byzance. Actes du Quatrième Colloque International Philologique 'EPMHNEIA' Paris, 23–24–25 Février 2006 Organisé par l'E.H.E.S.S. et l'Université de Chypre* (Paris: Centre d'études byzantines, néo-helléniques et sud-est européennes, 2009), pp. 141–55.

Gilson, Etienne, 'Avicenne en Occident au Moyen Âge', *Archives d'Histoire Doctrinale et Littéraire du Moyen Âge* 36 (1969) pp. 89–121.

Gísli Sigurðsson, *The Medieval Icelandic Saga and Oral Tradition. A Discourse on Method* (Cambridge, MA/London: Harvard University Press, 2004) (Publications of the Milman Parry Collection of Oral Literature 2).

Glorieux, Palémon, *Répertoire des maîtres de théologie de Paris du XIIIe siècle* (Paris, 1933).

Görich, Knut, *Die Ehre Friedrich Barbarossas. Kommunikation, Konflikt und politisches Handeln im 12. Jahrhundert* (Darmstadt: Wissenschaftliche Buchgesellschaft, 2001).

Grágás. Islændernes Lovbog i Fristatens Tid. Förste Del. Text I, ed. Vilhjálmur Finsen (København: Berlings, 1852).

Greban, Arnoul, *Arnoul Gréban, the Mystery of the Passion. The Third Day*, trans. Paula Giuliano (Asheville, 1996).

Greban, Arnoul, *Le Mystère de la Passion d'Arnoul Gréban*, ed. Omer Jodogne (Bruxelles, 1965).

The Greek New Testament, ed. Barbara Aland et al. (Stuttgart: Deutsche (Bibelgesellschaft, 1994).

Gregory of Nyssa, *Homilies on the Song of Songs*, ed. and trans. Richard A. Norris, Jr (Atlanta: Society of Biblical Literature, 2012).

Grosdidier de Matons, José, 'Liturgie et Hymnographie: Kontakion et Canon', *DOP* 34, no. 35 (1980–81), pp. 31–43.

Grosdidier de Matons, José, *Romanos le Mélode et les Origines de la Poésie Religieuse à Byzance* (Paris: Beauchesne, 1977).

Gross, Daniel M., *The Secret History of Emotion: From Aristotle's Rhetoric to Modern Brain Science* (Chicago: University of Chicago Press, 2006).

'Guðmundar saga dýra', in Jón Jóhannesson, Magnús Finnbogason and K. Eldjárn (eds.), *Sturlunga saga. Fyrra bindi* (Reykjavík: Sturlungaútgáfan, 1946), pp. 160–212.

Haki Antonsson, *Damnation and Salvation in Old Norse Literature* (Cambridge: Brewer, 2018).

Hallander, L. G., *Old English Verbs in '-sian': A Semantic and Derivational Study* (Stockholm: Almqvist & Wiksell, 1966).

'Hallfreðr vandræðaskáld Óttarsson, Erfidrápa Óláfs Tryggvasonar', ed. K. Heslop, in ed. D. Whaley, *Poetry from the Kings' Sagas 1,1* (Turnhout: Brepols, 2012) (Skaldic Poetry of the Scandinavian Middle Ages 1), pp. 400–41.

Hamilton, Sarah, *The Practice of Penance, 900–1050* (Bury St Edmunds: St Edmundsbury Press, 2001).

Hanna, Ralph, 'Lambeth Palace Library, MS 487: Some Problems of Early Thirteenth-century Textual Transmission', in Cate Gunn and Catherine Innes-Parker (eds.), *Texts and Traditions of Medieval Pastoral Care: Essays in Honour of Bella Millett* (York, 2009), pp. 78–88.

Hanna, Ralph, and Sarah Wood, *Richard Morris's Prick of Conscience: A Corrected and Amplified Reading Text* (Oxford, 2013).

Harkianakis, Archbishop Stylianos, *On Prayer* (Athens: Armos, 1999).

Harl, Marguerite, 'Les Origines Grecques du Mot et de la Notion de Componction dans la Septante et chez ses Commentateurs'. *Revue des Études Augustiniennes* 32 (1986), 3–21.

Harris, Oliver J. T., and Tim Flohr Sørensen, 'Rethinking Emotion and Material Culture'. *Archaeological Dialogues* 17, no. 2 (2010), pp. 145–63.

Harris, Yolande, 'The Building as Instrument', in Ros Bandt, Michelle Duffy and Dolly MacKinnon (eds.), *Hearing Places: Sound, Place, Time and Culture* (Newcastle: Cambridge Scholars Publishing, 2009), pp. 404–12.

Harrison, Carol, *The Art of Listening in the Early Church* (Oxford: Oxford University Press, 2013).

Harrison, Carol, 'Augustine and the Art of Music', in Jeremy S. Begbie and Steven R. Guthrie (eds.), *Resonant Witness: Conversations between Music and Theology* (Grand Rapids, MI: Eerdmans, 2011), pp. 27–45.

Harrison, Carol, 'Enchanting the Soul: The Music of the Psalms', in Andreas Andreopoulos, Augustine Casiday and Carol Harrison (eds.), *Meditations of the Heart: The Psalms in Early Christian Thought and Practice. Essays in Honour of Andrew Louth* (Turnhout: Brepols, 2011), pp. 205–24.

Hartley, L. P., *The Go-Between* (London, 1953).

Harvey, Susan Ashbrook, '2000 NAPS Presidential Address. Spoken Words, Voiced Silence: Biblical Women in Syriac Tradition', *Journal of Early Christian Studies* 9, no. 1 (2001), pp. 105–31.

Harvey, Susan Ashbrook, 'Why the Perfume Mattered: The Sinful Woman in Syriac Exegetical Tradition', in Paul M. Blowers (ed.), *In Dominico Eloquio/In Lordly Eloquence: Essays on Patristic Exegesis in Honour of Robert Louis Wilken* (Grand Rapids, MI: Eerdmans, 2002), pp. 69–89.

Harvey, Susan Ashbrook, *Scenting Salvation: Ancient Christianity and the Olfactory Imagination* (Berkeley: California University Press, 2006).

Hasenfratz, Robert J., 'The Theme of the "Penitent Damned" and Its Relation to *Beowulf* and *Christ and Satan*', *Leeds Studies in English* 20 (1990), pp. 45–69.

Haskins, Charles H., 'A List of Texts-books from the Close of the XIIth century', *Harvard Studies in Classical Philology*, 20 (1909), pp. 75–94.

Haskins, Susan, *Mary Magdalen: Myth and Metaphor* (London, 1993).

Hastrup, Kirsten, *Culture and Society in Medieval Iceland. An Anthropological Analysis of Structure and Change* (Oxford: Clarendon Press, 1985).

Hatfield, Elaine, Megan Carpenter, and Richard L. Rapson, 'Emotional Contagion as a Precursor to Collective Emotions', in Christian von Scheve and Mikko Salmela (eds.), *Collective Emotions* (Oxford: Oxford University Press, 2014), pp. 108–22.

Hausherr, Irénée, *Penthos: The Doctrine of Compunction in the Christian East* (Kalamazoo, MI: Cistercian Publications, 1982).

'Heiðarvíga saga', in Sigurður Nordal (eds.), *Borgfirðinga sǫgur. Hœnsa-Þóris saga. Gunnlaugs saga ormstungu. Bjarnar saga hítdœlakappa. Heiðarvíga saga. Gísls þáttr Illugasonar* (Reykjavík :Hið íslenzka fornritafélag, 1938) (Íslenzk fornrit 3), pp. 213–328.

Helle, Knut, *Gulatinget og Gulatingslova* (Leikanger: Skald, 2001).

Helle, Knut, *Norge blir en stat, 1130–1319* (Bergen/Oslo/Tromsø: Universitetsforlaget, 1974) (Handbok i Norges historie 3).

Hemmerdinger-Iliadou, Démocratie, 'Éphrem Grec', in *Dictionnaire de Spiritualité*, vol. 4 (Paris: Beauchesne, 1960), pp. 800–15.

Henderson, George, 'Narrative Illustration and Theological Exposition in Medieval Art', in Keith Robbins (ed.), *Religion and Humanism* (Oxford, 1981).

Heusler, Andreas, *Germanentum. Vom Lebens- und Formgefühl der alten Germanen* (Heidelberg: Winter, 1934) (Kultur und Sprache 8).

Heusler, Andreas, *Zum isländischen Fehdewesen in der Sturlungenzeit* (Berlin: Verlag der Königlichen Akademie der Wissenschaften, 1912) (Abhandlungen der Königlich Preußischen Akademie der Wissenschaften, Philosophisch-Historische Classe 1912, 4).

Hill, Thomas, 'Njáll's Comforting Words: *Brennu-Njáls saga*, chapter 129', *Saga-book of the Viking Society* 41 (2017), pp. 71–8.

Hinterberger, Martin, 'Autobiography and Hagiography in Byzantium', *Symbolae Osloenses: Norwegian Journal of Greek and Latin Studies* 75, no. 1 (2000), pp. 139–64.

Hinterberger, Martin, 'Emotions in Byzantium', in Liz James (ed.), *A Companion to Byzantium* (Chichester, UK: Wiley-Blackwell, 2010), pp. 123–34.

Hinterberger, Martin, 'Tränen in der Byzantinischen Literatur. Ein Beitrag zur Geschichte der Emotionen', *JÖB* 56 (2006), pp. 27–51.

'Historia de profectione Danorum in Hierosolymam', in M. C. Gertz (ed.), *Scriptores minores historiae Danicae medii ævi 2* (København: Gad, 1918–22), pp. 457–92.

Hofstetter, Walter, 'Winchester and the Standardization of Old English Vocabulary', *Anglo-Saxon England* 17 (1988), pp. 139–62.

The Holy Bible, Douay Version: Translated from the Latin Vulgate (Douay, A. D. 1609: Rheims, A.D. 1582). (London: Catholic Truth Society, 1956). Available at http://www.drbo.org/.

The Holy Bible, Douay-Rheims Version, with revisions and footnotes by Bishop Richard Challoner, 1749–52 (Baltimore, 1899; reprint Charlotte, NC, 1971). Available at http://www.drbo.org/ (accessed 15 October 2019).

Hough, Carole, *An Ald Reht: Essays on Anglo-Saxon Law* (Cambridge: Cambridge Scholars, 2014).

Hough, Carole, 'Alfred's *domboc* and the Language of Rape: A Reconsideration of Alfred', *Medium Aevum* 66, no. 1 (1997), pp. 1–27.

Hough, Carole, 'Legal and Documentary Writings', in P. Pulsiano and E. Treharne (eds.), *Companion to Anglo-Saxon Literature* (Oxford: Blackwell, 2001), pp. 170–87.

Hough, Carole, 'Penitential Literature and Secular Law in Anglo-Saxon England', *Anglo-Saxon Studies in Archaeology and History* 11 (2001), pp. 133–41.

'Hrafnkels saga Freysgoða', in Jón Jóhannesson (ed.), *Austfirðinga sǫgur. Þorsteins saga hvíta. Vápnfirðinga saga. Þorsteins þáttr stangarhǫggs. Ǫlkofra þáttr. Hrafnkels saga Freysgoða. Droplaugarsonar saga. Brandkrossa þáttr. Gunnars þáttr Þiðrandabana. Fljótsdæla saga. Þorsteins saga Síðu-Hallssonar. Draumr Þorsteins Síðu-Hallssonar. Þorsteins þáttr Austfirðings. Þorsteins þáttr sǫgufróða. Gull-Ásu-Þórðar þáttr* (Reykjavík: Hið íslenzka fornritafélag, 1950) (Íslenzk fornrit 11), pp. 95–133.

Hunt, Hannah, *Joy-bearing Grief: Tears of Contrition in the Writings of the Early Syrian and Byzantine Fathers* (Leiden: Brill, 2004).

Hunt, Hannah, 'The Monk as Mourner: St. Isaac the Syrian & Monastic Identity in the 7th C. & Beyond', in John A. McGuckin (ed.), *Orthodox Monasticism Past and Present* (Piscataway, NJ: Gorgias Press, 2015), pp. 331–42.

Hunt, Hannah, 'The Tears of the Sinful Woman: A Theology of Redemption in the Homilies of St. Ephraim and his Followers'. *Hugoye: Journal of Syriac Studies* 1, no. 2 (1998), pp. 165–84.

Hupka, Ralph B., Alison P. Lenton and Keith A. Hutchison, 'Universal Development of Emotion Categories in Natural Language', *Journal of Personality and Social Psychology* 77, no. 2 (1999), pp. 247–78.

'Íslendinga saga', in Jón Jóhannesson, Magnús Finnbogason and K. Eldjárn (eds.), *Sturlunga saga. Fyrra bindi* (Reykjavík: Sturlungaútgáfan, 1946), pp. 229–534.

Íslenskt textasafn. Stofnun Árna Magnússonar í íslenskum fræðum. Available at http://corpus.arnastofnun.is/leit.pl?hreinsaform=N%C3%BD+leit (accessed 20 November 2019).

'Ívarr Ingimundarson, Sigurðarbálkr', ed. K. E. Gade, in *Poetry from the Kings' Sagas 2,2*, ed. M. Clunies Ross (Turnhout: Brepols, 2009) (Skaldic Poetry of the Scandinavian Middle Ages 2), pp. 501–27.

Izard, C. E., *Human Emotions* (New York, 1977).

Izdebska, Daria, 'The Curious Case of *TORN*: The Importance of Lexical-semantic Approaches to the Study of Emotions in Old English', in A. Jorgensen, F. McCormack, and J. Wilcox (eds.), *Anglo-Saxon Emotions: Reading the Heart in Old English Language, Literature and Culture* (Burlington: Ashgate, 2015), pp. 53–74.

Izdebska, Daria, *The Semantic field of ANGER in Old English*. University of Glasgow, 2014. unpublished PhD thesis.

Jakobsson, Ármann, 'King Sverrir of Norway and the Foundations of His Power: Kingship Ideology and Narrative in *Sverris saga*', *Medium Ævum* 84 (2015), pp. 109–35.

Jakobsson, Ármann, *A Sense of Belonging. Morkinskinna and Icelandic Identity, c. 1220* (Odens: University of Southern Denmark Press, 2014) (The Viking Collection 22).

Jankélévitch Vladimir, *Valeur et signification de la mauvaise conscience* (Paris, F. Alcan, 1933).

Jansen, Katherine Ludwig, *The Making of the Magdalen: Preaching and Popular Devotion in the Later Middle Ages* (Princeton, 2000).

Jeffreys, Elizabeth M., 'Kontakio', in *ODB*, 1148.

Jeremias, Jörg, 'Reue I: Biblisch', in H. Balz et al. (eds.), *Theologische Realenzyklopädie 29* (Berlin/New York: De Gruyter, 1998), pp. 99–101.

John Chrysostom, *A Companion for the Sincere Penitent: Or, a Treatise on the Compunction of the Heart. In Two Books*, trans. John Veneer (London: Judge's-Head, St. Dunstan's Church, 1728).

John Chrysostom, *To Demetrius, on Compunction* and *to Stelechius, on Compunction*. PG 47, pp. 393–422.

John Chrysostom, *Homilies on Matthew*, 55. PG 58, 539–50. Translated in *St John Chrysostom. The Homilies of S. John Chrysostom, Archbishop of Constantinople, on the Gospel of St. Matthew. Part 2. Hom. 26–58* (Oxford: John Henry Parker, 1844).

John Chrysostom, *Homily on the Apostolic Saying That States: But Know This, That in the Last Days Perilous Times Will Come*. PG 56, pp. 271–80.

John Chrysostom, *Homilies on the Epistles to the Corinthians*. PG 61, 9–610. Translated by Philip Schaff in *Saint Chrysostom: Homilies on the Epistles of Paul to the Corinthians* (New York: Christian Literature Company, 1899), pp. 7–741.

John Chrysostom, *Homilies on the Statues*. PG 49, pp. 15–222.

John Klimakos, *The Ladder of Paradise*. PG 88, pp. 631–1161.

Jón Viðar Sigurðsson, *Chieftains and Power in the Icelandic Commonwealth* (Odense: Odense University Press, 1999).

Jónsbók. Kong Magnus Hakonssons Lovbog for Island vedtaget paa Altinget 1281 og Réttarbœtr. De for Island givne Retterbøder af 1294, 1305 og 1314, ed. Ólafur Halldórsson (København: Møller, 1904).

Jorgensen, Alice, 'It Shames Me to Say It': Ælfric and the Concept and Vocabulary of Shame', *Anglo-Saxon England* 41 (2012), pp. 249–76. doi: https://doi.org/10.1017/S0263675112000117 (accessed 20 November 2019).

Juslin, Patrik N., László Harmat, and Tuomas Eerol, 'What Makes Music Emotionally Significant? Exploring the Underlying Mechanisms'. *Psychology of Music* 42, no. 4 (2014), pp. 599–623.

Kassia, *On the Sinful Woman*. In Sinai Graecus 734–5, folio 159r-v; Vaticanus Graecus 771, folio 162v; Grottaferrata Δβ I, folio 161r.

Kaster, Robert, *Emotion, Restraint and Community in Ancient Rome* (Oxford: Oxford University Press, 2005).

Kastovsky, Dieter, 'Old English Word-format and Loan Translations', in J. Martín Arista, R. Torre Alonso, A. Canga Alonso, and I. Medina Barco (eds.), *Convergent Approaches to Mediaeval English Language and Literature. Selected Papers from the 22nd Conference of SELIM* (Cambridge: Cambridge Scholars, 2012), pp. 29–43.

Kazhdan, Alexander P., *A History of Byzantine Literature (650–850)* (Athens: National Hellenic Research Foundation, 1999).

Kazhdan, Alexander P., and Anthony Cutler, 'Emotions', in *ODB*, 691–2.

Kempe, Margery, *The Book of Margery Kempe*, ed. Sanford Brown Meech (London, 1997).

Keynes, Simon, 'King Alfred and the Mercians', in M. Blackburn and D. N. Dumville (eds.), *Kings, Currency and Alliances: History and Coinage of Southern England in the Ninth Century* (Woodbridge: Boydell Press, 1998), pp. 1–46.

Kirchberger, Clare, 'Some Notes on the *Ancrene Riwle*', *Dominican Studies* 7 (1954), pp. 215–38.

Kitson, Peter, 'Topography, Dialect and the Relation of Old English Psalter-glosses (I)', *English Studies* 83, no. 6 (2002), pp. 474–503.

Knight, Kimberley-Joy, '*Si Puose Calcina a' Propi Occhi*: The Importance of the Gift of Tears for Thirteenth-century Religious Women and Their Hagiographers', in Elina Gertsman (ed.), *Crying in the Middle Ages: Tears of History* (New York: Routledge, 2012), pp. 136–55.

Knuuttila, Simo, *Emotions in Ancient and Medieval Philosophy* (Oxford: Clarendon, 2004).

Koder, Johannes, 'Imperial Propaganda in the *Kontakia* of Romanos the Melode'. *DOP* 62 (2008), 275–91.

Kohnen, Thomas, 'Anglo-Saxon Expressives: Automatic Historical Speech-act Analysis and Philological Intervention', *Anglistik: International Journal of English Studies* 28, no. 1 (March 2017), pp. 43–56.

König-Pralong, Catherine, *L'Avènement de l'aristotélisme en terre chrétienne* (Paris, 2005).

Konstan, David, *The Emotions of the Ancient Greeks: Studies in Aristotle and Classical Literature* (London: University of Toronto Press, 2006).

Konstan, David, 'Rhetoric and Emotion', in Ian Worthington (ed.), *A Companion to Greek Rhetoric* (Oxford: Blackwell Publishing, 2007), pp. 411–25.

Koselleck, Reinhart, 'Hinweise auf die temporalen Strukturen begriffsgeschichtlichen Wandels', in Idem, *Begriffsgeschichten. Studien zur Semantik und Pragmatik der politischen und sozialen Sprache. Mit zwei Beiträgen von Ulrike Spree und Willibald Steinmetz sowie einem Nachwort zu Einleitungsfragmenten Reinhart Kosellecks von Carsten Dutt* (Frankfurt am Main, 2006), pp. 86–98.

Kramp, Iosef, 'Des Wilhelm von Auvergne *Magisterium divinale*', *Gregorianum*, II (1921), pp. 42–78 (Latin version pp. 79–114).

Krans, Jan, and Joseph Verheyden (eds.), *Patristic and Text-critical Studies: The Collected Essays of William L. Petersen* (Leiden: Brill, 2012).

Krueger, Derek, *Liturgical Subjects: Christian Ritual, Biblical Narrative and the Formation of Self in Byzantium* (Philadelphia: University of Pennsylvania Press, 2014).

Krueger, Derek, 'Liturgical Time and Holy Land Reliquaries in Early Byzantium', in Cynthia Hahn and Holger A. Klein (eds.), *Saints and Sacred Matter: The Cult of Relics in Byzantium and Beyond* (Washington, DC: Dumbarton Oaks Research Library and Collection, 2015), pp. 111–32.

Krueger, Derek, 'Romanos the Melodist and the Early Christian Self', in Elizabeth Jeffreys (ed.), *Proceedings of the 1st International Congress of Byzantine Studies: London, 21–26 August 2006* (Aldershot: Ashgate, 2006), pp. 255–74.

Kuhn, Sherman, M., 'Synonyms in the Old English Bede', *The Journal of English and Germanic Philology* 46, no. 2 (1947), pp. 168–76.

L' Histoire d'Erec en prose: roman du xve siècle, ed. M. Colombo Timelli (Geneva, Droz, 2000).

La Châtelaine de Vergy, ed. J. Dufournet et L. Dulac (Paris: Gallimard, 1997).

La Passion du Palatinus, ed. G. Frank (Paris: H. Champion, 1992).

Laing, Margaret and Angus McIntosh, 'Cambridge, Trinity College, MS 335: Its Texts and Their Transmission', in Richard Beadle and A. J. Piper (eds.), *New Science Out of Old Books: Studies in Manuscripts and Early Printed Books in Honour of A. I. Doyle* (Aldershot, 1995), pp. 14–52.

'Lambeth Homilies', in Richard Morris (ed.), *Old English Homilies*, First Series. EETS O.S. 29, 34 (London, 1867–8).

Lampe, G. W. H., *Patristic Greek Lexicon* (Oxford: Clarendon Press, 1961).

Lancelot, ed. A. Micha (Geneva; Paris: Librairie Droz, 1978).

Lancelot du lac, ed. F. Mosès (Paris, Libr: Générale Française, coll. « Le livre de poche Lettres gothiques », 1998).

Landman, Janet, 'Regret: A Theoretical and Conceptual Analysis', *Journal of the Theory of Social Behaviour* 17, no. 2 (1987), pp. 140–60.

Langé, Santino and Alberto Pensa, *Il Sacro Monte. Esperienza del reale e spazio virtuale nell'iconografia della Passione a Varallo* (Milan, 1991).

Largier, Niklaus, 'Inner Senses – Outer Senses: The Practice of Emotions in Medieval Mysticism', in C. Stephen Jaeger and Ingrid Kasten (eds.), *Codierungen von Emotionen im Mittelalter/Emotions and Sensibilities in the Middle Ages* (Berlin: De Gruyter, 2003), pp. 3–15.

Largier, Niklaus, Medieval Mysticism. *The Oxford Handbook of Religion and Emotion*, ed. John Corrigan (Oxford: Oxford University Press, 2008), pp. 364–79.

Largier, Niklaus, 'The Plasticity of the Soul: Mystical Darkness, Touch, and Aesthetic Experience'. *MLN* 125, no. 3 (2010), 536–51.

Larin, Vassa, '"Active Participation" of the Faithful in Byzantine Liturgy'. *St. Vladimir's Theological Quarterly* 57, no. 1 (2013), pp. 67–88.

'Laxdœla saga', in Einar Ólafur Sveinsson (ed.), *Laxdœla saga. Halldórs þættir Snorrasonar. Stúfs þáttr* (Reykjavík: Hið íslenzka fornritafélag, 1934) (Íslenzk fornrit 5), pp. 1–248.

Lazikani, A. S., *Cultivating the Heart: Feeling and Emotion in Twelfth- and Thirteenth-century Religious Texts* (Cardiff, 2015).

Le Roman d'Enéas: édition critique d'après le manuscrit B.N. fr. 60, ed. A. Petit (Paris, Libr. Générale Française, coll. « Le livre de poche Lettres gothiques », 1997).

Le Roman de Partonopeu de Blois, ed. A. Paris (Paris: Librairie générale française, 2005).

Le Roman de Tristan en prose, t. 1, ed. R. L. Curtis (München, M. Hueber, 1963).

Le Roman de Tristan en prose, ed. R. L. Curtis (Woodbridge, Suffolk, D.S. Brewer, 1985).

Le Roman de Tristan en prose t.1, éd. Ph. Ménard, (Geneva, Librairie Droz, 1987).

Le Typicon de la Grande Église, ed. Juan Mateos. 2 vols. OCA 165, 166 (Rome: Pontificum Institutum Orientalium Studiorum 1962–3).

Le Typicon du Monastère du Saint-Sauveur à Messine, ed. M. Arranz. OCA 185 (Rome: Pontificum Institutum Orientalium Studiorum, 1969).

Leclercq, Jean, *The Love of Learning and the Desire of God*, trans. Catharine Misrahi (NY, 1961).

Leduc, Francis, 'Penthos et Larmes dans l'œuvre de Saint Jean Chrysostome'. *Proche-Orient Chrétien* 41 (1991), pp. 220–57.

Lemke, Andreas, *The Old English Translation of Bede's* Historia Ecclesiastica Gentis Anglorum *in Its Historical and Cultural Context*. Göttinger Schriften zur Englischen Philologie, vol. 8 (Göttingen: Universitätsverlag Göttingen, 2015).

Lendinara, Patrizia, 'The Kentish Laws', in J. Hines (ed.), *The Anglo-Saxons from the Migration Period to the Eighth Century* (Woodbridge, 2003), pp. 211–30.

Levy, Kenneth, and Christian Troelsgård, 'Byzantine Chant', in S. Sadie and J. Tyrell (eds.), *The New Grove Dictionary of Music and Musicians*, vol. 4 (London: Macmillan, 2001), pp. 734–56.

Liddell, H. G., and R. Scott, *A Greek-English Lexicon* (Oxford: Clarendon Press, 1996).

Liddell, H. G., and R. Scott, *An Intermediate Greek-English Lexicon* (Oxford: Clarendon Press, 2002).

Lied, Laurel Joy, *A Meeting of Worlds. An Investigation into the Development of a Christian Vocabulary Set within the Old Norse Language Using a New Statistical Methodology* (Oslo, 2016) University of Oslo. Master Thesis.

Lingas, Alexander, 'From Earth to Heaven: The Changing Musical Soundscape of the Byzantine Liturgy', in Claire Nesbitt and Mark Jackson (eds.), *Experiencing Byzantium: Papers from the 44th Spring Symposium of Byzantine Studies, Newcastle and Durham, April 2011* (Farnham: Ashgate, 2013), pp. 311–58.

Lingas, Alexander, 'How Musical Was the 'Sung Office'? Some Observations on the Ethos of the Byzantine Cathedral Rite', in Ivan Moody and Maria Takala-Roszczenko (eds.), *The Traditions of Orthodox Music: Proceedings of the First International Conference on Orthodox Church Music, University of Joensuu, Finland, 13–19 June 2005* (Joensuu: International Society for Orthodox Church Music, 2007), pp. 217–34.

Lingas, Alexander, 'Hymnography', in G. Speake (ed.), *The Encyclopedia of Greece and the Hellenic Tradition*, vol. 1 (Chicago: Fitzroy-Dearborn, 2000), pp. 786–87.

Lingas, Alexander. 'The Liturgical Place of the *Kontakion* in Constantinople', in C. C. Akentiev (ed.), *Liturgy, Architecture and Art of the Byzantine World: Papers of the XVIII International Byzantine Congress (Moscow, 8–15 August 1991) and Other Essays Dedicated to the Memory of Fr. John Meyendorff* (St Petersburg: Vizantinorossika, 1995), pp. 50–7.

Lingas, Alexander, 'Medieval Byzantine Chant and the Sound of Orthodoxy', in Andrew Louth and Augustine Casiday (eds.), *Byzantine Orthodoxies: Papers from the Thirty-sixth Spring Symposium of Byzantine Studies, University of Durham, 23–25 March 2002* (Aldershot: Ashgate, 2006), pp. 131–50.

Lingas, Alexander, 'Music', in Nigel Wilson (ed.), *Encyclopedia of Ancient Greece* (New York: Routledge, 2010), pp. 484–6.

Lingas, Alexander, 'Sunday Matins in the Byzantine Cathedral Rite: Music and Liturgy'. PhD diss., University of British Columbia, 1996.

'Ljósvetninga Saga', in Björn Sigfússon (ed.), *Ljósvetninga saga með þáttum. Reykdœla saga ok Víga-Skútu. Hreiðars þáttr* (Reykjavík: Hið íslenzka fornritafélag, 1940) (Íslenzk fornrit 10), pp. 1–106.

Löbner, Hans-Werner, *Reden und Träume als strategische Elemente der Geschichtsschreibung des Mittelalters. Eine Untersuchung am Beispiel der Reden und Träume der Sverris-Saga* (Freiburg: [n. pub.], 1992).

Lombard, Peter, *Sententiae in IV libris distinctae*, 2 vols (Rome, 1971–81).

Loraux, Nicole, 'La métaphore sans métaphore: à propos de l'Orestie', *Revue philosophique de la France et de l'Etranger* 180, no. 2 (1990), pp. 247–68.

Lossky, Nicolas, *Essai sur une Théologie de la Musique Liturgique* (Paris: Les Éditions du Cerf, 2003).

Lossky, Vladimir, *Essai sur la Théologie Mystique de l'Église d'Orient* (Aubier: Éditions Montaigne, 1944).

Louth, Andrew, 'Byzantium Transforming (600–700)', in Jonathan Shepard (ed.), *The Cambridge History of the Byzantine Empire c. 500–1492* (Cambridge: Cambridge University Press, 2008), pp. 221–48.

Louth, Andrew, *Denys the Areopagite* (London: Continuum, 1989).

Louth, Andrew. 'The Ecclesiology of Saint Maximus the Confessor', *International Journal for the Study of the Christian Church* 4, no. 2 (2004), pp. 109–20.

Louth, Andrew, 'Justinian and His Legacy', in Jonathan Shepard (ed.) *The Cambridge History of the Byzantine Empire c. 500–1492* (Cambridge: Cambridge University Press, 2008), pp. 99–129.

Louth, Andrew, 'Mystagogy in Saint Maximus', in Paul Van Geest (ed.), *Seeing Through the Eyes of Faith: New Approaches to the Mystagogy of the Church Fathers* (Leuven: Peeters, 2016), pp. 375–88.

Louw, J. P., and Eugene A. Nida, *Greek-English Lexicon of the New Testament: Based on Semantic Domains* (New York: United Bible Societies, 1988).

Love, Nicholas, *The Mirror of the Blessed Life of Jesus Christ: A Reading Text*, ed. M. G. Sargent (Exeter, 2004).

Lust, J., Erik Eynikel, and K. Hauspie, *A Greek-English Lexicon of the Septuagint* (Stuttgart: Deutsche Bibelgesellschaft, 1992).

Maas, Michael, 'Roman Questions, Byzantine Answers: Contours of the Age of Justinian', in Michael Maas (ed.), *The Cambridge Companion to the Age of Justinian* (Cambridge: Cambridge University Press, 2005).

Magennis, Hugh, 'Contrasting features in the Non-Ælfrician Lives in the Old English *Lives of Saints*', *Anglia* 104 (1986), pp. 316–48.

Maguire, Henry, *Art and Eloquence in Byzantium* (Princeton, NJ: Princeton University Press, 1981).

'Markús Skeggjason, Eiríksdrápa', ed. J. Carroll, in M. Clunies Ross (ed.), *Poetry from the Kings' Sagas 2,1* (Turnhout: Brepols, 2009) (Skaldic Poetry of the Scandinavian Middle Ages 2), pp. 432-60.

Marrone, Steven P., 'Magic and the Physical World in the Thirteenth-century Scholasticism', in E. Sylla and W. Newman (eds.), *Evidence and Interpretation in Studies on Early Science and Medicine. Essays in Honor of John E. Murdoch* (Leiden, 2009), pp. 158-85.

Marrone, Steven P., 'The Philosophy of Nature in Early Thirteenth Century', in L. Honnefelder, R. Wood, M. Dreyer, M.-A. Aris (eds.), *Albertus Magnus und die Anfänge der Aristoteles-Rezeption im lateinischen Mittelalter von Richardus Rufus bis zu Franciscus de Mayronis/Albertus Magnus and the Beginnings of Aristotle Reception in the Latin West from Richardus Rufus to Franciscus de Mayronis* (Münster, 2005), pp. 115-58.

Marrone, Steven P., 'William of Auvergne on Magic in Natural Philosophy and Theology', in J. A. Aersten, A. Speer (eds.), *Wast ist Philosophie im Mittelalter?* (Berlin, 1998), pp. 741-8.

Martin, Hervé, *Le Métier de prédicateur à la fin du moyen âge (1350–1520)* (Paris, 1988).

Martin, Jean-Pierre, *Les Motifs dans la chanson de geste: définition et utilisation*, Villeneuve d'Ascq, Centre d'Études Médiévales et Dialectales, Univ. de Lille III, coll. « Discours de l'épopée médiévale », n° 1, 1992.

McNeill, John T., 'Medicine for Sin as Prescribed in the Penitentials', *Church History* 1 (1932), pp. 14–26.

McCann, Daniel, *Soul-health: Therapeutic Reading in Later Medieval England* (Cardiff, 2018).

McCloskey, Deirdre N., *The Bourgeois Virtues: Ethics for an Age of Commerce* (Chicago, 2006).

McCormack, Frances, 'Those Bloody Trees: The Affectivity of *Christ*', in A. Jorgensen, F. McCormack, and J. Wilcox (eds.), *Anglo-Saxon Emotions: Reading the Heart in Old English Language, Literature and Culture* (Burlington: Ashgate, 2015), pp. 143-61.

McEntire, Sandra J., *The Doctrine of Compunction in Medieval England: Holy Tears* (Lewiston: E. Mellen Press, 1990).

McEntire, Sandra, 'The Doctrine of Compunction from Bede to Margery Kempe', in Marion Glasscoe (ed.), *The Medieval Mystical Tradition in England IV* (Cambridge, 1987), pp. 77-90.

McEntire, Sandra, *The Doctrine of Compunction in Medieval England: Holy Tears* (Lewiston, NY, 1991).

McGinn, Bernard, '*Unio Mystica*/Mystical Union', in Amy Hollywood and Patricia Z. Beckman (eds.), *The Cambridge Companion to Christian Mysticism* (Cambridge: Cambridge University Press), pp. 200–10.

McGrath, Alister E., *Iustitia Dei: A History of the Christian Doctrine of Justification* (Cambridge, 1998).

McKinnon, James (ed.), *Music in Early Christian Literature* (Cambridge: Cambridge University Press, 1987).

McNamer, Sarah, *Affective Meditation and the Invention of Medieval Compassion* (Philadelphia: University of Pennsylvania Press, 2010).

McNamer, Sarah, 'Feeling', in Paul Strohm (ed.), *Oxford Twenty-first Century Approaches to Literature: Middle English* (Oxford: Oxford University Press, 2007), pp. 241–57.

McNamer, Sarah, 'The Literariness of Literature and the History of Emotion'. *PMLA* 130, no. 5 (2015), pp. 1433–42.

McTaggart (now Schuurman), Anne, *Shame and Guilt in Chaucer* (Basingstoke, 2012).

Meens, Rob, *Penance in Europe, 600–1200* (Cambridge, 2014).

Mellas, Andrew, *Liturgy and the Emotions in Byzantium: Compunction and Hymnody* (Cambridge: Cambridge University Press, 2020).

Mellinkoff, Ruth, *Outcasts: Signs of Otherness in Northern European Art of the Late Middle Ages* (Berkeley/Los Angeles/Oxford, 1994).

Merback, Mitchell B., *The Thief, the Cross and the Wheel. Pain and the Spectacle of Punishment in Medieval and Renaissance Europe* (Chicago, 1998).

Meyendorff, John, *Byzantine Theology: Historical Trends and Doctrinal Themes* (New York: Fordham University Press, 1983).

Meyendorff, John, *Imperial Unity and Christian Divisions* (Crestwood, NY: St Vladimir's Seminary Press, 1989).

Michaud-Quantin, Pierre, *Sommes de casuistique et manuels de confession au moyen âge, XIIe–XVIe siècles* (Louvain, Lille, Montréal, 1962).

Michel, Jean, *Le Mystère de la Passion (Angers 1486)*, ed. Omer Jodogne (Gembloux, 1959).

Middle English Dictionary, ed. Hans Kurath and S. M. Kuhn. Available at http://quod.lib.umich.edu/m/med/.

Milfull, Inge B., *The Hymns of the Anglo-Saxon Church: A Study and Edition of the 'Durham Hymnal'* (Cambridge: Cambridge University Press, 1996).

Miller, James, '"Let us Sing to the Lord": The Biblical Odes in the Codex Alexandrinus'. PhD diss., Marquette University, 2006.

Miller, William I., *Bloodtaking and Peacemaking. Feud, Law and Society in Saga Iceland* (Chicago: The University of Chicago Press, 1990).

Miller, William I., 'Emotions and the Sagas', in Gísli Pálsson (ed.), *From Sagas to Society: Comparative Approaches to Early Iceland* (Enfield Lock: Hisarlik Press, 1992), pp. 89–109.

Miller, William I., *Humiliation. And Other Essays on Honor, Social Discomfort, and Violence* (Ithaca, NY/London: Cornell University Press, 1993).

Millett, Bella, '*Ancrene Wisse* and the Conditions of Confession', *English Studies* 80 (1999), pp. 193–215.

Millett, Bella, 'The Discontinuity of English Prose: Structural Innovation in the Trinity and Lambeth Homilies', in Akin Oizumi, Jacek Fiscal and John Scahill (eds.), *Text and Language in Medieval English Prose: A Festschrift For Tadao Kubouchi* (Frankfurt, 2005), pp. 129–50.

Millett, Bella, 'The Pastoral Context of the Trinity and Lambeth Homilies', in Wendy Scase (ed.), *Essays in Manuscript Geography: Vernacular Manuscripts of the English West Midlands from the Conquest to the Sixteenth Century* (Turnhout, 2007), pp. 43–64.

Miner, Dorothy, *Illuminated Books of the Middle Ages and Renaissance* (Baltimore, 1949).

Möhlig-Falke, Ruth, *The Early English Impersonal Construction. An Analysis of Verbal and Constructional Meaning* (Oxford, 2012).

Moller, Herbert, 'Affective Mysticism in Western Civilization'. *Psychoanalytic Review* 52, no. 2 (1965), pp. 115–30.

Momma, Haruko, 'The Old English Metrical Psalms: Practice and Theory of Translation', in L. Brady, and M. J. Toswell (eds.), *Early English Poetic Culture and Meter: The Influence of G.R. Russom* (Kalamazoo: Medieval Institute Publications, 2016), pp. 93–110.

Moore, Sophie V., 'Experiencing Mid-Byzantine Mortuary Practice: Shrouding the Dead', in Claire Nesbitt and Mark Jackson (eds.), *Experiencing Byzantium: Papers from the 44th Spring Symposium of Byzantine Studies, Newcastle and Durham, April 2011* (Burlington, VT: Ashgate, 2013), pp. 195–212.

Moran, Neil, 'The Choir of Hagia Sophia'. *Oriens Christianus* 89 (2005), pp. 1–7.

Morkinskinna, ed. Ármann Jakobsson and Þórður Ingi Guðjónsson, 2 vols (Reykjaví: Hið íslenzka fornritafélag, 2011) (Íslenzk fornrit 23-4).

Morrison, Karl F., and Ruldoph M. Bell (eds.), *Studies on Medieval Empathies* (Turnhout, 2013).

Morrison, Stephen (ed.), *A Late Fifteenth-century Dominical Sermon Cycle, Edited from Bodleian Library MS E Museo 180 and Other Manuscripts*, 2 vols (Oxford: 2012 for 2011).

Morse, Stephen J., 'Commentary: Reflections on Remorse', *Journal of American Academy of Psychiatry Law* 42 (2014), pp. 49–55.

Mulchahey, M. Michèle, '*First the Bow Is Bent in Study*': *Dominican Education before 1350* (Toronto, 1998).

Muraoka, T., *A Greek-English Lexicon of the Septuagint* (Leuven: Peeters, 2009).

Murray, Alexander, *Suicide in the Middle Ages*, 2 vols (Oxford, 1998).

Nagy, Piroska, *Le Don des Larmes au Moyen Âge. Un Instrument en Quête d' Institution, ve–xiiie Siècle* (Paris: Albin Michel, 2000).

Nagy, Piroska, 'Religious Weeping as Ritual in the Medieval West', *Social Analysis: The International Journal of Social and Cultural Practice* 48 (2004), pp. 110–37.

Nave, Guy D., Jr, *The Role and Function of Repentance in Luke–Acts* (Leiden: Brill, 2002).
Neidorf, Leonard (ed.), *The Dating of Beowulf. A Reassessment* (Woodbridge: D.S. Brewer, 2014).
Nellas, Panayiotis, *Deification in Christ: The Nature of the Human Person*, trans. Norman Russell (New York: St Vladimir's Seminary Press, 1997).
Nesbitt, Claire, and Mark Jackson, 'Experiencing Byzantium', in Claire Nesbitt and Mark Jackson (eds.), *Experiencing Byzantium: Papers from the 44th Spring Symposium of Byzantine Studies, Newcastle and Durham, April 2011* (Farnham: Ashgate, 2013), pp. 1–16.
Netútgáfan. Available at https://www.snerpa.is/net/fornrit.htm (accessed 24 July 2020).
Neu, Jerome, *A Tear Is an Intellectual Thing: The Meanings of Emotion* (New York: Oxford University Press, 2000).
Nicholson, Simon, 'The Expression of Emotional Distress in Old English Prose and Verse', *Culture, Medicine and Psychiatry* 19, no. 3 (1995), pp. 327–38.
Nordal, Guðrún, 'The Contemporary Sagas and Their Social Context', in M. Clunies Ross (ed.), *Old Icelandic Literature and Society* (Cambridge: Cambridge University Press, 2000) (Cambridge Studies in Medieval Literature 42), pp. 221–41.
Nordal, Guðrún, *Ethics and Action in Thirteenth-century Iceland* (Odense: Odense University Press, 1998) (The Viking Collection 11).
Nussbaum, Martha C., *The Therapy of Desire: Theory and Practice in Hellenistic Ethics* (Princeton, NJ: Princeton University Press, 2009).
Nussbaum, Martha C., *Upheavals of Thought: The Intelligence of Emotions* (Cambridge: Cambridge University Press, 2001).
'Nyere Christenret, udgiven af Erkebiskop Jon den Yngre', in R. Keyser and P. A. Munch (eds.), *Norges gamle Love indtil 1387 2. Lovgivningen under Kong Magnus Haakonssöns Regjeringstid fra 1263 til 1280, tilligemed et Supplement til förste Bind* (Christiania: Grøndahl, 1848), pp. 339–86.
Oddr Snorrason, 'Óláfs saga Tryggvasonar', in Ólafur Halldórsson (ed.), *Færeyinga saga. Óláfs saga Tryggvasonar eptir Odd munk Snorrason* (Reykjavík: Hið íslenzka fornritafélag, 2006) (Íslenzk fornrit 25), pp. 123–380.
Oetgen, Jerome, 'The Trinity College Ascension Sermon: Sources and Structure', *Medieval Studies* 45 (1983), pp. 410–17.
Ogura, Michiko, 'The Variety and Conformity of Old English Psalter Glosses', *English Studies* 83, no. 1 (2003), pp. 1–8.
Ohly, Friedrich, *The Damned and the Elect: Guilt in Western Culture*, trans. Linda Archibald (Cambridge, 1992).
Okon-Singer, Hadas, Hendler, Talma, Pessoa, Luiz, and Shackman, Alexander J., 'The Neurobiology of Emotion–Cognition Interactions: Fundamental Questions and Strategies for Future Research', *Frontiers of Human Neuroscience* 9, no. 58 (2015), pp. 1–14. doi: 10.3389/fnhum.2015.00058.
The Old Norse Elucidarius. Original Text and Translation, ed. E. Scherabon Firchow (Columbia: Camden House, 1992).

Oliver, Lisi, 'Æthelberht's Code'. *Early English Laws* (London, 2020). Available at https://earlyenglishlaws.ac.uk/laws/texts/Abt/ (accessed 7 January 2020).
Ordbog over det norrøne prosasprog. Available at https://onp.ku.dk/ (accessed 24 July 2020).
Orkneyinga saga. Legenda de Sancto Magno. Magnúss saga skemmri. Magnúss saga lengri. Helga þáttr ok Úlfs, ed. Finnbogi Guðmundsson (Reykjavík: Hið íslenzka fornritafélag, 1965) (Íslenzk fornrit 34).
Orning, Hans J., *Unpredictability and Presence. Norwegian Kingship in the High Middle Ages* (Leiden: Brill, 2008) (The Northern World 38).
Owst, G. R., *Literature and Pulpit in Medieval England*, 2nd ed. rev. (New York, 1961).
The Oxford Dictionary of English Etymology, ed. C. T. Onions (Oxford, 1996).
Oxford English Dictionary (OED). Available at www.oed.com.
The Oxford English Dictionary: The Definitive Record of the English Language (Oxford, 2010). Available at http://www.oed.com/ (accessed 20 November 2019).
Palmer, James. M., 'Compunction and the Heart in the OE Poem *the Wanderer*', *Neophilologus* 88 (2004), pp. 447–60.
Panofsky, Erwin, *Early Netherlandish Painting*, 2 vols (Cambridge, MA, 1953).
Panofsky, Erwin, 'Jan van Eyck's *Arnolfini* Portrait', *Burlington Magazine* 64 (1934), pp. 117–27.
Papalexandrou, Amy, 'The Memory Culture of Byzantium', in Liz James (ed.), *A Companion to Byzantium* (Chichester, UK: Wiley-Blackwell, 2010), pp. 108–22.
Papalexandrou, Amy, 'Perceptions of Sound and Sonic Environment across the Byzantine Acoustic Horizon', in Susan Ashbrook Harvey and Margaret Mullett (eds.), *Knowing Bodies, Passionate Souls: Sense Perceptions in Byzantium* (Washington, DC: Dumbarton Oaks Research Library and Collection, 2017), pp. 67–85.
Papanikolaou, Aristotle, and George E. Demacopoulos, 'Augustine and the Orthodox: The "West" in the East', in Aristotle Papanikolaou and George E. Demacopoulos (eds.), *Orthodox Readings of Augustine* (Crestwood, NY: St Vladimir's Seminary Press, 2008), pp. 11–40.
Pascual, Rafael J., 'Material Monsters and Semantic Shifts', in L. Neidorf (ed.), *The Dating of Beowulf. A Reassessment* (Woodbridge: D.S. Brewer, 2014), pp. 202–18.
Patton, Kimberley Christine. '"Howl, Weep and Moan, and Bring It Back to God": Holy Tears in Eastern Christianity', in Kimberley Christine Patton and John Stratton Hawley (eds.), *Holy Tears: Weeping in the Religious Imagination* (Princeton, NJ: Princeton University Press, 2005), pp. 255–73.
Patton, Kimberley Christine, and John Stratton Hawley, *Holy Tears: Weeping in the Religious Imagination* (Princeton, NJ: Princeton University Press, 2005).
Payen Jean-Charles, *Le Motif du repentir dans la littérature française médiévale* (Geneva, Droz, 1967).
Pegon, Joseph, 'Componction', in Charles Baumgartner (ed.), *Dictionnaire de Spiritualité ascétique et mystique*, III (Paris, 1953), pp. 1312–21.
Pelikan, Jaroslav, *The Christian Tradition. A History of the Development of Doctrine, 2: The Spirit of Eastern Christendom (600–1700)* (Chicago: University of Chicago Press, 1974).

Pelle, Stephen, 'Source Studies in the Lambeth Homilies', *Journal of English and Germanic Philology* 113 (2014), 34–72.

Pellegrin, Elisabeth, 'Les *Remedia amoris* d'Ovide, texte scolaire médiéval', *Bibliothèque de l'Ecole des Chartes*, 115 (1957), pp. 172–9.

Pentcheva, Bissera V. (ed.), *Aural Architecture in Byzantium: Music, Acoustics, and Ritual* (New York: Routledge, 2017).

Pentcheva, Bissera V., *Hagia Sophia. Sound, Space and Spirit in Byzantium* (Pennsylvania: Pennsylvania State University Press, 2017).

Pentcheva, Bissera V., 'Hagia Sophia and Multisensory Aesthetics', *Gesta: International Centre for Medieval Art* 50, no. 2 (2011), pp. 93–111.

Pentcheva, Bissera V., 'Performing the Sacred in Byzantium: Image, Breath and Sound', *Performance Research* 19, no. 3 (2014), pp. 120–8.

Pentcheva, Bissera V., *The Sensual Icon: Space, Ritual, and the Senses in Byzantium* (Pennsylvania: Pennsylvania State University Press, 2010).

Pentiuc, Eugen J., *The Old Testament in Eastern Orthodox Tradition* (Oxford: Oxford University Press, 2014).

Perceforest, ed. G. Roussineau, 3 vol (Geneva, Droz, 1988).

Petersen, William L., *The Diatessaron and Ephrem Syrus as Sources of Romanos the Melodist*. CSCO 475 (Leuven: Peeters, 1985).

Philippe de Remi, *La Manekine*, ed. M.-M. Castellani (Paris: H. Champion, 2012).

Pizzone, Aglae (ed.), *The Author in Middle Byzantine Literature: Modes Functions and Identities* (Berlin: De Gruyter, 2014).

Plamper, Jan., *The History of Emotions: An Introduction*, trans. Keith Tribe (Oxford: Oxford University Press, 2015).

Plesch, Véronique, *Le Christ peint: Le Cycle de la Passion dans les chapelles peintes du XVe siècle dans les États de Savoie* (Chambéry, 2004).

Plesch, Véronique, *Painter and Priest: Giovanni Canavesio's Visual Rhetoric and the Passion Cycle at La Brigue* (Notre Dame, 2006).

'Þórarinn loftunga, Glælognskviða', ed. M. Townend, in *Poetry from the Kings' Sagas 1,2*, ed. D. Whaley (Turnhout: Brill, 2012) (Skaldic Poetry of the Scandinavian Middle Ages 1), pp. 863–7.

'Þórarinn stuttfeldr, Stuttfeldardrápa', ed. K. E. Gade, in *Poetry from the Kings' Sagas 2,2*, ed. M. Clunies Ross (Turnhout: Brill, 2009) (Skaldic Poetry of the Scandinavian Middle Ages 2), pp. 473–9.

'Þórðar saga kakala', in Jón Jóhannesson, Magnús Finnbogason and K. Eldjárn ed., *Sturlunga saga. Síðara bindi*, (Reykjavík: Sturlungaútgáfan, 1946), pp. 1–86.

'Þorgils saga ok Hafliða', in Jón Jóhannesson, Magnús Finnbogason and K. Eldjárn (eds.), *Sturlunga saga. Fyrra bindi* (Reykjavík: Sturlungaútgáfan, 1946), pp. 12–50.

Pott, Thomas, *Byzantine Liturgical Reform: A Study of Liturgical Change in the Byzantine Tradition*, trans. Paul Meyendorff (Crestwood, NY: St Vladimir's Seminary Press, 2010).

Pourrat, P., 'Affections', in Marcel Viller et al. (eds.), *Dictionnaire de spiritualité: ascetique et mystique, doctrine et histoire*, 17 vols, I (Paris, 1937), pp. 235–40.

Quasten, Johannes, *Music and Worship in Pagan and Christian Antiquity*, trans. Ramsay Boniface (Washington, DC: National Association of Pastoral Musicians, 1983).

Quinlan, Andrew John, *Sin. Gr. 734–735. Triodion. Excerpta ex Dissertatione ad Doctorum* (Newberry Springs: Pontificium Institutum Orientalium, 2004).

Ramelli, Ilaria, 'Tears of Pathos, Repentance and Bliss: Crying and Salvation in Origen and Gregory of Nyssa', in Thorsten Fögen (ed.), *Tears in the Graeco-Roman World* (Berlin: De Gruyter, 2009), pp. 367–96.

Rapp, Claudia, 'Literary Culture under Justinian', in Michael Maas (ed.), *The Cambridge Companion to the Age of Justinian* (Cambridge: Cambridge University Press, 2005), pp. 376–97.

Ray, Walter D., *Tasting Heaven on Earth: Worship in Sixth-century Constantinople* (Grand Rapids, MI: Eerdmans, 2012).

Réau, Louis, *Iconographie de l'art chrétien*, 3 vols (Paris, 1955–9).

Reddy, William M., *The Making of Romantic Love: Longing and Sexuality in Europe, South Asia and Japan, 900–1200 CE* (Chicago and London, 2012).

Reddy, William M., *The Navigation of Feeling: A Framework for the History of Emotions* (Cambridge: Cambridge University Press, 2001).

Régamey, Pie-Raymond, 'La componction du cœur', in *Portrait spirituel du chrétien* (Paris, 1963), pp. 67–116.

'Reykdœla saga ok Víga-Skútu', in Björn Sigfússon (ed.), *Ljósvetninga saga með þáttum. Reykdœla saga ok Víga-Skútu. Hreiðars þáttr* (Reykjavík: Hið íslenzka fornritafélag, 1940) (Íslenzk fornrit 10), pp. 149–243.

Rice, Robert, 'Hreowcearig "Penitent, Contrite"', *English Language Notes* 12, no. 4 (June 1975), pp. 243–50.

Richter, Lukas, 'Antike Überlieferungen in der Byzantinischen Musiktheorie', *Acta Musicologica* 70, no. 2 (1998), 133–208.

Riehle, Alexander, 'Authorship and Gender (and) Identity. Women's Writing in the Middle Byzantine Period', in Aglae Pizzone (ed.), *The Author in Middle Byzantine Literature: Modes Functions and Identities* (Berlin: De Gruyter, 2014), pp. 245–62.

Robert, Aurélien, 'Médecine et théologie à la cour angevine de Naples', in J. Chandelier, A. Robert (eds.), *Frontières des savoirs en Italie à l'époque des premières universités (XIIIe–XVe siècles)* (Rome, 2015), pp. 285–349.

Roberts, Jane, and Christian Kay, 'Classification', *About a Thesaurus of Old English* (Glasgow, 2017). Available at http://oldenglishthesaurus.arts.gla.ac.uk/classification (accessed 30 October 2018).

Rochow, Ilse, *Studien zu der Person, den Werken und dem Nachleben der Dichterin Kassia* (Berlin: Akademie-Verlag, 1967).

Romanos the Melodist, *Romanos le Mélode. Hymnes*, ed. José Grosdidier de Matons, 5 vols. SC 99, 110, 114, 128, 283 (Paris: Éditions du Cerf, 1964–81).

Romanos the Melodist, *Sancti Romani Melodi Cantica: Cantica Dubia*, ed. Paul Maas and C. A. Trypanis (Berlin: De Gruyter, 1970).

Romanos the Melodist, *Sancti Romani Melodi Cantica: Cantica Genuina*, ed. Paul Maas and C. A. Trypanis (Oxford: Clarendon Press, 1963).

Romanos the Melodist, *On the Life of Christ: Chanted Sermons by the Great Sixth-century Poet and Singer St. Romanos*, trans. Ephrem Lash. Sacred Literature Series: AltaMira Press, 1998.

Rosaldo, Renato, 'Grief and the Headhunter's Rage', in Stuart Plattner and Edward Bruner (eds.), *Text, Play and Story: The Construction and Reconstruction of Self and Society* (Washington, DC: American Ethnological Society, 1984), pp. 178–98.

Rosenwein, Barbara H., *Emotional Communities in the Early Middle Ages* (Ithaca, NY/London: Cornell University Press, 2006).

Ross, Woodburn O. (ed.), *Middle English Sermons, Edited from British Museum MS. Royal 18 B. xxiii* (London, 1940).

Roy, Émile, *Le Mystère de la Passion en France du XIVe au XVIe siècle* (Dijon, 1903–04, reprint, Geneva, 1974).

Rusconi, Roberto, 'De la prédication à la confession: transmission et contrôle de modèles de comportements au XIII^{e}s', in *Faire croire. Modalités de la diffusion et de la réception des messages religieux du XIIe au XVe siècle. Actes de table ronde de Rome (22–23 juin 1979)* (Rome, 1981), pp. 67–85.

Salvesen, Astrid, *Studies in the Vocabulary of the Old Norse Elucidarium* (Oslo: Universitetsforlaget, 1968).

Sauer, Hans, 'Language and Culture: How the Anglo-Saxon Glossators Adapted Latin Words and Their World', *Journal of Medieval Latin* 18 (2009), pp. 437–68.

Sävborg, Daniel, *Sorg och elegi i Eddans hjältediktning* (Stockhol: Almqvist & Wiksell International, 1997) (Acta Universitatis Stockholmiensis. Stockholm Studies in History of Literature 36).

Schechner, Richard, and Willa Appel, *By Means of Performance: Intercultural Studies of Theatre and Ritual* (Cambridge: Cambridge University Press, 1990).

Scheel, Roland, 'Byzantium – Rome – Denmark – Iceland: Dealing with Imperial Concepts in the North', in C. Scholl, T. R. Gebhardt and J. Clauß (eds.), *Transcultural Approaches to the Concept of Imperial Rule in the Middle Ages* (Frankfurt am Main et al.: Peter Lang, 2017), pp. 245–94.

Scheel, Roland, *Skandinavien und Byzanz. Bedingungen und Konsequenzen mittelalterlicher Kulturbeziehungen*, 2 (Göttingen: Vandenhoeck & Ruprecht, 2015) (Historische Semantik 23).

Scheer, Monique, 'Are Emotions a Kind of Practice (and Is That What Makes Them Have a History)? A Bourdieuian Approach to Understanding Emotion'. *History and Theory* 51, no. 2 (2012), pp. 193–220.

Schieffelin, Edward L., 'Performance and the Cultural Construction of Reality'. *American Ethnologist* 12, no. 4 (1985), pp. 707–24.

Schiller, Gertrud, *Iconography of Christian Art*, 2 vols (London, 1968).
Schmitt, Jean-Claude, 'Le Suicide au moyen âge', *Annales. Economies, Sociétés, Civilisations* 31, no. 1 (1976), pp. 3–28.
Searle, John R., *Speech Acts: An Essay in the Philosophy of Language* (London: Cambridge University Press, 1969).
Septuaginta: Id est Vetus Testamentum Graece iuxta LXX Interpretes, ed. Alfred Rahlfs (Stuttgart: Privilegierte Württembergische Bibelanstalt, 1935).
Shaver, P., J. Schwartz, D. Kirson, and C. O'Connor, 'Emotional Knowledge: Further Exploration of a Prototype Approach', in G. Parrott (eds.), *Emotions in Social Psychology: Essential Readings* (Philadelphia, PA: Psychology Press, 2001), pp. 26–56.
Sheldrake, Philip, 'Mysticism: Critical Theological Perspectives', in Julia Lamm (ed.), *Blackwell Companion to Christian Mysticism* (Oxford: Wiley-Blackwell, 2012), pp. 531–49.
Sif Rikhardsdottir, *Emotion in Old Norse Literature. Translations, Voices, Contexts* (Cambridge: Brewer, 2017).
'Sigvatr Þórðarson, Erfidrápa Óláfs helga', ed. J. Jesch, in D. Whaleyed (ed.), *Poetry from the Kings' Sagas 1,2* (Turnhout: Brepols, 2012) (Skaldic Poetry of the Scandinavian Middle Ages 1), pp. 663–98.
Silvas, Anna M., 'Kassia la Melode e il suo uso delle Scritture'. in Franca Ela Consolino and Judith Herrin (eds.), *Fra Oriente e Occidente: Donne e Bibbia nell' Alto Medioevo (secoli VI–XI): Greci, Latini, Ebrei, Arabi* (Trapani: Il Pozzo di Giacobbe, 2015), pp. 53–68.
Silvas, Anna M., 'Kassia the Nun c. 810–c. 865: An Appreciation', in Lynda Garland (ed.), *Byzantine Women: Varieties of Experience AD 800–1200* (Aldershot: Ashgate, 2006), pp. 17–39.
The Skaldic Project. Available at http://skaldic.abdn.ac.uk/db.php?if=default&table=home.
Smith, J. Warren, *Passion and Paradise: Human and Divine Emotion in the Thought of Gregory of Nyssa* (New York: The Crossroad Publishing Company, 2004).
Smith, Lesley, 'William of Auvergne and Confession', in P. Biller, A. J. Minnis (eds.), *Handling Sin: Confession in the Middle Ages* (York, 1998), pp. 95–107.
Snorri, Sturluson, *Heimskringla*, ed. Bjarni Aðalbjarnarson, 3 vols (Reykjavík: Hið íslenzka fornritafélag, 1941–51) (Íslenzk fornrit 26–28).
Sorabji, Richard, *Emotion and Peace of Mind: From Stoic Agitation to Christian Temptation* (New York: Oxford University Press, 2002).
Sørensen, Preben Meulengracht, *Fortælling og ære. Studier i islændingesagaerne* (Aarhus: Aarhus University Press, 1993).
Špidlík, Tomáš, *La Spiritualité de l'Orient Chrétien* (Roma: Pontificium Institutum Orientalium Studiorum, 1978).
Sprenger, Ulrike, *Die altnordische heroische Elegie* (Berlin/New York: De Gruyter, 1992) (Ergänzungsbände zum Reallexikon der germanischen Altertumskunde 6).

Spyrakou, Evangelia C., *Οἱ Χοροὶ τῶν Ψαλτῶν κατὰ τὴν Βυζαντινὴ Παράδοση* [Singers' Choirs according to the Byzantine Tradition]. Institute of Byzantine Musicology Studies, 14 (Athens: University of Athens, 2008).

Stanley, Eric Gerald, 'Did the Anglo-Saxons Have a Social Conscience Like Us?' *Anglia. Journal of English Philology* 121, no. 2 (2003), pp. 38–264. doi: https://doi.org/10.1515/ANGL.2003.238 (accessed 20 November 2019).

Stearns, Carol Z., and Peter N. Stearns, 'Emotionology: Clarifying the History of Emotions and Emotional Standards', *The American Historical Review* 90, no. 4 (1985), pp. 813–36.

Steenbrugge, Charlotte, *Drama and Sermon in Late Medieval England: Performance, Authority, Devotion* (Kalamazoo, 2017).

Stewart, Columba, 'Evagrius Ponticus and the "Eight Generic *Logismoi*"', in Richard Newhauser (ed.), *In the Garden of Evil: The Vices and Culture in the Middle Ages* (Toronto: Pontifical Institute of Medieval Studies, 2005), pp. 3–34.

Stewart, Columba, 'Evagrius Ponticus and the Eastern Monastic Tradition on the Intellect and the Passions', *Modern Theology* 27, no. 2 (2011), pp. 263–75.

Suter, Ann, 'Tragic Tears and Gender', in Thorsten Fögen (ed.), *Tears in the Graeco-Roman World* (Berlin: De Gruyter, 2009), pp. 59–83.

Sverris saga, ed. Þorleifur Hauksson (Reykjavík: Hið íslenzka fornritafélag, 2007) (Íslenzk fornrit 30).

The Synaxarion of the Monastery of the Theotokos Evergetis: March–August, the Movable Cycle, trans. Robert Jordan (Belfast: Belfast Byzantine Enterprises, 2005).

Taft, Robert F., *The Byzantine Rite: A Short History* (Minnesota: The Liturgical Press, 1992).

Taft, Robert F., 'Christian Liturgical Psalmody: Origins, Development, Decomposition, Collapse'. in Harold W. Attridge and Margot Elsbeth Fassler (eds.), *Psalms in Community: Jewish and Christian Textual, Liturgical, and Artistic Traditions* (Leiden: Brill, 2004), pp. 7–32.

Taft, Robert F., 'The Liturgy of the Great Church: An Initial Synthesis of Structure and Interpretation on the Eve of Iconoclasm'. *DOP* 34, no. 35 (1980/1981), pp. 45–75.

Taft, Robert F., *Through Their Own Eyes: Liturgy as the Byzantines Saw It* (Berkeley: InterOrthodox Press, 2006).

Taylor, Larissa Juliet, *Soldiers of Christ: Preaching in Late Medieval and Reformation France* (New York/ Oxford, 1992).

The Taste of Maryland. Art Collecting in Maryland, 1800–1934 (Baltimore, 1984).

Tentler, Thomas, *Sin and Confession on the Eve of the Reformation* (Princeton, 1977).

Teske, Roland J., *Guillaume d'Auvergne, The Universe of Creatures* (Milwaukee, 1998).

Teske, Roland J., 'William of Auvergne's Debt to Avicenna', in J. L. Janssens, D. de Smet (eds.), *Avicenna and His Heritage. Acts of the International Colloquium, Leuven-Louvain la neuve, 8–11 sept 1999* (Leuven, 2002), pp. 153–70.

Theodore the Stoudite, *Letters. Theodori Studitae Epistulae*, ed. George Fatouros, vol. 2 (Berlin: De Gruyter, 1992).

Theodoricus monachus, 'Historia de antiquitate regum Norwagiensium', in G. Storm (ed.), *Monumenta historica Norvegiæ. Latinske Kildeskrifter til Norges Historie i Middelalderen* (Kristiania: Brøgger, 1880), pp. 3–68.

Thijs, Christine B., 'Early Old English Translation: Practice before Theory', *Neophilologus* 91 (2007), pp. 149–73. doi: 10.1007/s11061-006-9011-2.

Þórir, Óskarsson, 'Rhetoric and Style', in R. McTurk (ed.), *A Companion to Old Norse-Icelandic Literature and Culture* (Malden, MA/Oxford: Blackwell, 2005, 2005), pp. 354–71.

Timofeeva, Olga, 'Anglo-Latin and Old English. A Case for Integrated Bilingual Corpus Studies of Anglo-Saxon Registers', in P. Bennett, M. Durrell, S. Scheible, and R. J. Whitt (eds.), *New Methods in Historical Corpora* (Tübingen: Narr verlag, 2013), pp. 195–204.

Timofeeva, Olga, 'Anglo-Latin Bilingualism before 1066: Prospects and Limitations', in A. Hall, O. Timofeeva, A. Kiricsi, and B. Fox (eds.), *Interfaces between Language and Culture in Medieval England: A Festschrift for Mattio Kilpio*. The Northern World 48 (Leiden: Brill, 2010), pp. 1–36.

Timofeeva, Olga, 'Latin Loans in Old English and Finnish Loans in Modern English: Can We Distinguish Statistics from Myth?', in R. W. McConchie (ed.), *Selected Proceedings of the 2012 Symposium on New Approaches in English Historical Lexis (HEL-LEX 3)* (Somerville, MA: Cascadilla Proceedings, 2013), pp. 166–76.

Tkacz, Catherine Brown, 'Singing Women's Words as Sacramental Mimesis'. *Recherches de Théologie et Philosophie Médiévales* 70, no. 2 (2003), 275–328.

Topping, Eva Catafygiotu, *Sacred Song: Studies in Byzantine Hymnography* (Minneapolis: Light and Life Publications, 1997).

Torrance, Alexis., *Repentance in Late Antiquity. Eastern Asceticism and the Framing of the Christian Life* (Oxford: Oxford University Press, 2012).

Traube, Ludwig, *Vorlesungen und Abhandlungen* (München, 1911).

'Trinity homilies', *Old English Homilies*, Second Series, ed. Richard Morris, EETS O.S. 53 (London, 1873).

Triodion, trans. Kallistos Ware and Mother Mary, *The Lenten Triodion* (Boston: Faber, 1978).

Triodion, Τριώδιον Κατανυκτικόν, περιέχον ἅπασαν τὴν ἀνήκουσαν αὐτῷ ἀκολουθίαν τῆς ἁγίας καὶ μεγάλης Τεσσαρακοστῆς (Rome: [n.p.], 1879).

Tripolitis, Antonia, *Kassia: The Legend, the Woman and Her Work* (New York: Garland Press, 1992).

Troelsgård, Christian, *Byzantine Neumes: A New Introduction to the Middle Byzantine Notation* (Copenhagen: Museum Tusculanum Press, 2011).

Troelsgård, Christian, 'Kanon Performance in the Eleventh Century, Evidence from the Evergetis Typikon Reconsidered', in Nina Gerasimova-Persidkaia and Irina Lozovaia (eds.), *Byzantium and Eastern Europe: Liturgical and Musical Links – In Honour of the 80th Birthday of Dr Miloš Velimirović* (Moscow: State Conservatory of Moscow 'Piotr Tjajkowskij', 2004), pp. 44–51.

Turner, Victor W., *The Anthropology of Performance* (New York: PAJ Publications, 1986).

Turner, Victor W., *The Ritual Process: Structure and Antistructure* (Chicago: Aldine, 1969).

Turner, Victor, 'Pilgrimage as a Liminoid Phenomenon', in Victor Turner and Edith Turner (eds.), *Image and Pilgrimage in Christian Culture: Anthropological Perspectives* (New York, 1978), pp. 1–39.

Turville-Petre, Gabriel, *Origins of Icelandic Literature* (Oxford: Clarendon Press, 1953).

Úlfar Bragason, *On the Poetics of Sturlunga* (Ann Arbor, MI: University Microfilms International, 1986).

Vecchio, Silviana, '*Passio, affectus, virtus*: il sistema delle passioni nei trattati morali di Guglielmo d'Auverne', in F. Morenzoni, J. Y. Tilliette (eds.), *Autour de Guillaume d'Auvergne* (Turnhout, 2005), pp. 173–87.

Veraldar saga, ed. Jakob Benediktsson (København: Luno, 1944) (Samfund til Udgivelse af gammel nordisk Litteratur 61).

Ólason, Vésteinn, *Dialogues with the Viking Age. Narration and Representation in the Sagas of Icelanders* (Reykjavík: Heimskringla, 1998).

Ólason, Vésteinn, 'Gísli Súrsson – A Flawless or a Flawed Hero?', in S. Toftgaard Andersen (ed.), *Die Aktualität der Saga. Festschrift für Hans Schottmann* (Berlin/New York: De Gruyter, 1999) (Reallexikon der Germanischen Altertumskunde. Ergänzungsband 21), pp. 163–75.

Viarre, Simone, *La survie d'Ovide dans la littérature scientifique des XIIe et XIIIe siècles* (Poitiers, 1966).

Viller, Marcel et al., *Dictionnaire de Spiritualité ascétique et mystique. Doctrine et Histoire*, 17 vols (Paris, 1932–95).

Vǫlsunga saga. The Saga of the Volsungs. The Icelandic Text According to MS Nks 1824 b, 4°. With an English Translation, Introduction and Notes, ed. K. Grimstad (Saarbrücken: AQ-Verlag, 2000) (Bibliotheca Germanica. Series Nova 3).

Von See, Klaus et al., *Kommentar zu den Liedern der Edda 7. Heldenlieder. Atlakviða in grœnlenzka. Atlamál in grœnlenzko. Frá Guðrúno. Guðrúnarhvǫt. Hamðismál* (Heidelberg: Winter, 2012).

Von See, Klaus et al., *Kommentar zu den Liedern der Edda 6. Brot af Sigurðarkviðo. Guðrúnarkviða I. Sigurðarkviða in skamma. Helreið Brynhildar. Dráp Niflunga. Guðrúnakviða II. Guðrúnarkviða III. Oddrúnargrátr. Strophenbruchstücke aus der Vǫlsunga saga* (Heidelberg: Winter, 2009).

Von See, Klaus, 'Skaldenstrophe und Sagaprosa. Ein Beitrag zum Problem der mündlichen Überlieferung in der altnordischen Literatur', in Klaus Von See, *Edda, Saga, Skaldendichtung. Aufsätze zur skandinavischen Literatur des Mittelalters* (Heidelberg: Winter, 1981) (Skandinavistische Arbeiten 6), pp. 461–85.

Von See, Klaus, 'Snorris Konzeption einer nordischen Sonderkultur', in A. Wolf (ed.), *Snorri Sturluson. Kolloquium anläßlich der 750. Wiederkehr seines Todestages* (Tübingen: Narr, 1993) (ScriptOralia 51), pp. 141–77.

von Simson, Otto G., '*Compassio* and *Co-Redemptio* in Roger van der Weyden's *Descent From the Cross*', *Art Bulletin* 35, no. 1 (1953), pp. 9–16.

Vries, Jan de, *Altnordisches etymologisches Wörterbuch*. 2. verbesserte Aufl. (Leiden: Brill, 1977).

Wagner, Karen, 'Cum aliquis venerit ad sacerdotem: Penitential Experience in the Central Middle Ages', in A. Firey (ed.), *A New History of Penance* (Leiden/Boston, 2008) (Brill's Companion to the Christian Tradition 14), pp. 201–18.

Walter, Ernst, *Lexikalisches Lehngut im Altwestnordischen. Untersuchungen zum Lehngut im ethisch-moralischen Wortschatz der frühen lateinisch-altwestnordischen Übersetzungsliteratur* (Berlin: Akademie-Verlag, 1976) (Abhandlungen der Sächsischen Akademie der Wissenschaften zu Leipzig. Philologisch-Historische Klasse 66, 2).

Wanner, Kevin J., *Snorri Sturluson and the Edda. The Conversion of Cultural Capital in Medieval Scandinavia* (Toronto: University of Toronto Press, 2008).

Ward, 'John L., Disguised Symbolism as Enactive Symbolism in Van Eyck's Paintings', *Artibus et Historiae* 15/29 (1994), pp. 9–53.

Ward, Benedicta, *Harlots of the Desert: A Study of Repentance in Early Monastic Sources* (London, 1987).

Ware, Kallistos, '"Forgive Us … as We Forgive": Forgiveness in the Psalms and the Lord's Prayer', in Andreas Andreopoulos, Augustine Casiday and Carol Harrison (eds.), *Meditations of the Heart: The Psalms in Early Christian Thought and Practice. Essays in Honour of Andrew Louth* (Turnhout: Brepols, 2011), pp. 53–76.

Ware, Kallistos, 'The Meaning of "Pathos" in Abba Isaias and Theodoret of Cyrus', *Studia Patristica* 20 (1989), pp. 315–22.

Ware, Kallistos, 'The Meaning of the Divine Liturgy for the Byzantine Worshipper', in Rosemary Morris (eds.), *Church and People in Byzantium* (Birmingham: Centre for Byzantine, Ottoman and Modern Greek Studies, University of Birmingham, 1990), pp. 7–28.

Ware, Kallistos, '"An Obscure Matter": The Mystery of Tears in Orthodox Spirituality', in Kimberley Christine Patton and John Stratton Hawley (eds.), *Holy Tears: Weeping in the Religious Imagination* (Princeton, NJ: Princeton University Press, 2005), pp. 242–54.

Ware, Kallistos, 'The Orthodox Experience of Repentance', *Sobornost* 2 (1980), pp. 18–28.

Ware, Kallistos, 'Symbolism in the Liturgical Commentary of St. Germanos of Constantinople', in Paul Van Geest (ed.), *Seeing through the Eyes of Faith: New Approaches to the Mystagogy of the Church Fathers* (Leuven: Peeters, 2016), pp. 423–42.

Webb, Ruth, Ekphrasis, Imagination and Persuasion in Ancient Rhetorical Theory and Practice (Aldershot: Ashgate, 2009).

Webb, Ruth, 'Imagination and the Arousal of the Emotions in Greco-Roman Rhetoric', in Susanna Morton Braund and Christopher Gill (eds.), *The Passions in Roman Thought and Literature* (Cambridge: Cambridge University Press, 1997), pp. 112–27.

Webb, Ruth, 'Spatiality, Embodiment and Agency in Ekphraseis of Church Buildings', in Bissera V. Pentcheva (eds.), *Aural Architecture in Byzantium: Music, Acoustics, and Ritual* (New York: Routledge, 2017), pp. 163–75.

Weill-Parot, Nicolas, *Les 'images astrologiques' au Moyen Âge et à la Renaissance. Spéculations intellectuelles et pratiques magiques (XII*ᵉ*-XV*ᵉ *siècle)* (Paris, 2002).

Weill-Parot, Nicolas, *Points aveugles de la nature: la rationalité scientifique médiévale face à l'occulte, l'attraction magnétique et l'horreur du vide (XIII*ᵉ*-milieu du XV*ᵉ *siècle)* (Paris, 2013).

Weill-Parot, Nicolas, 'Pouvoirs lointains de l'âme et des corps: éléments de réflexion sur l'action à distance entre philosophie et magie, entre Moyen Âge et Renaissance', *Lo Sguardo*, 10, no. III (2012), pp. 85–98.

Weisl, Angela Jane, 'Confession, Contrition, and the Rhetoric of Tears: Medievalism and Reality Television', in G. Ashton and D. T. Kline (eds.), *Medieval Afterlives in Popular Culture* (New York, 2012).

Wellesz, Egon, *A History of Byzantine Music and Hymnography* (Oxford: Clarendon Press, 1961).

White, Andrew Walker, *Performing Orthodox Ritual in Byzantium* (Cambridge: Cambridge University Press, 2015).

Wierzbicka, Anna, *Imprisoned in English: The Hazards of English as a Default Language* (New York, 2013).

William of Auvergne, *Opera omnia* (Orléans-Paris, 1674, repr. Frankfurt a M., 1963).

Williams, Graham, *Sincerity in Medieval English Language and Literature* (London: Palgrave Macmillan, 2018).

Wolf, Kirsten, 'Body Language in Medieval Iceland. A Study of Gesticulation in the Sagas and Tales of Icelanders', *Scripta Islandica* 64 (2013), pp. 99–22.

Wolf, Kirsten, 'Somatic Semiotics: Emotion and the Human Face in the Sagas and þættir of Icelanders', *Traditio* 69 (2014), pp. 125–45.

Würth, Stefanie, 'Die mittelalterliche Übersetzung im Spannungsfeld von lateinischsprachiger und volkssprachiger Literaturproduktion. Das Beispiel der Veraldar saga', in V. Johanterwage and S. Würth (eds.), *Übersetzen im skandinavischen Mittelalter* (Wien: Fassbaender, 2007) (Studia medievalia septentrionalia 14), pp. 11–32.

Zeelenberg, Marcel, 'Anticipated Regret: A Prospective Emotion about the Future Past', in G. Oettingen, A. T. Sevincer, and P. M. Golliwitzer (eds.), *The Psychology of Thinking about the Future* (London: Guildford Press, 2018), pp. 276–95.

Zernack, Julia, 'Vorläufer und Vollender. Olaf Tryggvason und Olaf der Heilige im Geschichtsdenken des Oddr Snorrason Munkr', *Arkiv för nordisk filologi* 113 (1998), pp. 77–95.

Zweig, Benjamin Russell, 'Depicting the Unforgivable Sin: Images of Suicide in Medieval Art', PhD diss., Boston University, 2014.

Manuscripts

Grottaferrata Δβ I (eleventh to twelfth centuries).
Sinai Graecus 734–735 (tenth century).
Vaticanus Graecus 771 (eleventh century).

Dictionaries, Corpora and Thesauri

Anglo-Norman Dictionary (AND) = Available at http://www.anglo-norman.net/ (accessed 20 November 2019), gate/BNC = British National Corpus XML Edition (Oxford, 2007). Available at http://www.natcorp.ox.ac.uk/corpus/index.xml (accessed 15 November 2018).

B-T = Bosworth, Joseph and T. Northcote Toller, *An Anglo-Saxon Dictionary based on the manuscript collections of the late Joseph Bosworth* (London: Oxford University Press, 1898).

Cleasby, Richard and Gudbrand Vígfusson, *An Icelandic-English Dictionary*. 2nd ed. (Oxford, 1957).

Corpus of Middle English Prose and Verse (CMEPV) = Available at https://quod.lib.umich.edu/c/cme/ (accessed 20 November 2019).

DMLBS = *Dictionary of Medieval Latin from British Sources* (Oxford, 2012). Available at http://www.dmlbs.ox.ac.uk/web/welcome.html (accessed 20 November 2019).

DOE = Cameron, Angus, Ashley Crandell Amos, Antonette diPaolo Healey et al. (eds.), *Dictionary of Old English: A to I online* (Toronto, 2018). Available at http://www.doe.utoronto.ca (accessed 30 October 2019).

DOEC = *Dictionary of Old English Web Corpus*, compiled by Antonette diPaolo Healey with John Price Wilkin and Xin Xiang (Toronto, 2009).

HTE = *The Historical Thesaurus of English*. version 4.21. 2017 (Glasgow, 2017). Available at http://historicalthesaurus.arts.gla.ac.uk/ (accessed 30 October 2018).

Kronen, Guus, *An Etymological Dictionary of Proto-Germanic* (Leiden, 2013).

Köbler, Gerhard, Indogermanisches Wörterbuch. 5th ed. (2014). Available at https://www.koeblergerhard.de/idgwbhin.html (accessed 25 November 2019).

Lewis and Short = Lewis, Charlton T., and Charles Short, *A Latin Dictionary, Founded on Andrews' Edition of Freund's Latin Dictionary* (Oxford: Clarendon Press, 1975).

OED = *Oxford English Dictionary Online* (Oxford University Press, 2019). Available at www.oed.com (accessed 30 October 2019).

Orel, Vladimir, *A Handbook of Germanic Etymology* (Leiden: Brill, 2003).

Pfeifer, Wolfgang, *Etymologisches Wörterbuch des Deutschen* (Berlin: Akademie Verlag 1992).

Pons.eu (Stuttgart, 2020), available at https://en.pons.com/translate?q=%C5%BCal&l=enpl&in=&lf=pl#dict (accessed 5 January 2020).

Posner, Philip, Ethan Della Rocca, and Josh Day, *Logeion* (Chicago, 2018). Available at https://logeion.uchicago.edu (accessed 15 November 2018).

PWN-Oxford English-Polish Dictionary (Warszawa, 2004). Available at https://oxford.pwn.pl/about_the_dictionary.html (accessed 5 January 2020).

TOE = *A Thesaurus of Old English* (Glasgow, 2007). Available at http://oldenglishthesaurus.arts.gla.ac.uk/ (accessed 30 October 2018).

Translations

Mary Paul Macpherson, trans., 'A Rule for the Life of a Recluse', in *Treatises: The Pastoral Prayer*, ed. M. Basil Pennington (Kalamazoo, MI, 1982), pp. 41–102.

Millett, Bella, trans., *Guide for Anchoresses: A Translation Based on Cambridge, Corpus Christi College, MS 402* (Exeter, 2009).

Unpublished Material

O'Brien, Sarah M., 'An Edition of Seven Homilies from Lambeth Palace Library MS. 487' (unpublished doctoral thesis, University of Oxford, 1985).

Tibber, P. H., 'The Origins of the Scholastic Sermon, c. 1130–c. 1210' (unpublished doctoral thesis, University of Oxford, 1983).

Index

Ælfric 35, 48, 55, 178 n.39, 179 n.52
Æthelberht's code 42, 181 n.77
Þórarinn loftunga (Praise-tongue) 71, 189 n.58
Þórðr Andréasson 81
Þorgils saga ok Hafliða 78, 81, 84, 192 n.98, 193 n.105, 193 n.106
Þorvarðr Hǫskuldsson 82
ÞRÆST 37, 39, 44, 45, 48, 182 n.86
Þróttr 72–3
Abélard, Pierre 120, 151–2, 215 n.46

Accarie, Maurice 147, 213 n.18, 213 n.22, 214 n.26
affective
   potency 111–16
   richness 105, 107–11, 117
'afgørðir' (crimes) 77
Ágrip af Nóregs konunga sögum 70, 74, 189 n.51, 191 n.74
Albert the Great 96
Alcuin 33, 64, 75
   De virtutibus et vitiis 33, 64, 88
Alþingi 78
ambiguity 6, 11, 95–6
Anciaux, Paul 90, 106, 117, 198 n.29, 198 n.31, 199 n.36, 199 n.39, 206 n.27, 206 n.29
anger 5, 6, 27, 46, 50, 52, 61, 62, 136
Anglo-Saxons 31–3, 58
   penance and compunction 33–4
Aquinas, Thomas 106, 112, 206 n.28
Arches and springs 164
Aristotle 24, 88–9, 174 n.81, 174 n.83
armhertnesse 107, 108, 207 n.38
Arnold of Villanova 96
Ascension 91, 169 n.15
Athanasius of Alexandria 24
Atlamál in grænlenzko 66, 68, 69
attrition 8, 90, 91, 106
Augustine 24, 42, 47, 174 n.82
   On Music 24
Avicenna 89, 196 n.9, 199 n.36
Axa (story of) 93

Bede 44, 46, 47, 54, 65, 183 n.89, 206 n.23, 206 n.24
   Historia Ecclesiastica 44, 46, 47, 54, 182 n.88, 183 n.89
Begriffsgeschichte 65, 187 n.24
behreowsung 36, 56, 107, 179 n.52
Beowulf 49, 52, 53
bētan 42, 56
Bible 9, 11, 93, 97, 217 n.76
bireusing(e) 107, 206 n.33
Blake, William 25
Bliss, Jane 110
'boðorðabrot' (violation of God's commandments) 77
Bǫðvarr Ásbjarnarson 79
Bonaventure, St. 214 n.26
bōt 42, 43
Brennu-Njáls saga 83, 194 n.127
Brot af Sigurðarkviðo (Fragment of the Poem about Sigurðr) 68
Brynhildr 67–9, 188 n.41
BRYRD 37, 39, 41, 44, 45
   glosses 48
   prose 46–8
   verse 45–6
BRYT 39
Byzantine 5, 19
   faithful 15, 16, 25
   hymns 16, 17, 22, 23, 168 n.3, 170 n.28
   patristic texts 24
   worship 23

Canavesio, Giovanni 143–8, 152, 153, 155–64, 212 n.12, 213 n.16, 213 n.21, 214 n.29, 218 n.79
'canonical' sagas 61
Chaucer, Geoffrey 9, 10
   Canterbury Tales 10, 11
   Parson's Tale 10, 11
   Tale of Melibee, The 10
Christ 20, 25, 72, 73, 94, 103, 106, 110, 114–16, 143–9, 151, 154, 167 n.1,

211 n.6, 213 n.19, 214 n.25, 216 n.54, 217 n.67, 217 n.76
  before Caiaphas 145, 159
  death 114
  emotions 16
  enemies 154
  footsteps 21
  forgiveness 110, 150, 154, 155, 215 n.46
  grief and sadness 50
  life and praise 72, 169 n.15
  love for 109
  prophecy 144
  salvific acts of 22
  sufferings 145, 153
  Washing the Feet of the Apostles 146, 161, 163
Christendom 80–2, 169 n.22
Christianity 7, 13, 17, 25, 28, 32, 42, 61, 62, 69, 76, 81, 83, 84, 92, 99, 152
Christian, William A. Jr. 152–3
Chrysostom, John 15–16, 18
church 33, 76, 77, 80, 87, 168 n.6, 169 n.22
  body 99
  of Constantinople 18, 22
  discourse 97
  doctrine 7
cliché 123, 124, 127–8, 133, 137, 141, 142
Codex regius 67, 188 n.37
Comfort Spirit 115, 117
compassion 2, 3, 18, 21–3, 32, 36, 37, 51, 54, 103, 108, 110, 111, 117, 204 n.2, 217 n.67
compunct 8, 9, 11, 12
compuncti' 92
compunctio 8, 38, 47, 48, 65, 180 n.60
compunctio cordis 64, 105
compunctio lacrimarum (compunction of tears) 92
condemnation 88, 127–30, 135, 142
confessio 90, 214 n.26
confessio cordis 113
confession 1–3, 20, 28, 33, 47, 55, 56, 62, 68, 71, 76, 80, 85, 87, 90, 91, 97, 99, 112, 113, 120, 130, 133, 142, 145, 148, 151, 156, 195 n.3, 197–8 n.17, 203 n.92, 212 n.12, 214 n.26, 215 n.46
confessio oris 112, 113
conscience 13, 25, 62, 63, 66, 68, 69, 71–4, 76, 77, 79, 82–4, 119–21, 124, 127, 130, 134, 135, 137, 140, 188 n.41, 193 n.112
Constantinople 16, 18–20, 22, 26
Contemporary Sagas (*Samtíðarsögur*) 78–82, 192 n.97, 193 n.112
contiguity 89
contrite 3, 4, 8–11, 25, 27, 28, 39
contritio 8, 38, 39, 45, 48, 90, 113, 180 n.60, 199 n.37, 214 n.26
contritio cordis 108, 112
contrition 1–13, 27, 28, 30, 31, 33, 34, 36, 38, 39, 48, 54, 59, 91–3, 98–101, 103, 106–8, 111–13, 120, 122, 143, 145, 148–51, 153, 154, 178 n.43, 199 n.38, 217 n.76
  penance and 87, 90–1
contritus 8, 45
corpus 9, 11, 18, 27–9, 31, 35, 39, 48, 55, 64, 66, 89, 121, 175 n.2, 180 n.64, 181 n.69, 186 n.13, 196 n.12, 209 n.3
  iWeb 12
  Old French Frantext 120
  prose 41, 69, 82
  verse 66, 82
  word-families in 40–2
Corpus of Middle English Prose and Verse 11, 12
Crowning with thorns 145, 158, 216 n.54
Crucifixion 22, 72, 114, 147, 149, 154, 162, 169 n.15, 213 n.19
crusades 71
cultivated land (peasant) 93

DǢDBŌT 37, 39, 41, 181 n.71
  and compensation 42–4
death 16, 22, 44, 52, 61, 67–9, 71, 74–6, 80, 81, 88, 95, 106, 114, 120–3, 125, 127–9, 131, 132, 134, 135, 137, 141, 146, 171 n.37, 189 n.59, 193 n.112
Deguileville, Guillaume de 152, 153
  Pèlerinage de vie humaine 152, 216 n.49
Delaurenti, Béatrice 4
Denial of Peter 143–5, 149, 150, 154, 156, 157, 163, 211 n.6, 211 n.8, 214 n.23
Denoyelle, Corinne 7, 155, 217 n.78
Descent into Limbo 147, 162
Desesperance 150–1, 215 n.41

Díaz-Vera, Javier E. 179 n.47
Dictionary of Old English (DOE) 36–7, 42
Dictionary of Old English Web Corpus (DOEC) 35, 179 n.48
Diller, Hans-Juergen 179 n.47
Dionysius the Areopagite 168 n.4, 168 n.5
divine 15, 16, 22, 23, 25, 33, 46, 89, 168 n.6, 173 n.68, 174 n.83
  emotion 5, 15
  forgiveness 210 n.21
  grace 17, 46, 48, 90, 99
  inspiration 47, 48
  mercy 151
  punishment 129
Dupront, Alphonse 153, 216 n.55, 216 n.56
duty and condemnation 127–30, 142

earmlice 58
Easter 91, 107, 114, 167 n.1, 169 n.15
Ecce Homo 149
Ecclesiasticus 30:24 108
Eddic poem 66–71, 82, 187–8 n.33
edification 62, 72
Egill Skalla-Grímsson
  Sonatorrek 84, 194 n.129
Egils saga Skalla-Grímssonar 84, 195 n.131
Eiríkr, King 84
Elucidarius in Old Norse Translation 64, 186 n.19, 186 n.20
embodiment 5, 109
emotion 1–4, 7, 12, 15, 24, 51, 59, 61–3, 66, 68, 69, 71, 75, 79, 83, 84, 87, 88, 90, 91, 99, 101, 103, 117, 131, 154, 155, 167 n.14, 168 n.2, 174 n.83, 176 n.14, 178 n.43, 181 n.71, 183 n.95, 184 n.107, 187 n.33, 196 n.5, 200 n.54, 204 n.3, 204 n.98, 217 n.76
  Beowulf 52
  Christ 16
  complexity 29–32
  cross-cultural universality 4–5
  levels 29–30
  liturgical 25
  music on 24
  painful 38, 49
  potential 85
  senses 45
  vocabulary 6, 84
Enide 125, 126, 128, 129, 131, 132, 139–41, 210 n.28
enumeration 98–9
Ephrem 18, 19
Erec and Enide 131, 139–41, 210 n.28
Ereignislied 67, 82
Erik Ejegod, King 71
Eucharist 20, 22
expression 3, 29–30, 39, 44, 45, 48, 54, 59, 62, 65, 83, 92, 98, 125, 136, 147, 151, 154, 155, 176 n.14, 179 n.47, 196 n.12, 209 n.3, 210 n.15, 210 n.27, 214 n.23
  facial 5, 6, 29, 62, 154, 176 n.14
  impersonal 127
  linguistic 5, 6, 31, 59, 115
  medieval homiletic 117
  metonymic 126
  pragmatic 30, 31
  of repentance 18, 99
  universalities of 4–8
  verbal 51, 123
  violent 146
Eysteinn, King 77

facial expressions 5, 6, 29, 62, 154, 176 n.14
Family Sagas (*Íslendingasögur*) 61–3, 66, 69, 74, 77, 79, 81–5, 186 n.11, 194 n.121
'first robe' 20, 21
forbisne 109
forgiveness 20, 21, 30–3, 55, 56, 62, 76–81, 85, 116, 121, 128, 150, 151, 154, 155, 191 n.83, 210 n.21, 215 n.45, 215 n.46
FORGNID 37, 39, 48
Fourth Lateran Council 87, 97, 111, 120, 130, 202 n.79, 212 n.12
Fornaldarsögur 63
FOR/TŌBRŸT* 37, 45, 48
Fragment of the Poem about Sigurðr (*Brot af Sigurðarkviðo*) 68
Fulkerson, Laurel 31–2

Gamli kanóki 72, 190 n.67
gebētan 44
Genesis 3:21 173 n.64
Gennep, Arnold van 155, 217 n.70, 217 n.71, 217 n.73, 217 n.75, 217 n.77

Georgianna, Linda 113, 208 n.54
Gerrits, G. H. 106, 107, 206 n.30
getrēowian 43
Gilson, Etienne 199 n.36
Gizurr Þorvaldsson, Jarl 81
God 9, 19, 22–5, 50, 53, 65, 66, 70, 72, 75,
    76, 81–3, 94, 105–8, 112, 120, 126,
    147, 149, 152, 154, 191 n.83, 208 n.58
  commandments 77
  compassion, incarnation and sacrifice
    22
  and faithful 25, 45
  forgiveness 21, 33, 55, 56, 76
  grace 46, 47
  love of 8, 33, 79, 110, 116, 129
  man's relationship to 72
  mercy 10, 74, 193 n.105
  transgressions 51
grace 17, 20, 25, 33, 46–8, 51, 90, 99, 106,
    120, 152
Grágás 73, 189 n.53, 190 n.70
Great Lent 15, 16, 19, 20, 22, 167 n.1, 171
    n.41, 172 n.50, 173 n.64
Greban, Arnoul 146–8, 150, 151, 210 n.21,
    214 n.27
  Passion 148, 150, 210 n.21
Gregory of Nyssa 18, 170 n.33, 174 n.83
Gregory the Great 33, 66, 92, 93, 100, 199
    n.47, 200 n.53
  Dialogi 33
  Pastoral Care 33, 47, 55
Gregory the Theologian
  On His Own Verses 24
Guðmundr 80, 81
Guðmundar saga dýra 80, 193 n.107, 193
    n.110, 193 n.113
guilt 1, 6, 9, 10, 68, 79, 114, 120, 130–2,
    140, 142, 188 n.41
  Church doctrine 7
  dynamics of 13
  medievalism of 2–4
  violence of 121
Gulaþingslǫg 73
Guthlac 50, 52

Hafliði 78–80, 193 n.105
Hagia Sophia 19, 22
Hákon inn góði, King 74
Hákon Pálsson, Jarl 75

happiness 5, 27, 62, 130, 133, 139, 142,
    210 n.28
Haraldr, King 76–7, 84
harmr (pain/grief) 83–4
Harmsól ('Sun of Sorrow') 72
Hartley, L. P. 4
Heiðarvíga saga 84, 195 n.130
Helreið Brynhildar 68
Henderson, George 144, 211 n.4
Heusler, Andreas 81, 194 n.115, 194 n.119,
    194 n.121
*Historia de antiquitate regum
    Norwagiensium* 70, 189 n.50
Historia Ecclesiastica (Bede) 44, 46, 47, 54,
    182 n.88, 183 n.89
Historical Thesaurus of English (HTE) 32,
    34
Holofernes 46, 52, 112–13
Holy Ghost 113, 115, 116, 208 n.61
Holy Spirit 47, 53, 115, 116
Holy Week 15, 19, 22
homo interior 69, 77, 82, 85
Hough, Carole 43
HRĒOW 36, 38–41, 48–9, 59
  glosses 57–8
  prose 55–7
  verse 49–55
hreowlice 58
humanity 20, 111, 114, 119, 147
Hunt, Tony 110
Hupka, Ralph B. 6
hymnody 15, 25, 172 n.46
hymnography 15, 16, 20, 168 n.3, 170 n.28
hymns 5, 9, 15–23, 25–6, 170 n.29, 171
    n.37, 171 n.41, 171–2 n.41, 172
    n.45, 173 n.74

Icelandic mentality. *See* Old Norse-
    Icelandic literature
iðran 62–6, 69, 73, 75, 193 n.113
iðrask 62–73, 82, 84, 195 n.133
irreversibility 133, 137, 140, 141
irriguum inferius 105
irriguum superius 105
Íslendinga saga 81, 193–4 n.113,
    194 n.116
Íslendingasögur (Family Sagas) 61–3, 66,
    69, 74, 77, 79, 81–5, 186 n.11, 194
    n.121

Íslenskt textasafn. Stofnun Árna Magnússonar í íslenskum fræðum 186 n.13
iWeb corpus 12
Izdebska, Daria 4, 8, 9, 107, 176 n.13, 178 n.46, 180 n.63, 183 n.93

Jankélévitch, Vladimir 121, 123, 129, 131, 134, 135, 138, 140–1, 155, 209 n.8, 209 n.11, 210 n.23
Jónsson, Karl 75
Judith 45, 52, 112, 113

kanon 18, 170 n.28, 170 n.29
Kassia 21, 173 n.61
　On the Sinful Woman 21
Kempe, Margery 3, 5
　Book of Margery Kempe, The 5–6
Ketill 78–9, 193 n.105
　exemplum 78, 79, 84, 193 n.105
Kohnen, Thomas 31
Konstan, David 131, 209 n.1, 210 n.24
kontakion 5, 15, 19–22, 168 n.3, 169 n.18, 171 n.41, 172 n.43, 172 n.45
Konungasögur 77

La Brigue's Passion cycle 143–8, 150, 151, 153–6, 211 n.1, 212–13 n.13, 213 n.21, 214 n.25, 214 n.28
Lambeth and Trinity homilists 103, 117
　affective richness 107–11
　potency 111–16
　terms and scholarship 105–7
　texts and audiences 104
Lampe, G. W. H. 167 n.2, 170 n.24
　Patristic Greek Lexicon 17
Last Judgment 154–5, 164, 165, 169 n.16
Lateran Council. *See* Fourth Lateran Council
Laxdæla saga 83, 184 n.2, 194 n.126, 195 n.132
Lazikani, Ayoush 6, 8, 9
Leclercq, Jean 105, 107, 108, 117, 205 n.17
　Love of Learning and the Desire for God 105, 205 n.17
lexical labels 7
liturgical calendar 16, 19, 167 n.1
liturgy 15–16, 18–23, 25, 26, 98, 168 n.10, 173 n.74
Logos 16
Lombard, Peter 113, 208 n.53

Loraux, Nicole 93, 200 n.49, 204 n.100
love 2, 8, 17, 23, 28, 33, 48, 64, 67, 68, 79, 83, 103, 105, 106, 109, 110, 116, 117, 126, 129, 138–40, 171 n.37, 208 n.61, 210 n.28
Love, Nicholas
　Myrrour of the Blessed Lyf of Jesu Christ 10–11
Lukan parable 15, 17

McEntire, Sandra J. 33, 105, 107, 117, 166 n.3, 177 n.31, 178 n.35, 178 n.38, 205 n.15, 206 n.23–206 n.25
　Doctrine of Compunction in Medieval England, The: Holy Tears 105–6, 166 n.3, 177 n.31, 178 n.35, 178 n.38, 205 n.15, 206 n.25
Magi 94
Magnús Erlingsson, King 75–6
Mark, King 134
Markús Skeggjason 71, 189 n.60
Martin, Hervé 148, 212 n.12
Martin, Jean-Pierre 123, 209 n.10
Mary Magdalene 109–11, 147, 151, 152, 154, 207 n.41, 215 n.47
Matthew 144, 171 n.37
Mellas, Andrew 4–5
Mellinkoff, Ruth 154, 216 n.65
mesalliance 67, 83
'metaphorical game' 92, 93, 204 n.100
metaphors 39, 53, 100, 101, 136, 145, 152, 153, 180 n.60, 182 n.86, 183 n.94, 200 n.49, 204 n.100, 212 n.10, 212 n.13
　agricultural 92–6
　bodily 96–9, 203 n.92
Michel, Jean 146–7, 213 n.17, 213 n.22, 214 n.23
　Passion 146–7
Middle English 9–13, 28
Middle English Dictionary (MED) 9
mildhertnesse (mild-heartedness) 107
Miller, William I. 79, 184 n.1, 185 n.3, 185 n.6, 193 n.104, 193 n.105, 194 n.115, 194 n.121
Millett, Bella 104, 111, 205 n.5, 205 n.7, 205 n.10, 205 n.11, 205 n.13, 207 n.40, 207 n.47, 207 n.50–207 n.52
　Ancrene Wisse 104, 107, 112, 113, 207 n.50, 207 n.51, 208 n.54

mind 29, 30, 47, 49, 50, 56, 64, 66, 76, 77, 79, 93, 97, 101, 145, 148, 195 n.133, 212 n.12
mind-body relations 89, 101
Minstrels' Passion, The (Hunt and Bliss) 110, 115, 116
mirabilia 89
misconception 63
miserere 108
miserior 58
Mocking of Christ 145, 158, 159
Morkinskinna 70, 72, 75–7, 186 n.13, 189 n.52, 190 n.64, 191 n.86, 191 n.87, 192 n.89
Morse, Stephen J. 182 n.80
Motif of Repentance in Medieval French Literature, The *(Le Motif du repentir dans la littérature française médiévale)* 120, 209 n.6, 212 n.10
Murray, Alexander 154, 214 n.36, 215 n.37, 216 n.63, 218 n.79
myrrh and incense 94, 95, 200 n.61

Nagy, Piroska 152, 154, 195 n.4, 196 n.5, 199 n.41–199 n.43, 199 n.47, 200 n.53, 200 n.59, 204 n.99, 216 n.60
Nativity 91, 167 n.1
'natural magic' 89, 101, 197 n.15
nature 15, 16, 20, 34, 66, 70, 84, 88, 89, 100, 103, 105, 111, 117, 156, 174 n.83
Nicole Oresme 96, 100
Nicholson, Simon 32, 184 n.100
night vigil 19, 22
normalized frequencies (NF) 40–1
Notre-Dame des Fontaines 143–8, 150, 152–4, 156, 211 n.1, 213 n.15

Óláfr Tryggvason, King 74–7
Old English 28, 29, 31–5, 38, 39, 42, 43, 45–7, 49, 54, 55, 58, 59, 180 n.65, 181 n.71, 182 n.87
Old English Homilies 206 n.34, 206 n.36
Old High German 38, 59
Old Norse 5, 10, 38, 180 n.60
Old Norse Elucidarius, The 64, 186 n.19, 186 n.20
Old Norse-Icelandic literature 61–2
  Eddic and Skaldic poetry 66–71
  Family Sagas 61–3, 66, 69, 74, 77, 79, 81–5, 186 n.11, 194 n.121
  iðran and *iðrask* 62–6
  Kings' sagas 74–7
  Samtíðarsögur 78–82, 192 n.97, 193 n.112
  sin, praise, edification 71–4
Old Saxon 38, 49
onbryrded 46, 47
Ǫnundr Þorkelsson 80
Origen 18, 106, 170 n.33
Orkneyinga saga 75, 191 n.77
Ovid 95–6, 201 n.69, 201 n.73
Oxford Dictionary of the Christian Church, The (ODCC) 8
Oxford English Dictionary (OED) 9, 11

Pact of Judas 148, 160
pain 4, 8, 9, 28, 32, 38, 49, 50, 52, 61, 83, 95–7, 107, 117, 126, 128, 135, 137, 139, 141, 142, 174 n.83, 201 n.65, 204 n.98
Partonopeu 128, 133, 135, 136
Pascha 16, 169 n.15
Pascual, Rafael J. 32
passion 15, 19, 20, 88, 91, 93, 94, 96, 97, 139, 174 n.83, 195 n.5, 211 n.1
Passion cycle 143–51, 153–6, 211 n.1, 212 n.13, 213 n.21, 214 n.25, 214 n.29, 217 n.76
Patristic literature 97, 100, 202 n.80
Payen, Jean-Charles 120, 122, 209 n.6, 212 n.10, 212 n.13, 215 n.46
'pedagogy of passions' 91, 97
Pelle, Stephen 104, 205 n.12
penance 5, 10, 13, 33–4, 36–7, 41, 42, 44, 53, 55, 56, 62, 65, 71, 73–5, 77, 80, 87, 88, 90–3, 97, 99, 106, 113, 128, 141, 143, 152, 154, 156, 182 n.84, 203 n.92, 208 n.53, 211 n.8, 212 n.10, 212 n.13
  sacrament of 148–51
penitence 10, 17, 28, 31, 33, 39, 48, 51, 54, 55, 57, 59, 71, 95, 103, 105, 111, 116, 136, 148, 178 n.43, 212 n.10, 215 n.44
Pentecost 91, 113–16, 208 n.56
Peter of Abano 96, 201 n.73
Pfeifer, Wolfgang 38
pilgrimage 71, 75, 82, 143, 152, 153, 155, 216 n.55, 216 n.58
pleasure 3, 19, 24, 25, 68, 95, 96, 127, 138, 174 n.83
Plesch, Véronique 5, 157–64, 211 n.1

Poema Morale 104
poenitantia 65
poenitentia 57
potency 103, 111–16
Pourrat, P. 103, 205 n.4
praise 18, 34, 42, 52, 69–72, 77, 115, 125
Present-Day English (PDE) 7, 11, 12, 27, 28, 31, 38, 54, 59
present state 136–7
prestsfundr 80, 193 n.113
Prick of Conscience (Ralph and Wood) 10
prima aetas 65
prodigal son 15, 25, 26
    Romanos's hymns 19–23
    sacred music 23–5
    in *Triodion* 16–19
prophecy 68, 69, 144
psalmody 18, 19, 24
Psalms 18, 24
Psalter glosses 41–2, 44, 45, 57, 181 n.70

rapture of the soul *(raptus animae)* 96
raw frequencies (RF) 40–1
regret 1, 5, 9, 27–32, 50, 51, 53, 55, 57–9, 69, 74
religion 7, 27, 32, 34, 79, 97, 129, 130, 155
Remedia amoris (Ovid) 96, 201 n.69
remordre 121, 122
remorse 2, 7, 27, 28, 30, 43, 44, 58, 61, 73, 79, 99, 106, 119–24, 133–5, 142, 146, 155, 156, 182 n.80, 209 n.3
    admission of sin 130–3
    defined 120
    duty and condemnation 127–30
    past and present 137–41
    in pre-Christian Classical Antiquity 31–2
    present state 136–7
    regret and 32, 58
    self-loathing 124–30
    suffering of 134
    uncertainty 141–2
Remorse of Judas 151, 160
reowlic 58
reowsumnesse 107
repentance 5, 7, 8, 10, 15, 17–19, 21–3, 25, 26, 28, 32, 33, 36, 38, 39, 42, 53–8, 64, 87, 90, 99, 105, 106, 119–23, 129, 130, 136, 142, 145–9, 151, 152, 155, 169 n.22, 178 n.43, 179 n.49, 181 n.71, 184 n.100, 209 n.1, 212 n.12, 214 n.23, 215 n.46
repentir 7, 121, 129
restitutio/satisfactio 64, 90, 214 n.26
reversibility 95–6
Reykdœla saga ok Víga-Skútu 84, 195 n.130
Rice, Robert 54
richness
    and activity 103
    affective 105, 107–11, 117
    emotional 63
'ring-Þróttr' 72–3
Roger Bacon 100
Romanos 15, 173 n.66
    On the Harlot 21
    hymns 19–23, 25
    On the Prodigal 20, 21, 23, 25, 171 n.41, 173 n.71

sacred music 23–5
salvation 15, 19, 21, 25, 66, 87, 92, 123, 142, 151, 152
Samtíðarsögur 78–82, 192 n.97, 193 n.112
samvizka (conscience) 62, 66, 73
San Fiorenzo 145, 159
satisfactio 64, 90, 214 n.26
satisfactio operis 112
Scheel, Roland 4, 5
scholarship 2, 13, 79, 105, 117, 183 n.91
schrift (confession) 112, 113
Scripture 15, 17
seawater 109
self-loathing 124–30
sermons 1, 10, 72–3, 104
shame 1, 2, 4, 6, 7, 9, 13, 30, 61, 79, 113, 119–22, 124, 126, 129, 135, 142
short lay of Sigurðr, The *(Sigurðarkviða in skamma)* 66, 67, 69
Sigurðr Fáfnisbani 67–9
Sigurðr Jórsalafari, King 71, 72, 77, 189 n.62
Sigvatr Þórðarson 69–71, 188 n.49, 189 n.54
    Erfidrápa Óláfs helga 69, 70, 188 n.49, 189 n.59
sin 7, 8, 15, 42, 50, 53, 62, 65, 70, 71, 73, 75, 77, 83, 95, 103, 105, 107–13, 116, 117, 120, 122, 125, 126, 129,

136, 137, 141, 142, 145–52, 154–6,
  215 n.41, 218 n.79
 admission of 130–3
 Christian obsession 81
 individual guilty 119
 remission of 106
Sinai Graecus 16–17, 169 n.18, 173 n.61,
  175 n.89
Skaldic poem 66–71, 75, 76
 and law 71–4
 praise and edification 72
Smith, Lesley 91, 198 n.28, 198 n.34, 199
  n.36, 203 n.92, 204 n.97
Snorri Sturluson 66, 70, 72, 77, 80, 82, 187
  n.31, 190 n.65, 192 n.94, 192 n.95
 Heimskringla 70, 72, 77, 184 n.1, 187
  n.31, 190 n.65
sorrow 8, 25, 31, 33, 36–8, 49–55, 57, 72,
  84, 99, 106–13, 115, 117, 180 n.52,
  184 n.100, 208 n.61
soul 24, 25, 66, 71, 76, 88, 89, 93, 96, 97,
  100, 105, 108, 109, 112–13, 116,
  129, 130, 136–7, 140, 146, 152, 171
  n.37, 174 n.80, 174 n.82, 189 n.59,
  195 n.5, 204 n.98
spirit 8–10, 18, 19, 24, 25, 33, 38, 43, 44,
  46, 47, 53, 66, 89, 92, 97–9, 101,
  106, 113–17, 147, 168 n.6, 208 n.57,
  212 n.12
Steenbrugge, Charlotte 1, 154
storytelling 81, 82, 94
Sturlunga saga 78, 81, 192 n.98, 193 n.107,
  193 n.113
suffering 49, 50, 59, 63, 67, 69, 98, 99, 106,
  114, 123, 125–7, 129, 134, 141, 142,
  210 n.27, 217 n.67
 Christ 145, 153
 intensification of 136–7
Suicide of Judas 161, 213 n.15
Sverrir, King 75–6, 80
Sverris saga 75, 76, 191 n.79, 191 n.80, 191
  n.83, 191 n.84

tármelti (melting into tears) 64, 75
tears 3, 5, 6, 10, 12, 13, 15, 18–20, 25, 26, 33,
  47, 53, 55–7, 64, 75, 92–4, 105, 106,
  108–11, 121, 122, 143–5, 166 n.9,
  169 n.16, 170 n.33–170 n.35, 171
  n.37, 175 n.93, 177 n.34, 178 n.37,
  204 n.99, 212 n.13, 215 n.46, 215
  n.47, 216 n.48, 217 n.76, 218 n.79
 efficacious 151–2
 penitential 152
 pilgrimage 152–5
 religious 152–3
 repentance at Notre-Dame des
  Fontaines 145–8
 sacrament of penance 148–51
 water of 152, 153
term compunction 105–7
Thesaurus of Old English, A (TOE)
  34
Thorn 158, 216 n.54
TÕBRŸT 45
Trinity. *See* Lambeth and Trinity homilists
Triodion 15–21, 25
Turner, Victor W. 155, 217 n.69, 217 n.72
Typikon of the Great Church 16, 20

universality of emotion 4–8
Upstairs Downstairs series 12

Value and Meaning of Bad Conscience,
  The *(La Valeur et signification de la
  mauvaise conscience)* 121, 209 n.8,
  209 n.11, 210 n.23
Vápnfirðinga saga 83
Veraldar saga 65, 187 n.25, 187 n.26
vernacular homilies 103, 117
'Viking lifestyle' 81
vocabulary 6, 7, 28, 29, 32, 34, 48, 50, 54
Vǫlsunga saga 67, 69, 84, 188 n.36, 188 n.45
Vulgate 8, 65, 204 n.1, 211 n.2

Weisl, Angela Jane 3
wergild 42–4
William of Auvergne 4, 87, 99–101,
  195 n.5, 196 n.9–196 n.12, 197
  n.14–197 n.16, 198 n.18, 198 n.20,
  198 n.28, 198 n.34, 199 n.36, 199
  n.38, 199 n.40, 199 n.46, 200 n.52,
  200 n.55, 200 n.58, 200 n.60, 201
  n.63–201 n.65, 201 n.69, 201 n.73,
  201 n.74, 202 n.76–202 n.78, 202
  n.81, 202 n.83, 203 n.92, 204 n.97
 Acts of the Apostles 92, 103, 204 n.1,
  209 n.62
 compuncti' 92

compunction, definition 91–2
De anima 88, 196 n.6
De sacramentis 88, 90, 198 n.20
De sacramento penitentie 95, 96, 198 n.28, 199 n.38, 199 n.40, 199 n.46, 200 n.52, 200 n.55, 200 n.58, 200 n.60, 201 n.64, 201 n.69, 202 n.78, 202 n.83, 203 n.92
De trinitate 88, 196 n.10
De universo 88, 89, 96, 97, 196 n.11, 196 n.12, 197 n.14, 201 n.74, 202 n.76, 202 n.81
Liber Catonianus 96
Magisterium divinale sive sapientale 88, 90, 196 n.6, 196 n.7
penance and contrition 90–1
theology, pastoralism and philosophy 88–9
Tractatus novus de penitentia 90, 95, 198 n.18, 201 n.63
Williams, G. 1, 31, 43, 154
word-family 29, 36–42, 44, 48, 49, 57, 59, 179 n.47
wpm (word per million) count 27, 175 n.2
Wulfstan 35, 43

Yvain 127, 132

żal 31, 54

www.ingramcontent.com/pod-product-compliance
Lightning Source LLC
Chambersburg PA
CBHW072133290426
44111CB00012B/1866